Protest and Resistance in the Chinese Party State

Protest and Resistance in the Chinese Party State

Edited by
Hank Johnston and Sheldon Zhang

ROWMAN & LITTLEFIELD
Lanham • Boulder • New York • London

Published by Rowman & Littlefield
An imprint of The Rowman & Littlefield Publishing Group, Inc.
4501 Forbes Boulevard, Suite 200, Lanham, Maryland 20706
www.rowman.com

86-90 Paul Street, London EC2A 4NE

Copyright © 2022 by The Rowman & Littlefield Publishing Group, Inc

All rights reserved. No part of this book may be reproduced in any form or by any electronic or mechanical means, including information storage and retrieval systems, without written permission from the publisher, except by a reviewer who may quote passages in a review.

British Library Cataloguing in Publication Information Available

Library of Congress Cataloging-in-Publication Data

Names: Johnston, Hank, 1947– editor. | Zhang, Sheldon, editor.
Title: Protest and resistance in the Chinese Party state / edited by Hank Johnston and Sheldon Zhang.
Description: Lanham : Rowman & Littlefield, [2021] | Includes bibliographical references and index. | Summary: "Although contemporary China is a repressive state, protests and demonstrations have increased almost tenfold between 2005 and 2015. This is an astounding statistic when one considers that Marxist-Leninist regimes of the past tolerated little or no public dissent. How can protests become more common as the state becomes more repressive? This collection helps to answer this compelling question through in-depth analyses of several Chinese protest movements and state responses. The chapters examine the opportunities and constraints for protest mobilization, and explains their importance for understanding contemporary Chinese society"— Provided by publisher.
Identifiers: LCCN 2021060041 (print) | LCCN 2021060042 (ebook) | ISBN 9781538165003 (cloth ; alk. paper) | ISBN 9781538165027 (paperback ; alk. paper) | ISBN 9781538165010 (epub)
Subjects: LCSH: Protest movements—China. | Political participation—China. | Communism and liberty—China. | Authoritarianism—China. | China—Politics and government—2002–
Classification: LCC HN733.5 .P76 2021 (print) | LCC HN733.5 (ebook) | DDC 303.60951—dc23/eng/20220118
LC record available at https://lccn.loc.gov/2021060041
LC ebook record available at https://lccn.loc.gov/2021060042

∞™ The paper used in this publication meets the minimum requirements of American National Standard for Information Sciences—Permanence of Paper for Printed Library Materials, ANSI/NISO Z39.48-1992.

Contents

Foreword   vii
    Hank Johnston (San Diego State University)

PART I: THE PROTEST LANDSCAPE

1   Nonviolent Protest in Party-State China   3
    Hank Johnston (San Diego State University) and
    Sheldon Zhang (University of Massachusetts, Lowell)

2   Popular Protests in China, 2000–2019   31
    Chih-Jou Jay Chen (Academia Sinica, Taiwan)

3   Troublemaking Repertoires in a Grassroots Petitioning Campaign   61
    Wing-Chung Ho (City University of Hong Kong)

PART II: POLITICAL OPPORTUNITIES AND CONSTRAINTS

4   Civic and Noncivic Activism under Autocracy   91
    Xi Chen (The Chinese University of Hong Kong)

5   Bureaucrat-Assisted Contention in China   120
    Kevin J. O'Brien (University of California, Berkeley),
    Lianjiang Li (Chinese University of Hong Kong), and
    Mingxing Liu (Peking University)

6   "Lawyering Repression" and Protest Demobilization under
    Rule of Law Authoritarianism   142
    Yue Xie (Shanghai Jiatong University)

PART III: ENVIRONMENTAL PROTEST

7 State Elites and Movement Alliances against the Nu River Dam   169
Setsuko Matsuzawa (The College of Wooster)

8 Relational Mechanisms of NGOs in Environmental Protests   192
Yang Zhang (American University)

PART IV: HONG KONG

9 How Protests Evolve: The Umbrella Legacy of the Anti-Extradition Movement   223
Ming-sho Ho (National Taiwan University)

10 Memory Making in Hong Kong's Tiananmen Vigils   248
Edmund W. Cheng and *Samson Yuen* (Hong Kong Baptist University)

PART V: RELIGION

11 The Public Transcript and the Rise and Fall of Urban Churches   279
Carsten T. Vala (Loyola University, Maryland)

12 Religion and Protest Participation   304
Chengzhi Yi (Shanghai Jiaotong University),
Geping Qiu (East China University of Political Science and Law),
and *Tao Liang* (Beijing Normal University)

Index   327

Foreword

This volume is the third in the Hansen Collection of Peace and Nonviolence Research. It has been my honor to occupy San Diego State University's (SDSU) Hansen Chair of Peace and Nonviolence for the past five years. The social science of protest, nonviolence resistance, and—the other side of the coin—how protest descends into violent confrontation are important foci in understanding contemporary societies. The appointment afforded generous resources to address contemporary topics about peace and nonviolence and, broadly, to promote world peace through scholarship and academic engagement. Supporting a collection of research monographs on these topics is one part of a robust Hansen program on our campus. Sponsoring conferences is another dimension of the program, and this volume is based on a conference on nonviolent resistance in nondemocracies and authoritarian states held at SDSU in 2019. I am grateful to the Hansen Foundation and its trustee, Anton Dimitroff, for supporting these conferences.

This volume in the series touches on an area of study that has come to the foreground of contentious politics research recently: the challenges to democracy that one-party authoritarian systems of governance pose. It is a theme, I believe, that will gain momentum in the coming decades of the twenty-first century and, especially, the violence-nonviolence dynamic as states employ more intensive modes of policing and surveillance based on new technologies. These are topics that are highly relevant because democracies are challenged in the twenty-first century, and insights from contemporary China are compelling because protests there wax and wane and because state methods of social control are sophisticated and intrusive.

Although a focus on China has always been present in the contentious politics field, the preponderance of research concentrates on the democracies of the West, where protest is normatively accepted, frequent, and protected by law. The goal of this volume is to cast a brighter light on the protest horizon in China, which broadened significantly during the 1990s and continued to expand in unprecedented numbers until 2012. Then, limited by Xi Jinping's more authoritarian approach to governance, the number of protests events began to diminish. Many protests in China are small expressions of anger at officials and local governments, mostly nonviolent, and never directly challenging the authority of the Chinese Communist Party (CCP). The vast majority of them remain relatively constrained events or campaigns. The Hansen-SDSU conference in 2019 hosted a thematic thread of several sessions focusing on the unique repertorial characteristics of protests in China and their relations to the state. This collection is partly the fruit of that initiative. A stronger synergy of the social movement field and China-area research has been underway for more than a decade, and our intention is to contribute to its enrichment.

When China began its modernization after the death of Mao Zedong, events of "mass incidents" and "troublemaking" were quite limited, but as the economy and society opened and modernized, protests increased rapidly. Chih-Jou Jay Chen has constructed an important data set of protest events in China. His finds that there was an increase in collective-action events between 2005 and 2014 at a rate of 9.5 times (see chapter 2). Another study estimated that the number of protests in 2010 could have been as high as 230,000. Although most were small gatherings at a village police headquarters or party offices to voice complaints or deliver petitions, these totals also included larger protests against chemical plants and toxic waste incinerators. Chen's chapter shows that the number of large protests (more than one thousand participants) increased during the same period. He refers to China as a "protest society," recasting the term popularized twenty-five years ago by David Meyer and Sidney Tarrow regarding Western democracies, "social movement societies."

To contextualize these numbers, we can consider protest figures from the U.S., where politics was especially contentious during the Trump administration. In the first three years after his election, there were an estimated 16,500 protests, with about 11.7 million total participants, including the massive Women's Marches at the outset of the new administration with 3 to 5 million participants. More recently, the wave of Black Lives Matter (BLM) protests in 2020 sparked by the killing of George Floyd during an arrest by the Minneapolis police, peaked on June 6, 2020, when five hundred thousand people mobilized on a single day. One study suggests that as many as 26 million people participated in 2020 BLM campaign, which would make it the largest social movement in the history of the U.S. While the absolute number of protests events in China and the U.S. may be comparable, participation in China is more constrained, and overall figures for participation are not available.

We can be certain that on a per-population basis, protest rates are not as high. Mass protests characteristic of BLM—campaigns that span the country—are highly unlikely in China. Protesters there have a keen awareness of what we could characterize as the KISS principle: Keep it small and segmented. Protests there are self-limited. Large events and campaigns that potentially could extend in geographic scope—suggesting major faults in CCP leadership—would be severely repressed in China as threatening to the party's power.

Another way to contextualize the high number of protests in China is with comparisons with other communist party regimes. In the Leninist regimes of the twentieth century, high levels of repression and surveillance meant that social movements and citizen protest campaigns—at least as we know them in the West—were not common. Like China, the organization of society and civic life in the Soviet Union, East Germany, Poland, Hungary, and the other Eastern bloc countries was highly constrained, less open, and widely surveilled. The development of any independent civil society groups or organizations was seen as highly suspicious. When large movements did occur, they were crushed by state repression: Hungary (1956) and Czechoslovakia (1968) and martial law in Poland (1981)—state responses reminiscent of Tiananmen Square. China, like the communist states of Eastern Europe, monitors any networked relations among groups and individuals who might express shared collective grievances. For social movement theorists, China stands out today when seen in the context of protest incidence from the Cold War era. The high levels of protest in China raise questions about different configurations of repertorial characteristics that might operate there, which are major thematic threads developed in this collection of research.

I close with the observation that the twenty-first century will be China's century. Researchers of contemporary societies must pay attention to its model of governance, state security, and geopolitics to fully understand trends in the future. One of these trends is especially portentous: how the People's Republic of China applies cutting-edge surveillance technologies with goal of maintaining social harmony. Digital technologies are unprecedented in their potential for monitoring citizens, and Chinese party-state uses social media strategies to shape public opinion and promote official perspectives and propaganda intensively. It also applies them extensively for social control. The need for social scientists to comprehend and analyze these trends is compelling. Moreover, as political parties in Poland, Hungry, Turkey, Brazil, and the U.S. erode both the rule of law and the institutional protections characteristic of liberal democracies, this weakening of citizen protections opens the door even more for the use of digital surveillance. Johnston and Zhang's introduction discusses the chilling implications of real-time virtual surveillance in which, hypothetically, a smartphone could capture a frown on someone's face when a story comes across a WeChat feed. If the story is about Xi Jinping, we might have a "face crime," to borrow from the Orwellian newspeak lexicon. In the early 2020s, this kind of monolithic and coordinated web of surveillance does yet not exist. The People's Republic of China is not alone in the use of new surveillance technologies, but today it seeks to take a global lead in their application.

Hank Johnston
Professor of Sociology
San Diego State University
December 22, 2021

Part I

THE PROTEST LANDSCAPE

Chapter One

Nonviolent Protest in Party-State China

Hank Johnston (San Diego State University) and
Sheldon Zhang (University of Massachusetts, Lowell)

Research on protest and social movements recently has been growing among China-area scholars. Nevertheless, it is fair to say that most social scientists in the contentious politics field have only a general awareness of the contemporary protest arena in China.[1] The goal of this chapter is to contextualize the chapters that follow by painting a picture of the protest landscape in China and consider why it is theoretically important for the field of protest studies. Protests grew significantly during the 1990s and continued increasing during the 2000s. In the last five years, they have decreased in the face of state repression. Although many protests demonstrate anger at officials and local governments, they remain mostly nonviolent.

Overt protest movements sometimes occurred the Marxist-Leninist regimes of the last century but never at the frequency in China today. Those were high-capacity authoritarian (HCA) states.[2] Their organization of society and civic life was highly constrained, less open, and widely surveilled. Often, large movements, when they did occur, were crushed by state repression, such as workers' strikes in East Berlin (1953) and Polish Solidarity (1981), and, in the case of Hungary (1956) and Czechoslovakia (1968), by foreign armies. The past regimes of Eastern Europe inhibited the development of networked relations among groups and individuals who might express shared collective grievances—the constituent elements of most social movements in the West (Della Porta and Diani 2006, Diani 1997)—by prohibiting an independent civil society, a pattern that also prevailed in China for many decades. In the Leninist regimes of the twentieth century, patterns of social control ensured that social movements and outbursts of citizen protest—at least as we know them in the West—were not common. The case of China stands out because just the opposite is the case. As we will discuss shortly, protests are numerous there.

Researchers of the repression-mobilization relationship have long recognized the interactive nature of state-protester relations in repressive states (Clarke 2011; Hoover and Kowaleswki 1992; Lichbach 1987; Moore 1998; Rasler 1996; Soule and Davenport 2009). In different regime settings and in different ways, actors seek to influence each other's behavior by, on the one side, bringing attention to grievances through protest mobilization and, on the other, by the state's actions of preemption and coercion. Overall, research reveals a consistent pattern in HCAs: protest movements, especially those that challenge state security, are met with strong repression that limits overt collective actions significantly (Cingranelli and Richards 1999; Davenport 2005; Regan and Henderson 2002). More fine-grained effects seem variable depending on the kind of movement and type of repressive tactics. In authoritarian South Korea, Chang (2008) found that repression decreased overt protests, as one would expect, but increased network alliances within movements. Starr and colleagues (2008) suggest that state surveillance tends to destabilize dissident groups, but others find that it radicalizes them (Varon 2004; Zwerman and Steinhoff 2005). Military repression stimulated protests actions in several South American authoritarian regimes, indicating blowback effects of disproportional repression (Loveman 1998). Knowing where this line of proportionality lies is the "dictators' dilemma" (Francisco 2005), namely, applying levels of repression sufficient to quell protest but not too much to undermine the quiescence of the majority of citizens.

In the absence of widespread marches, rallies, and demonstrations, research on resistance in repressive contexts has uncovered patterns of collective action that take other forms, identified as "street politics" (Bayat 1997, 2003, 2013), "weapons of the weak" (Scott 1985, 1990), and a "resistance repertoire" (Johnston 2006, 2011, 2018). These studies emphasize forms of resistance that contrast with recognizable collective actions such as marches, rallies, demonstrations, petitions, sit-ins, and so on—which fall under the rubric of the modern social movement repertoire (Tilly 1995, 2008). These fine-grained studies of resistance in repressive societies complimented a large bibliography of comparative politics research that often used aggregate measures and statistically modeled the complexity of the repression-mobilization relationship (Maher and Peterson 2008; Ortiz 2013). Yet, such approaches often missed the less obtrusive forms of collective resistance, which are "smaller" and difficult to measure. The point here is not to debate the ways of studying the repression-mobilization relationship but, rather, to establish a jumping off point for the case of China based on two observations. First, the widely supported proposition that overt protest mobilization is dampened by state repression is not operative in China. Indeed, many protests occur every year. Second, the resistance repertoire—those patterns of small, often symbolic, resistant collective actions that characterized the Marxist-Leninist states of the last century—do not seem to be applicable in contemporary China either. These two compelling and counterfactual observations suggest that research on protest movements in China hold the potential for deeper understanding and theoretical refinement.

COLLECTIVE ACTION IN CONTEMPORARY CHINA

When China began its modernization program in the late 1970s and into the 1980s, cases of "mass incidents" were initially quite limited, but soon thereafter the number of protests began to rise. One study recorded 8,700 mass incidents in 1993, which increased to 87,000 by 2005. Göbel and Ong (2012) placed the number of public protests in 2010 between 180,000 and 230,000. However, care is needed in interpreting these figures. Official statistics can include reports of small gatherings at a village police headquarters or party office to voice complaints to deliver petitions to larger protests against chemical plants.

In 2020, researchers of protest in China were working to collect data that would allow comprehensive assessments of big-picture protest patterns. In this vein, Chen (see his analysis in chapter 2) has assembled an important data set for Chinese protests using protest event methods based on newspaper reports that chronicle protests. His data offer figures that show protests increasing between 2005 and 2014 at an astonishing rate of 9.5 times (see figure 2.1). In mainland China, a number of protests are small, and organized demonstrations of 100,000 plus—not uncommon in the West—simply do not occur. Still, Chen's report shows that the number of large protests (more than one thousand participants) also increased during the same period. Recently Zhang and Pan (2019) analyzed social media data to identify more that 136,000 collective action events between 2010 and 2017. Their data show a peak in early 2013 when monthly protests rose above three thousand and more rural, land-related protests, an important finding that synchronizes with our analysis—more on this shortly.

Zhang and Pan observe that no data set of collective action in China should be considered complete (2019, 38) and they analyze several, but we can close this overview by asserting with fair confidence several observations: (1) The number of collective actions in China grew significantly as the country modernized its economy. (2) However, most measures show that the frequency of protests have fallen since 2014, when the policies of Xi Jinping began to restrict the space for dissent and protest actions. Accounts of shutting down nongovernmental organizations (NGOs), prohibition of new ones, comprehensive surveillance, arrests of rights lawyers and dissidents, tighter controls on the press, increased propaganda, and severe repression in minority national regions all attest to this trend. (3) Overall, protest actions, when they do occur, tend to be smaller than those in the West and less formally organized. Zhang analyzes urban environmental protests, noting that, prior to 2014, some mobilized as many as ten thousand participants and had NGO participation, a pattern familiar to protests observed in the West (see chapter 8). The landscape of contentious politics is complex in China. It reflects the opportunities and constraints of a Chinese party-state that is trying to accommodate a rapidly changing market-based economy and a society much more open and dynamic than during Maoist times. These factors impart distinct patterns to the field of play of contentious politics in China. Most significantly, they give rise to a protest repertoire that has unique characteristics when compared to the one that predominates in the West and that differs from the resistance repertoire characteristic of historical Marxist-Leninist regimes.

GOVERNANCE STRUCTURE AND PROTEST REPERTOIRE

An element of the structure of opportunities and threats for collective action is that civil society is developed unevenly in China. Metropolitan areas often host vibrant local neighborhood, community groups, some of which coalesce around shared interests, but, in general, the landscape of independent civic life in China is constrained when compared with the West.[3] Restrictions on nonprofits mean many must register as private businesses, rendering them liable to closing as an illegal business should they participate in activities deemed disruptive or "quarrelsome." The ecosystem of independent NGOs is complex and has been shrinking for several years. Some exist in a corporatist and symbiotic relationship with the regime, as Matsuzawa's study in chapter 7 demonstrates regarding environmental activism (see also Zhang's chapter 8). Other NGOs, say, human rights groups with foreign ties or labor rights organizations, are threatened, and still other charitable and welfare NGOs exist in a netherworld between legality and illegality. Activists who lead civil society groups are sometimes detained by security forces and charged for "picking quarrels and provoking trouble."

A further dimension of civil society development is that significant parts of Chinese society remain anchored in rural villages where peasant life and traditions persist alongside a rapidly changing landscape of economic and social development. Formal civic associations are less developed outside of cities, and party and kinship relations remain important structures in rural areas. We will have more to say about rural protests in a later section, but for now the persistence of the rural demographic, plus the complexities of urban civic and social organization and the Chinese Communist Party's (CCP) influence there, mean that the structure of political opportunities and constraints for protest, despite high levels of occurrence, is distinct from Western polities. Notably, the hiatus between the central leadership and local authorities, which imparted administrative and political flexibility during the reform era, also provided space for collective action as well as the breakdowns in local governance that motivate a lot of protest today.

These observations make the occurrence of high levels of protest in China interesting, both substantively and theoretically, and raise questions if, perhaps, different configurations or distributions of repertorial characteristics are operative there. In the West, established community organizations and active civic life outside of state and party scrutiny are fundamental for the development of social movements. Research has consistently shown that social movements are organized, networked, and resource dependent. They do not "spring full grown from the head of Zeus," as the old collective behavior approaches to protest movements had it—namely, that they emerge spontaneously and self-organize as grievances mount and shared dissatisfaction bring people together.[4] Today, the field of protest studies takes as axiomatic that most movement participation in the West comes via prior association, networked social relations, and histories of engagement in contentious issues. These are seeds of organized civic life—at least in modern democracies—that give bud to protest activism. Different configurations of independent civic organization in China mean that many of the data points in the surge of mass incidents described in the last section have different origins. Suggestive of the self-organization of old collective behaviorist perspectives, many protests gather headway spontaneously as rural villagers and urban dwellers make appeals and petitions to officials, party congresses, and state bureaus. When denied, ignored, or repressed, grievances grow, get emotionally charged—often with stories of police brutality—and transform into larger collective actions, spawned by social media and internet communication technologies. These roots suggest a different shape for mobilization trajectories and different characteristics of the protest repertoire—spontaneous, emotional, and emergent.

We see aspects of a unique form of contestation in O'Brien and Li's (2006) seminal study of rural protests. The collective action events they describe start as "contained contention," referring to a normative awareness of the boundaries within which the actors press their claims and the "mediated tactics" they use. As such, claim making often begins benignly enough within institutional channels, such as a written petition or a collective trip to the offices of local officials to present demands or grievances. Protesters' awareness of limits is reminiscent of trajectory of the Solidarity union in Poland (1981) and how it had a "self-limiting" quality (Touraine et al. 1983). Solidarity's leaders were always clear about accepting the leading role of the communist party and the geopolitical realities of Poland's place in the Warsaw Pact.[5] Solidarity grew to be a movement of national scope and was eventually repressed by martial law. In contrast, "rightful resistance," the term O'Brien and Li introduce for this repertorial configuration, mostly remains constrained and local, which helps deflect repression, although not avoid it completely. Importantly, the "rightful" dimension of these protests, an emphasis on how claimants' rights have been transgressed based on their understanding of official policy and its illegal (or corrupt) misapplication, also embraces a recognition of the legitimacy of the CCP and central state institutions. The logic of rightful resistance is that central leaders of state and party are not the problem but the solution: They are seen as legitimate authorities and guarantors against local malfeasance, illegality, and repression.

THE LOGIC OF PETITIONS AND APPEALS

Present in most collective action is the logic of petitions, appeals, and letters of request to authorities who are assumed to be dedicated to building Chinese socialism and whose responsiveness will lead to satisfaction of grievances, policy change, and reform. This contrasts with a logic operative in most Western protests, which is to mobilize large numbers of participants and to demonstrate their worthiness, unity, and commitment (Tilly 2008). The key assumption here is that protesters have an eye on the next election cycle, with the message, "be responsive or else." Beginning in 1949 as part of Maoist "mass line" politics, workers could send letters and petitions to work unit leaders when grievances or injustices arose in farms and factories (Wang 2012). Petitioning the emperor was a tradition that existed in prerevolutionary times, and the CCP used it to its benefit so that the masses had a way of sending information to higher-level cadres as a mechanism to adjust and fine-tune state policies. This synchronized with the principle of the mass line and was integral to the party's ideological commitment to the welfare of the people. Petitions and appeals also were ways that the activities of lower cadres could be monitored by higher party officials through reports from the grassroots. Today, these entreaties can be directed at numerous targets in the state and party administrative system: village administrative offices, environmental offices, police headquarters, party offices and Party Discipline Inspection Committees, Letters and Visits Office of the Central Committee, local and regional offices of numerous ministries, union offices, forums for public consultation about new policies, and municipal and provincial levels, and so on. In the general absence of elections, these multiple points of access are critical elements of governance to maintain CCP's legitimacy and to gather information about its performance.

Notable is the *xinfang* system (Letters and Visits Offices), a state bureau that has become an important vehicle of grievance articulation. Lee (2003) reports that millions of petition and letter claims are lodged each year within the xinfang system, and that the traffic in the system increased 115 percent during the 1990s, not surprising given the pace of economic and social restructuring at that time. The system provides opportunities not only for individual appeals but also for small collective performances, which, if greater than five petitioners, becomes a "collective petition." These visits often start small to deliver a petition but can gather the participation of bystanders by tapping social psychological processes, whereby the situation is defined provocatively and—in many cases—with heated responses. Importantly for our purposes, the number can grow to scores of participants and even hundreds. Chen argues that "turning up the heat" in these collective actions is a strategy to get a claim heard by officials and get a favorable response (see also Cai 2010: 41–42). If grievances are widely shared, such episodes may develop into campaigns that persist for long periods, but generally they maintain a particular focus and rarely extend more widely geographically. Petitioners can build on neighborhood, workplace, friendship, and familial ties to express anger collectively at local officials and to seek redress based on understandings of citizen rights under the Chinese state (O'Brien 1996; O'Brien and Li 2006).

Local cadres are often the source of injustices or unresponsiveness, leading to another unique element in the topography of Chinese protests. Claimants can "skip a level" and take the letters and petitions over the heads of local officials to provincial or national leaders. This threat has always been more theoretical than practical and, for the most part, remains that way today, but the idea is to hold lower-level officials accountable out of fear of scrutiny by their superiors. Attempts to jump a level, especially the national leaders in Beijing, invoke the wrath of lower officials and bring detentions, beatings, kidnappings, diversions, and pressure put on family members. The career advancement of local officials is based in part on preventing petitions reaching higher levels, and it is not uncommon that petitioners are intercepted and detained extrajudicially in "black jails" (Economist 2013: 45).[6] Alternatively, group petitions are often dealt with by divide-and-conquer tactics to peel off supporters through monetary buy offs. Petitioners know that most local and midlevel officials will not give them satisfaction, but "seem to possess an abiding faith in the center's desire . . . to halt policy violations" (O'Brien and Li 2006: 90). For our purposes, there are two key points: (1) the system is an institutional and routinized means to encourage feedback and claims for purposes of responsive governance, allowing group petitions up to a point but discouraging large collective actions by limiting the number of claimants (Chen 2011); (2) however in practice, the system is also used to stifle and channel citizen claims as much as to hear them and respond to them.

DIMENSIONS OF CLAIMS

Most protests are guided by the belief that higher-level cadres will correct the malfeasance of corrupt ones, and the power and legitimacy the CCP is almost never challenged directly. As such, the information function of protest lies at the heart of the repertoire. Grievances and claims are mostly presented as appeals and petitions regarding the failures of lower-level administrators, not the political center, and justified as mechanisms to inform higher-level officials. Of the different protest categories listed here, most are related to how this institutional lag between governance and institutional development at decentralized levels of state and party administration give rise to discontinuities and injustices caused by lapses in control. Although often denied by participants, collective protests imply questions about the top-to-bottom integrity regarding implementation of the party's leading role, and the occurrence of protests are matters of great concern among state and party leadership. Local officials know that they must minimize them or pay the price. To organize and describe the horizon of protest events in China, we offer the categorization of types as follows, although there are differences among scholars about where to draw the boundaries for each group.[7]

1. *Rural transformation.* This large and heterodox category is a unique feature of the protest horizon in China. It hinges, in part, on historical underdevelopment and Mao's ideological emphasis on the peasantry and its revolutionary potential. This urban-rural divide has always been a key characteristic of demographics in China. The sociological elements of town and village life, kin and neighbor, friend relations and homogeneity of experience help define rural society and become elements of collective actions there. Currently about 60 percent of the population is urban, which compares to about 80 percent in the U.S. A significant urban-rural transition has been underway since 1980, when almost 80 percent of the population lived in rural villages. As discussed, the elaboration of rightful resistance tactics was based on research in Hunan and other provinces in China's central farming region (O'Brien and Li 2006).

Protests in this category include actions against high taxation and arbitrary or burdensome fees on farmers by local officials, unlawful appropriation of harvests, undemocratic procedures in village committees' elections, and environmental issues from rapid modernization (Bernstein and Lü 2003a, 2003b). Also, immorality, conspicuous consumption, and corruption of village or township cadres become local grievances. These latter behaviors might go unnoticed in urban Gesellschaft, but Gemeinschaft relations in the countryside mean they are hard to conceal and easily transformed to topics of village-life discussions. Unjust land expropriations also have emerged as a focus of rural protests since the 1990s, when land-related revenues became a key strategy of meeting provincial and local fiscal shortfalls. Local cadres charged with development of local manufacturing, housing construction, and infrastructure development often compensated locals inadequately for confiscated property and for the hardships caused by removal. Large sums of money change hands and socialist principles of living simply and serving the people can get so obviously transgressed that they spark outrage. Also included here are large national infrastructural projects, such as the monumental Three Gorges Dam, which required the relocation of more than a million rural villagers. Those displaced faced marginalization, unemployment, landlessness, and fragmentation of communities. A protest campaign of petitioning in Beijing by dislocated persons is analyzed by Wing-Chung Ho in chapter 3.

2. *Labor issues*. This a category that also embraces a number of collective actions, which have been increasing significantly over the past decade. From less than one hundred at the outset of 2014, the count rose to almost five hundred 2 years later. Notably, the urban settings of most strikes, the critical-mass quality of the factory floor, and the compelling presence of the targets (business owners and management) produce a configuration of protests that is more recognizable when compared to other categories of protest.

Low wages, poor working conditions, unemployment from restructured state-owned enterprises, and a massive wave of (marginalized) migratory laborers are obviously contradictory to socialist values—more on this in our conclusion. Many strikes are about unpaid or underpaid wages resulting from too rapid growth and fiscal mismanagement of new enterprises. Labor conflicts are today geographically widespread, and tend to be, and tend to be concentrated in private, domestically owned businesses (China Labor Bulletin 2019). In the booming economy, many businesses break labor laws, avoid social insurance payments for workers, and have workers in unsafe production settings. When selling businesses, closing them, or relocating them, factory owners frequently ignore legal obligations to workers. The construction industry, which takes advantage of rural-to-urban labor migration, is reported to be the worst offender (China Labor Bulletin 2019). The report continues that the recent repression of civil society groups that aid workers and worker organizations is designed to curtail labor unrest. Also, the highly competitive informal markets in large cities have been severely constrained and regulated by municipal governments, and workers and taxi drivers are regularly harassed by municipal security forces and *chengguan*.

Economists estimate that 5 million workers could be unemployed in the future as factories continue to automate and the economy slows, increasing the likelihood of more strikes and labor unrest (Thomlinson 2018). Reports indicate that the bureaucratic All-China Federation of Trade Unions seems to avoid the issues of worker welfare for the most precarious sectors, which means that institutional channels to address worker grievances are closed. As Eisinger's classic study (1973) on political opportunities demonstrated, blocked channels of participation can translate to collective violence. We speculate that the contradiction of worker unrest in the context of China's twenty-first-century socialism is not lost on the best thinkers in the CCP, and awareness of workers' potential for social change, as in Poland forty years ago, enters the calculations of party planners as they ponder China's social harmony.

3. *Frauds, Misrepresented Products, and Consumer Safety.* This category derives from the rapidly growing consumer market and weak regulatory oversight. In 2008, for example, a milk and infant formula scandal occurred when supplies were discovered to be contaminated with melamine. Several infants developed kidney stones in Gansu Province as a result, precipitating protests by outraged parents. Shoddy construction of school buildings was revealed by the Sichuan earthquake in May 2008, which resulted in the deaths of thousands of students and, again, gave rise to widespread protests (Wong 2008).

Recently, many small investors were hurt by the collapse of numerous peer-to-peer (P2P) lending firms. At that time the market was unregulated—and even lauded by some officials and state media (Li, Stevenson, and Wee 2018). Nevertheless, the search for high returns produced a bubble. Some firms turned out to be mere Ponzi schemes (Cho 2019). One of the largest, Ezubao, was closed by the government in 2016 for its Ponzi structure of $7.6 billion with 900,000 investors. At the nadir of the P2P crisis, some lenders disappeared with clients' money, and others closed accounts, amounting to tens of billions of yuan. Widespread losses precipitated outbreaks of collective action, social media activism, and coordination of aggrieved citizens in different cities—a development that brought swift response by authorities (Economist 2013).

The rapid growth of an urban middle class in China has also given rise to discontinuities in the housing market. The demand for housing was met by investors in the construction of large suburban housing tracts, often with parks, recreation centers, and other amenities and services to help market the homes. The rapid growth of housing construction over the past twenty years caused gaps in both governance and taxation—in terms of state administration—and tract management—in terms of fulfilling promises made by the builders and by the private management companies that run the services. For our purposes, these gaps get translated into NIMBY-like protests and petition campaigns that sometimes get unruly but, for the most part, are peaceful and given wider leeway by authorities and police. Wright (2019) cites more than 1,200 such mass incidents in Guangzhou related to grievances associated with home ownership, and 600 in Beijing during the five years, 2003 to 2008.

4. *Health, education and welfare issues.* This broad category reflects the transition away from a form of state socialism where all elements of citizen welfare were publicly provided to a more investor-driven market economy in which profit-seeking motives rise to the surface and cause inequities. A major subgroup in this category embraces numerous protests over unpaid or inadequate pensions for workers of closed state-owned enterprises. Included here too are protests of veterans, often about fairness of retirement benefits but also relating to unemployment and difficulties in adjustment (Diamant and O'Brien 2015). Two years ago, protests occurred in several cities, which became volatile because of social media reports of police brutality (Buckley 2018). Earlier in 2016 and early in 2017, thousands of veterans staged protests in Beijing at the People's Liberation Army (PLA) headquarters and the Communist Party Central Military Commission. Veterans, like other aggrieved groups, stay in communication with each other and coordinate protests via WeChat.

Other public welfare services that in the past were exclusively managed by the state, such as health care and education, are also major arenas of grievance because the intrusion of profit-seeking motives affects access and availability. Regarding education, grievances against excessive fees, enrollment in prestigious schools, and perceived biases and inequalities in admissions are common. Parents connect and network via social media in the absence of independent parent-teachers associations. Similarly with health care, aggrieved groups connect regarding poor access, limited resources, grievances of malpractice, corruption, and lack of information.[8]

5. *Environmental protest.* Some of the largest collective actions in China are urban NIMBY-like mobilizations against the construction of polluting factories, especially petrochemical plants (Deng and Yang 2013). In 2007 in Xiamin and again in 2011 in Dalian (Bradsher 2011), thousands of mostly middle-class protesters gathered to protest the construction of PX petrochemical plants. These were large and notable environmental protests and were organized through social media platforms such as Sina Weibo and Renren despite authorities' efforts to block calls for action. Göbel and Ong (2012) point out that these protests are distinct from environmental protests in the countryside, which tend to be directed against water contamination and threats to means of subsistence posed by pollution. In the countryside, the protests are also are smaller and more emotionally charged, while the Dalian protest were convened as causal and peaceful "strolls" as a tactic and had participation of environmental NGOs. These urban campaigns reflect postmodern values of quality of life, a nonmaterial focus characteristic of "new social movements" (Johnston, Laraña, and Gusfield 1994; Kriesi, Koopmans, Duvendak, and Giugni 1995; Melucci 1985), as well as protection of property values—a materialist, NIMBY-like claims. They also exhibit recognizable modern protest repertoire tactics, reminiscent of collective actions in differentiated postmodern societies—not rural villages in the hinterland. Xi Chen's chapter in this volume reviews the distinction between materialist and nonmaterialist contention and how the state responds to protests differently. Repression of environmental protests tends to be lighter.

Chen's chapter also probes the intersection of nonmaterial issues with the dimension civic activism. He reviews the feminist movement, which appeared only in the post-Maoist era as a nonmaterialist new social movement in the civic domain. He notes that feminist groups' tendencies to organize independently and with foreign NGO funding are traits not welcomed by government officials. Many feminist groups are unable find sponsors to officially register. Thus, their impact is limited, and we do not accord them prominent position in our review in this section—despite recent activities of #MeToo activism (Hernández and Mou 2018a, 2018b).

THE SECURITY STATE IN THE TWENTY-FIRST CENTURY

This section focuses on the other side of the mobilization-repression relationship: the state, its repressive apparatus, and its patterns of social control. As HCAs go, the broad landscape of social control in China shows great variability—according to size, activity, focus, geographical scope, and level of state hierarchy to which appeals are directed. For some areas, times, places, and topics, there are degrees of freedom and openness—especially when compared to the Marxist-Leninist regimes of the past century. In 2013 there was a campaign against press censorship by editors and reporters in Guangzhou, something that would have never happened in the Soviet Union or East Germany (Demick and Pierson 2013; Wong 2013; see also Buckley 2013).[9] In 2020, social media chatter criticizing the state's coronavirus coverup in Wuhan shows gaps in censorship. Most Chinese citizens go about their daily lives experiencing latitude in what they do and say and do not feel the oppressive weight of the state. Work, family, friends, shopping, and recreational activities are mostly apolitical activities. The same generalizations cannot be applied to citizens who pursue activist causes—whether labor, environmental, women's issues, consumer issues, or any of the other grievances/claims mentioned in the last section. They encounter the state in ways more reminiscent of the old KGB and Stasi.[10]

In these cases, fear is a mechanism of social control. Sanctions by authorities tend to start lightly, say, being called to police offices for a talk and warning, then shift to punishments such as hours of questioning, unexpected detentions—sometimes for days on end—and prison terms for widely followed activist bloggers who are persistent and unrepetitive. One report, based on a recorded interrogation, describes a police officer's warning that offers a vivid portrait of how social control works:

> Delete all your tweets, and shut down your account. Everything on the internet can be monitored, even the inappropriate comments in WeChat groups. This is truly wholehearted advice for you. If this happens a second time, it will be handled differently. It will affect your parents. You are still so young. If you get married and have kids, it will affect them (quoted in Mozur 2019).

These words echo other statements encountered in our research in Poland, in the Soviet Union, and in East Germany. Although this example is just a warning, it is backed up by threats of imprisonment, life-course-altering sanctions such as denial of employment and discrimination against family (Deng and O'Brien 2013). Notch these up to include the police beatings, reeducation camps, the "knock on the door" and disappearances into "black jails," and the analyst finds all the elements the familiar modern HCA repressive repertoire.[11]

In recent years, however, the Chinese party state has turned to digital dimensions of social control, which is a significant new addition to the repressive repertoire when compared with the twentieth-century Marxist-Leninist HCAs. On the one hand, digital repression and control may seem "softer" (Ferree 2005) than the brute force last century's tactics, but, on the other, it is important to recognize that digital repression too ultimately derives its power from fear (Johnston and Carnesecca 2014). It is common that persistent and outspoken activists in China—power bloggers on WeChat and other platforms or human rights lawyers (Palmer 2017)—end up in detention centers, arrested for spreading rumors or dismissed from employment (Buckley 2013; Jacobs 2010; Li et al. 2018; Wines 2011).

Recently, the growth of the economy synchronizes with increasing possibilities for living one's life digitally. Today, Sina Weibo is a hugely popular app that allows citizens to multitask much of their lives online, all within the same platform. Last year it had more than 450 million total users, and the number of engagements—ranging from sharing gossip and trending topics, to shopping and placing orders, to rating movies and sharing pictures—approached 100 trillion. Millions of new, mostly young users are available via these new platforms for marketing and commerce as China's consumer-based economy develops. Weibo and Tencent are platforms that put China years ahead of the West in developing alternatives for using currency and credit cards for purchases. China's giant tech companies have built ecosystems based on mobile payment platforms that embrace astonishingly robust levels of commercial activity. For the connected young generation, few areas of everyday life escape digital penetration: On your smartphone you can go shopping, order food, rent a car, get a loan, reserve a bike, even schedule a doctor's appointment, and pay for it all (Deyner 2016a).

Like Google and Amazon in the U.S., China's leading tech companies are located at the apex of digital commerce. There is one difference, however. Although Google, Apple, and Amazon mine user data for mostly for marketing and profit (Zuboff 2019), Sina Weibo, Tencent, Alibaba, Baidu, and other leading corporations must also answer to the politics of the CCP. It is simply a cost of doing business, one recognized and accepted. On the one hand, they endeavor to comply with censorship orders regarding keeping forbidden talk and ideas off their platforms. Increasingly, foreign corporations doing business in China must accommodate this, too (Ansfield 2012). On the other hand, the vast and continual data stream that these platforms produce about purchases, who contacts whom, what they say, where they are, where they go, and what they are doing are all accessible by the state. All these are points of data that the state can use to monitor and control its citizens.

Techno-Authoritarianism

China today is poised to be a leader in blanketing society with "sharp eyes" of artificial intelligence (AI) surveillance. In recent years, China has been the world's largest consumers of high-definition surveillance cameras. Estimates place the number of cameras at more than 150 million—one for every nine people.[12] A decade ago, an ambitious program was commenced in Suining County, Jiangsu Province, that attempted combine metadata about activities from social media sources with other data inputs such as GPS location, visual tracking, and facial recognition to create an overall "social credit" score for citizens (Denyer 2016a). Credit ratings are widely used in the West to measure punctuality and consistency in paying bills, but these social credit scores aim to measure of one's moral fiber—reflections of the kind of person you are, good or bad or in between—and go beyond credit scores to touch the core of social identity. The program was partly aimed at the area of consumer fraud, scammers, and businesses that sell unsafe products, goals that, superficially, seem quite benign and uncontroversial. Similar programs have started elsewhere, for example in Rongcheng on the coast of the Yellow Sea and in Langfang in Hebie Province. According to Denyer (2016a), these programs reflect CCP's desire to build a "harmonious socialist society" and a "culture of sincerity."

These programs shrink the distinction between public and private lives and submit a broad range of behaviors to state scrutiny. Based on a total of 1000 points, citizens who jaywalk, smoke on trains, fail to clean up after their dog, carry excessive debt, and—importantly, for our purposes—create disturbances at state offices or skip-level petition, lose points. Other offenses might include spending too much time playing video games, fighting with a neighbor, or talking to the wrong people—say, human rights lawyers or environmental activists. People get points added for good behaviors like giving blood or helping to clean up after a snowstorm. The penalties are so far relatively mild, at least in eastern regions of the country: one's access and functionality on Weibo might be restricted, ratings on dating sites besmirched, limitations on travel can be imposed on, say, the ability to buy first-class train tickets or obtain airline tickets. Doing this for China's 1.4 billion citizens is a daunting task, but implementation of these citywide programs suggest the state is moving ahead.

Added to content dredging of social media and tracking phone-generated GPS locations, street surveillance and facial recognition algorithms provide powerful additional data inputs to the system. The goal is that every citizen has a numbered identity that gives access to the full array of social contacts, behaviors, and measures of trustworthiness, all linked with real-time recognition/tracking of who is where and doing what. The ostensible rationale for this program is public security—the apprehension of criminals, fugitives, and known swindlers identified by constant street surveillance. Campbell (2019) reports that the application of gait-recognition software, which plots thousands of data points about a person's stride and can identify individuals using these patterns, is being used by security services.

Applying such cutting-edge technologies for policing seems to be generally supported: Citizens recognize that when cameras are present, petty crimes decrease and neighborhoods become safer. There are small benefits too, such as vehicles stopping for pedestrians in crosswalks. Anecdotal evidence suggests concerns about privacy are less salient in China, but when legal safeguards are absent, the state can use this ecosystem of surveillance to repress political criticism, track known activists, and intrude deeply in private lives. Uighurs (also Kazakhs, Uzbeks, and Kyrgyz) are required to surrender biometric data like photos, fingerprints, DNA, blood and voice samples (Wee 2019), a reflection of state concerns about ethno-nationalism. Phone tracking and facial recognition apps mean that those who grow beards or go to mosques are identified by the system and interrogated. Heavy video surveillance was instituted in Tibet and Urumqi after ethnic riots (Wines 2010), which has continued to be applied as new technology develops.

The Great Firewall[13]

In January 1996, the internet became available to Chinese citizens. It took just a few months for certain sites to be deleted, for example, about the fall of Eastern European communism, repression at Tiananmen Square, and Islamic terrorism. However, the extent of today's Great Firewall took shape about a decade ago when authorities closed down Google, YouTube, and Twitter after violent ethnic riots in Tibet and Xinjiang (internet access was cut entirely to Xinjian for six months). Google's retreat in 2010 meant that the domestic search engines could be more closely regulated and scrutinized with existing resources, and homegrown alternatives to Facebook, YouTube, and Twitter were easier to control. In the past decade, police and other agencies of state administration expanded the number of censors and amped up the regulation of domestic internet platforms. Also, foreign businesses were required to install chips to block thousands of prohibited sites and track the web history of hundreds of thousands of computers. Such hardware had been on computers of hotels, coffee chains, and internet cafés for years, which linked them with local police servers where they were automatically scanned for access to prohibited sites.

Compared to the technological sophistication of the previous section's programs, blocking websites, posts, and blogs may appear to be mere digital extensions media censorship, police surveillance, bugging, state propaganda, and restrictions on creative freedoms à la KGB and other Soviet-style security agencies. However, as part of the state's repressive repertoire, today's Great Firewall (or Golden Shield as the party calls it) is an extensive, multitiered, and evolving effort. Its strategic objective is to manage a three-pronged dilemma that confronts the Chinese party state: (1) as a leading economic power deeply integrated in a digitally connected word market, (2) it seeks to manage the flow of internet information to limit political criticism and stifle reports on current events that might reflect unfavorably on it, and (3) it also wants to amplify its internet participation to manage domestic policy, foster legitimacy, and positively promote the party's power (Denyer 2016b; Yang 2011).

The Great Firewall's intent is to create "internet sovereignty" that allows for expansive development of commerce and benign social communications among citizens but which also reflects the moral and social management of the CCP. This refers, on the one hand, to limiting pornography, celebrity gossip, and offensive, profane material, as well as ideas deemed alien to Chinese cultural traditions. Added to this are limits on sharing of information about news events that could cascade politically (Stockmann and Luo 2017). Officials have been highly sensitive for the past decade about the speed with which information diffuses through social media and microblogs. Wildfires of popular anger spread on topics like structural failures in new buildings, consumer fraud, or stories of venality and corruption of officials—and recently about the COVID-19 response in Wuhan (Yuan 2020; Wang 2020). When people vent their anger, cybersecurity departments identify them and track their posts to gauge the topography of a gathering collective incident, intercept the opinion leaders or "Big V bloggers" (with millions of followers—V stands for verified account), and delete their accounts—and, in many cases, detain them.

These tactics of internet administration were reinforced and codified in a new cybersecurity law passed in 2017 that established legal parameters for internet censorship, stopped leaks in the flow of uncensored information, and extended supervision of domestic online postings, and not just foreign websites. Administration of Great Firewall policing was extended downward from national-level agencies such as the Ministry of Public Security and the Cyberspace Administration of China, which supervises the internet, to local enforcement agencies that "touch the ground" (Mozur 2019, 7). As a result of this law, internet companies were also required to increase self-censorship of their own content, which has given rise to a secondary market for "censorship factories," and research and development efforts to use more AI-based censorship. Last year it was reported that one online media company had 120 AI learning models applied to monitoring content (Yuan 2019). The law also required that internet companies store user data domestically and make it available for security review. As of December 2019, telecommunications companies were required to obtain facial scans of new internet or mobile phone users as part of the real-name registration process, synchronizing internet use with the metadata programs of social control discussed in the last section.

We close by noting that the state's online involvement also includes (1) the use of propaganda, patriotic and nationalist appeals, and public relations tactics to shape popular opinion through social media tools; (2) a digitized version of mass line politics in which social media postings are reviewed and analyzed, so that the party can be responsive to current trends, and (3) so that it can react quickly to negative news events to prevent a downward spiral of social media comments. Repnikova (2017) discusses departments in the Ministry of Propaganda that analyze social media postings. Her study traces how journalists and reporters get orders how to cover trending topics. It also chronicles how outrage on WeChat about the deadly 2012 floods in Beijing were countered by microblogging state agents portraying the party as responsive to emergencies, for example, by posting that the state's infrastructural development really saved lives. Regarding the floods, official guidance to the mass media was to focus on heroic rescue efforts by dedicated emergency personnel—a strategy used today to counter criticism of the state's coronavirus response. The state also supports paid netizens and volunteers—retired cadres, for example—who report critical and offensive posts and engage as pro-government participants on WeChat, QQ, Baidu Teiba, and Weibo. Repnikova and Feng (2018) observe that officials encourage the coproduction of microblogs for persuasion and propaganda, and state-connected netizens are then called to repost, share content, and shape discussions. Wong (2011) notes that these kinds of actions increased after a Party Central Committee meeting that focused on culture and ideology—presumably reflecting a decision to engage more in these areas. Netizens are encouraged to partake in the life of the top leader, Xi Jinping, through fawning posts and reposts (Repnikova and Feng 2018).[14]

In sum, the scope and depth of internet scrutiny have been expanding for the last decade. On Weibo and WeChat, if one searches, one can still find posts from small investors about financial fraud, videos of land seizures and violence by hired thugs posted by farmers, or social media chatter by unemployed veterans, but many are quickly taken down. Moreover, those who post them are identified, called in for visits with the police, interrogated, warned, and mostly sent on their way—but not always. Internet restrictions are tighter and more intensely monitored in the western provinces of the country, especially references to the Dalai Lama, Islam, and the World Uighur Congress. Although still available in the eastern seaboard cities, virtual private network (VPN) access is highly restricted in the West. There are reports that these digital free spaces have recently been contracted, too.[15]

CONCLUSION

A thread that weaves through the previous discussion is the contrast of contemporary China with the twentieth-century Marxist-Leninist states. Although Polish Solidarity might have been a warning, most social scientists were surprised by the quick collapse of those regimes. The generally accepted equation then was that heavy repression plus high-capacity monitoring of society plus official propaganda and attempts to exclude information from the West equaled a veil of silence that precluded the collective articulation of claims and grievances. Social life was infused with what Timur Kuran (1995) called "preference falsification," essentially an emperor-has-no-clothes explanation of popular quiescence. When no one speaks up, everyone assumes that others are mostly content with how things are and thus choose to "pass" rather than to "voice" their grievances collectively (Hirschman 1972).

Subsequent studies showed that, although this mechanism may have limited civic discourse for many, it did not for everyone. Collective actions of resistance still occurred in these HCAs, just not in the forms that social scientists readily recognized and measured. The term we invoked previously in our essay was the "resistance repertoire"—small-scale, hidden or backstage mobilizations that rely heavily on creativity and symbolism to make a statement of discontent. These small collective actions (1) teach activist skills as the opposition gathers public momentum. Importantly, (2) they break the veil of silence in these HCAs and (3) eventually may "trigger" the broader resistance and larger (and eventually more recognizable) collective actions once political opportunities open. Notably, we have emphasized that this triggering function of resistance repertoire does not strictly apply to China. Indeed, Chinese society is already "triggered," so to speak. As we discussed, public collective actions occur frequently and almost everywhere, although we have noted a downturn since 2014. Our "triggered China" hypothesis means that many citizens can see collective action unfolding. They can learn about it in their social media networks and are thus primed to understand the feasibility and practicality of making themselves heard this way and presume that national leaders will be responsive. This is not to say that a veil of silence does not exist in China; many people watch their words and many others simply avoid politics—but it is more like a net with gaps than a veil that covers completely.

To close then, what can we say about the future? Here too insights from studies in the resistance repertoire tradition can suggest directions for further investigation. First, research suggests care regarding assumptions of an all-seeing omnipotent techno-security regime. Studies shows that despite high-capacity intrusion in daily lives, citizens in the HCAs of the past were able to carve out islands of freedom where the truth could be spoken and room for maneuver claimed. Research suggests that there are several reasons for this. The state itself permits free spaces to exist, for reasons of legitimacy, saving resources, or information gathering. The church in Poland, the theater in Prague, and the women's groups and peace groups in East Germany were examples. We see these sites throughout contemporary Chinese society: charitable groups, environmental NGOs, independent Protestant churches, neighborhood groups, and a few areas of freedom in social media. China could close down access to all VPNs if it wanted to. Also, lapses among the various security services often allows free spaces to blossom. Comprehensive social control is resource dependent, and it must be exercised at numerous levels of the state administration. This means that there are overlaps; but when gaps occur they can lead to a keystone-cops-like scenario in which multiple levels of security agencies compete for turf or steer clear of enforcement, creating interstices where activism can occur. Multiply this by the complexity of social control functions in a country of 1.4 billion people with a vibrant economy and an exponentially expanding virtual reality online, and it is axiomatic that free spaces are bound to exist in China as they did elsewhere.

Second, the various technological monitoring programs that we discussed in the last section, as foreboding a future as they portend, can be circumvented by human creativity, symbolism, duplicity, and deploying the complexities and subtilties of human language. This can move political blogs and voices of dissent just beyond the ability of algorithms to identify them and automatically shut them down. Such tactics constitute a fundamental insight of the resistance repertoire and weapons-of-the-weak literature: subterfuge, subtilty, duplicity, and double-entendre have always been ways of making political statements to avoid getting caught (Wines 2009). On this dimension at least, the police and security agencies seem to be in a weaker position—always reacting to new creative tactics and forced to guess what might come next. It is a game of symbolic whack-a-mole in which bureaucratic and multilayered authoritarian security agencies confront the artistic élan and innovation of activists. This suggests a somewhat more optimistic view for the future, one that counters the brave new world of techno-totalitarianism—a hopeful view that is multiplied by our third and final observation.

By this we refer to the creative force unleashed as younger generations come of age and bring their new perspectives to public discourse. Mannheim observed (1952: 300) that youth can more clearly see injustices in society due to their "fresh contact" with society and history. Protest research has noted that youths have a unique structural availability, being relatively less encumbered by family and work commitments, especially students, which helps explain their commitment and militancy to social change causes. To this we add the general observation that youth seem to be more risk averse. Thus, for a generation born after Tiananmen Square repression, it is plausible that many youths in China may be more willing to risk speaking up for their ideals (Hernández 2018). To this we add that youth are less cognitively encumbered, opening new ways of seeing opportunities but also sharply seeing contradictions in society.[16]

These qualities of youthful participation are reflected in the huge Hong Kong mobilizations of 2019, widely supported by all age groups but driven by committed militant youths who took to the streets. Ming-sho Ho's chapter 9 in this volume shows the creativity, tactical flexibility, and commitment of these activists. But our final point is not about demands for democracy but, rather, about the impact of a younger generation's presence, who mobilize their guile, passion, bravery, and creativity. We project to these events to the mainland, where there too is a sleeping giant of a young generation having come of age with rising expectations, altruism, and love of country but also with "fresh contact with society and history" to give them new perspectives. True, many are apolitical, but many others are not only "triggered" for collective action, as we have mentioned, but also participating themselves in triggering—if only via social media engagement about perceived injustices or failures of the state to live up to its word. Reports about their reactions to COVID-19 coverups and propaganda campaigns are suggestive (Yuan 2020), and it may be that a current of criticism and dissatisfaction flows in some sectors of youth (Wang 2020). How this might manifest is far from certain, but for protest researchers, the long-term prospects of more collective action in China and the countermeasures by the state would seem to be fertile grounds for research and theory.

NOTES

1. Among the monographic studies of protest and social movements in China with a strong contentious-politics focus, scholars can consult Xi Chen (2011), Yongshun Cai (2010), Diana Fu (2017), Ching Kwan Lee (2007), and Kevin O'Brien and Lianjiang Li (2006).

2. To distinguish them from low-capacity states such as Nicaragua under Somoza or Uganda under Amin—"sultanistic regimes"—Weber's concept elaborated by Linz and Stepan (1996) regarding authoritarian states (see Johnston 2012).

3. In the "resistance repertoire" of twentieth-century Marxist-Leninist regimes, such organizations were smaller and often functioned duplicitously to avoid monitoring, claiming to be one thing, such as a hiking club or a jazz society, but sowing the seeds of resistance in their talk, criticism, and jokes (Johnston 2006).

4. An interesting aspect of this period—today, mostly forgotten history in our field—was the intersection of disaster research and the collective behavior focus as it was practiced then. The overlap resided in the processes of spontaneous and emergent organization of disaster responses by affected communities. In cities, towns, and neighborhoods, disasters are clearly "suddenly imposed grievances," a concept that Walsh and Warland (1983) introduced that bridged thinking in the two fields—a quarter-century after Turner and Killian's first edition of *Collective Behavior* (1957) and a time when the resource mobilization perspective de-emphasized the spontaneity and emergent organization of protest movements.

5. Regarding the Marxist-Leninist states of the twentieth century, O'Brien and Li compare their "rightful resistance" concept with Straughn's "consentful contention" in East Germany (Straughn 2005).

6. See note 11.

7. We do not include ethno-nationalist movements here. The macrostructural conditions for their mobilization are different from the domestic, social-problem issues that are the basis of our list here, and, for that reason, we do not discuss the history, resistance, violence, and state respression in Tibet and Xanjiang. Nor do we discuss here the regional autonomy issues that have driven protests in Hong Kong, but we will have a few words about the movement's youthful militants in the conclusion.

8. For example, in 2003, the *Southern Metropolis Daily* reported cover-up of the SARS epidemic (Pierson 2013), paralleling the outpouring of social media anger regarding the coverup and propaganda regarding the COVID-19 outbreak in Wuhan (Yuan 2020; Wang 2020).

9. Editors and reporters from *Southern Weekly* and *Southern Metropolis Daily* struck over revisions made to the traditional New Year's address calling for greater adherence constitutional rights. Guangzhou's propaganda director took it upon himself to rewrite the address, transforming it to praise for Xi's vision for China's future (Pierson 2013).

10. Everyday life is highly constrained in the western ethnic-minority provinces, where mundane aspects of life are intensely scrutinized (Montefiore 2013; Wong 2009).

11. The *laojiao* system of reeducation through labor was officially ended several years ago, but it has since been resurrected in different raiment in Xinjiang as a tactic to quash Islamism there.

12. As of this writing, the U.S. still is the leader per capita in number of cameras.

13. The "Great Firewall" label was introduced in 1997 by an article that appeared in the magazine *Wired*, where issues of Internet freedom in China and how US websites were becoming unavailable there were reported.

14. This has also opened up spaces for lively symbolic humor and scatological postings about Xi and other officials and satire about the state's covert propaganda practices.

15. During the 2010s, VPNs were widely used work-arounds of the Great Firewall. The technology is relatively simple. Users log in to a VPN service and are able to access the internet for outside China through a double link. Google, Twitter, YouTube, *New York Times*, Netflix, and everything was available this way, although at slower speeds. Internet administrators were well aware of them and permitted their existence.

Access waxes and wanes according to the domestic political climate, say, impending Party Congresses, pandemics, or unrest in western provinces. Since 2017 the space for VPNs has shrunk.

16. Lively Maoist-Marxist chat rooms exist today where students challenge growing inequality based on "true" socialist ideals. Leftist sites host topics such as environmental issues, labor protests, unemployment, globalization, and economic theory. Recently, a group of young leftists traveled to Huizhou to help organize an independent labor union, apart from the All-China Federation of Trade Unions, and protest for greater worker protections. On several dimensions this is reminiscent of Solidarity in Poland and was not welcomed by authorities. Many were detained and accused of acting for foreign NGOs (Hernández 2018). Here, youthful idealism confronts the limits of politics.

REFERENCES

Ansfield, Jonathan. 2012. "Chinese Authorities Putting Pressure of Businesses to Help Censor the Web." *New York Times*, November 14: A9.

Bayat, Asef. 1997. *Street Politics: Poor People's Movements in Iran.* New York: Columbia University Press.

———. 2003. "The Street and Politics of Dissent in the Arab World." *Middle East Report* 226: 10–17.

———. 2013. *Life as Politics.* Stanford, CA: Stanford University Press.

Bernstein, Thomas, and Xiaobo Lü. 2003a. *Taxation without Representation in Contemporary China.* New York: Cambridge University Press.

———. 2003b. "Taxation without Representation: Peasants, the Central and the Local States in Reform China." *China Quarterly* 163: 742–63.

Bradsher, Keith. 2011. "Dalian, China, Chemical Plant to Close After Protests." *New York Times*, August 14. Accessed March 7, 2020. https://www.nytimes.com/2011/08/15/world/asia/15dalian.html.

Buckley, Chris, 2013. "Outspoken Chinese Prof Says He Was Dismissed." *New York Times*, October 20: A-10.

———. 2018. "Marching across China, Army Veterans Join Ranks of Protesters." *New York Times*, June 25. Accessed February 8, 2020. https://www.nytimes.com/2018/06/25/world/asia/china-veterans-protests.html?searchResultPosition=1.

Cai, Yongshun. 2010. *Collective Resistance in China: Why Popular Protests Succeed or Fail.* Stanford, CA: Stanford University Press.

Campbell, Charlie. 2019. "'The Entire System Is Designed to Repress Us': What the Chinese Surveillance State Means for the Rest of the World." *Time Magazine*, November 21. Accessed April 9, 2020. https://time.com/5735411/china-surveillance-privacy-issues/.

Chang, Paul Y. 2008. "Unintended Consequences of Repression: Alliance Formation in South Korea's Democracy Movement (1970–1979)." *Social Forces* 87(2): 651–77.

China Labour Bulletin. 2019. "Understanding and Resolving Fundamental Problems in China's Construction Industry." March 18. Accessed March 10, 2020.

https://clb.org.hk/content/understanding-and-resolving-fundamental-problems-china%E2%80%99s-construction-industry.

Chen, Xi. 2011. *Social Protests and Contentious Authoritarianism in China*. New York: Cambridge University Press.

Chen, Chih-Jou Jay. 2020. "A Protest Society Evaluated: Popular Protest in China, 2000–2019." *Mobilization: An International Quarterly* 25(5): 643–62.

Cho, Yusho. 2019. "China's Peer-to-Peer Lenders Fight for Survival." *Nikkei Asian Review*, February 18, 2019. Accessed March 10, 2020. https://asia.nikkei.com/Business/Business-trends/China-s-peer-to-peer-lenders-fight-for-survival2.

Cingranelli, David L., and David Richards. 1999. "Respect for Human Rights after the End of the Cold War." *Journal of Peace Research* 44: 669–87.

Clarke, Killian. 2011. "Saying 'Enough': Authoritarianism in Egypt's Kefaya Movement." *Mobilization: An International Quarterly* 16: 397–416.

Davenport, Christian. 2005. "Understanding Covert Repressive Action: The Case of the U.S. Government against the Republic of New Africa." *Journal of Conflict Resolution* 43: 92–116.

Della Porta, Donatella, and Mario Diani. 2006. *Social Movements. An Introduction*, 2nd ed. Malden, MA: Blackwell.

Demik, Barbara, and David Pierson. 2013. "In China, Press Censorship Demonstrations Continue." *Los Angeles Times*, January 10: A3.

Deng, Yanhua, and Guobin Yang. 2013. "Pollution and Protest in China: Environmental Mobilization in Context." *The China Quarterly* 214: 321–36. https://doi.org/10.1017/S0305741013000659.

Deng, Yanhua, and Kevin J. O'Brien. 2013. "Relational Repression in China: Using Social Ties to De-mobilize Protesters." *The China Quarterly* 215(3): 533–52.

Denyer, Simon. 2016a. "China's Plan to Organize Its Society Relies on 'Big Data' to Rate Everyone." *Washington Post*, October 22. Accessed April 4, 2020. https://www.washingtonpost.com/world/asiapacific/chinas-plan-to-organize-its-whole-society-around-big-data-a-rating-for-everyone/2016/10/20/1cd0dd9c-9516-11e6-ae9d-0030ac1899cd_story.html.

———. 2016b. "China's Scary Lesson to the World: Censoring the Internet Works." *Washington Post*, May 23. Accessed May 25, 2016. https://www.washingtonpost.com/world/asia_pacific/chinas-scary-lesson-to-the-world-censoring-the-internet-works/.

Diamant, Neil J., and Kevin J. O'Brien. 2015. "Veterans Political Activism in China." *Modern China* 41(3): 275–312.

Diani, Mario. 1997. "Social Movements and Social Capital: Network Perspective on Social Movements." *Mobilization: An International Quarterly* 2(2): 129–47.

Economist. 2013. "Treating the Symptoms." March 2: 45.

Eisinger, Peter K. 1973. "The Conditions of Protest Behavior in American Cities." *American Political Science Review* 67: 11–28.

Ferree, Myra Marx. 2005. "Soft Repression: Ridicule, Stigma, and Silencing in Gender-Based Movement." In Christian Davenport, Hank Johnston, and Carol Mueller, eds., *Repression and Mobilization*, 138–55. Minneapolis: University of Minnesota Press.

Francisco, Ronald A. 2005. "After the Massacre: Mobilization in the Wake of Harsh Repression." *Mobilization: An International Quarterly* 9: 107–26.

Fu, Diana. 2017. *Mobilizing without the Masses.* New York: Cambridge University Press.

Göbel, Christian, and Lynette H. Ong. 2012. *Social Unrest in China.* London: ECRAN.

Hernández, Javier C. 2018. "Chinese Fight for Mao's Ideals, to the Chagrin of the Communist Party." *New York Times*, September 29: A1.

Hernández, Javier C., and Zoe Mou. 2018a. "Account of Police Brutality Gives Rise to a #MeToo Movement in China." *New York Times*, October 12. Accessed February 13, 2020. https://www.nytimes.com/2018/10/12/world/asia/china-police-metoo.html?searchResultPosition=3.

———. 2018b. "MeToo Chinese Women Say. Not So Fast. Say Censors." *New York Times*, June 23. Accessed February 13, 2020. https://www.nytimes.com/2018/01/23/world/asia/china-women-me-too-censorship.html.

Hirschman, A. O. 1972. *Exit, Pass, and Loyalty.* Cambridge, MA: Harvard University Press.

Hoover, Dean, and David Kowalewski. 1992. "Dynamic Models of Dissent and Repression." *Journal of Conflict Resolution* 36: 150–82.

Jacobs, Andrew. 2010. "Satirical Post Earns a Year in a Chinese Labor Camp." *New York Times*, November 19: A-10.

Johnston, Hank. 2006. "The Dynamics of 'Small' Contention in Repressive States." *Mobilization: An International Quarterly* 11: 195–212.

———. 2011. *States and Social Movements.* Cambridge, UK: Polity Press.

———. 2012. "State Violence and Oppositional Protest in High-Capacity Authoritarian Regimes." *International Journal of Collective Violence.* 6: 55–74.

———. 2018. "Repertoires of Resistance in the Authoritarian Governance Arena." *Journal for Human Rights* 12(1): 20–45.

Johnston, Hank, and Cole Carnesecca. 2014. "Fear Management in Contemporary Antiauthoritarian Oppositions: 'Taking a Stroll' in China." In Frédéric Royall and Didier Chabanet, eds., *From Silence to Protest*, 27–50. Farnham, UK: Ashgate.

Johnston, Hank, Enrique Laraña, and Joseph Gusfield. 1994. "Identity, Grievances, and New Social Movements." In Enrique Laraña, Hank Johnston, and Joseph R. Gusfield, eds., *New Social Movements*, 13–35. Philadelphia: Temple University Press.

Kriesi, Hanspeter, Ruud Koopmans, Jan-Willem Duyvendak, and Marco Giugni. 1995. *New Social Movements in Western Europe.* Minneapolis: University of Minnesota Press.

Kuran, Timur. 1995. *Private Truths, Public Lies.* Cambridge, MA: Harvard University Press.

Lee, Ching Kwan. 2003. "Pathways of Labour Insurgency." In Elizabeth J. Perry and Marc Selden, eds., *Chinese Society: Change, Conflict, and Resistance*, 115–38. London: Routledge.

———. 2007. *Against the Law: Labor Protests in China's Rustbelt and Sunbelt.* Berkeley: University of California Press.

Li, Cao, Alexandra Stevenson, and Sui-Lee Wee. 2018. "In China, Losing Their Savings on Iffy Apps, Then Their Voice." *New York Times*, August 11: A1.

Lichbach, Mark Irving. 1987. "Deterrence or Escalation? The Puzzle of Aggregate Studies of Repression and Dissent." *Journal of Conflict Resolution* 31: 266–97.

Linz, Juan J., and Alfred Stepan. 1996. *Problems of Democratic Transition and Consolidation.* Baltimore, MD: Johns Hopkins Press.

Loveman, Mara. 1998. "High-Risk Collective Action: Defending Human Rights in Chile, Uruguay, and Argentina." *American Journal of Sociology* 104(2): 477–525.

Maher, Thomas V., and Lindsey Peterson. 2008. "Time and Country Variation in Contentious Politics: Multilevel Modeling of Dissent and Repression." *International Journal of Sociology* 38(3): 52–81.

Mannheim, Karl. 1952. "The Problem of Generations." In Paul Kecskemeti, ed., *Essays in the Sociology of Knowledge*, 276–320. London: Routledge and Kegan Paul.

Melucci, Alberto. 1985. "The Symbolic Challenge of Contemporary Movements." *Social Research*, 52, 789–816.

Montefiore, Clarissa. 2013. "How China Distorts Its Minorities through Propaganda." *BBC* December 15. http://www.bbc.com/culture/story/20131215-how-china-portrays-its-minorities.

Moore, Will. 1998. "Repression and Dissent: Substitution, Context and Timing." *American Journal of Political Science* 42: 851–73.

Mozur, Paul. 2019. "He Was Chained to a Chair in China. His Offense: Posting on Twitter." *New York Times*, January 11: A1–7.

O'Brien, Kevin J. 1996. "Rightful Resistance." *World Politics* 49(1): 31–55.

———. 2006. *Rightful Resistance in Rural China.* New York: Cambridge University Press.

Ortiz, David G. 2013. "Rocks, Bottles, and Weak Autocracies: The Role of Political Regime Settings on Contention-Repression Interactions." *Mobilization: An International Quarterly* 18: 289–312.

Palmer, Alex W. 2017. "The Last Line of Defense." *New York Times Magazine*, July 30: 26–51.

Pierson, David. 2013. "Chinese Decry Press Censorship." *Los Angeles Times*, January 8: A3.

Rasler, Karen. 1996. "Concessions, Repression, and Political Protest in the Iranian Revolution." *American Sociological Review* 61(1): 132–52.

Regan, Patrick M., and Errol Henderson. 2002. "Democracy, Threats and Political Repression in Developing Countries: Are Democracies Internally Less Violent?" *Third World Quarterly* 23(1): 119–36.

Repnikova, Maria. 2017. *Media Politics in China.* New York: Cambridge University Press.

Repnikova, Maria, and Kecheng Feng. 2018. "Authoritarian Participatory Persuasion 2.0: Netizens and Thought-Work Collaborators in China." *Journal of Contemporary China* 27(113): 763–79.

Scott, James C. 1985. *Weapons of the Weak.* New Haven, CT: Yale University Press.

———. 1990. *Domination and the Arts of Resistance.* New Haven CT: Yale University Press.

Soule, Sarah A., and Christian Davenport. 2009. "Velvet Glove, Iron Fist or Even Hand?" *Mobilization: An International Quarterly* 14: 1–22.

Starr, A., L. A. Fernandez, R. Amster, L. J. Wood, and M. J. Caro. 2008. "The Impacts of State Surveillance on Political Assembly and Association: A Socio-Legal Analysis." *Qualitative Sociology* 31(3): 251–70.

Stockmann, Daniela, and Luo, Ting. 2017. "Which Social Media Facilitate Online Public Opinion in China?" *Problems of Post-Communism* 64(3–4): 189–202. DOI: 10.1080/10758216.2017. 1289818.

Straughn, Jeremey Brooke. 2005. "Taking the State at Its Word: The Arts of Consentful Contention in the German Democratic Republic." *American Journal of Sociology* 110(6): 1598–650.

Thomlinson, Harvey. 2018. "China's Communist Party Is Abandoning Workers" *New York Times*, April 2. Accessed March 2, 2020. https://www.nytimes.com/2018/04/02/opinion/china-communist-party-workers-strikes.html?searchResultPosition=5.

Tilly, Charles 1995. *Popular Contention in Great Britain 1758–1834.* Cambridge MA: Harvard University Press.

———. 2008. *Contentious Performances.* New York: Cambridge University Press.

Touraine, Alain, Francois Dubet, Michel Wieviorka, and Jan Strzelecki. 1983. *Solidarity: The Analysis of a Social Movement, 1980–1981.* Cambridge, UK: Cambridge University Press.

Turner, Ralph, and Lewis Killian. 1957. *Collective Behavior*, 1st ed. Englewood Cliffs, NJ: Prentice Hall.

Varon, Jeremy. 2004. *Bringing the War Home.* Berkeley: University of California Press.

Walsh, Edward J., and Rex H. Warland. 1983. "Social Movement Involvement in the Wake of a Nuclear Accident: Activists and Free Riders in the TMI Area." *American Sociological Review* 48(6): 764–80.

Wang, Juan. 2012. "Shifting Boundaries between the State and Society: Village Cadres as New Activists in Collective Petitions." *The China Quarterly* 211: 697–717.

Wang, Vivian. 2020. "The Documented the Coronavirus Crisis. Then They Vanished." *New York Times*, February 20. Accessed April 30, 2020. https://www.nytimes/2020/02/14/business/wuhan-coronavirus-journalists.html?action=click&module=RelatedLinks&pgtype=Article.

Wee, Sui-Lee. 2019. "China Uses DNA to Track Its People, with the Help of American Expertise." *New York Times*, February 21. Accessed April 4, 2020. https://www.nytimes.com/2019/02/21/business/china-xinjiang-uighur-dna-thermo-fisher.html.

Wines, Michael. 2009. "Dirty Pun Tweaks China's Online Censors." *New York Times*, March 11: A4.

———. 2010. "China Keeps Millions of Tireless Eyes on Its People." *New York Times*, August 2. Accessed April 2, 2020. https://www.nytimes.com/2010/08/03/world/asia/03china.html?searchResult Position=1.

———. 2011. "Scatological Mockery of Chinese Official Brings Swift Penalty." *New York Times*, June 6: A5.

Wong, Edward. 2008. "China Admits Building Flaws in Quake" *New York Times*, September 4. Accessed March 7, 2020. https://www.nytimes.com/2008/09/05/world/asia/05china.html.

———. 2009. "China Tightens Security in Tibet." *New York Times.* March 9: A6.

———. 2011. "Beijing Imposes New Rules on Social Networking." *New York Times*, December 12: 9.

———. 2013. "Protest Grows over Censoring of China Paper." *New York Times*, January 8, A1–9.

Wright, Theresa, 2019. "Assessing Collective Contention in China and Beyond: Opportunities, Resources, Behavior, and Outcomes." Paper prepared for the Mobilization Conference on Nonviolent Social Movements in China, San Diego, California, May 10–11, 2019.

Yang, Guobin. 2011. *The Power of the Internet in China.* New York: Columbia University Press.

Yuan, Li. 2019. "China Turns Censorship into Lucrative Factory Work." *New York Times*, January 13: B1–5. Available at: https://www.nytimes.com/2019/01/02/business/china-internet-censor.html?auth=login-email&login=email&searchResultPosition=13.

———. 2020. "Widespread Outcry over Death of Coronavirus Doctor." *New York Times*, February 7. Accessed April 30, 2020. https://www.nytimes.com/2020/02/07/business/china-coronavirus-doctor-death.html.

Zhang, Han, and Jennifer Pan. 2019. "CASM: A Deep Learning Approach for Identifying Collective Action Events with Text and Image Data from Social Media." *Sociological Methodology* 49: 1–57.

Zuboff, Shoshana. 2019. *The Age of Surveillance Capitalism.* New York: Public Affairs Press.

Zwerman, Gilda, and Patricia Steinhoff. 2005. "When Activists Ask for Trouble: State-Dissident Interactions and the New Left Cycle of Resistance in the United States and Japan." In Christian Davenport, Hank Johnston and Carol Mueller, eds., *Repression and Mobilization*, 85–107. Minneapolis: University of Minnesota Press.

Chapter Two

Popular Protests in China, 2000–2019

Chih-Jou Jay Chen (Academia Sinica, Taiwan)

The experience of collective resistance in contemporary Chinese society greatly varies from that of democracies and other authoritarian countries. This study shows that social protests in China occur frequently among a wide range of social groups, in various locations, and take on a variety of claims and forms. However, despite their high frequency and momentum, most popular protests in China are disorganized, dispersed, and short-lived. Still, they are widely used as an instrument to put pressure on the government to meet the protesters' demands.

This study examines key features of popular protests in China over the past two decades, identifying the dynamic relationship between protests and repression. Over the course of the past two decades, intensifying social conflicts and widespread popular protests have occurred all over China. Diverse sectors of society are participating (e.g., students, public employees, industrial workers, farmers, etc.) in popular protests and are employing increasingly confrontational tactics. An underlying source of these social conflicts has been the growing social grievances, frustrations, and tensions of Chinese society. China's fast-growing economy has created a powerful government and a nouveau-riche upper class, leading to a profound divide between the haves and the have-nots. Widening social inequality has become a plain fact of everyday life. At the same time, Chinese citizens have become more aware of their rights and interests. When their rights and interests are impaired, especially due to government corruption or abuse of power, complaints surge and protests intensify. As this study shows, protests soared from the early 2000s to the mid-2010s, before rapidly shrinking in the mid-2010s under Xi Jinping's rule.

To keep social conflict at bay and ensure stability, the government has relied on a series of *weiwen* (stability maintenance) and social governance measures, ranging from generous financial incentives to rigorous surveillance and ruthless crackdowns of protesters. Repression remains an essential measure for social and political control in China. Since Xi Jinping came to power in 2012, the Chinese government has become more aggressive in dealing with political dissidents and those who engage in civil resistance (Franceschini and Nesossi 2018; Fu and Distelhorst 2017). In January 2019, China's Minister of Public Security stated that China's police must focus on withstanding "color revolutions" (popular uprisings) and treat the defense of China's political system as their central mission (Reuters 2019). However, the sheer use of brute force is not the routine practice when dealing with contentious daily incidents. Surprisingly, the government has sometimes tolerated or accommodated protesters to serve its own interests (Lee and Zhang 2013). On the one hand, protests function as a source of information for high-level authorities who tend to lack knowledge due to restrictions on the free flow of information in society. On the other, protests can help reveal the severity of an issue and its potential for more disruption if it remains unaddressed (Huang, Boranbay, and Huang 2019).

As Tilly pointed out, "The repressiveness of a government is never a simple matter of more or less. It is always selective and always consists of some combination of repression, toleration, and facilitation" (Tilly 1978: 106). Therefore, it is imperative to identify the triggers of the Chinese government's selective use of repression or toleration of social protests. In other words, what type of protesters are more likely to be repressed or tolerated by the government? What are the implications of the different configurations of protests and repression on China's institutional transformation?

Based on an analysis of more than twelve thousand protests in China that occurred between 2000 and 2019, this study first reports the trends and characteristics of social unrest in China, exploring how and why protests had become frequent despite the government's efforts to maintain social order and how protests have declined significantly since the mid-2010s. It then examines the extent of violence and forceful policing during protests, during different time periods, and across rural and urban areas. The configurations of collective protests and government responses illustrate the institutional arrangements of contentious politics and social-conflict resolution in China. This study concludes that the dynamics of social protest in an authoritarian regime like China are highly associated with the state's capacity to institutionalize contentious politics, impacting the changing state-society relations in China.

WHY PROTESTS ESCALATED

Since the 1990s, China's institutional changes and market reforms have produced weak mechanisms to protect citizens' interests from being violated. Although unorganized citizens became vulnerable to abusive state and nonstate actors, the state encountered difficulties in demobilizing them for a period of time because of its limited resources and ability to control them. Beginning in the 1990s, China's collective resistance first originated with the reform of the state-owned enterprise system in urban areas, which led to mass protests by laid-off workers. Rural peasants also repeatedly engaged in collective petitioning or collective resistance to protest raising taxes or the corruption of local cadres. Since 2000, private enterprises and foreign investment enterprises have developed rapidly, hiring a large number of migrant workers. However, because labor security was insufficient and labor disputes were frequent, protests by workers had heightened. At the same time, based on financial needs and urban development, local governments stepped up urban expansion and demolition projects that resulted in a growing number of mass protests. During this period, except for a few Falun Gong protests, most instances of collective resistance did not challenge the legitimacy of the Chinese communist regime. They mostly focused on economic demands, personal rights, maladministration, or executive corruption.

How can the rapid increase in collective protests in China over the past two decades be explained? This study shows that social protests had recurred in China because state authority—while constantly threatening the interests of social groups—had limited capacity to demobilize the aggrieved. The literature on collective resistance in China rarely connects Chinese experiences to the study of social movements in Western democracies. However, social movement literature in democratic countries provides useful insights into understanding collective protests in authoritarian China. Protest groups in China are usually those whose rights and interests have been harmed during institutional transformation and the market transition processes. On the one hand, emotional grievances and interest demands drive protest actions. On the other hand, the social movement literature suggests that political opportunity, resource mobilization, and framing processes are often more important factors in the formation and development of collective actions. The surge of popular protests in China has been linked to these factors (O'Brien 2008).

Political Opportunity

Collective protests and contentious action occur when political opportunities arise and when protest participants have access to resources (McAdam

1999 [1982]; Tarrow 1998; Tilly 1978). Political opportunities refer to those aspects of the political system that affect the possibilities for protest groups to mobilize effectively (Tarrow 1996). Among many aspects of the Chinese political system, decentralization—a certain degree of autonomy of local governments given by the central government—has been the most crucial factor driving economic development and maintaining effective rule in China. Given the formidable scale of governance in China, the central government is in charge of policy making, and local authorities have to implement policies. However, this separation gives rise to a fundamental tension between the central government and local governments. The extent of the authority of the central government is achieved at the expense of local governance effectiveness. Therefore, the strengthening of local governance capacities implies the expansion of local authority, which often leads to an acute threat to the central authority (Zhou 2014).

Maintaining social stability has been the primary political responsibility of both the central and local governments in China. However, the central-local separation in Chinese bureaucracy has paved the way for political opportunities facilitating protest mobilization and claims making. Political opportunities arise from two starting points. One point highlights the disparities among state authorities or among authorities of different levels in the political echelon, especially the disparities of interests and priorities between the central and local levels (Bernstein and Lü 2003; O'Brien and Li 2006). The other point asserts that the central government tolerates social protests because they serve as a source of information on local agents, helping the central government identify social grievances and instances of corruption and maladministration by local cadres (Huang et al. 2019; Lorentzen 2013).

For example, the labor department in local governments prefers enhanced enforcement of labor laws, and the environmental department aims to control industrial pollution. Yet, the industrial and commercial department is concerned about corporate profits and government revenue. Different government departments have diverse goals that result in various behavioral patterns, so inconsistency among government departments provides political opportunities for protesters to exploit for the purpose of protecting or pursuing their interests. For example, during the late 1990s and early 2000s, the State Environmental Protection Administration (SEPA) of the Chinese central government acted as a crucial ally of the environmentalists. The environmental movements were successful in several campaigns mostly because of the support of SEPA (Sun and Zhao 2007).

Also, opportunities may arise in part from "the central-local divide," as protesters use the threat of disruption to increase the possibility of intervention from higher-level authorities (O'Brien and Li 2006; Cai 2010). For example, since the 1990s, the "rightful resistance" in rural China has hinged on peasant protesters making use of the legal system and central government directives, thus securing support at higher levels for their efforts to check local misconduct (O'Brien and Li 2006). Labor protests, labor laws, and regulations issued by the central government (including pension contributions, overtime pay, and housing allowances) give workers leverage points to launch strikes demanding more financial reimbursement from employers and local governments (Chen 2015; Elfstrom and Kuruvilla 2014).

The Chinese government is not popularly elected and lacks procedural legitimacy. Therefore, it has to rely heavily on good performance to buttress its power. The central government is more concerned with regime legitimacy and stability, and thus, it is more tolerant of citizens' nonpolitical actions if repressing such activities damages the regime's legitimacy (Cai 2008). With this belief in the central authority's willingness to accommodate people's nonpolitical claims and rightful demands, Chinese citizens commonly cite legitimate grounds for pursuing their interests (O'Brien and Li 2006). On the other hand, local governments tend to focus on local economic interests and their performance appraisals by higher levels of government. Local authorities are willing to make concessions if they realize that their own interests will be at stake or that higher levels of government will intervene.

Another reason why local protests are tolerated by higher levels of government is due to information constraints. Higher-level authorities usually face difficulties in gathering reliable information about the policy implementation of local governments and the underlying grievances of the masses. Social protests can provide information about whether local governments have gone against the central government's directives and bring social discontent to the surface rather than keeping it underground (Lorentzen 2013). In addition, large and disruptive protests are often reported by the media and are an important source of information for higher-level governments to identify grievances and social conflicts in grassroots society.

As mentioned previously, disparities between the central and local authorities shape the political opportunity structure for social protests. The central government considers its own legitimacy and information constraints, and therefore, its inclination on whether to intervene or to suppress local collective protests often depends on these considerations. Local governments must follow the directives of the central government and fulfill its various political and economic requirements. The central government's attitude to social protest is thus crucial to local governments when dealing with social resistance. The local governments become more repressive when the central government becomes less tolerant of social protests or encourages repression. The interaction between the central and local authorities thus shapes the political space for collective action.

Mobilizing Structures

In addition to political opportunities, mobilizing structures—the ties that connect individuals to groups that organize action—come in many forms and facilitate the mobilization of collective protests in China. Communist regimes understandably prohibit independent organizations to preempt political threats. In China, the party-state discourages or prohibits the formation of organizations aimed at protecting citizens' interests. For example, although trade unions may occasionally help mediate disputes between workers and their employers, they are far from assertive when defending workers' rights (Chen 2003). Trade unions and professional organizations are official organs of the party-state; they are not the mobilizing base for collective actions. Although collective actions rarely challenge the legitimacy of the state, they are not legally institutionalized nor officially sanctioned, and usually not initiated or orchestrated by resourceful organizations. Popular protests are mostly spontaneous, mobilized through existing social or religious networks or institutions among the citizens such as villagers or coworkers (Pun 2007; Deng 2014; Luo and Andreas 2016; Lu and Tao 2017). Since the mid-2000s, when the internet and mobile phones gained popularity, social media have played a crucial role in facilitating the mobilization of collective actions.

Community associations, nongovernmental organizations (NGOs), and work or hometown relations have brought people together to launch collective protests. Labor strikes in China are typically initiated by unorganized workers rather than by trade unions—whose task is to mediate, not only between workers and the government but also between workers and employers (Chen 2010). Although worker NGOs will not take the lead in confrontations with the state and usually avoid developing cross-regional networks, their contribution is to provide information or consultation on specific policy areas (e.g., labor regulations, organizing of trade unions, labor disputes) and also assist individual workers in negotiations and formulating requests in labor disputes (Elfstrom 2019; Chan 2013; Lee and Shen 2011; Friedman 2009; Friedman and Lee 2010). In addition to providing daily consultation services for workers, some NGO activists will actively provide online assistance and legal advice when they encounter cases of collective resistance or worker strikes and encourage workers to establish trade unions. Some even offer assistance to ensure the release of detained worker leaders (Li and Duan 2013; Chen 2019).

Trade unions and worker NGOs in factories in China rarely take the lead in organizing collective resistance. The main mobilizing structures can be found in the workers' daily community and their social relations in the workplace. The development of civic organizations in Chinese society is heavily restricted by the state. Therefore, the mobilization of collective action often carries a high degree of spontaneity and relies on the living and working environments of the mobilized group. For example, during instances of collective resistance in rural China, protesting villagers often rely on the leadership of capable cadres in the village. Associations of village elders, kinship organizations, and neighborhood relations also play an essential role in mobilizing citizens for collective action (Deng 2014).

Many aspects of social conflicts in China also carry an emotional charge. Research found that shared understandings and emotional activities were crucial in shaping the dynamics of collective actions during riots or poorly organized social movements in the U.S. before the 1960s (Jasper 2011). Similarly, in authoritarian China, where collective actions are not institutionalized and are not well organized, rumors and high-running emotions have played a significant role in shaping the dynamics of social protests (Zhao 2000, 2001; Perry 2002; Yang 2009). Also, people in a poorly organized social movement are more likely to follow specific cultural scripts or even their culturally embedded emotions and instincts to pursue their demands (Zhao 2010a).

Many of China's collective protests rely on mobilization of emotions. Collective resistance arises when shared values are being violated (Perry 2002). In this sense, social movements are motivated by concern for due honor, pride, and recognition of one's basic humanity (Honneth 1995). Take China's petitioning peasants, veterans, ethnic minorities, and religious groups for example. Even if they seek compensation for economic interests, what pushes them to overcome difficulties and continue to fight is not an instrumentalized, rational calculation. Their motivation is to receive fair treatment and an apology for the humiliation they were subjected to. In the age of the internet and social media, the emotional mobilization of collective action in China has spread like wildfire (Yang 2009).

WHY PROTESTS DIMINISHED

As the performance evaluation of local leaders in China is linked to their ability to maintain social stability, local governments have tried to minimize or prevent social protests by improving information collection and by creating, strengthening, and coordinating state institutions to better handle disputes (Meng 2016; Hu 2011; Yang 2017; Chung 2012). Concessions and repression (or threat of repression) have been the primary methods employed by local governments to demobilize protests, thereby reversing the upward protest trend from the mid-2010s. The strategy of "buying stability" (*hua qian mai pingan*, literally meaning "paying cash for peace") has been the most prevalent means of pacifying aggrieved citizens involved in labor, land rights, and property disputes (Lee and Zhang 2013; Su and He 2010; Elfstrom and Kuruvilla 2014; Heurlin 2016; Yan 2016). Buying stability reflects the local government's eagerness to preserve stability before aggrieved protesters swarm the streets or block office buildings of higher-level government agencies. The practice seems to have effected some positive change, and it has become a lasting mechanism (Lee and Zhang 2013; Heurlin 2016).

The essence of buying stability does not lie in the payment amount but the processes leading to it. It is through grassroots efforts of "mass work, thought work, and education work" that state power is practically realized (Lee and Zhang 2013). For protesters, their family and social relationships may put them under unbearable pressure. For example, before resorting to violent suppression, local officials may quell resistance by deploying intermediaries such as hired thugs (X. Chen 2017; Ong 2018), relatives and acquaintances (Deng and O'Brien 2013; O'Brien and Deng 2015), as well as neighborhood committees and clan organizations (Deng 2017; Mattingly 2016). These methods are the most prevalent means of pacifying the aggrieved in social conflicts in China's grassroots society. Consequently, the cost for the state is believed to be "enormous and rising" (Chen 2013). However, buying stability and resorting to relational connections cannot be easily applied on a large-scale basis because of the high costs involved. Hence, many local authorities fail to fully accommodate protesters because financial resources are inadequate, and all possible connections have been used up.

Apart from concessions, repression has been equally—if not more—important in creating the downward trend of collective protests in China after the mid-2010s. Under Xi Jinping's leadership, local governments have been more repressive in coping with protests against land seizures and, therefore, more likely to arrest protesters. The state's crackdown on certain disadvantaged groups, including peasants who lost their land, has become particularly severe. Chinese peasants are considered subordinate both socially and economically and, thus, are more likely to be met with fierce repression during protests (C-J Chen 2017). Furthermore, thanks to sophisticated digital technology, the Chinese government has established a surveillance state of immense scale (see Johnston and Zhang chapter 1 in this volume). It has enhanced information collection and internal security, elevating mass surveillance to cope with collective protest and resistance (Shahbaz 2018). Intensified surveillance has advanced the state's capacity for preventive repression.

Information facilitates preventive repression because it not only reveals citizens' underlying preferences but also identifies individuals for the type and level of grievance they possess (Greitens 2019). During collective protests, local mobile networks are shut down, and social media apps blocked. A broad use of these repressive tactics may have effectively reduced the number and scale of peasant protests.

The Chinese government has also attempted to preempt collective action by strengthening the monitoring of citizens and by instituting information-collection mechanisms. From Xi Jinping's rise to power in late 2012 to the eruption of the COVID-19 pandemic in spring 2020, the most critical change in Chinese politics and society has been the authoritarian regime's accelerated oppression of civil rights and the public sphere and its realization of a digital governance of total surveillance. In response to increasing resistance and dissent, the regime has treated collective protest as a national security issue.

The central and local authorities have established nationwide surveillance and intelligence networks, tightening internet controls and codifying policies within the law (Lei 2017). Specifically, the National Security Law and the Cybersecurity Law have been introduced, and the new government agency, the State Information Office, has been established. They provide legitimacy and facilitation of the government's gathering of intelligence and monitoring of the situation on the ground across the country (Chung 2012). China's censors have reined in blogs, social media, and search engines and effectively eradicated any "incorrectly oriented" information. Information and blog posts on provocative collective protests are blocked on social media platforms. The collusion between the state and a group of powerful internet companies, along with real-name registration, labor-intensive censorship, and the social credit system, all have contributed to the deep infiltration of the state into society. Various stability-preservation offices are tasked to screen and detect social conflicts at the grassroots level. Such activities include field investigations, information gathering and analysis, household visits, and discussions with pertinent parties (Yan 2016). The result is that the government has been able to monitor and suppress disadvantaged protest groups, such as petitioners, ethnic minorities, and religious groups more comprehensively and effectively than ever before.

THE DYNAMICS OF COLLECTIVE PROTEST

Social protests challenge authoritarian rulers in part because the dynamic process of collective action may produce unpredictable outcomes. In a repressive regime, social protests signal not only societal grievances but also the limitations of the state's control. The dynamic process of collective protest in a country depends on its state-society relationship on the basis of which the state may shape collective resistance. The extent of the state's capacity to channel protest activities into more institutionalized forms is critical to a country's state-society relationship and its national development.

In Western and East Asian democratic countries, riots and public disturbances are rare; popular protests and social movements moved from a stage of chaotic insurgencies and severe repression into a process of institutionalization and legalization, transforming the whole society into a "social movement society" (Meyer and Tarrow 1998; Soule and Earl 2005). However, in authoritarian China, the state has a much weaker capacity and incentive to institutionalize social conflicts. The government has been much less tolerant of contentious activities that directly challenge the central government's legitimacy (Chen and Cai, 2021). Protest activities in China vary widely in terms of groups, claims, size, targets, forms, as well as government responses. Some of them operate like chaotic insurgencies, while others act peacefully and follow the rules. Similar forms of protest activities occurring across China may present different dynamics depending on the local political contexts. The Chinese authoritarian state behaves differently when facing different kinds of protest activities. It can prohibit or hamper some but facilitate other forms of social protest, and it can also be seen either as a unitary actor or an entity of multiple interests and voices, all depending on the kind of social conflicts concerned (Zhao 2010b).

With China's rapid economic development over the past four decades, many opportunities were created, but many contradictions were also spawned. The Chinese government regularly emphasizes that its national development is impossible without a stable environment. However, stability does not necessarily exclude social conflicts or collective protest. It requires that the country's ability to reduce social conflicts is continually extended and improved, thereby eliminating the possibility of large-scale, massively destructive movements.

DATA AND METHODS

Systematic data on social protests in China is lacking. This study draws on data from my collection of more than twelve thousand protest news events that occurred in China from 2000 to 2019. Since 2007, my research assistants have been collecting cases of social protests from fifteen online sources, including newspaper databases—six of which are located outside of mainland China.[1] For a news event to be included in the database, four nominal criteria had to be met: It had to involve more than ten participants; it had to present either a grievance against some target or a demand made to some institution; it had to take on confrontational form; and it had to be located in the public sphere. Based on these criteria, nonconfrontational events (i.e., complaints, letter-writing campaigns, lawsuits, and press conferences) have been excluded. Petitioning (*shangfang*) events were included only if they escalated into public protests (e.g., holding demonstrations or sit-ins in front of government offices); legal and routine petitioning activities were not included in our database.[2]

It is difficult to assess whether the cases I collected are representative of the overall protest landscape in China, but to my knowledge, my database includes the largest number of publicly accessible news reports from the past decade. However, relying solely on media reports may introduce bias into the data (see Earl, Martin, McCarthy, and Soule 2004; Koopmans and Rucht 2002; Koopmans and Statham 1999; Ortiz, Myers, Walls, and Diaz 2005; Rucht and Neidhardt 1999). First, in regard to contemporary Chinese news reports, the fluctuation in the number of protests over the years may be caused by selective editing by the media or state censorship. Hence, the number of reported protests may not accurately reflect the actual number of protests. Second, protests by some groups (e.g., urban workers) may be more likely to gain media attention than others (e.g., peasants in remote areas). Small-scale protests are also less likely to be reported than large-scale ones. Therefore, certain kinds of protests may be underrepresented in the database. These possibilities certainly exist, but they do not necessarily invalidate the analysis in this study because I have been carefully maintaining the validity and reliability of the database.

To maintain data reliability, the data sources were kept the same and cases were drawn systematically from the same newspaper databases and news agencies. Protest news solely from the internet or social media sources were not included to prevent introducing another layer of bias. My data set comprises more than 2,500 large-scale protests with 1,000 or more participants each. Because large-scale protests are less likely to be covered up, they can be suggestive of the nature and trend of social protests in China. Another study on protest events in China drawing on data from social and news media also finds that reporting bias in the news media is substantially reduced for large events (Goebel and Steinhardt, 2019). Thus, I compared my collection of all cases with the collection of only large-scale protests and found that the distribution of protests across different social groups over different periods displays similar patterns across the two collections. This result implies the data is not biased and its overall quality is satisfactory. However, this study is not limited to large-scale cases. As it is necessary to examine protests of different sizes, small-scale protests were also included in the analysis.

Furthermore, considering the political sensitivity of protest news in China, description bias may exist in the news events data. The news stories published in Chinese newspapers tend to present a government perspective, whereas some of those outside China may present the government in less favorable light. For example, while protest activists might seek to attract media attention to expose government officials' wrongdoings, news reports might frame the coverage in ways that underscore the disruption and violence of the protest. These possibilities certainly exist, but they do not necessarily invalidate the analysis because key variables included in this study were mostly objective protest characteristics, such as date, location, protest groups, the number of participants, the type of demands, the protest target and tactics, and the government's response. Although data from reported protest events cannot be relied on for a description of the whole country along any single dimension, this unrepresentativeness does not necessarily affect the generalizability of findings regarding the relationships between variables (cf., Manion 1994). Existing research on contentious politics in China is mostly based on case studies or small samples.[3] This study examined the characteristics and trends of protests with a large sample. In this way, it can make a significant contribution to advance systematic research in this area.

DYNAMICS OF SOCIAL PROTESTS IN CHINA

This section first presents the development and expansion of popular protests in China. From the news events data of 12,585 cases from 2000 to 2019, it can be ascertained that collective resistance in China had rapidly increased with regard to the number of events, spatial expansion, and regional distribution. Figure 2.1 shows the frequency distribution of protest events from 2000 to 2019, including protests that occurred in urban and rural areas. By and large, there was a rising tendency of social protests from 2000 to 2014. During the period of 2004–2005, an initial rise in the frequency can be observed. In 2007, protest frequencies reached their first peaks, continuing their climb in 2009 only to regress around 2011–2012. The annual number and increasing rates of protests in cities were far greater than those in rural areas. Nevertheless, they reveal similar trends, with their frequencies reaching a peak of 2,212 in 2014.[4] In 2015, however, the number began to decline to 1,703, shrinking to a twelve-year low of 195 in 2019.

Meanwhile, large-scale protests revealed a similar pattern; their numbers increased from 25 in 2000 to 90 in 2005 to 116 in 2010, before reaching 311 in 2014 (figure 2.2). They started to decline and reached 266 in 2015, falling to a twelve-year low of 26 in 2019. Both the collections of all protest

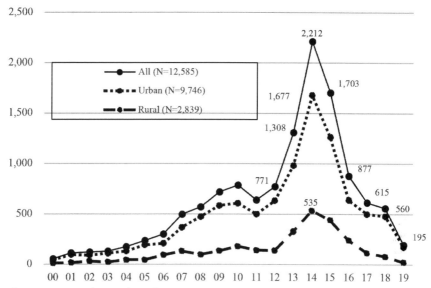

Figure 2.1. Yearly Number of Protest Events, 2000–2019

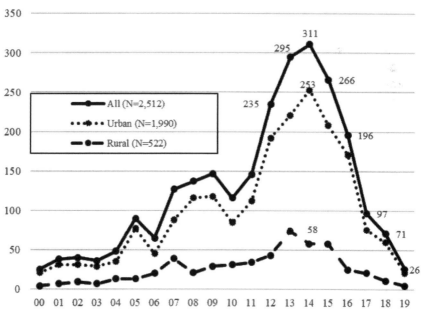

Figure 2.2. Large-scale Protest Events (> 1000 participants), 2000–2019

Table 2.1. Distribution of Participants in Social Protests in China, 2000–2019

	2000–2019		2000–2002	2003–2007	2008–2012	2013–2015	2016–2019
	N	%	%	%	%	%	%
Public-sector employees	1,407	11	31	18	13	7	12
State-owned firm workers	694	6	27	13	6	3	4
Military veterans	341	3	0	2	3	2	6
Civil servants, teachers, etc.	372	3	3	3	5	2	2
Private-sector employees	2,949	23	17	24	25	25	18
Private-sector workers	2,334	19	13	18	18	20	16
FDI workers	615	5	4	6	7	5	1
Urban residents harmed	4,210	33	20	24	30	36	40
Homeowners	1,121	9	1	6	7	12	9
Petitioners	1,176	9	0	5	7	12	11
Displaced residents	361	3	3	4	4	2	2
Students	214	2	5	3	2	1	1
Ad hoc groups (masses)	837	7	6	8	8	5	8
Minorities and religious groups	343	3	6	1	4	2	2
Peasants	2,839	23	21	25	20	25	20
Total	12,585	100	289	1,338	3,488	5,223	2,247

FDI, foreign direct investment.

incidents and of the large-scale ones showed that the number of social protests in China reached its climax in 2014, only to fall dramatically during the 2016–2019 period.

Table 2.1 presents the distribution of social groups in popular protests during different eras of Chinese leadership: 2000–2002 (i.e., Jiang Zemin administration); 2003–2007 (i.e., Hu Jintao's first term); 2008–2012 (i.e., Hu Jintao's second term); 2013–2015 (i.e., the first three years of Xi Jinping's rule) and 2016–2019 (i.e., the period when Xi Jinping's power consolidated). I differentiated these five periods with the aim of understanding the broader processes of social protest and social control employed by the Chinese government and its agencies under the leadership of Jiang Zemin, Hu Jintao, and Xi Jinping. Highlighting how state authorities respond to protest events can help us understand the state's incentives and illustrates the extent to which state authorities and citizens view protest as a legitimate mechanism for political participation. Especially after Xi Jinping came to power in late 2012, civic organizations, media freedom, and rights activists have all been subject to severe suppression and control by the state. The shrinking space for protest activities and suppression of collective protests have notably changed in comparison to past administrations. To highlight the impact of the Xi Jinping administration even further, I divided his tenure (2013–present) into the first three years (2013–2015) and the following four years (2016–2019).

Protest participants were divided into the following categories: (1) public-sector employees; (2) private-sector employees; (3) urban residents; (4) ad hoc groups or groups of people with mixed backgrounds; (5) minorities and religious groups; and (6) peasants. Public-sector employees included civil servants, military veterans, workers at state-owned and collective firms, and those working in public institutions (schools and banks). Private-sector employees included self-employed individuals, workers at private firms, and workers at foreign direct investment (FDI) firms. Urban residents refer to those who come from the same group with their interests or rights harmed, including homeowners, petitioners, displaced residents, and students. Ad hoc groups consisted of previously unassociated protest participants who joined protests because of issues of common concern (e.g., environmental pollution) or as participants of riots.

The data showed that some groups protested more frequently than others, and the same groups might participate in collective protests differently at different times. As presented in table 2.1, workers at state-owned firms frequently protested in the early 2000s, accounting for 27 percent of all protests during 2000–2002, reflecting a large number of labor disputes and workers' protests caused by the transformation and privatization of state-owned firms during that period (Lee 2007; Hurst 2009; Chen 2009). Workers' protests at state-owned firms significantly declined in later years, accounting for 3 percent of total protests in 2013–2015 and 4 percent in 2016–2019, respectively. In contrast, protests staged by private-sector employees accounted for a major part of the protests: their protests had become more frequent from 2008–2015 (about 25 percent) but declined from 2016–2019 (18 percent). The protest group of urban residents harmed—including homeowners, petitioners, displaced residents, and students—staged the most protests, accounting for 33 percent of the total number of protest events over twenty years. In particular, during the recent 2016–2019 period, their protests further increased, accounting for 40 percent of the total number of protest events, which were disputes with businesses or claims for their rights and interests. Peasant protests accounted for 20 percent to 25 percent of the total number of protest events over the twenty years. Rural residents protested mainly because of disputes over tax and fee collection (before the 2004 tax reform) and their loss of farmland, which has been a constant source of grievances among peasants in many localities (Chen 2020; Cai 2003; Guo 2001; Zweig 2000).

Protest Targets and Claims

The challenge to the state authority is measured by the target at which a protest is directed. I divided the targets of complaints into five categories: (1) high-level government, including ministries of the central government, provincial government, and municipality government (i.e., Beijing, Shanghai, Tianjin, and Chongqing); (2) low-level government, including prefecture-level, county-level, and township-level government, except village government in rural areas; (3) state-owned firms; (4) nonstate firms; and (5) village government.

As table 2.2 shows, 13 percent of the protests of the 2000–2019 period targeted the central and provincial governments, 30 percent were directed against governments at the prefecture-city level and lower, 13 percent against village governments, 14 percent against state-owned firms, and 30 percent against nonstate firms. The distribution of protest targets showed significant changes between 2016–2019 and previous periods. During the 2016–2019 period, the proportion of protests directed at different levels of government increased. The proportion of protests targeting the central and provincial governments grew from 11 percent in 2013–2015 to 18 percent in 2016–2019, while the proportion of protests targeting local governments rose from 29 percent in 2013–2015 to 32 percent in 2016–2019. In contrast, protests targeting nonstate firms decreased from 36 percent in 2013–2015 to 29 percent in 2016–2019. During 2016–2019, protesters became more likely to appeal to the central government or provincial (municipal) governments than during previous periods, implying that their grievances could not be resolved by lower-level governments, with no alternative but to seek help from higher-level governments.

The protesters' claims were divided into five categories: (1) economic claims (i.e., monetary issues such as wages, pensions, layoff compensations, property, investments, and other economic demands); (2) administration claims (including issues with government policies and regulations, officials' malpractice and corruption, and disputes over village elections); (3) rights

Table 2.2. Protest Target in China, 2000–2019

	2000–2019 N	2000–2019 %	2000–2002 %	2003–2007 %	2008–2012 %	2013–2015 %	2016–2019 %
High-level government	1,569	13	10	10	15	11	18
Low-level government	3,440	30	30	28	30	29	32
State firms	1,612	14	38	22	15	10	12
Nonstate firms	3,465	30	12	23	25	36	29
Village government	1,566	13	10	17	15	14	9
Total	11,652	100	273	1,230	3,246	4,971	1,932

Table 2.3. Protest Claims in China, 2000–2019

	2000–2019		2000–2002	2003–2007	2008–2012	2013–2015	2016–2019
	N	%	%	%	%	%	%
Economic claims	5,115	41	38	39	41	42	38
Administration claims	2,394	19	30	20	19	18	18
Rights issues	2,792	22	20	22	23	19	27
Rural land seizures	1,652	13	6	13	11	16	11
Incidental events	631	5	6	5	6	4	5
Total	12,584	100	289	1,338	3,488	5,222	2,247

claims, including disputes over individual rights ranging from property rights (e.g., relocation/dislocation, forced eviction, pollution, and environmental issues, etc.) to individual rights (e.g., community safety, medical malpractice, occupational injury, job rights, gender equality, and others); (4) rural land seizures; and (5) incidental events.

Table 2.3 presents the distribution of protest claims. During the 2000–2019 period, the most widely reported protest claims focused on economic issues (41 percent of all claims), followed by rights issues (22 percent), administration issues (19 percent), and issues of rural land seizures (13 percent). There was a significant change in the trend of protest claims over the past seven years from 2013–2015 to 2016–2019. Although protest events responding to general economic discontent had been declining from 42 percent in 2013–2015 to 38 percent in 2016–2019, the protests triggered by rights issues increased from 19 percent in 2013–2015 to 27 percent in 2016–2019. That is, protesters in China were primarily driven by concrete interests, such as economic rights. However, people's grievances were not limited to monetary issues. Growing discontent was also caused by violations of individual rights, bad government policies, and officials' wrongdoings. In rural areas, the most important protest issue that emerged in the early 2000s and accelerated after the mid-2000s was linked to land seizures in suburban agricultural villages, where local cadres underpaid or embezzled compensations originally awarded to displaced peasants (Chen 2020; Heurlin, 2016).

Disruption and Repression of Social Protests

Table 2.4 presents the forms of collective protest in urban and rural China. Over the 2000–2019 period, violent actions accounted for 28 percent and 57 percent in urban cities and rural villages, respectively. Violent tactics were more frequently seen in rural villages than in urban areas. More than half of rural protests concluded in violence, representing 59 percent and 55 percent of all reported rural events in 2013–2015 and 2016–2019, respectively. In

Table 2.4. Protest Forms in Urban and Rural China, 2000–2019

	2000–2019	2000–2002	2003–2007	2008–2012	2013–2015	2016–2019
Urban Protests (N)	9,746	229	1,004	2,799	3,922	1,792
Nonviolent %	72	69	69	72	70	78
Violent %	28	31	31	28	30	22
Rural Protests (N)	2,839	60	334	689	1,301	455
Nonviolent %	43	37	43	48	41	45
Violent %	57	63	57	52	59	55

comparison, more than half of all urban protests (72 percent) adopted nonviolent means, and the overall level of violence was much lower than at rural protests, although still accounting for 28 percent of all events. In urban areas, nonviolent protests slightly increased from the early 2000s to the 2010s, climbing to their highest level (78 percent) during the period of 2016–2019.

The data reveal that repression has been commonly employed by the Chinese government in dealing with social protests, especially since 2013. As my collection includes information on whether arrests were made, I use the arrest of protesters as a proxy for repression. It merits mentioning that not all of the arrested protest participants face criminal charges, and some are released without any charges filed against them. Table 2.5 presents police presence and action at protest scenes, showing notable variations in the application of different police approaches between urban cities and rural villages. In urban cities, the number of no-shows (i.e., events police were not reported to have attended) in 2000–2019 is high—39 percent of reported protest events occurred without police presence; the other three types of police responses were standing guard (17 percent), dispersing protesters (15 percent), and making arrests (29 percent). In comparison, only 21 percent of reported protest events from 2000–2019 in rural regions occurred without police presence. However, more importantly, the percentage of instances where police resorted to arrests in rural villages was overwhelming—48 percent of events involved arrests. This proportion was much higher than that in urban cities, where 29 percent of events resulted in arrests. In rural villages, the approach of standing guard was the least frequent response (12 percent) to protests, whereas the least frequent (15 percent) police response in cities was crowd dispersal.

These descriptive statistics reveal that the use of force had been vigorously adopted in China, either to disperse crowds or to arrest protesters. These two approaches together accounted for 44 percent of events in urban areas and 67 percent of events in rural villages, respectively. Despite this, an important difference is that city police relied on preventive and tolerant approaches much more than their rural counterparts, where there existed a high incidence of repressive police actions.

Table 2.5. Police Presence and Action at Protest Events in Urban and Rural China, 2000–2019

	2000–2019	2000–2002	2003–2007	2008–2012	2013–2015	2016–2019
Urban Protests (N)	9,746	229	1,004	2,799	3,922	1,792
Police Presence %	61	53	66	61	61	57
Arrest %	29	20	25	24	33	31
Disperse %	15	14	18	15	14	15
Stand guard %	17	19	23	22	14	11
No-show %	39	47	35	38	39	43
Rural Protests (N)	2,839	60	334	689	1,301	455
Police Presence %	79	73	78	73	84	77
Arrest %	48	38	35	40	53	56
Disperse %	19	23	25	18	21	13
Stand guard %	12	12	18	15	10	8
No-Show %	21	27	22	27	16	23

With regard to historical trends, there have been notable changes after Xi Jinping's ascent to power, as well as between the first three years (2013–2015) and the following four years (2016–2019) of his tenure. Compared to the four years (2008–2012) preceding the Xi administration, during the first three years of his tenure (2013–2015), nonviolent protests in both urban and rural areas slightly declined from 72 percent to 70 percent in cities and from 48 percent to 41 percent in rural areas (table 2.4). However, in the following period of 2016–2019, nonviolent protests in both urban and rural areas increased significantly, gaining 8 percent (from 70 percent to 78 percent) in urban centers and 4 percent (41 percent to 45 percent) in rural areas. This shows that while the aggression of protesters had slightly increased in the early days of the Xi Jinping administration, violent protests were reduced and conflicts remained comparatively peaceful during the following four years of his tenure. However, over the 2000–2019 period, the proportion of police using force to arrest protesters has continued to increase, showing that the Chinese government's degree of tolerance toward collective protests is shrinking even though the percentage of peaceful protests had increased significantly.

A Typology of Repression and Violence

The dynamic relationship between protests and repression is the focus of this study. Peaceful protests and rallies are clear manifestations of institutionalized collective resistance. That is, in democratic societies with a high degree of institutionalized collective protests, peaceful protests and tolerant police often go hand in hand and are the mainstay of collective action. However, in China, the trend does not seem to be moving in that direction; it is more diverse.

Empirically, I used the combination of protest forms and police responses to show the dynamic relationship between protest and repression. Presumably highly institutionalized protests include nonviolent protests with tolerant police at the scene. One reason for using the combination of protest forms and police response as a measurement rather than measuring protest forms and police response separately is that at the scene of protests in China, the disruption caused by protesters and the responses of the police are often highly correlated to one another. For example, protests that were originally nonviolent could quickly turn violent as a result of police brutality. Police responses also often vary depending on how protesters behave.

Table 2.6 presents a cross tabulation of police responses and violent protests. In this 2×2 framework, the raw variable is "police responses to protests"

Table 2.6. A Typology of Repression and Violence

	Tolerant police + Nonviolent protesters			Tolerant police + Violent protesters		
	Year	Urban	Rural	Year	Urban	Rural
Tolerant Police (No Arrests)	2000–2019	5,647 (58%)	843 (30%)	2000–2019	1,269 (13%)	627 (22%)
	2000–2002	142 (62%)	16 (27%)	2000–2002	41 (18%)	21 (35%)
	2003–2007	556 (55%)	107 (32%)	2003–2007	198 (20%)	111 (33%)
	2008–2012	1,685 (60%)	255 (37%)	2008–2012	435 (16%)	157 (23%)
	2013–2015	2,204 (56%)	341 (26%)	2013–2015	423 (11%)	264 (20%)
	2016–2019	1,060 (59%)	124 (27%)	2016–2019	172 (10%)	74 (16%)
	Forceful police + Nonviolent protesters			Forceful police + Violent protesters		
	Year	Urban	Rural	Year	Urban	Rural
Forceful Police (Arrests)	2000–2019	1,385 (14%)	390 (14%)	2000–2019	1,445 (15%)	979 (34%)
	2000–2002	16 (7%)	6 (10%)	2000–2002	30 (13%)	17 (28%)
	2003–2007	138 (14%)	38 (11%)	2003–2007	112 (11%)	78 (23%)
	2008–2012	339 (12%)	75 (11%)	2008–2012	340 (12%)	202 (29%)
	2013–2015	555 (14%)	191 (15%)	2013–2015	740 (19%)	505 (39%)
	2016–2019	337 (19%)	80 (18%)	2016–2019	223 (12%)	177 (39%)

divided into two categories: no arrest and arrest. The column variable is "forms of protest" with two categories: nonviolent protests and violent protests. The observations of each cell are further divided into urban and rural areas, and across the five different time periods. The values in parentheses are total percentages. Thus, certain protest combinations can be compared as a proportion of all protests during a certain period. The four combinations were: (1) tolerant police + nonviolent protesters; (2) tolerant police + violent protesters; (3) forceful police + nonviolent protesters; and (4) forceful police + violent protesters.

The number of observations corresponding to row 1 and column 1 is the combination of tolerant police coexisting with nonviolent protesters, which is the most common scenario of collective protest in contemporary democracies, representing a highly institutionalized form of collective protest. In China, 58 percent of urban protests and 30 percent of rural protests fell into this category, indicating that collective protests in urban areas were more orderly and predictable than those in rural areas, and were less likely to result in government crackdowns. There has been no tendency for this type of "highly civilized" protest scene to increase in China. Even in urban areas, its proportion had declined from 62 percent in 2000–2002 to 59 percent in 2016–2019. In rural areas, such "civilized" protest scenes had also dropped from 37 percent in 2008–2012 to 27 percent in 2016–2019. Collective protests in contemporary China are still a long way from institutionalization and legalization, as observed in most democracies. It is worth noting that although the combination of nonviolent protesters and tolerant police accounted for the majority of protests in urban areas, its share and growth had not only not progressed, but also regressed after the 2008–2012 period, especially in rural areas.

The second protest scenario is when violent protesters encounter tolerant police. This situation was the least common in urban areas, accounting for only 13 percent of the total number of protests in urban areas and 22 percent in rural areas. Moreover, they had continued to decrease over time. In 2003–2007, 20 percent of protests in cities and 33 percent in rural areas belonged to this category; but by 2016–2019, this share had shrunk to 10 percent in cities and only 16 percent in rural areas. In the past, this kind of protest scene was generally a situation where "resistance had legitimate grounds, and the government was in the wrong." Hence, the government tried to tolerate the intense behavior of the protesters. Or, when the scale of the protest was too large (e.g., in the early years, when peasants protested in rural areas and the government's police force could not respond in time), the local authorities adopted a more passive attitude. However, in recent years, as the government's stability maintenance resources and workforce have rapidly expanded, it no longer tolerates collective resistance, especially if protesters use violent means.

The third protest scenario describes a situation where nonviolent protesters were arrested by the police. This combination had been growing over the years. For example, in 2008–2012, 12 percent of collective resistance in cities and 11 percent in rural areas belonged to this category, but by 2016–2019, the proportion rose to 19 percent in cities and 18 percent in rural areas. The police were increasingly inclined to use force to arrest protesting crowds, even when there were no violent tactics involved.

The fourth combination, "forceful police coexisting with violent protesters," could be described as "fighting violence with violence." It was the second most common type in urban areas, accounting for 15 percent of urban protests and second only to the "civilized" institutionalized form. In rural areas, this type accounted for the highest percentage of the four combinations (34 percent of all rural protests over the past twenty years). In the face of collective resistance, the Chinese government was much more repressive in the villages than in the cities. And the confrontations between the government and the peasants had further intensified under the Xi Jinping administration between 2013 and 2019.

Table 2.7 presents results from logistic regression analysis, modeling two kinds of combinations between police arrests and protest forms. Model 1 is the combination of tolerant police coexisting with nonviolent protesters, representing highly "civilized" collective protest. Model 2 is the opposite combination—forceful police coexisting with violent protesters—indicating mutual distrust and hostility between protesters and the police. In addition to variables discussed in previous sections, a dummy variable was included to examine the effects of big cities, such as Beijing, Chongqing, Shanghai, Tianjin, Shenzhen, and provincial capital cities, on police intervention in protest activities.

First, both model 1 and model 2 show that different leaders had significant effects on the relationship between protest and repression. Other things being equal, compared to the Hu Jintao administration (2008–12), the first combination of collective resistance with tolerant police coexisting with nonviolent protesters was less likely to occur during both periods of the Xi Jinping administration; also, the combination of forceful police coexisting with violent protesters was more likely to occur. These trends are quite consistent with table 2.6, even when not controlling for other variables. Regardless of whether protests remained peaceful or turned violent, the trend under Xi Jinping's rule of strong repression was clear and profound. Other things being equal, collective protests using nonviolent tactics and peaceful police had been significantly less common under Xi Jinping than under Hu Jintao; meanwhile, in protest scenes, instances where state violence was used to curb protesters' violence had increased significantly.

The two models in table 2.7 show that protest groups significantly affected the relationship between protest and repression. Simply stated, the identity

Table 2.7. Logistic Regression Coefficients Predicting Protest Typology, 2000–2019

Period (2008–2012)[a]	(1) Tolerant Police + Nonviolent Protesters	(2) Forceful Police + Violent Protesters
2000–2002	−.079	.051
2003–2007	−.159 *	−.121
2013–2015	−.167 ***	.478 ***
2016–2019	−.155 *	.257 **
Protest size (100–1000)[a]		
Less than 100	.252 ***	−.419 ***
More than 1000	−.412 ***	.247 ***
Protest target (firms and others)[a]		
High-level government	.236 **	−.493 ***
Low-level government	.171 ***	−.261 ***
Protest groups (public-sector employees)[a]		
Private-sector workers	−.279 ***	.528 ***
FDI workers	−.097	.411 *
Ad hoc groups	−1.182 ***	1.070 ***
Students	−.772 ***	−.221
Urban residents harmed	−.950 ***	1.143 ***
Petitioners	−.658 ***	.008
Minorities/religious group	−1.438 ***	1.806 ***
Peasants	−1.550 ***	1.630 ***
Big cities	.295 ***	−.297 ***
Intercept	.723 ***	−2.279 ***
χ^2	902.4 ***	772.1 ***
df	17	17
N	9,820	9,820

df = degrees of freedom; FDI = foreign direct investment.
[a]Reference groups in parentheses.
* $P < .05$.
** $P < .01$.
*** $P < .001$.

of the protesters affected the interactions between protesters and the police. As can be seen from model 1, the likelihood for police tolerating nonviolent protesters who worked in the public sector, including state firm workers, military veterans, schoolteachers, etc., were significantly higher than for police tolerating other nonviolent groups (except FDI workers). For example, all other things being equal, the odds for police tolerating nonviolent protesters who worked in the public sector were about $e^{1.550} = 4.71$ times (371 percent) higher than for police tolerating nonviolent peasant protesters.

Model 2 shows that some groups (including private-sector workers, FDI workers, ad hoc groups, urban residents, minorities, religious groups, and peasants) were more likely than public-sector employees to be situated in protests in which police force was used against protesters. For instance, the odds for police arresting violent minority and religious group protesters were about $e^{1.806} = 6.09$ times (509 percent) higher than for police to arrest violent protesters employed in the public sector.

Finally, location also affects the relationship between protest and repression. Municipalities directly under the central government and provincial capitals have access to higher levels of administrative power and adequate resources. They have more room for decision-making and are better equipped to deal with mass protests. Also, they can respond to mass protests more effectively and in a timely manner. All other things being equal, the odds for police tolerating nonviolent protesters in big cities are about $e^{295} = 1.34$ times (34 percent) higher than for police tolerating nonviolent protesters elsewhere. Also, in large cities, forceful police and violent protesters are less likely to coexist than in other cities. All other things being equal, the odds of police arresting violent protesters were multiplied by $e^{-.297} = 0.74$ (reduced by 26 percent) in large cities compared with protests in other cities.

CONCLUSION

This study presents trends and key features of social unrest in China, examining the dynamics of repression and protest and the extent of the state's capacity to channel protest activities into more institutionalized forms. It shows that social protest in China has diffused widely throughout different social groups, covering a huge variety of issues across a wide geographical area. The data reveal the ups and downs of China's social protests over the past two decades.

Since the 1990s, China's institutional changes and market reforms have produced a mass society with weak mechanisms protecting citizens' interests and rights from being violated. Chinese citizens are vulnerable to abusive state and nonstate actors. Social grievances, frustrations, and tensions have been growing and have become the causes of soaring popular protests. However, the Chinese party-state has prohibited people from establishing organizations independent from its control. A disorganized society is believed to be incapable of posing a crucial challenge to the government. Meanwhile, the central-local relations in the Chinese political system had paved the way for political opportunities facilitating mobilization and claims making in collective protests. State penetration is limited because unorganized citizens are not subjected to the government's direct control. Discrete mobilization remains possible. With social conflict persisting, the government increases repression efforts in order to contain social protests.

In China, although popular protests have not threatened social stability because they are often short-lived and isolated, the persistence of grievances keeps constant pressure on the government. The government can certainly respond to popular protests by tackling the sources of grievances. However, accommodating protesters' demands can be costly for the government. At the same time, the government's organizational control over the people is also limited. Consequently, repression has become an important measure the government has employed to contain protests, especially in recent years. However, sustaining repression also proves to be costly to the government because it requires substantial resources and may sacrifice regime legitimacy.

Since 2013, under Xi Jinping's rule, the Chinese government has been more committed to cracking down on collective protests. Compared with the previous Jiang Zemin and Hu Jintao eras, Xi's regime has shown an even greater tendency toward strongman rule and centralized decision-making. The party-state has strengthened its control of civil society, and media and internet censorship have been tightened. In addition to traditional party-state organizations, the party-state also mobilizes technology manufacturers and incorporates digital technology to advance its mass surveillance and social control (Greitens 2019; Xiao 2019). Faced with increasing challenges by political dissidents, rights defense lawyers, NGO activists, as well as various types of collective protests, the regime has responded with severe and comprehensive crackdowns. This is the main reason why mass protests have been shrinking in China since the mid-2010s.

This study suggests that the Chinese government has been capable of suppressing collective resistance in recent years under Xi Jinping. However, although the government's resources and capacity to contain social resistance have been growing tremendously, there seems to be a ceiling on the Chinese state's ability—and probably willingness—to institutionalize collective resistance in the country. Under Xi Jinping's rule, the regime has been relying on increasing surveillance and repression to squash protest activities; the police are more inclined to arrest protesters. This study concludes that the dynamics of social protest in China are contingent on its state-society relations and the state's institutionalization capacity with regard to contentious politics. This study also shows that a strong authoritarian state has important implications for people's political participation and social stability. Centralized states aggrandize themselves by destroying intermediate bodies and reducing local autonomy, which then leaves few openings for institutionalized participation (Tarrow 1998: 78). Without intermediate associations and institutionalized collective protest, an authoritarian state is likely to face instabilities or even chaos, which can lead to its downfall. Such chaos is not necessarily the concern of governments that take all possible means to retain power. However, when a strong authoritarian state prohibits social organizations and stifles the progress of institutionalized collective action, it makes itself the major target of social grievances and actions throughout its rule.

NOTES

1. The cases were collected from a news database, Wisers (http://wisenews.wisers.net/wisenews), three online news services published in China, and two newspapers in Hong Kong, including *Zhongguo Xinwenwang* [China News Service], *Xinjingbao* [The Beijing News], *Nanfang Ribao* [Nanfang Daily], *Nanfang Zhoumo* [Southern Weekly], *Nanfang Dushi-bao* [Southern Metropolis Daily], *Huaxi Dushibao* [West China Metropolis Daily], *Guangzhou Ribao* [Guangzhou Daily], *Shenzhen Wanbao* [Shenzhen Evening News], *Lanzhou Chenbao* [Lanzhou Morning News], *Pingguo Ribao* [Apple Daily], and *Mingbao* [Ming Pao]. The four online news agencies based out of mainland China include The Central News Agency, Radio Free Asia, *Boxun* [Boxun], and *Dajiyuan* [The Epoch Times].

2. Reports that met these criteria were then coded for content. In collecting and coding the data, the procedures were subject to intensive reliability and validity checks.

3. A new way of case collection is online data mining. See Zhang and Pan (2019).

4. This tendency of persistent protests is in line with the numbers released by sanctioned sources in China. The number of publicly reported collective actions rose from 8,700 in 1993 to about 127,500 in 2008. But sanctioned sources stopped releasing the aggregated statistics after 2008 (Chung 2012).

REFERENCES

Bernstein, Thomas, and Xiaobo Lü. 2003. *Taxation without Representation in Contemporary Rural China*. New York: Cambridge University Press.

Cai, Yongshun. 2003. "Collective Ownership or Cadres' Ownership? The Nonagricultural Use of Farmland in China." *China Quarterly* 175: 662–80.

———. 2008. "Power Structure and Regime Resilience: Contentious Politics in China." *British Journal of Political Science* 38(3): 411–32.

———. 2010. *Collective Resistance in China: Why Popular Protests Succeed or Fail*. Stanford, CA: Stanford University Press.

Chan, Chris King-Chi. 2013. "Community-Based Organizations for Migrant Workers' Rights: The Emergence of Labour NGOs in China." *Community Development Journal* 48(1): 6–22.

Chen, Chih-Jou Jay. 2009. "Growing Social Unrest and Emergent Protest Groups in China." In Hsin-Huang Michael Hsiao and Cheng-Yi Lin, eds., *Rise of China: Beijing's Strategies and Implications for the Asia-Pacific*, 87–106. London: Routledge.

———. 2015. "Popular Protest in an Authoritarian Regime: A Wildcat Strike in Southern China" [Zhongguo Weiquan Zhengti Xia de Jiti Kangyi: Taizichang da Bagong de Anli Fenxi]. *Taiwanese Sociology [Taiwan Shehuixue]* 30: 1–53.

———. 2017. "Policing Protest in China: Findings from Newspaper Data" [Youxiao Zhili de Zhigu: Dangdai Zhongguo Jiti Kangzheng yu Guojia Fanying]. *Taiwanese Sociology [Taiwan Shehuixue]* 33: 113–64.

———. 2019. "Deriving Happiness from Making Society Better: Chinese Activists as Warring Gods." In Becky Yang Hsu and Richard Madsen, eds., *The Chinese Pursuit of Happiness: Anxieties, Hopes, and Moral Tensions in Everyday Life*, 131–54. Berkeley: University of California Press.

———. 2020. "Peasant Protests over Land Seizures in Rural China." *The Journal of Peasant Studies* 147: 327–47.

Chen, Chih-Jou Jay, and Yongshun Cai. 2021. "Upward Targeting and Social Protests in China." *Journal of Contemporary China* 30(130): 511–25.

Chen, Feng. 2003. "Between the State and Labour: The Conflict of Chinese Trade Unions' Double Identity in Market Reform." *The China Quarterly* 176: 1006–28.

———. 2010. "Trade Unions and the Quadripartite Interactions in Strike Settlement in China." *The China Quarterly* 201: 104–24.

Chen, Xi. 2013. "The Rising Cost of Stability." *Journal of Democracy* 24(1): 57–64.

———. 2017. "Origins of Informal Coercion in China." *Politics and Society* 45(1): 67–89.

Chung, Jae Ho. 2012. "Managing Political Crises in China: The Case of Collective Protests." In Jae Ho Chung, ed., *China's Crisis Management*, 25–42. London: Routledge.

Deng, Yanhua. 2014. "Societies of Senior Citizens and Popular Protest in Rural Zhejiang." *China Journal* 71: 172–88.

———. 2017. "Autonomous Redevelopment: Moving the Masses to Remove Nail Households." *Modern China* 43(5): 494–522. DOI: 10.1177/0097700416683901.

Deng, Yanhua, and Kevin J. O'Brien. 2013. "Relational Repression in China: Using Social Ties to Demobilize Protesters." *The China Quarterly* 215: 533–52.

Earl, Jennifer, Andrew Martin, John McCarthy, and Sarah Soule. 2004. "The Use of Newspaper Data in the Study of Collective Action." *Annual Review of Sociology* 30: 65–80.

Elfstrom, Manfred. 2019. "A Tale of Two Deltas: Labour Politics in Jiangsu and Guangdong." *British Journal of Industrial Relations* 57(2): 247–74.

Elfstrom, Manfred, and Sarosh Kuruvilla. 2014. "The Changing Nature of Labor Unrest in China." *Industrial and Labor Relations Review* 67(2): 453–80.

Franceschini, Ivan, and Elisa Nesossi. 2018. "State Repression of Chinese Labor NGOs: A Chilling Effect?" *China Journal* 80: 111–29.

Friedman, Eli. 2009. "External Pressure and Local Mobilization: Transnational Activism and the Emergence of the Chinese Labor Movement." *Mobilization: An International Journal* 14(2): 199–218.

Friedman, Eli, and Ching Kwan Lee. 2010. "Remaking the World of Chinese Labour: A 30-Year Retrospective." *British Journal of Industrial Relations* 48(3): 507–33.

Fu, Diana, and Greg Distelhorst. 2017. "Grassroots Participation and Repression under Hu Jintao and Xi Jinping." *China Journal* 79: 100–22.

Goebel, Christian, and Christoph Steinhardt. 2019. *Better Coverage, Less Bias: Using Social Media to Measure Protest in Authoritarian Regimes.* Department of East Asian Studies, University of Vienna.

Greitens, Sheena Chestnut. 2019. "Surveillance with Chinese Characteristics: The Development and Global Export of Chinese Policing Technology." Accessed June 15, 2020. http://ncgg.princeton.edu/IR percent 20Colloquium/GreitensSept2019.pdf.

Guo, Xiaolin. 2001. "Land Expropriation and Rural Conflicts in China." *The China Quarterly* 166: 422–39.

Heurlin, Christopher. 2016. *Responsive Authoritarianism in China: Land, Protests, and Policy Making*. New York: Cambridge University Press.

Honneth, Axel. 1995. *The Struggle for Recognition*. Cambridge, MA: MIT Press.

Hu, Jieren. 2011. "Grand Mediation in China: Mechanism and Application." *Asian Survey* 51(6): 1063–89.

Huang, Haifeng, Serra Boranbay, and Ling Huang. 2019. "Media, Protest Diffusion, and Authoritarian Resilience." *Political Science Research and Method* 7 (1): 23–42.

Hurst, William. 2009. *The Chinese Workers After Socialism*. New York: Cambridge University Press.

Jasper, James M. 2011. "Emotions and Social Movements: Twenty Years of Theory and Research." *Annual Review of Sociology* 37: 285–303.

Koopmans, Ruud, and Dieter Rucht. 2002. "Protest Event Analysis." In Bert Klandermans and Suzanne Staggenborg, eds., *Methods of Social Movement Research*, 231–59. Minneapolis: University of Minnesota Press.

Koopmans, Ruud, and Paul Statham. 1999. "Political Claims Analysis: Integrating Protest Event and Political Discourse Approaches." *Mobilization: An International Quarterly* 4(2): 203–21.

Lee, Ching Kwan. 2007. *Against the Law: Labor Protests in China's Rustbelt and Sunbelt*. Berkeley: University of California Press.

Lee, Ching Kwan, and Yuan Shen. 2011. "The Anti-Solidarity Machine? Labor Nongovernmental Organizations in China." In Sarosh Kuruvilla, Ching Kwan Lee, and Mary E. Gallagher, eds., *From Iron Rice Bowl to Informalization: Markets, Workers, and the State in a Changing China*, 173–87. Ithaca, NY: ILR Press.

Lee, Ching Kwan, and Yaonghong Zhang. 2013. "The Power of Instability: Unraveling the Microfoundations of Bargained Authoritarianism in China." *American Journal of Sociology* 118(6): 1475–508.

Lei, Ya-Wen. 2017. *The Contentious Public Sphere: Law, Media, And Authoritarian Rule in China*. Princeton, NJ: Princeton University Press.

Li, Chunyun, and Yi Duan. 2013. "Between Labor and the State: The Origin and Transformation of Chinese Labor NGOs." Paper presented at Chinese Association of Work and Labor Studies Annual Meeting, Beijing, China, December 28.

Lorentzen, Peter. 2013. "Regularizing Rioting: Permitting Public Protest in an Authoritarian Regime." *Quarterly Journal of Political Science* 8(2): 127–58.

Lu, Yao, and Ran Tao. 2017. "Organizational Structure and Collective Action: Lineage Networks, Semiautonomous Associations, and Collective Resistance in Rural China." *American Journal of Sociology* 122(6): 1726–74.

Luo, Qiangqiang, and Joel Andreas. 2016. "Using Religion to Resist Rural Dispossession: A Case Study of a Hui Muslim Community in Northwest China." *The China Quarterly* 226: 477–98.

McAdam, Doug. 1999 [1982]. *Political Process and the Development of Black Insurgency, 1930–1970*, 2nd ed. Chicago: University of Chicago Press.

Manion, Melanie. 1994. "Survey Research in the Study of Contemporary China: Learning from Local Samples." *The China Quarterly* 139: 741–65.

Mattingly, Daniel C. 2016. "Elite Capture: How Decentralization and Informal Institutions Weaken Property Rights in China." *World Politics* 68(3): 383–412.

Meng, U. I. 2016. "The Development of Grand Mediation and Its Implications for China's Regime Resilience: The Li Qin Mediation Office." *China Review* 16(1): 95–119.

Meyer, David S., and Sidney Tarrow. 1998. *The Social Movement Society: Contentious Politics for a New Century*. Lanham, MD: Rowman & Littlefield.

O'Brien, Kevin J. 2008. "Introduction: Studying Contention in Contemporary China." In Kevin J. O'Brien, ed., *Popular Protest in China*, 11–25. Cambridge, MA: Harvard University Press.

O'Brien, Kevin J., and Lianjiang Li. 2006. *Rightful Resistance in Rural China*. New York: Cambridge University Press.

O'Brien, Kevin J., and Yanhua Deng. 2015. "The Reach of the State: Work Units, Family Ties and 'Harmonious Demolition.'" *China Journal* 74: 1–17.

Ong, Lynette. 2018. "Thugs and Outsourcing of State Repression in China." *China Journal* 16(3): 680–95.

Ortiz, David G., Daniel J. Myers, Eugene N. Walls, and Maria-Elena D. Diaz. 2005. "Where Do We Stand with Newspaper Data?" *Mobilization: An International Quarterly* 10(3): 397–419.

Perry, Elizabeth. 2002. "Moving the Masses: Emotion Work in the Chinese Revolution." *Mobilization: An International Quarterly* 7(2): 111–28.

Pun, Ngai. 2007. "Gendering the Dormitory Labor System: Production, Reproduction, and Migrant Labor in South China." *Feminist Economics* 13(3–4): 239–58.

Reuters. 2019. "Chinese Police Must Guard Against 'Color Revolutions,' Says Top Official." January 18. *Reuters.* Accessed June 15, 2020. http://www.gn.apc.org/rts/mcw00.cgi-bin/cgi.

Rucht, Dieter, and Friedhelm Neidhardt. 1999. "Methodological Issues in Collecting Protest Event Data: Units of Analysis, Sources and Sampling, Coding Problems." In Dieter Rucht, Ruud Koopmans, and Friedhelm Neidhardt, eds., *Acts of Dissent: New Developments in the Study of Protest*, 65–89. Lanham, MD: Rowman & Littlefield.

Shahbaz, Adrian. 2018. "Freedom on the Net 2018. The Rise of Digital Authoritarianism." *Freedom House.* Accessed June 15, 2020. https://freedomhouse.org/sites/default/files/FOTN_2018_Final%20Booklet_11_1_2018.pdf.

Soule, Sarah A., and Jennifer Earl. 2005. "A Movement Society Evaluated: Collective Protest in the United States, 1960–1986." *Mobilization: An International Quarterly* 10(3): 345–64.

Su, Yang, and Xin He. 2010. "Street as Courtroom: State Accommodation of Labor Protest in South China." *Law & Society Review* 44(1): 157–84.

Sun, Yanfei, and Dingxin Zhao. 2007 "Multifaceted State and Fragmented Society: The Dynamics of the Environmental Movement in China." In Dali Yang, ed., *Discontented Miracle: Growth, Conflict, and Institutional Adaptations in China*, 111–60. Singapore: World Scientific Publisher.

Tarrow, Sidney. 1996. "States and Opportunities: The Political Structuring of Social Movements." In D. McAdam, J. McCarthy, and M. Zald, eds., *Comparative Perspectives on Social Movements*, 41–61. Cambridge: Cambridge University Press.

———. 1998. *Power in Movement*. New York: Cambridge University Press.

Tilly, Charles. 1978. *From Mobilization to Revolution*. New York: Random House.

Xiao, Qiang. 2019. "The Road to Digital Unfreedom: President Xi's Surveillance State." *Journal of Democracy* 30(1): 53–67.

Yan, Xiaojun. 2016. "Patrolling Harmony: Pre-emptive Authoritarianism and the Preservation of Stability in W County." *Journal of Contemporary China* 25(99): 406–21.

Yang, Dali. 2017. "China's Troubled Quest for Order: Leadership, Organization and the Contradictions of the Stability Maintenance Regime." *Journal of Contemporary China* 26(203): 35–53.

Yang, Guobin. 2009. *The Power of the Internet in China: Citizen Activism Online*. New York: Columbia University Press.

Zhang, Han, and Jennifer Pan. 2019. "CASM: A Deep-Learning Approach for Identifying Collective Action Events with Text and Image Data from Social Media." *Sociological Methodology* 49(1): 1–57.

Zhao, Dingxin. 2000. "State-Society Relations and the Discourses and Activities during the 1989 Beijing Student Movement." *American Journal of Sociology* 105(6): 1592–632.

———. 2001. *The Power of Tiananmen: State-Society Relations and the 1989 Beijing Student Movement*. Chicago: University of Chicago Press.

———. 2010a. "Theorizing the Role of Culture in Social Movements: Illustrated by Protests and Contentions in Modern China." *Social Movement Studies:* 9(1): 33–50.

———. 2010b. "Authoritarian State and Contentious Politics." In K. T. Leicht and J. C. Jenkins, eds., *Handbook of Politics*, 459–76. New York: Springer.

Zhou, Xueguang. 2014. *The Institutional Logic of Governance in China: An Organizational Approach* [Zhongguo guojia zhili de zhidu luoji: yige zuzhixue yanjiu]. Beijing: SDX Joint Publishing Company.

Zweig, David. 2000. "The 'Externalities of Development': Can New Political Institutions Manage Rural Conflict?" In Elizabeth Perry and Mark Selden, eds., *Chinese Society: Change, Conflict and Resistance*, 120–42. London: Routledge.

Chapter Three

Troublemaking Repertoires in a Grassroots Petitioning Campaign

Wing-Chung Ho (City University of Hong Kong)

According to Charles Tilly, "repertoires of contention" refer to the historical relevance of the protest methods actors adopt in particular societal contexts:

> The word repertoire identifies a limited set of routines that are learned, shared and acted out through a relatively deliberate process of choice. Repertoires are learned cultural creations, [and also . . .] emerge from struggle. (Tilly 1995: 26)

Conceptually connecting activists' repertoires with Bourdieu's theory of practice, Crossley (2002: 53) coins the term "radical habitus" in his study of the psychiatric survivors' movement. To Bourdieu, habitus refers to "a system of lasting, transposable dispositions" (1977: 72) internalized among a class of actors that "generates meaningful practices and meaning-giving perceptions" (1984: 170). Crossley's application of the radical habitus concept refers to actors' pre-reflective and pre-reflexive structures that "demarcate a particular profile or style of reasoning and acting . . . and which seemed to influence [the activists] . . . choices of repertoire" (2002: 53). Following Crossley's approach, this chapter aims to further our understanding of the processes whereby actors select and play out particular tactics and framings from societal repertoires of contention to fight against the repressive state. Speaking of the more constrained and less open environments under authoritarian rule, Johnston (2015: 619) has highlighted the "novel configurations" of activists' mobilization tactics as compared to those commonly practiced under open democracies, such as demonstrations, marches, and rallies. Labeling it the "resistance repertoire," Johnston points to the various forms of collective action that reside between the abeyance phase of a movement, when heavy repression or recent memories of it drive oppositional sentiments into private spaces, and their dramatic expression via mobilization according to the modular repertoire. Thus, the repertoire represents this phase of collective action where crucial first steps are taken—creatively and intentionally—to socially organize dissatisfaction and slowly move oppositional sentiments into more public forms (2015: 626). This chapter endeavors to illustrate how Chinese petitioners select and actively play out their societal-specific "resistance repertoire" (i.e., "the unique early patterns of challenge and claim-making [tactics] . . . characteristic of repressive contexts" [Johnston 2015: 620])against the authoritarian regime of China.

I empirically analyze a particular case of grassroots mobilization that involved at its maximum about thousand petitioners who had been displaced and forced to relocate to different parts of China due to the building of the Three Gorges Dam (hereafter, TGD, 1994–2006). I use a unique data set captured from a discussion group with 140 participants in an instant messenger app—WeChat.[1] The data comprise all the verbal, textual, visual, and online information recorded during eight consecutive days (June 12–19, 2017) during which the petitioning occurred and was eventually dispersed by different state repression strategies. Such records of real-time exchanges among petitioners and other displaced persons online reveal the petitioners' tactics, the state's counterpetition moves, and the motives behind the petitioners' repertoire selection (i.e., how they used different tactics and framings).[2]

This study engages and hopefully enriches the existing literature by probing the actors' experiences in the mobilization process. My emphasis on the activists' experiences in repertoire selection is perhaps more justifiable here than former studies due to the availability of processual data I have at hand. The present study also possesses a novel theoretical perspective to understand China's grassroots resistance in terms the concept of habitus. Following Crossley (2002, 2003), I echo some social movement studies that theorize activism in terms of habitus in the context of the animal rights (Munro 2005) and environmentalist movements (Haluza-DeLay 2008; Alam, Nilan, and Leahy 2019). Here, I concur with Haluza-DeLay (2008: 210) that such an approach possesses the advantages of offering "an improved conception of agency [in fueling a mobilization, and addressing] . . . the free-rider problem better than theories of rational choice or collective identity." To this end, this study argues that the TGD petition campaign reflects more the actors' parochial and rent-seeking motives—as symbolized in the discourse of "making trouble" (*nao/naoshi,* 鬧/鬧事)—than the defense of one's legal and constitutional rights as a citizen. Both the characteristics and outcomes of such repertoire selection shaped by what I call the habitus of *nao* will be discussed. In illustrating its characteristics, I endeavor to address specific questions including: What are the tactics used by subordinates to deal with repressive strategies and to sustain a mobilization? What rationalities are used to determine a particular set of tactics? Are these tactics effective? I aim to address these questions in relation to the conventional repression-concession-escalation dynamics in the social movement literature, namely, have the authorities yielded to the pressure of the movement or have they imposed effective repressive measures to contain its effects? And, if repressive measures are taken, do they lead to effective suppression of the movement or unintended escalation that might challenge the political status quo?

TGD MIGRANTS AND THEIR GRIEVANCES

The grievances of TGD migrants originated in the building of the dam named after three adjacent gorges along the middle section of China's longest river (6,300 km), the Yangtze (Heggelund 2004: 15). With a length of 181 meters and a total installed capacity "exceeding 22,000 MWe," TGD is the world's tallest gravity dam and has the greatest hydropower production (Jackson and Sleigh 2000: 225). It represents China's largest engineering and infrastructure project since the communist takeover in 1949 (Zhang and Lou 2011). TGD is arguably the most contested development project in communist China as twenty counties or municipal districts, 227 townships, and 1,680 villages were affected by inundation (Duan and Steil 2003). When the water level reached its final level of 175 meters in late 2009, the dam not only flooded 17,200 hectares of farmland, prompted the relocation of 1,500 enterprises, destroyed many historical relics, but also created 1.35 million forced migrants (Wilmsen et al. 2011: 22). Scholars' estimates of the number of people being resettled were higher than the official statistics, ranging from 1.4 million (Wong 2007) to 2 million (Padovani 2006a: 99). Since the adjacent reservoir region was "overpopulated and environmentally pressed" (Heggelund 2004: 113), the central government made the decision in 1999 to relocate 166,000 peasants beyond the reservoir region. These villagers who "migrated beyond the reservoir region" (*waiqian,* 外遷) consisted of 45,000 who were relocated to relatively nearby Chongqing and Hubei nonreservoir areas; 25,000 to more than twenty provinces or cities based on their own decision; and 96,000 to eleven provinces or cities, namely Hubei, Sichuan, Anhui, Jiangsu, Zhejiang, Shanghai, Shandong, Hainan, Hunan, Jiangxi, Fujian, and Guangdong, which were to benefit from the electricity generated by the dam (Wang 2010: 153).

In the literature, reports of pre- and postmigration lives of TGD migrants generally describe dissatisfaction over four types of "impoverishment risks"—following after Cernea's typology of risks faced by forced migrants (2000)—namely, marginalization, joblessness, landlessness, and community disarticulation (Hsu, Ma, and Ho 2019). Marginalization refers to the difficulties the migrants encounter—psychologically or economically or both—in adapting to the mainstream culture of the receiving communities. TGD resettlers usually express problems of being discriminated against by the locals (Li, Waley, and Rees, 2001; Jim and Yang 2006). When migrants are displaced to geographically far and culturally different regions, they also complain about the presence of language barriers (low proficiency in the local dialect) and their incapability to socially and culturally integrate with the local community (Padovani 2006b; Heggelund 2006). Economic marginalization is usually due to the migrants' relatively low educational level. The cash compensation promised by the state for the loss of homes and livelihoods had been found to be inadequate in maintaining migrants' livelihoods in the receiving areas (Duan and Wilmsen 2012). Furthermore, the cash compensation that migrants received seldom tallied with what had been promised due to the suspected misappropriation of funds by officials at all levels (Xi et al. 2007).

Marginalization by locals has increased migrants' likelihood of becoming unemployed. Scholars have suggested that the state's initiative of the Partnership Support Scheme to turn the TGD migrants into the active labor force of local factories in the receiving areas failed its mission (Padovani 2006a; Heggelund 2006; Wilmsen et al. 2011). Jackson and Sleigh (2000: 234–35) had already documented the failure of the scheme such that the plan on the part of the Chongqing municipal government to relocate 180 factories was found to be incapable of absorbing its 100,000 unemployed residents in Chongqing, let alone to absorb 67,000 additional displaced residents from TGD areas.

The problem of landlessness was primarily caused by the inundation of migrants' original farmlands and aggravated by the lack of either the availability of agricultural land or good quality land in the receiving areas and the presence of state regulations (e.g., state restrictions on deforestation) that disallows certain land to be used for farming (Jackson and Sleigh, 2000, 2001; Jim and Yang 2006; Xi et al. 2007). Individual studies also extended the definition of landlessness to include those cases where migrants experienced substantial reduction in plot size in the receiving areas (e.g., Jackson and Sleigh 2000: 232–34). Scholars in one way or another have cast doubt over the official optimistic claim that 60 percent of displaced peasants would obtain "land-for-land" compensation (e.g., Duan and Wilmsen 2012).

Another problem that most TDG migrants report is community disarticulation that refers to the fragmentation of previously established social networks caused by forced displacement. Studies generally document a strong nostalgic sentiment of the migrants for their original lifestyle, which was endowed with rich cultural and symbolic meaning (Li et al. 2001; Padovani 2006a; Yu and Xiang 2006). Padovani (2006b: 6) points out that the official action of putting only a maximum of three families in a certain destination had resulted in serious social disintegration problem among the relocatees.

On the whole, despite some explicit improvement in the livelihood of migrants being reported in one specific site (Wilmsen 2016), most TGD migrants' postmigration lives generally report problems, rather than improvements. This explains the motivation behind some migrants deciding to take their discontent to the streets by staging protests and even traveling vast distances to petition Beijing despite these actions being suppressed by the authoritarian regime (Wilmsen et al. 2011: 22). In the literature, Ying (2013) has traced the collective petitions of TGD migrants relocated to Shandong Province from 1997 to the early 2010s and by migrants relocated to Hubei from 1996 to 2006. Other reports also observe that TGD migrants have continued to petition the government from the 1990s until the present (Leavenworth 2016). Alongside espousing sympathy on migrants' petitions, articles published by mainland scholars, however, usually portray the migrants' resistance as manifestations of over-reliance-on-the-state psychology on the part of the migrants who lack an "agentic subjectivity" (*zhuguan nengdongxin*, 主觀能動性) (e.g., Liu and Lei 2001: 15).

PETITIONING BEIJING

I have been conducting fieldwork on TGD migrants since September 2014. My research focus has been on the postmigration lives of second-generation, young adult migrants in Guangdong. In December 2014 when visiting Zhaoqing,[3] I met a thirty-six-year-old TGD migrant, whom I will call Guoji.[4] Since then, Guoji has become a key informant and has referred many of his native fellows to me for interviews. On June 12, 2017, Guoji texted me via WeChat and said that a collective petitioning campaign was taking place in Beijing that comprised thousands of TGD migrants from different places. He invited me to join the "big" (*daqun*, 大群) or "main" (*zhuqun*, 主群) WeChat group of 140 participants[5] comprising both the Beijing-bound petitioners and other forced migrants who were not on the scene. This big WeChat group was supposed to discuss petitioning tactics and share important information among key persons of different migrant groups to make the petition a coordinated collective action. Guoji was not heading to Beijing, but he claimed to be a leader who mobilized migrants resettling in Zhaoqing to participate in the petitioning. He told me that his intention in letting me join the "big" WeChat group was to help me better understand the hardships of the TDG migrants. To avoid arousing unnecessary suspicion and tension, Guoji advised me not to say or type anything to the group but just to observe. I took his advice in due course.

One should note that in contemporary authoritarian China, petitioning is an ambivalent and paradoxical system that allows social actors to voice grievances that have not been properly addressed at one level of state authority and to seek redress from the authorities at upper levels. I call the system "ambivalent" because it is "in-between," both *within* and *outside* the formal institutions. It is within state institutions because the institutional foundation of the petition system was laid down starting in 1949 when the Communist Party "established a political secretariat to handle people's letters to the ruling party," and Letters and Visits Offices (*xinfang*, 信訪) were eventually established at various levels for "social actors to [formally] report situations and suggest proposals to governments . . . through letters, telephone, or personal appearance." (Wang 2012: 710) However, in reality, petitioning is usually considered by the state as "illegal" (e.g., a collective petition involving more than four persons without state approval is considered illegal), and only a tiny fraction of petitions succeed in having their complaints addressed.[6] All these factors contribute to the understanding among the general public that petitions represent extrainstitutional and even irrational resistance against the state in the sense that they are unlikely to succeed (Pils 2011). I also call the system paradoxical—and even counterintuitive—because its existence is actually based on petitioners' "trust" (rather than resentment) that the state leaders who will listen to their demands and rectify the wrongdoings of local officials (Li 2008). Also, it is paradoxical because the system serves several ostensibly mutually conflicting state functions, including: (a) the provision of a channel for public discontent that does not threaten the regime (Cai 2004), (b) the collection of people's feedback on existing policies (Peerenboom 2001; Wang 2015; Dimitrov 2015); and (c) evaluation of cadres' performance based on the number of petition incidents recorded and their ability to reduce petitioning incidents (Minzner 2006; Gui 2017). All this being said, and despite its overt dispute-resolution function apparently being limited in practice (He and Feng 2016: 234), the masses are nevertheless willing to take their chances. Lee (2014: 128–29) has indicated that there is "an annual average of 11.5 million petitions, in the forms of individual letters, . . . organized demonstrations, large-scale marches, and public speeches." The main reason for large collective petitions is that aggrieved claimants can put pressure on local officials, for whom the number and scale of collective petitioning incidents can have a significant negative effect on their career advancement. Thus, eliminating incidents of "petitioning Beijing" is a top priority (Gui 2017: 164). It is against this backdrop that the TGD collective petition analyzed in the present study took place.

DATA STRUCTURE

Consisting of information recorded on eight consecutive days, the data set involves 140 individuals (by unique WeChat identities) who participated in the big WeChat group discussion at least once. All these participants were assigned a number in an ascending order beginning with the first message of the data set labeled "participant#1" and so on so forth. Based on the information I could ascertain from the data, the participants were TGD migrants resettled in ten provinces or cities, namely, Hubei, Anhui, Jiangsu, Zhejiang, Shandong, Hunan, Jiangxi, Fujian, Guangdong, and Chongqing. All the messages totaled 29,394 Chinese words, excluding words incorporated in fifteen photos, six documents, three hyperlinks, and two maps. All this information constitutes the main corpus of data used in my analysis, which was supplemented by two face-to-face in-depth interviews with internet police officers, one from Guangzhou (September 2018) and another from Chongqing (October 2018).

The data span an unfolding campaign that can be divided into three distinct chronological stages. Specifically, days one and two are the action stage; days three and four, the retreat stage; and days five to eight, the evaluation and repercussion stage.

The action stage was when most petitioners arrived in Beijing. On day one they headed to the Letters and Visits Office of the Three Gorges Project Construction Committee (LVOTG) and on day two to the Letters and Visits Office of the Central Government (LVOCG) and the Central Commission for Discipline Inspection (CCDI). The goal was to launch their complaints and submit relevant documents as a single group of victims to the aforementioned petitioning agencies. In the retreat stage, owing to the many counterpetition strategies launched by the local governments, many petitioners had been "retrieved" or "intercepted" (*jiefang*, 截訪). They were either persuaded or forced to return to their hometowns. Messages at this stage indicated that many petitioners were either on their way home or on the run to avoid being picked up. The spirits of the petitioners plummeted, and both the number of messages and participants involved fell substantially. In the evaluation and repercussion stage, many of the petitioners had returned home or were still on their way back. Participants began to evaluate whether their action was a success or failure and to share how they were treated by local governments on their return. The evaluation was enriched by two incidents: First, a group of petitioners from Jiangxi was assaulted by a group of thugs once they returned. One petitioner was badly beaten and hospitalized (day five). Second, a female petitioner from Hubei was sexually harassed by a gangster hired by the local government to escort the petitioners back home. The local government yielded to the migrants' pressure, and the police turned over the harasser to

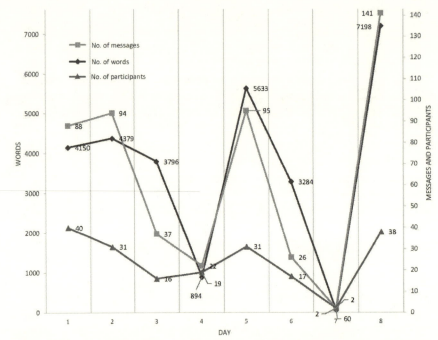

Figure 3.1. Words, Messages, and Participants in WeChat Discussions, Days One to Eight

the migrants. The harasser gave an open apology and offered 5,000 yuan in compensation to the victim (day eight). These two incidents triggered heated discussion among the participants, and the number of messages and participants involved surged on both days. After day eight, the discussion began to die down and the topics began to drift away from those related to the petition in Beijing. The data after day eight were thus considered irrelevant to the present study. The number of messages, words, and unique participants involved each day across three different stages are summarized in figure 3.1.

PETITIONERS' TACTICS AND FRAMINGS AGAINST THE STATE POWER

As previous studies suggest, local government officials, fearing that their career prospects are jeopardized, often send out cadres or to hire private security companies or gangsters to retrieve dissenters who endeavor to lodge complaints in Beijing (Fu and Distelhorst 2018: 104; Ong 2018a). The primary objective of the counterpetition strategies is to prevent petitioners from reaching the designated petitioning agencies in the capital city and haul them back to their hometowns. The WeChat messages indicated that the local governments sent their people to Beijing, using cars to tempt or force petitioners—already exhausted by the hot weather—to get into the cars on day one. Petitioners urged others to refuse the temptation and pressure. For example, participant #9 said, "Comrade, don't get into the cars. Stay together! Don't get dispersed. It will be difficult [to get together again] if you get dispersed" (participant #9, day one). Some local cadres adopted softer methods of persuasion or offered monetary rewards as bait to get hold of petitioners. These actions prompted a number of participants to issue warnings to their fellow petitioners not to believe the cadres or accept the money they offered:

> When the local government [cadres] came to find you, don't believe in their words. Seventeen years have passed. Will they realize their words when you return!? No, they won't! (participant #7, day one)

> Here, I just want to tell our migrant fellows and compatriots. Between individual interests [i.e., accepting monetary offerings] and the interest of millions of suffering folks, I am sure that we all know which option is just! The local cadres are just working hard to protect their positions. We migrant compatriots should never compromise or retreat. . . . For those who do not return [i.e., implying that some had already accepted the offering] and suffer on the frontline, you are all good children of China and heroes of migrant compatriots. (participant #22, day one)

Previous studies have suggested that Beijing's control over popular resistance is effectively boosted by the use myriad online technologies, including "controlling the technological infrastructure, co-opting private Internet companies, documenting the 'real-name' access, and developing sophisticated censorship systems" (Tang and Huhe 2014: 563; Zhou and Yan 2014). The regime's effective grip on cyberspace has constituted what some scholars call a "networked authoritarianism" (Hassid 2008; MacKinnon 2008; Hung 2010). In the present case, petitioners claimed that their actions had been effectively traced and subsequently constrained by a number of online surveillance methods, including screening of WeChat messages, checking of online purchases of train tickets, and scrutinizing e-records of hotel room booking systems.[7] For example, on day one, a participant said:

> People in this group, please don't type anymore. The Beijing police station just called someone in the group, asking him why he had to make trouble. The internet police has been monitoring our action. (participant #14, day one)

On day two, some petitioners suspected that their phone records had been tapped because it appeared that their plans were being monitored. Participant

#67 posted, "Your ID card is being monitored. They all know where you take transport and which hostel you stay in" (participant#67, day two).

WeChat discussions also suggested that that there were moles hidden among the petitioners who betrayed the crowd by leaking information about the petition to local government cadres. As a result, many petitioners were intercepted before reaching Beijing, and many who had reached Beijing were taken away by local government cadres before reaching the petitioning agencies on day one and two.

And, for the estimate of three to four hundred petitioners who finally reached the petitioning agencies in Beijing, some reported to be bullied by the armed police. For example, a petitioner from Jiangxi complained on day two:

> In this morning, we, together twelve migrants from Jiangxi, went to the CCDI for petitioning. We were immediately surrounded by the armed police. . . . Finally, we were sent away by the local government cadres. . . . For those who are still petitioning, just do it slowly and deliberately. We will be sent back to Jiangxi tonight. You should take action regardless whether it will rain [later] today. (participant #65, day two)

For others who could actually made contact with officials in Beijing, they complained that the officials only received their materials without any concern about their demands, not to mention resolving their problems. Some officials at the LVOCG even denied that they were in any official capacity to receive the petitioners. Rather, they were there just to "take their materials"; a petitioner spoke of what had happened in day one:

> In the afternoon of 12 June [i.e., day one], we went to LVOCG as suggested by the LVOTG earlier [in the morning]. They received three groups of [TGD migrant] petitioners. For the first group, they got nothing, not even a formal acknowledgement of their visit. For the second group, they got a piece of paper which printed the address of the Three Gorges Project Construction Committee office. We are already here and how can we not know the address?! For the third group, our people requested that the officials follow the formal procedures of Letters and Visits such that they [i.e., the officials] needed to reveal their identification. The officials said that they were not [from] LVOCG; rather, they were from the Three Gorges Project Construction Committee office. Therefore, they were not there to receive petitioners [officially], but only to take our materials. (participant #37, day three)

One should note that petitioners seldom accepted these counterpetition strategies subserviently. In fact, petitioners had been suggesting and, at times, adopted tactics to countervail different repression strategies. For example, a participant suggested that for those who were forced to enter the cars arranged by local governments, they should "just open the window and threaten to jump out of it!" (Participant #10, day one); or "tell them that you need to go the toilet and run away." (participant #58, day two). To avoid being illegally repressed, participants suggested adopting a soft position when being chased or seized by the retrievers.[8] To protect the leaders of the petition, participants kept reminding each other to frame their action as being purely voluntary and without leaders when asked by officials.[9] To align themselves with the rational and nonviolent frame, participants suggested repeatedly that petitioners should kneel down in front of the officials in Beijing and refuse to leave before their grievances were addressed.[10] To avoid being chased by the internet monitors, participants suggested (a) not sending text messages but rather voice messages in WeChat;[11] (b) not to reveal too many details of the petition in the "big" WeChat group;[12] and (c) not to use transportation that required ID card registration.[13] To increase the impact of the petition, participants kept calling on other participants to share their stories, photos, and films to journalists in Beijing or friends outside China via WeChat.[14] Because visual files in WeChat are more likely than text messages to avoid state surveillance, petitioners used photos and screen-captured maps to share with others important information about the collective petition in the action stage (e.g., the address of LVOTG and its pertinent map). At the retreat stage, photos were also used to convey a common, bitter past by reminiscing about how they had been forced to leave their native home seventeen years ago and how they had been struggling in recent years to pursue their rights. These pictures were effective in reinforcing shared similarities and, hence, solidarity among the petitioners when their spirits were at their lowest point.

The petitioners' repertoires of contention, however, seemed to have had little impact on the state's repressive measures. Data suggested that the effectiveness of the petition had been further compromised by poor weather (e.g., being a hot and humid on day one and rainy from day two onward), and resource constraints such as costly accommodations (e.g., participants reported resting only in massage parlors or underground stations on days one and two), insufficient battery and memory capacity of mobile phones, and expensive digital data for WeChat communication.[15] All this evidence points to the often neglected resource dimension in studies of petitioning in Beijing, and seems to rebut Lee's claim, "For the aggrieved populace . . . petitioning [is] free of charge" (2014: 129).

Consequently, petitioners from different migrant resettlements failed to reach the petitioning destinations as a united crowd, and many were said to have been stopped from going forward by local government cadres. This explains why during day three and day four participants began to register frustration over the poor communication and coordination among petitioners. For example, an irritated participant angrily stated in the WeChat group:

> Things just couldn't work out this way! Some said that we should meet in one place at one time, then, another one we meet at another place at another time. You guys went there today, and I was not informed. How could I get there!? At the beginning, I said that I would send a representative from our group to submit materials or whatever, and then to let them electronically read the ID card. Then, some advised that there was no rush to let them electronically read the ID card at this stage. You tell me what is going on here!? Damn! If you guys do not go there tomorrow, I shall send my folks to go there anyway! (participant #56, day three)

Some participants complained that the disruptive the actions of the local governments divided the groups, and some got lost. For example, a participant said:

> Five of us were [taken by the local officials] back home. One was still outside with other people. For another group of five, two were detained, two were [taken] back, and one was waiting to be found [by the local cadres] and be [taken] back. (participant #10, day three)

Later on day three, a petitioner suggested participating less in the big WeChat group because people who had lost contact might use the platform to report more urgent issues, and unnecessary chats would cause wasteful consumption of mobile phone battery and memory.[16] Afterward, the number messages in the group decreased drastically. The collective spirit of the petitioners remained low until day four, as reflected in the words of a female participant who expressed in a saddened tone, "I feel really upset and am about to shed tears.... All the police are sons of bitches!" (participant #12, day four). This message was immediately followed by two posts saying that one should not use such emotional language. One participant stated, "The police are monitoring this group" (participant #37, day four). Another even claimed that "the center (*zhongyang*, 中央) is attending to our matters, so don't say anything that may cause misunderstanding" (participant #37, day four). This was how the retreat stage ended, and from day five onward, the campaign entered the final evaluation and repercussion stage when the WeChat discussions offered a better glimpse of the motives behind the activists' repertoires of contention.

On day five, there was a significant shift as participants began to talk about their postreturn treatment. Also, the discussion quickly turned to an incident when a group of returning petitioners was beaten by a group of thugs in Jiangxi. Eleven petitioners had been put into a car arranged by the local government and accompanied by a female vice-chief of the county migrant bureau. The car reached its destination at around 11 p.m. Two minutes after the vice-chief got out of the car, two cars arrived their license plates covered. A dozen of men got out of the cars and beat the returning migrants. Several migrants were injured, and one who failed to run away from the scene was seriously injured and hospitalized. Greatly disturbed by the incident, talk on WeChat became heated and turned quickly into a discussion about using collective violence as the tactic to gain justice for the victims. Here are some examples:

> You guys must carry knives [when asking for justice at the migrant bureau]. Just stab them recklessly in case of emergency (participant #50, day five).
>
> There must be consequences [for the local government] this time! We will go with a big crowd. If things do not work out, we shall fight (*da*, 打)! (participant #87, day five).
>
> The local government is too corrupt. If you do not kill (*sha*, 殺) a few people and make a big scene (*gaoda*, 搞大), President Xi will not know (participant #106, day five).

A participant even proposed following the female vice bureau chief secretly and gathering information about where she lived and worked. Once known, the migrants were to organize a group and surround her home or office, forcing her to give an explanation (participant #21, day five). Afterward, the discussions focused on the use of physical assault against the bureau chief and the gangsters, and in case the migrants were accused of using violence, participants agreed to either to "donate money to defend the migrants" in court (participant #110, day five) or to "take care of" the accusers' families, if "they end up in jail" (participant #9, day five).

At one point, a participant called for using the legal system rather than violence. However, this did not mean that he possessed a strong consciousness of legality or justice. As the discussion below quickly reveals, participants only consider the legal procedures as a means—a superficial formality—that could serve as a pretext for subsequent violent actions:

> Don't be so reckless. We should take "peaceful measures before using force" (*xianli houbing*, 先禮後兵). We should follow the [legal] procedures first. If the procedures cannot solve the problem, we then fight (participant# 62).
>
> Does this society follows procedures!? Why did the damn migrant bureau chief send people to beat the petitioners!? If you don't fight back, will they attend to the matter!? It is not about monetary compensation [to the victims], it is just about fighting (participant #99).

I know, procedures do not work in this society. But, this formality (*guchang*, 過場) needs to be done, and must be done. We need to make a big scene, then we have a solid reason (*zhanliyou le*, 站理由了) [to act militantly]. To report to the police is to give them time to solve the problem. If they cannot solve the problem, we can find a bunch of people to smash the police station (participant #62).

In discussing the migrants who were beaten, participants use many extra-legal (including illegal) terms to frame their actions, including "fighting," "beating up," "killing," and "making a big scene," which, I argue, refer to the discourse of "making trouble" (*nao/ naoshi*, 鬧/鬧事). Such discursive usage of nao contrasts with the discursive use of legality, including the terms "legal" (*hefa*, 合法) and "rights maintenance" (*weiquan*, 維權), to frame their collective actions a couple of days before. The same drift of framing was also observed on day eight when the case of a female returning petitioner to Hubei who was sexually harassed by a local-government-hired gangster was discussed. In this case, migrants went to the local police station in Hubei to protest at after the incident was exposed. The police yielded to the pressure of protesters a couple of days later and turned the harasser over to them on day eight. The photo of the kneeling harasser was quickly posted in the WeChat group. It was said that the harasser apologized publicly to the victim in front of the angry migrants and offered the victim 5,000 yuan as compensation. The victim accepted the money and settled the issue after slapping the harasser's face twice. Once again, on that day, the discursive usage of nao disproportionately outnumbered that of legality in the discussion (figure 3.2).

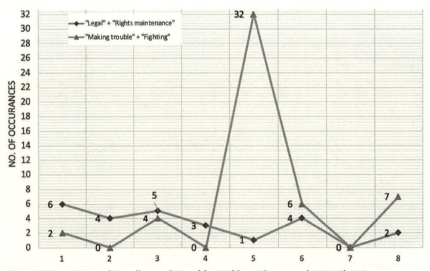

Figure 3.2. Usage of Legality and Trouble-Making Discourse in WeChat Posts

THE RESISTANCE LOGIC OF *NAO*

The participants' use of *nao* toward the end of the campaign was not an ad hoc response to two incidents of harassment on days five and eight. Rather, I suggest that it reflects a general logic that governed their resistive struggles against authority. It is the logic that—in theoretical terms—turned resistance into a game behavior, with the expectation that the state would eventually yield to pressure due to persistent troublemaking by a sizable and united crowd. "Trouble" means behavior that is usually illegal (e.g., physical assaults) but not serious criminal offenses (such as murder) or regime-threatening acts. Furthermore, the logic of nao was not merely a game-theory hypothesis in participants' heads that required empirical testing. Rather, it was portrayed as a mechanism with abundant confirming evidence. For example, in evaluating different postreturn experiences, participants interpreted more lenient receptions by local governments as the result of the trouble they caused. In fact, unlike what has been commonly understood in the literature that petitioners would "face brutal retaliation from local officials when they attempt to make their grievances heard by higher authorities" (Wong and Peng 2015: 57), most returning petitioners had received a relatively mild backlash such as being detained from five to twenty-four hours. One participant even noted a positive" reception by the local government, including "politeness and meals" (participant #95, day five). Another noted that the local government convened an official meeting to discuss the migrants' demands (participant #118, day five). Some even had their expenses in Beijing reimbursed (participant #115, day six; participant #119, day eight). Participants unanimously attributed the relatively mild backlash and even the positive receptions to the government's concerns that the migrants would make trouble again. For example:

> We are the fiercest of them all. When I went to Beijing, the county head said publicly that he would arrest me [when I returned]. When I returned, migrants here came to receive me. [The local government took no action.] On the next day, the police came and detained me for 5 hours. They threatened to put me in jail. Then, all the migrants arrived [at the police station]. They said that if I was jailed, they would be too. They [i.e., the police] had to release me. If migrants just looked at each other and did nothing, nothing would have changed over the past 17 years. (participant #99, day five)

> TGD brothers, I am not bluffing. We have fought all our way through. We migrants have continuously fought with people here forty times in the first year when we came. The party secretary dared not came down from his office. He even said good things about us. It is all about if we are united (*qixin*, 齐心) or not. Look what happened this time! Who dared to arrest us [when returning

from Beijing]!? They not only said good things about us, but also reimbursed our expenses. (participant #143, day eight)

Note that such preference of nao tactics and framing based on nao also shaped the way participants evaluated the successfulness of their petitioning in Beijing. On day six, while a couple of participants complained explicitly or implicitly that they had gotten "no reward" out of the petition (participant #70, day six), participants quickly raised dissenting views. However, these "positive" participants evaluated their action's "success" without making reference to the originally stated action itineraries and goals on days one and three. Rather, they considered the petition as "successful" or "had a big reward" by claiming that their actions had "aroused the attention of the local government" (participant #130, day six), that the petition was part of the "[longer] process" and there would be good consequences "in the future" (participant #132, day six), and that the completion of the journey to Beijing to arouse the attention of the "center" itself had already been "a success" (participant #138, day seven).

If we take "arousing attention" of the state authorities as the goal of the petition, it is more in line with the resistance logic of nao than that of legality or rights consciousness. Although the former nao logic aims to shame on the ruling class by increasing its costs of governance, a legalistic logic aims to expose the loopholes of the institutional system; while the former points to more diffused outcomes, the latter is more on clear and distinct outcomes; the former more on individual, parochial interests, the latter more on benefit-to-all, systemic benefits. The petition campaign began with an emphasis on "lawfulness" and "righteousness," with the goal of benefiting "a million TDG migrants." However, it evolved into one using extralegal or illegal tactics to obtain individual gains akin to a personal vendetta, such as "to take down the county party secretary, make him get sacked!" (participant #99, day five) or to fight and "make a bigger scene otherwise, how can you guys stay in Jiangxi!?" (participant #115, day five). Over the course of the campaign the data show that the systemic, benefits-to-all arguments implied by the original legality discourse eventually retreated to the background of the discussion. In its place, participants generally adopted the tactical logic of "making trouble in order to make them [the government] compromise" (participant #105, day five), which became the key frame mechanism and tactic in the evaluation and repercussion stage (see figure 3.2). The following quotes represent typical use of the discourse of nao at this stage:

> The government is worried. If only one percent [TDG] of migrants go to Beijing, we will have ten thousand. In fact, what has our party-center (*dangzhongyang*, 黨中央) and the state worried is trouble making (*nao*). If we have ten

thousand people and can mobilize them at our disposal, what force can hinder us TGD migrants [from making demands]!? (participant #99, day five).

It all started two years ago. Now they [i.e., the local government] responded to our action. We went to the township government every week, and not less than two times per week. We smashed the township government plaque, and the police station as well. We said that we have no place to live and are about to live in the government building (participant #143, day eight).

People in Jiangxi, don't be afraid. The more you feel scared, the more you will be oppressed. It was like the first few years when we moved to Jiangxi. We beat up the party secretary, the township chief, and fought with the police. We arrived in 2004, and began to fight in 2005. I was sentenced to jail for 8 years [for physical assault]. My sentence [thanks to the continual pressure from the migrants] was later cut down to one and a half years, and I was changed from being the principal defendant in the case to the fourth (participant #10, day eight).

The foregoing quotes illustrate four key characteristics inherent in the resistance logic of nao, which shaped the petitioners' repertoire selection: (a) a sizable crowd, (b) unity in action, (c) repetition of tactics, and (d) committing petty crimes. Here, I would like to highlight a fifth one, (e) trust in the regime. As has been mentioned in the literature review that "trust" is an essential element inherent in collective petitioning in China, and that petitioners possess a bifurcated perception of the state such that the central government is caring and benevolent whereas the local government is mercenary and malevolent (Guo 2001: 435; O'Brien and Li 2006: 42; Lee 2014: 126). Such bifurcation of the state was evident in numerous posts:

We need to let our demands known to the center (*zhongyang*). Let the sunshine of the center shine on the TGD migrants (participant #18, day1).

This time, every provincial government was in action [to stop petitioners]. The local governments know what happens, only the central leaders (*zhongyang lingdao*, 中央領導) do not know. It was like "the mountain is high and the emperor is far away [to know what happen in the local government]" (*shangao huangdi yuan*, 山高皇帝遠). They [i.e., the central leaders] cannot see [our problems] (participant #69, day two).

In fact, it was the police from different provinces who messed things up in Beijing. How could the center and the state do these kinds of things!? (participant #95, day four).

The data also show that participants had different understandings of the central government. Their views ranged from generalities and less central institutions, such as LVOTG, LVOCG, CCDI, Beijing government, party-center, central leaders, or the politburo, to more specific and central authorities like individual leaders, namely, politburo member Wang Qishan, Premier Li Keqiang, and ultimately, President Xi Jinping. And, in line with the discourse of nao, the more central or higher up in the line of authority one goes, the more difficult it is to "hear," "see," and "know," the problems of the petitioners. The discourse of nao, which literally also means making noise and commotion, became an effective discursive resource to frame their actions that the "high-up center" could hear, see, and know their problems.

To the petitioners, such linkage between the noise made (by making troubles) and the noise heard (by the center) was not always hypothetical. Rather, at times, they considered it real in itself. For instance, on day eight, there was news that two politburo members Wang Qishan (also head of CCDI) and Zhang Gaoli would visit Jiangxi. Participants speculated that their visit was related to the beating of returning petitioners in Jiangxi.[17] Such a spectrum of perceived progressive centrality of the state potentially opens up possibilities for further state bifurcations. This explains why the petitioners turned to CCDI on day two after failing to get anything positive from VLOTG on day one; CCDI was considered more central.[18] Stemming from this logic, petitioners can conduct layers of bifurcations of the center; I call it, "nested bifurcations," that is, bifurcations of the state made on top of the original one(s). In doing so, if the demands of the resister were unheard at one level of the "center," efforts can be channeled to another level of "center" higher up in the political hierarchy, until in principle, President Xi rejects their demands, which in reality is an impossibility. The mental logic of nested bifurcations of the state thus generates hope that the petitioners' demands will be eventually heard should their trouble (nao) be noisy and noticeable enough to catch the attention of the "center" at one point along the line of authority.[19]

THE HABITUS OF NAO AND ITS OUTCOMES

The foregoing analysis shows that the repertoire selection emerging in the TGD petitioning campaign was shaped by the logic of nao, rather than rights consciousness. In this last section, I argue further that the logic of nao is not a context-based ad hoc means of resistance but an internalized, durable set of dispositions held by many activists and constitutes part of their "radical habitus"—to borrow the term from Crossley (2002, 2003). The conversations among the activists indicated their repertoire choices were shaped by their knowledge of their past struggles with local officials. Drawing similarity between the present petition campaign and other struggles in the past, the activists generally considered it normal to use minor law-breaking tactics to fight against the regime, such as scuffling, fighting, and smashing objects, which are subsumed under the taken-for-granted category of troublemaking. In Crossley's own wording, the petitioners spoke of their past "struggles in the same breath as" the present petition and categorized "the two under the same label" (2002: 55).

Support for the existence of a nao habitus—rather than that of legality—is also found in the fact that no one raised the possibility of punishing the sexual harasser through *impersonal* legal sanctions on day eight. Instead, everyone seemed to be satisfied—almost automatically—with using *personal* shame (i.e., photographing the kneeling harasser) and a physical response (i.e., two slaps to the face) to punish the harasser. The activists seemed to be naturally attuned to the tactic nao to attain a practical sense of acting—or getting "a feel for the game"—in this situation. All this leads me to agree with Perry's (2009) challenge to O'Brien's "rights awareness" (1996: 32) as the foundation of peasants' repertoires of contention. To Perry (2009), petitioning in China expresses a "politics as usual" featuring "rule awareness" rather than the "rights awareness" bred in Western open societies (2009: 18). It is true that the activists still on occasion frame their resistance in terms of the discourse of legality. However, in the TGD petition campaign I contend that such use was mainly to portray their action as not threatening to the regime and to avoid brutal repression rather than reflecting actors' rightful consciousness. Following this line of argument, I also concur with Lee, who observes, "State and protesters' engagement with the law as gamesmanship [in petitioning] does not necessarily produce a rule-of-law political culture, but instead nurtures a cynical and instrumental view of the law" (Lee 2014: 129). Put another way, the resistance generated from the habitus of nao is more akin to interest-based collective rent-seeking behavior rather than the defense of one's legal and constitutional rights with the concern for systemic change.

The use of nao in contemporary Chinese grassroots mobilization is found in patient-doctor clashes (Tu 2014), labor disputes (Pun and Lu 2010), land confiscations (Lian 2012), forced evictions (Chen 2017: 63), and grievances due to heavy taxation (Zhang 2015). However, these analyses generally deem nao as an ad hoc epiphenomenon generated by a larger systemic problem.[20] For example, Pun and Lu suggest that "a culture of violence [i.e., nao]" bred among construction workers is generated by the "labor subcontracting system ... of the construction industry" (Pun and Lu 2010: 158). I have been arguing here that nao refers to the general logic embodied in the actors and constitutes part of their habitus and shapes repertoire choices. In fact, to consider nao as activists' habitus can explain better not only the use of trouble making in a wide range of resistance settings but also activists' inclination to create and sustain instabilities in society rather than a level-playing ground in fighting against the authorities.[21]

Theoretically, the repertoire selection generated by the habitus of *nao* can be subsumed under Johnston's umbrella concept of resistance repertoire, which refers to a set of relatively less public and recognizable contentious tactics and framings that constitute seeds of future collective actions (2015: 629). Such linkages with future overt collective action leads to my final piece of analysis—the outcomes of the resistances shaped by the habitus of nao.

Here, one should note that the Chinese grassroots resistance based on making trouble does not really fit the conventional repression-concession-escalation dynamics between two parties, the resister and the state (Lichbach 1987; Moore 2000). Nor do they fit models that take into account "the strategic interaction between the government and the opposition" (Piserskalla 2010: 121). Chinese grassroots resistance generally involves three parties with the "state" being bifurcated into "local government" and the "central government." In this three-party game, or what Cai calls "divided power" (2008: 411), the central government can "'*pretend*' not to know of the repression [by the local government] when it does not want to intervene" (Cai 2008: 430; original emphasis). Therefore, the repression-concession dilemma mainly involves hesitations on the part of local government officials about whether their decisions would jeopardize their careers, rather than if they would escalate the resistance to an extent of shaking up the status quo. Since the "central government" is considered by the resisters as the real arbitrator (who seldom arbitrates in reality), it is unlikely that the aggrieved would escalate their resistance even in face of repression by the local government.

Based on this logic, grassroots resistance shaped by the habitus of nao in contemporary China is unlikely to escalate to an extent that it threatens the status quo of single-party rule. What the resisters have in mind is mainly to make constant trouble so as to make their grievances finally heard, seen, and known by the center. This logical inference is thus at odds with the claims that the regime will face a quick collapse (Shambaugh 2015), a "democracy or die" situation (Huang 2013: 47), or a grassroots-movement-turned-revolution "should the regime adopt more indiscriminate coercion rather than soft regulations" on popular resistance (Steinhardt 2017: 552). It also gives rise to serious doubts over the explicit and implicit claims made by experienced scholars that incessant grassroots resistance would cause erosion of the legitimacy of the party-state and eventually threaten the stability of the regime in times of crises, in particular, fiscal crises (e.g., Li 2008; Chen 2017: 63; Lee 2014: 133; Ong 2018a). Here, my view coincides with Hu, Wu, and Fei's that "authoritarian regimes are less reliant on legitimacy for survival than their democratic counterparts" (2018: 683).[22]

NOTES

1. Tu (2016: 343) has shown that the small closed networks on WeChat can facilitate social mobilization because it (a) provides a comfortable space for discussions and cultivate a series of alternative public spheres; (b) promotes online debates and popular protests despite strengthened internet censorship; (c) creates new ways for ordinary people to be associated with one another and to build solidarity; and (d) allows a high level of mobility for the user as it operates via mobile phones rather than computers.

2. One should note that social mobilization in terms of collective petitioning or mass protest in communist China has been a vastly explored topic. Previous studies have investigated the social, economic, and political conditions that make possible specific actors participate in collective action in support of or against the regime (Cai 2004, 2010; Ho 2010; Wang 2012); the use of tactics—both tactically and communicatively—that highlights the rightfulness or conceals the antiregime nature of the collective action (O'Brien 1996; O'Brien and Li 2006; Ho and Lu 2019); the fragmented mentality of the collective actors such that regime legitimacy (by association, its resilience) can be protested against at the expense of the local authorities (Guo 2001; Cai 2008); the nature of grassroots resistance as it ostensibly represents *both* challenge *and* compliance to the state authority (Li, Liu, and O'Brien 2012; Dimitrov 2015; Ho 2017); the rationalities and timeliness of the state intervention, which may lead to effective repression or tactical escalation of the resistance (O'Brien and Deng 2015); different roles played by online technologies such that they can both facilitate mobilization of the aggrieved (Tang and Huhe 2014; Lee and Ho 2014; Deluca, Brunner, and Sun 2016; Harris forthcoming) and allow the state to give room to public criticism while silencing regime-threatening collective expressions (King, Pan, and Roberts 2013); and different interventions adopted and constraints faced by nongovernmental organizations (NGOs) in grassroots mobilization (Lee and Shen 2009; Pun and Lu 2010; Xu 2013). Alongside these conventional themes, recent studies have witnessed the emergence of research foci that concern multifarious state strategies to absorb popular protests and pacify resisters. These foci range from the use of accommodative discourse to deflect the discontent from the regime (Steinhardt 2017); to the identification of typical actor-state interfaces in the course of popular resistance (Lee and Zhang 2013); to specific stability-maintenance strategies including the use of police (Wang and Minzner 2015; Wang 2014; Greitens 2017), thugs (Ong 2018a; Wang and Minzner 2015; Chen 2017), and other less formal ways of "buying peace with money" (Lee 2014: 130), such as building up community mediation forums (Hu 2011), deploying social workers (Hu et al. 2018) and lawyers (Zheng and Hu 2020), using profit-seeking brokers in state-society bargaining (Ong 2018b), and the use of informal human relationships (Deng and O'Brien 2013; O'Brien and Deng 2015, 2017) to temper the aggrieved and diffuse popular protests.

3. In Guangdong, most TGD migrants relocated to four areas, namely, Foshan, Zhaoqing, Jiangmen, and Huizhou.

4. To protect the informants, pseudonyms will be used throughout this chapter.

5. In parallel with this "main" WeChat group was an unknown number of sub-WeChat groups that were composed different groups of migrants from different places during the petition process.

6. For example, Bruun (2013: 256) states that only "a tiny fraction of the 12 million yearly petitions have positive outcomes and in many instances petitions are prevented by police interference." Citing Minzner (2006), Lee (2014: 128) writes that "fewer than 0.2 percent of petitions succeed in having their complaints addressed."

7. My interview with a senior internet policeman in Guangzhou confirmed all these surveillance strategies. He also revealed that these methods are common in preventing petitioners to lodge complaints to the central government. He said that anyone who carries a title of delegate chief or its equivalent in any district-level police station can order a thorough search of all WeChat messages and online purchasing records of a civilian. He gave an example that if an active dissenter bought a high-speed train ticket on the internet, the local police would immediately know it. Being one of the engineers of the online surveillance system, he said that "the system is more advanced than that in the US" (interviewed conducted in October 2018).

8. For example: "No need to tackle them hard. When they come, you just run away." (participant #28, day one); or "Don't make trouble or block roads." (participant #28, day one)

9. For example: "This petition is all about rights maintenance (*weiquan*, 維權). Our action is voluntary (*ziyuan*, 自願), there is nothing called leadership (*meiyao lingdao bu lingdao de*, 沒有領導不領導的)." (participant #14, day one).

10. For example: "Everyone in Beijing, when you arrive [at the petitioning agencies], you must meet the leaders. If you cannot meet them, everyone knee[ls] down" (participant #18, day one).

11. For example: "Fellows in this group, please don't type anymore" (participant #14, day one). One should note that my internet policeman informant confirmed to me that image and voice messages were "a lot more difficult" (*kunnan henduo*, 困難很多) to be monitored than text messages.

12. For example: "When you arrive [in Beijing], people will contact you. We will not tell you where we are in the big group" (participant #21, day two).

13. For example: "Don't use ID card to buy tickets! Those who bought tickets through this way could not make their way to Beijing" (participant #63, day two).

14. For example: "Share our stories to all big WeChat groups (participant #13, day one); "Keep calling the journalist from People's Station." (participant #25, day one); "Let the whole country and even people in the US to know we migrant groups have been unfairly treated" (participant #17, day one).

15. For example, a participant lamented to have spent 300 yuan on digital information for the three-day stay in Beijing (participants #22, day three).

16. On day one, a participant sent a text message outlining in several points the itinerary and action goals of the petition:

- Visit CCDI together. We cannot press on them. We need to pose ourselves as a group of the weak in order to beg for sympathy. We will rally by kneeing down in front of them.

- Action address: Beijing Western District Xianli Street 41.
- Materials [to be submitted]: The letter of demand and other evidences (evidences should be color-printed).
- Objective of action: To meet with the highest leaders (*zuigao lingdao*, 最高領導).
- Action time: Tomorrow at 8:30 am. (participant #18, day one)

And, in the letter of demand reposted on day three, it stated clearly the demands of the petitioners in six points (participant #37, day three): (a) premigration compensation; (b) postmigration support; (c) housing quality problems; (d) pension problem; (d) land problems; and (e) precise poverty alleviation (jingzhun fupin, 精準扶貧).

17. However, it was quickly found to be a wrong speculation.

18. "We should sustain what we believe. Success is hinged upon now on CCDI which as we all know is to investigate corrupt officials. That's why this place must have an influence [on our demands]. Please native fellows and relatives tell each other" (participant #37, day two).

19. It reminds me of the similar situation of sporadic struggles on the part of Mexican peasants against corrupt officials documented in Nuijten (2004). The ambivalent answer offered by the legal system controlled by corrupt officials has created to the peasants what Nuijten (2004: 211) terms as a "hope-generating governmentality machine" such that the peasants feel hope about to continue their struggles without concern for changing the political status quo.

20. Among these scholars, Lian (2012: 493) is more in line with my thinking, considering nao as a general logic of resistance (i.e., "to make a disturbance, to gain recognition"), an approach known as "crying children can be fed milk."

21. This phenomenon has intrigued even two most astute China experts who consider it "surprising" to see that the "aggrieved citizens actually share [with the grassroots stability maintenance officials] a common interest in sustaining a certain level of instability" (Lee and Zhang 2013: 1493).

22. This is also in line with Pierskalla (2010: 120) who states: "In strong autocracies, elites have a secure grip on power and generally do not fear popular protest, which in turn induces dissenting voices to remain silent."

REFERENCES

Alam, Meredian, Pam Nilan, and Terry Leahy. 2019. "Learning from Greenpeace: Activist Habitus in a Local Struggle." *Electronic Green Journal* 1(42): 1–18. https://escholarship.org/uc/item/41s879p5.

Bourdieu, Pierre. 1977. *Outline of a Theory and Practice*, trans. Richard Nice. New York: Cambridge University Press.

———. 1984. *Distinction: A Social Critique of the Judgment of Taste*, trans. Richard Nice. Cambridge, MA: Harvard University Press.

Bruun, Ole. 2013. "Social Movements, Competing Rationalities and Trigger Events: The Complexity of Chinese Popular Mobilizations." *Anthropological Theory* 13(3) 240–66.

Cai, Yongshun. 2004. "Managed Participation in China." *Political Science Quarterly* 119(3): 425–51.

———. 2008. "Power Structure and Regime Resilience: Contentious Politics in China." *British Journal of Political Science* 38(3): 411–32.

———. 2010. *Collective Resistance in China: Why Popular Protests Succeed or Fail.* Stanford, CA: Stanford University Press.

Cernea, Michael Mihail. 2000. "Risks, Safeguards and Reconstruction: A Model for Population Displacement and Resettlement." *Economic and Political Weekly* 35(41): 3659–78.

Chen, Xi. 2017. "Origins of Informal Coercion in China." *Politics and Society* 45(1): 67–89.

Crossley, Nick. 2002. "Repertoires of Contention and Tactical Diversity in the UK Psychiatric Survivors Movement: The Question of Appropriation." *Social Movement Studies* 1(1): 47–71.

———. 2003. "From Reproduction to Transformation: Social Movement Fields and the Radical Habitus." *Theory, Culture, and Society* 20(6): 43–68.

Deluca, Kevin Michael, Elizabeth Brunner, and Ye Sun. 2016. "Weibo, WeChat, and the Transformative Events of Environmental Activism on China's Wild Public Screens." *International Journal of Communication* 10: 321–39.

Deng, Yanhua, and Kevin O'Brien. 2013. "Relational Repression in China: Using Social Ties to De-mobilize Protesters." *China Quarterly* 215: 533–52.

Dimitrov, Martin K. 2015. "Internal Government Assessments of the Quality of Governance in China." *Studies in Comparative International Development* 50(1): 50–72.

Duan, Yuefang, and Shawn Steil. 2003. "China Three Gorges project: Policy, Planning and Implementation." *Journal of Refugee Studies* 16: 422–43.

Duan, Yuefang, and Brooke Wilmsen. 2012. "Addressing the Resettlement Challenges at the Three Gorges Project." *International Journal of Environmental Studies* 69(3): 461–74.

Fu, Diana, and Greg Distelhorst. 2018. "Grassroots Participation and Repression under Hu Jintao and Xi Jinping." *The China Journal* 79(1): 100–22.

Greitens, Sheena. 2017. "Rethinking China's Coercive Capacity: An Examination of PRC Domestic Security Spending, 1992–2012." *The China Quarterly* 232: 1002–25.

Gui, Xiaowei. 2017. "How Local Authorities Handle Nail-Like Petitions and Why Concessions Are Made." *Chinese Sociological Review* 49(2): 162–82.

Guo, Xiaolin. 2001. "Land Expropriation and Rural Conflicts in China." *The China Quarterly* 166: 422–39.

Haluza-DeLay, Randolph. 2008. "A Theory of Practice for Social Movements: Environmentalism and Ecological Habitus." *Mobilization: An International Quarterly* 13(2): 205–18.

Harris, Rachel. forthcoming. "Dissonant Voices in China's Harmonious Society." In Noriko Manabe, and Eric Drott, eds., *The Oxford Handbook of Protest Music*. Oxford, UK: Oxford University Press.

Hassid, Jonathan. 2008. "Controlling the Chinese Media: An Uncertain Business." *Asian Survey* 48(3): 414–30.
He, Xin, and Yuqing Feng. 2016. "Mismatched Discourses in the Petition Offices of Chinese Courts." *Law and Social Inquiry* 41(1): 212–41.
Heggelund, Gorild. 2004. *Environment and Resettlement Politics in China.* Burlington, UK: Ashgate Publishing Company.
———. 2006. "Resettlement Programmes and Environmental Capacity in the Three Gorges Dam Project." *Development and Change* 37(1): 179–99.
Ho, Wing-Chung, and Jian Lu. 2019. "Culture vs. the State? The 'Defend-My-Mother-Tongue' Protests in Guangzhou." *The China Journal* 81(1): 81–102.
Ho, Wing-Chung. 2010. *The Transition Study of Postsocialist China: An Ethnographic Study of a Model Community*. Singapore: World Scientific Publications.
Hsu, Ho, Kun Ma, and Wing-Chung Ho. 2019. "Forced Migration and Political Functions of the Three Gorges Project in China." *Journal of Comparative Asian Development* 17(2): 62–77.
Hu, Jieren. 2011. "Grand Mediation in China: Mechanism and Application." *Asian Survey* 51(6): 1065–89.
Hu, Jieren, Tong Wu, and Jingyan Fei. 2018. "Flexible Governance in China: Affective Care, Petition Social Workers, and Multi-Pronged Means of Dispute Resolution." *Asian Survey* 58(4): 679–703.
Huang, Yasheng. 2013. "Democratize or Die: Why China's Communists Face Reform or Revolution." *Foreign Affairs* 92: 47–54.
Hung, Chin-Fu. 2010. "China's Propaganda in the Information Age: Internet Commentators and Wen'an Incident." *Issues and Studies* 46(4): 149–81.
Jackson, Sukhan, and Adrian Sleigh. 2000. "Resettlement for China's Three Gorges Dam: Socioeconomic Impact and Institutional Tensions." *Communist and Post-Communist Studies* 33(2): 223–41.
———. 2001. "The Political Economy and Socioeconomic Impact of China's Three Gorges Dam." *Asian Studies Review* 25(1): 57–72
Jim, Chi Yung, and Felix Y. Yang. 2006. "Local Responses to Inundation and Defarming in the Reservoir Region of the Three Gorges Project" [in Chinese]. *Environmental Management* 38(4): 618–37.
Johnston, Hank. 2015. "'The Game's Afoot': Social Movements in Authoritarian States." In Donatella della Porta, and Mario Diani, eds., *The Oxford Handbook of Social Movements*, 619–33. New York: Oxford University Press.
King, Gary, Jennifer Pan, and Margaret E. Roberts. 2013. "How Censorship in China Allows Government Criticism but Silences Collective Expression." *American Political Science Review* 107(2): 326–43.
Leavenworth, Stuart. 2016. China May Shelve Plans to Build Dams on Its Last Wild River. *National Geographic*, May 12. https://news.nationalgeographic.com/2016/05/160512-china-nu-river-dams-environment/.
Lee, Ching Kwan. 2014. "State and Social Protest." *Daedalus* 143(2): 124–34.
Lee, Ching Kwan, and Y. Shen. 2009. "China: The Paradox and Possibility of a Public Sociology of Labor." *Work and Occupations* 36(2): 110–25.

Lee, Ching Kwan, and Yonghong Zhang. 2013. "The Power of Instability: Unraveling the Micro-foundations of Bargained Authoritarianism in China." *American Journal of Sociology* 118(6): 1475–508.

Lee, Kingsyhon, and Ming-Sho Ho. 2014. "The Maoming Anti-PX Protest of 2014." *China Perspectives* 3(1): 33–39.

Li, Heming, Paul Waley, and Phil Rees. 2001 "Reservoir Resettlement in China: Past Experience and the Three Gorges Dam." *Geographical Journal* 167(3): 195–212.

Li, Lianjiang. 2008. "Political Trust and Petitioning in the Chinese Countryside." *Comparative Politics* 40(2): 209–26.

Li, Lianjiang, Mingxing Liu, and Kevin J. O'Brien. 2012. "Petitioning Beijing: The High Tide of 2003–2006." *The China Quarterly* 210: 313–34.

Lian, Hongping. 2012. "The Resistance of Land-Lost Farmers in China: 'Interest-Striving' and 'Struggle by Order.'" *Journal of Community Positive Practices* 3(4): 478–99.

Lichbach, Mark I. 1987. "Deterrence or Escalation? The Puzzle of Aggregate Studies of Repression and Dissent." *Journal of Conflict Resolution* 31: 266–97.

Liu, Chengbin, and Hong Lei. 2001. "Role-Behavioral Obstacles of TGD Migrants" [*sanxia yimin de juese xingwei zhangai*]. *Society* [*Shehui*] 8: 13–16.

MacKinnon, Rebecca. 2008. "Flatter World and Thicker Walls? Blogs, Censorship and Civic Discourse in China." *Public Choice* 134(1/2): 31–46.

Minzner, Carl. 2006. "Xinfang: An Alternative to the Formal Chinese Judicial System." *Stanford Journal of International Law* 42: 103–79.

Moore, Will H. 2000. "The Repression of Dissent: A Substitution Model of Government Coercion." *Journal of Conflict Resolution* 44: 107–27.

Munro, Lyle. 2005. "Strategies, Action Repertoires and DIY Activism in the Animal Rights Movement." *Social Movement Studies* 4: 1, 75–94

Nuijten, Monique. 2004. "Between Fear and Fantasy: Governmentality and the Working of Power in Mexico." *Critique of Anthropology* 24(2): 209–30.

O'Brien, Kevin. 1996. "Rightful Resistance." *World Politics* 49(1): 31–55.

O'Brien, Kevin, and Yanhua Deng. 2015. "Repression Backfires: Tactical Radicalization and Protest Spectacle in Rural China." *Journal of Contemporary China* 24(93): 457–70.

———. 2017. "Preventing Protest One Person at a Time: Psychological Coercion and Relational Re-pression in China." *The China Review* 17(2): 179–201.

O'Brien, Kevin J., and Lianjiang Li. 2006. *Rightful Resistance in Rural China*. New York: Cambridge University Press.

Ong, Lynette H. 2018a. "Thugs and Outsourcing of State Repression in China." *The China Journal* 80(1): 94–110.

———. 2018b. "Engaging *Huangniu*. Brokers: Commodification of State-Society Bargaining in China." *Journal of Contemporary China*, 28(116): 293–307.

Padovani, Florence. 2006a. "Involuntary Resettlement in the Three Gorges Dam Area in the Perspective of Forced Migration Due to Hydraulic Planning in China." In F. Crepeau, D. Nakache, M. Collyer, N. H. Goetz, and A. Hansen, eds., *Forced Migration and Global Processes: A View from Forced Migration Studies*, 91–123. New York: Lexington Books.

———. 2006b. "Displacement from the Three Gorges Region: A Discreet Arrival in the Economic Capital of China." *China Perspectives* 66(2): 223–41.

Peerenboom, Randall. 2001. "Globalization, Path Dependency and the Limits of Law: Administrative Law Reform and Rule of Law in the People's Republic of China." *Berkeley Journal of International Law* 19: 161–264.

Perry, Elizabeth J. 2009. "A New Rights Consciousness?" *Journal of Democracy* 20(3): 17–20.

Pierskalla, Jan Henryk. 2010. "Protest, Deterrence, and Escalation: The Strategic Calculus of Government Repression." *Journal of Conflict Resolution* 54(1): 117–45.

Pils, Eva. 2011. "Taking Yuan Seriously: Why the Chinese State Should Stop Suppressing Citizen Protests against Injustice." *Temple International and Comparative Law Journal* 25: 285–327.

Pun, Ngai, and Huilin Lu. 2010. "A Culture of Violence: The Labor Subcontracting System and Collective Action by Construction Workers in Post-Socialist China." *The China Journal* 64: 143–58.

Shambaugh, David. 2015. "The Coming Chinese Crackup." *The Wall Street Journal*, March 6. http://www.wsj.com/articles/the-coming-chinese-crack-up-1425659198.

Steinhardt, H. Christoph. 2017. "Discursive Accommodation: Popular Protest and Strategic Elite Communication in China." *European Political Science Review* 9(4): 539–60.

Tang, Min, and Narisong Huhe. 2014. "Alternative Framing: The Effect of the Internet on Political Support in Authoritarian China." *International Political Science Review* 35(5): 559–76.

Tilly, C. 1995. "Contentious Repertoires in Great Britain, 1758–1834." In Marc Traugott, ed. *Repertoires and Cycles of Collective Action*, 15–42. Durham, NC: Duke University Press.

Tu, Fangjing. 2016. "WeChat and Civil Society in China." *Communication and the Public* 1(3) 343–50.

Tu, Jiong. 2014. "Yinao: Protest and Violence in China's Medical Sector." *Berkeley Journal of Sociology*, December 11, 2014. Accessed October 1, 2020. http://berkeleyjournal.org/2014/12/yinao-portest-and-violence-in-chinas-medialsector/.

Wang, Juan. 2015. "Managing Social Stability: The Perspective of a Local Government in China." *Journal of East Asian Studies* 15(1): 1–25.

———. 2012. "Shifting Boundaries between the State and Society: Village Cadres as New Activists in Collective Petition." *The China Quarterly* 211: 697–717.

Wang, Lei. 2010. "Guangdong Sanxia Yimin Yuyan Shiyong Qingkuang Diaocha" [A Survey on Guangdong TGD Migrants' Use of Language]. Academic Research [*Xueshu Yanjiu*] 4(2) 153–56.

Wang, Yuhua. 2014. "Empowering the Police: How the Chinese Communist Party Manages Its Coercive Leaders." *The China Quarterly* 219: 625–48.

Wang, Yuhua, and Carl F. Minzner. 2015. "The Rise of the Security State." *The China Quarterly* 222: 339–59.

Wilmsen, Brooke. 2016. "After the Deluge: A Longitudinal Study of Resettlement at the Three Gorges Dam, China." *World Development* 84(1): 41–54.

Wilmsen, Brooke, Michael Webber, and Duan Yuefang 2011. "Development for Whom: Rural to Urban Resettlement at the Three Gorges Dam, China" *Asian Studies Review* 35(1): 21-42.

Wong, John. 2007. "China's Major Economic Challenge: Sustaining High Growth whilst Fixing Its Growth Problems. In Wang Gungwu and John Wong, eds., *Interpreting China's Development*, 83-96. Hackensack, NJ: World Scientific Publishing.

Wong, Stan Hok-wui, and Minggang Peng. 2015. "Petition and Repression in China's Authoritarian Regime: Evidence from a Natural Experiment." *Journal of East Asian Studies* 15(1): 27–67.

Xi, Juan, Sean-Shong Hwang, Xiaotian Feng, Xiaofei Qiao, and Yue Cao. 2007. "Perceived Risks and Benefits of the Three Gorges Project." *Sociological Perspectives* 50(2): 323–37.

Xu, Y. 2013. "Labor Non-Governmental Organizations in China: Mobilizing Rural Migrant Workers." *Journal of Industrial Relations* 55(2): 243–59.

Ying, Xing. 2013. *A Study of the Stability of Contemporary Rural Chinese Society*. Berlin: Springer.

Yu, Cheng, and He Xiang. 2006. "Power Games and Migrant Adaptability in Migration Villages." *Chinese Sociology and Anthropology* 38(3): 71–89.

Zhang, Quanfa, and Zhiping Lou. 2011. "The Environmental Changes and Mitigation Actions in the Three Gorges Reservoir Region, China." *Environmental Science and Policy* 14(8): 1132–38.

Zhang, Wu. 2015. "Leadership, Organization and Moral Authority: Explaining Peasant Militancy in Contemporary China." *The China Journal* 73: 59–83.

Zheng, Rupting, and Jieren Hu. 2020. "Mediating State-Society Disputes in China: Outsourced Lawyers and their Selective Responses." *China Information* 34(3): 383–405. DOI: 10.1177/0920203X19887670.

Zhou Kai, and Xiaojun Yan. 2014. "The Quest for Stability." *Problems of Post-Communism* 61(3): 3–17.

Part II

POLITICAL OPPORTUNITIES AND CONSTRAINTS

Chapter Four

Civic and Noncivic Activism under Autocracy

Xi Chen (Chinese University of Hong Kong)

China under Xi Jinping is descending deeper into the depths of autocracy. Xi is not only amassing enormous power into his hands, his administration is also undertaking fierce attacks on society. Observers lament that Xi's administration conducted the "worst crackdown on lawyers, activists and scholars in decades" (Zeng 2015). The clampdown on civil society is so extensive that "even those used to a degree of immunity have found themselves target[s]" (Minzner 2015).

A consensus among many observers is that the Chinese state has become substantially more repressive toward society. In a recent study, however, Fu and Distelhorst (2017) put forth a somewhat different interpretation. They argue that although the transition from Hu Jintao to Xi Jinping severely restricted opportunities for contentious participation—defined as disruptive behavior ranging from grassroots advocacy to outright protests—formal institutions for participation that expanded under Hu Jintao continue to provide channels for dialogue among local officials and citizens. By distinguishing between institutionalized participation and contentious participation, Fu and Distelhorst paint a more accurate picture of recent political changes. I contend, however that this is still inadequate; further differentiation is needed to account for the changes in contentious politics in China.

In particular, this chapter argues that political opportunity structures for popular contention in China are essentially bifurcated: civic activism purported to promote public interests is sharply differentiated by the state from noncivic activism focusing on private interests. The Chinese state uses sophisticated different strategies to deal with popular contention. It is a widely accepted assumption that state strategies in China are often based on a distinction between materialist contention and nonmaterialist contention. The dichotomy between civic and noncivic contention has been rarely recognized as the basis for state strategies.

A clarification of the role of this dichotomy can help us answer many important questions regarding the dynamics and changes of contentious politics in China. For example, why did Xi's administration intensify state repression? Is the regime trying to close the space for all kinds of popular collective action? Fu and Distelhorst observed three important shifts in state repression under Xi—from sporadic harassment to criminalization, from post facto to preemptive, and from social stability to national security framing. Such shifts might be interpreted as a comprehensive change in state strategies for dealing with popular contention. If we distinguish between civic and noncivic activism it becomes clear that Xi's administration only substantially intensified its repression of civic activism, and its basic approach to noncivic activism remained largely unchanged. It is no coincidence that almost all the examples cited by Fu and Distelhorst are cases of assaults on civic activists or organizations such as rights lawyers or labor nongovernmental organizations (NGOs). Compared to noncivic activism, civic activism is more likely to be responded by the state with criminalization, preemptive measures and national security framing. Indeed, there is little evidence that state strategies for coping with social protests regarding private interests have systematically changed under Xi.

Identifying the patterns of state differentiating strategies can improve our understanding of political opportunity structure (POS), which is a key concept in the field of contentious politics. Most studies on POS are concerned about basic features of regime, such as the regime's openness or its propensity and capacity for repression (Tilly 1978; McAdam, Tarrow, and Tilly 2001). The importance of regime type for shaping political opportunity structure has been confirmed by plenty of empirical studies, including a few cross-national studies of political contexts (e.g., Kitschelt 1986). Some studies also suggest that each type of regimes will have different configurations based on the nature of the involved issues (Giugni 2004; Kriesi 2005; Johnston 2011). As Hank Johnston (2011) pointed out, for example, the former Soviet Union always allowed ecology protests but did not tolerate protests for independence among ethnonational republics. An important task for students of contentious politics is therefore to examine how a regime differentiates between popular contention with different types of claims and explain why.

In this chapter, I contend that the distinction between civic and noncivic activism has been the basis for state strategies not only under Xi, but throughout the history of People's Republic. To account for the patterns of differentiation, we need to investigate the functions that different types of popular collective action can fulfill and the threats they may pose to the regime. Civic activism tends to fulfill different functions and pose different threats from noncivic activism, and such functions and threats often change over time. China is an ideal case for studying how different regime types interact with the nature of claims to produce different patterns of state strategies. China experienced two dramatic regime transformations in the last four decades: the transition from totalitarianism to post-totalitarianism starting from the late 1970s and the transition from post-totalitarianism regime back to neototalitarianism under Xi.

It should be noted that the distinction between civic and noncivic activism is rarely relevant to political opportunities in democracies. Because civil society is open and free in such regimes, the government is unlikely to be particularly hostile toward civic activism. Moreover, few democratic governments are interested in aggressive mobilization of civic activism to achieve its social and political objectives. Unlike democracies, which treat civic and noncivic activism largely in the same way, authoritarian states are more sensitive to this distinction, often regarding civic activism as more threatening. Such a tendency was particularly manifested in the past two decades when a sizable group of authoritarian states waged war on NGOs with foreign connections.

Compared to ordinary authoritarian regimes, totalitarian or post-totalitarian regimes tend to differentiate between civic and noncivic activism more sharply. They often take a more polarized approach toward civic activism than noncivic activism. This is partly because such regimes tend to view civic activism through a lens of ideological war and partly because they often extensively use mass mobilization as a political tool. As Linz (2000, 70) noted, in a totalitarian society, citizen participation in and active mobilization for political and collective social tasks are encouraged, demanded, rewarded, and channeled through a single party and many monopolistic secondary groups. Passive obedience and apathy, retreat into the role of "parochials" and "subjects," characteristic of many authoritarian regimes, is considered undesirable by the rulers. The Soviet Union under Joseph Stalin, for example, exhorted people to become "men with big characters" who transcend "bourgeois" individualism (Fritzsche and Hellbeck 2009). Such tendencies can sometimes linger after the society has departed from totalitarianism. Vladimir Putin's Russia, for instance, sponsors a Komsomol-style youth organization, Nashi (Hemment 2015), which launched fierce attacks on NGOs in the mid-2000s as a response to what was perceived as foreign manipulations of the color revolutions (Howell 2015). Among communist and postcommunist regimes, China stands out for its particularly sharp differentiation between the two types of activism.

To be sure, there are huge variations within each category of civic and noncivic activism in China. Civic activism, for example, ranges from the

Charter 08 movement, which called for a change of the political system, to regime-friendly efforts to relieve poverty in the countryside or assist victims of domestic violence. No civic activism can possibly "represent" such a wide range of activist goals. In this chapter, although I will cite a variety of examples, for the convenience of comparisons across time my empirical evidence will mostly be focused on labor and feminist activism, neither of which is exclusively civic or noncivic activism. Labor activism can be found in all historical periods and had an important impact on regime legitimacy and stability. By contrast, feminism did not emerge until in post-Mao era, and is generally perceived as less politically sensitive. Labor activism and feminist activism can complement each other to illustrate the changing space for social activism in China.

DISAGGREGATING POLITICAL OPPORTUNITY STRUCTURES IN CHINA

Most recent studies of contentious politics in China focus on popular contention with economic claims, such as the reduction of taxes and fees for peasants, jobs and severance packages for laid-off workers, pensions for retirees, and compensation for people who lost their land or houses. Clearly, the Chinese government's approach to these types of popular contention is dramatically different than its approach to the student movement in 1989 or Falun Gong movement in 1999. Few studies, however, have tried to systematically elucidate the basic patterns of differential strategies and the rationales behind them. An important exception is Perry (2002), who observes that the party-state sharply distinguishes three types of popular contention: nationalist movements, protest movements with political or religious agendas, and localized protests on subsistence or other economic entitlements. Chinese Communist Party (CCP) leaders have been cautious in dealing with nationalist protests because they are well aware of their vulnerability in such events. As they learned from the May Fourth Movement and other nationalist movements in the past century, Chinese citizens could easily shift their target from foreigners to their own government. Although Chinese leaders were wary of student activism in general, they nevertheless sometimes "allowed, even encouraged, educated youths to take to the streets to express their patriotic outrage" (Perry 2002: xi).

In Perry's view, the party-state's strategies for coping with non-nationalist popular contention are essentially based on a dichotomy between economic and noneconomic protests. As she stated, "Claims to a basic subsistence that stay within local confines have seldom been deemed especially threatening by Chinese regimes, and so—in contrast to protests motivated by explicitly religious or political agendas—historically have not attracted a great deal of central anxiety or attention" (Perry 2002: xiv). As an authoritarian regime, the Chinese government's repressiveness toward politically motivated protests is hardly surprising: such protests are directly threatening to the regime. More puzzling is the Chinese government's usual tolerance of protests for basic subsistence or other economic entitlements. Perry attributes such tolerance to the political culture in China; from Mencius to Mao, there is a long tradition in China that recognizes "the natural propensity of those who are hard pressed economically to rebel against rapacious officials" (Perry 2002: 31). Perry's disaggregation of state strategies in China is illuminating. Although not all scholars agree with her cultural explanations, the assumption is widely accepted that in China, economic and economic protests involve quite different patterns of government-citizen interactions.

A somewhat similar conceptual framework has been proposed by Lee and Hsing (2010) who distinguish between the politics of (re)distribution and that of recognition (politics of representation is their third type about media expression of ideas and symbols). The politics of (re)distribution includes struggles and claims for material interests among social groups or between social groups and state actors that spring from their common or differential class locations, whether these are defined by property ownership or their roles in production (Lee and Hsing 2010: 3). By contrast, the politics of recognition is concerned with the discovery and articulation of needs previously denied or ignored, especially the demand for social recognition of certain groups' moral status, political position, and identity (Lee and Hsing 2010: 4). The similarities between this framework and Perry's typology are obvious: Perry's subsistence protests and politically or religiously motivated protests correspond to Lee and Hsing's protests on (re)distribution and those on recognition, respectively.

Lee and Hsing's distinction, however, reveals a rather different rationale for the state's differential strategies: The Chinese state is under international pressure to be more tolerant toward social activism focused on recognition rather than redistribution. This is because the Chinese government actively projects itself as a modern and civilized power, seeking the status and legitimacy bestowed through connections within the international community (Lee and Hsing 2010: 9). This makes the Chinese state subject to pressure from international society, which is often selective. As they explain, "While China is often targeted for its violation of environmental, gender, and religious rights, the sway of global neoliberalism leads to little criticism against rising inequality and redistributive injustice in China" (Lee and Hsing 2010: 9).

In recent years, however, their expectation seems to be at odds with the reality. Activists and organizations focusing on issues of recognition often experience considerably harsher repression than those protesting material loss. This is not because there is no international pressure on the Chinese government on gender, religious, or other human rights. The Chinese government nevertheless enjoys a strong position in global politics and is also determined to resist pressure from outside. External intervention may actually politicize social activism and, therefore, make it more vulnerable. Activist and NGO linkages to international society seldom bring about effective protection. Instead, they sometimes trigger government suspicion and repression. International intervention also has the unintended effect of helping the state create social organizations as repressive actors (Long 2018).

Despite the seemingly opposite conclusions, Perry's and Lee and Hsing's theories share one assumption: The dichotomy between claims to materialist and those to nonmaterialist interests is a basic boundary the Chinese state draws when it responds to popular contention. In this chapter, I posit that the differential strategies of the party-state in China are often based not so much on the distinction between materialist and nonmaterialist claims as on the distinction between civic activism and noncivic activism. The former is defined as activism advocating for the interest of the general population (public interest), and the latter as activism by specific individuals or small groups in defense of their particularistic interest (private interest). Although civic and noncivic activism involve systematically different patterns of state response, this distinction has often been overlooked by protesters, activists, as well as by observers of popular contention.

The lack of attention to the distinction between civic and noncivic activism in the study of popular contention in China is partly due to the confusion between this distinction and that between materialist and nonmaterialist contention. Indeed, there is considerable overlap between materialist contention and noncivic activism: a majority of materialist protests, such as laid-off workers' or retirees' protests during state-owned enterprise (SOE) restructuring and peasant protests over fees and taxes, were staged to defend private interests. Similarly, many nonmaterialist protests, such as the Charter 08 campaign for political reforms or feminist groups' demonstration against gender discrimination, were staged for public interest.

As figure 4.1 shows, however, these two dichotomies should not be confused with each other. Although most cases of well-known popular contention in recent years fall into either type B (noncivic activism on materialist interests) or type D (civic activism on nonmaterialist interests), types A and C ought not to be ignored. type A refers to civic activism that works on materialist interest claims. Examples include labor NGOs' support of workers in their struggle for better salaries or work conditions or environment activists'

Civic and Noncivic Activism under Autocracy 97

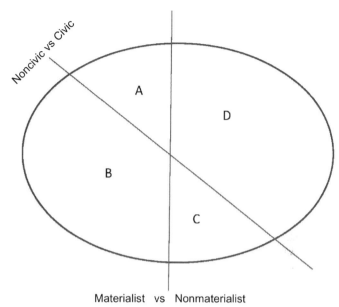

Figure 4.1. **Differentiating the Claims of Popular Contention**

assistance of villager victims of pollution to obtain compensations. Many civic organizations or activists, including so-called right defense lawyers such as Xu Zhiyong, regarded working on ordinary people's daily materialist grievances as one of their primary strategies. The government was not more lenient toward such activists because they focused on economic issues. On the contrary, the government found this approach especially alarming. As a party that rose to power by mobilizing on peasants' grievances, the CCP is certainly aware of the consequences of intellectuals and activists' reaching out to the masses. In an official document passed in the CCP's sixth plenum of the sixteenth Congress, for example, it is pointed out that two of the most alarming trends of the mass incidents in recent years are the tendency of politicizing economic issues, and some international and domestic enemies' efforts to take advantage of mass incidents and incite instability. Nor surprisingly some of the most high-handed recent crackdown cases targeted such activists. Obviously, government response to type A activism has been more similar to its response to other civic activism (type D) rather than its strategies to deal with type B activism on materialist interests.

Type C refers to noncivic activism focused on nonmaterialist interests. One example is villagers' protests against election irregularities in village elections. Such protests were often staged by failed candidates and their supporters who attributed the loss to alleged manipulations. Such protests clearly bear on nonmaterialist claims even though they may involve materialist interests indirectly. They are not civic activism either because the goal of protesters in such cases was simply to defend their own interest in the specific elections in a small community rather than pursue political change in general. The government's response to this type of protests was substantially different from its response to civic activists' advocacy of free and fair elections for the nation. Similarly, peasants who tried to pressure upper authorities to dismiss their corrupt village leaders tended to be treated in a quite different way than the activists who advocated assets disclosure by all government officials in China. The government treated them as noncivic protesters rather than civic protesters even though their claims are political in nature. Generally, unruly peasants protesting election irregularities or cadre corruption in their own communities tend to be treated by the government much more leniently than peaceful civic activists who advocate free elections or political leaders' assets disclosure.

In sum, conventional wisdom assumes the Chinese government treats type A (materialist and civic) activism and type B (materialist and noncivic) activism as the same category, while treating type C (nonmaterialist and civic) activism and type D (nonmaterialist and civic) as another category. The preceding examples, however, indicate that government responds to type A similarly to type C, while responding to B akin to type D. This is preliminary evidence to show that, from the government's point of view, the distinction between civic and noncivic activism is often more important than the distinction between materialist and nonmaterialist claims (table 4.1). Yet, more systematic research is needed to determine whether this has always been true, and if so, why.

Table 4.1. Examples of the Four Types of Claims of Popular Contention

	Materialist Interests	*Nonmaterialist Interests*
Civic Activism	Type A —Labor NGO assistance to worker protests on salary nonpayment —Environment NGO assistance of residents to obtain pollution compensations	Type D —Civic organizations demanding political reform —Feminist groups demanding protection against domestic violence
Noncivic Activism	Type B —Workers demanding higher salaries —Peasants demanding lowering taxes and fees	Type C —Villagers demand the investigation of election irregularities in the villagers —Parents demand fair college entrance exams

NGO, nongovernmental organization.

EXPLAINING HISTORICAL CHANGE AND VARIATION

The sharp differentiation between civic and noncivic activism by the state is not merely a temporary phenomenon but a consistent pattern throughout the seven decades of People's Republic. This is illustrated by figure 4.2, which depicts political spaces along Tilly's repression-toleration-facilitation continuum (1978). State response to popular collective action is often understood as either repression or toleration. Studies of autocracy have a strong tendency to overlook the state's role in facilitating popular collective action. State facilitation, however, is not only common but also constitutes an essential character of some political systems, especially totalitarian regimes. In this figure, state response is mapped between extreme repression (e.g., a massacre of participants of popular collective action) at the bottom and extreme facilitation (described by Tilly as compulsion: punishing nonperformance instead of rewarding performance) at the top. Political space is roughly divided into three zones. In the zone of repression, the costs of popular collective action imposed by the state are significantly higher than the rewards; and in the zone of facilitation, the imposed costs of popular collective action are considerably lower than the rewards. The zone of toleration is in between.

When we compare costs and rewards created by the state, we not only consider the size of costs and rewards but also their possibility. Figure 4.2 measures two key dimensions of repression-toleration-facilitation: (1) the probability and (2) the intensity of each type of response. The size of the area of each type of activism in the zones indicates the likelihood of the response. For example, if civic activism occupies a large area of facilitation, it means that the state is likely to facilitate civic activism by, say, providing resources

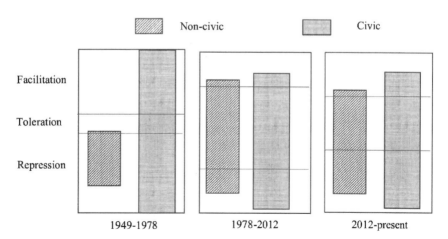

Figure 4.2. Shifting Political Space in Three Historical Periods in China.

to civil society organizations. The distance from the zone of toleration indicates the intensity. When civic activism extends far below the bottom line of toleration, for instance, it indicates that such mobilization possibly suffer very high-intensity repression. To measure the political space over time, in figure 4.2 the People's Republic of China (PRC) history is divided into Mao's era (1949–1978), the pre-Xi reform era (1978–2012), and Xi's era (after 2012). As a big picture painted with broad strokes, this chart leaves out the fine variations within each era. Despite this limitation, the figure helps to illuminate major changes in the basic patterns of state response to each type of social activism.

The figure also reveals a consistent feature of the political space over the three eras: the space for civic activism is more widely spread than the one for noncivic activism. In other words, compared to noncivic activism, civic activism is more likely to fall into either the zones of repression or facilitation rather than the zone of toleration. Moreover, civic activism is also more likely to suffer high-intensity repression or enjoy high-intensity facilitation than noncivic activism.

On the other hand, there have also been remarkable changes over time. In Mao's era, the contrast between the two types of popular collective action was particularly stark. State response to civic activism was highly polarized. The authorities often encouraged or even compelled people to participate in some mass activities while responding to other mass activities with imprisonment and even execution. By contrast, the response to noncivic activism was mostly limited to relatively moderate repression, supplemented with a small chance of toleration.

The transition to the post-Mao era brought about dramatic changes. The contrast between the two types of popular collective action became less striking. State response to civic activism became less polarized: The state has dramatically reduced its efforts to mobilize the masses in political campaigns and its response to unauthorized civic activism also became more lenient. Of course, the state still occasionally dealt with civic activism with extreme repression, and the massacre in response to the student movement in 1989 is a case in point. In the meantime, the political space for noncivic action began to spread more widely across the three zones. Such popular collective action became more likely to be tolerated. Remarkably, noncivic activism in the reform era sometimes enjoyed facilitation by the state, albeit mostly de facto rather than de jure. For example, in the waves of peasant protests in the 1990s against arbitrary fees and taxes, the central and provincial governments often showed their sympathy for protesters and empowered peasants by frequently issuing policy documents that peasants could use to resist village and township cadres.

Some aspects of such patterns continued into in Xi's era. There were, however, some noticeable changes. Both types of popular contention encountered harsher repression than before, but civic activism experienced more dramatic changes than noncivic activism. Many civic activists and organizations suffered brutal crackdown. The assault on defense lawyers in the "709" campaign in 2015 is a case in point. In the meantime, civic activism that fits government agendas began to enjoy stronger state facilitation than pre-Xi era. The governments at various levels invested immense resources to support or sponsor civic activism and organizations. To some extent the patterns of state response to civic activism in this era reversed some of the changes in the reform era and came closer to the more polarized patterns in Mao's era. By comparison, the response to noncivic activism experienced less remarkable changes except a moderate increase of the repressiveness.

How do we account for the change and variation in political space in PRC history? The shift of the basic regime character has certainly played a role. Tilly and many other scholars have long emphasized the role of regime type in shaping popular contention. Different regimes have different propensity for repression and facilitation, which is an essential aspect of political opportunity structure. Totalitarian regimes, for example, tend to actively mobilize the masses and also fiercely repress unauthorized social activism. This is well illustrated by figure 4.2. In Mao's era, China was a totalitarian regime, which features large zones for repression and facilitation and a small zone for toleration. The transition to a post-totalitarian regime after the late 1970s led to a dramatically different configuration: The zone of toleration considerably expanded, and the zones of facilitation and repression substantially shrank. Such general tendencies, at different degrees, affected every type of popular collective action.

In addition to their general propensity or capacity for repression, toleration and facilitation, regime types also shape political contention via their interaction with the nature of the claims. In authoritarian regimes popular collective action helps to fulfill three types of important functions. First, popular contention often acts as a main tool for the regime to attain its political and ideological goals. Mao's regime, for example, mainly rely on mass mobilization to achieve its goals of revolution and social transformation. Second, popular contention also fulfills basic functions for the political system. Upper authorities can garner information from such events to ensure lower-rank government officials' responsiveness and accountability. Third, popular contention can provide important resources and services that benefit the government. Civic organizations and activism are especially helpful for solving many social problems and governance tasks, such as environment protection and poverty relief.

At the same time, popular collective action can pose two main types of threats to the regime. First, popular contention may directly disrupt the regime's political and ideological agenda. Popular contention advocating an alternative political and ideological system is understandably viewed by any regime as a top threat. Second, popular contention may not directly intend to challenge the political order, but its disruption of social and economic order can also endanger the rule. Civic and noncivic activism tend to fulfill different functions and pose different threats, and the nature of the functions and threats have also changed over time. For example, in Mao's era, the regime relied on mass mobilization to achieve its political and ideological goals, while in post-Mao era the government especially value civic activism's function in social services such as social support to juvenile delinquents or disabled people. An analysis of functions and threats is thus especially helpful for accounting for variations across time and issues.

SOCIAL ACTIVISM UNDER MAO

Before discussing the political space for civic and noncivic activism in Mao's era, a note on the terminology is in order. When used to describe popular collective action in Mao's era, civic activism look like a misnomer for two reasons. First, it is often believed that most of such mass activities were heavily manipulated by Mao and other communist leaders. Second, they were often violent and detrimental to citizenship rights. It thus merits emphasis that civic activism is understood broadly in this study and is not confined to largely voluntary and peaceful actions.

Mao's China is a typical totalitarian regime with extraordinary propensity and capacity for mass mobilization. Maoist ideology made a sharp distinction between public and private interests, and ordinary people were discouraged from narrow-mindedly pursuing private interests. Since the revolutionary era, Mao and the communist party fervently exhorted ordinary people in China to fight for lofty goals such as national liberation or social transformation. As Perry (2002: 114) remarks, active mass involvement was a hallmark of Mao's revolution. Lieberthal (2003: 68) also notes, "Mao made the campaign style a prominent feature of Chinese politics—the country experienced at least one major campaign almost every year until his death in 1976. . . . The campaign form epitomized Mao Zedong's core belief that he could motivate people sufficiently to accomplish almost any goal he set for them."

Fierce mass mobilization in Mao's regime was accompanied with its strong propensity and capacity for repression. Frenzied mass campaigns and deep state penetration left no room for autonomous activities or organizations, let alone dissension and opposition. It should be noted that not only the targets of political campaigns or dissent groups were subject to brutal repression. Even the followers or activists of state-sponsored mass campaigns sometimes suffered harsh crackdowns. This happened to mass campaigns that were divided into factions, with some factions being attacked by their rivals or the authorities. It also happened to activists and participants when Mao found them no longer useful for his agenda. Red guards and rebels in the Cultural Revolution were abandoned or punished when Mao believed that his main objectives in the Cultural Revolution had been achieved. Although the Cultural Revolution is often understood as a political campaign targeted at party authorities, red guards and rebels suffered much more violence than party or government officials.

The regime's capacity to crack down on popular protests was built on a set of social and political institutions, especially a work-unit system that created "organized dependency" (Walder 1986). Ordinary people's heavy dependence on their work unit for all kinds of resources made it difficult for them to challenge the authority. Other institutions, such as the household registration system (*hukou*) and archive system (*dang'an*), worked together contain collective challenges. The deep penetration of the society left little space for unauthorized mobilization. The extensive mass mobilization itself constituted an important coercive tool. Tasks of repression was often accomplished by mobilizing ordinary people to attack the designated targets.

Compared to its polarized approach toward civic activism—either ardent facilitation or harsh repression, the regime under Mao was less dramatic toward noncivic activism. Popular collective action to pursue private interests was more consistently met with state repression, albeit not necessarily as severe. It should be noted that although the regime tried to prevent collective protests on private interests, it also strove to accommodate ordinary people's individualized petitions and complaints. Ever since the revolutionary era petitions and complaints were recognized by Mao's mass line as important tools for ensuring political responsiveness and accountability.

Ordinary people sometimes took advantage of such space to stage collective protests on private interests. Mao attributed such events to the limits of the masses' consciousness. When workers launched waves of protest mainly on wages, welfare, and labor conditions around 1956, for example, Mao (1971: 470) pointed out that, "it should be admitted that some people are prone to pay attention to immediate, partial and personal interests and do not understand, or do not sufficiently understand, long-range, national and collective interests."

Mao therefore put forth his famous theory on two types of contradictions under socialism, identifying antagonistic contradictions between the people and their enemies and nonantagonistic ones among the people. He labeled the latter as collective protests staged by ordinary people for their "immediate, partial and personal interests" and proposed to deal with them mainly with persuasion. To be sure, effective persuasion under Mao usually involved extensive coercion. Still the repression was expected to be considerably less harsh than the "means of dictatorship" stipulated for antagonistic conflicts. Indeed, Mao's theory of two types of contradictions set the limit to the government's response to collective protests on private interests. Such limits, to a large extent, continued to constrain the government's strategies even today, four decades after the end of Mao's era.

THE CULTURAL REVOLUTION AND PROTESTS OF "ECONOMISM"

An analysis of the wave of collective protests of "economism" in 1966–1967, at the outset of the Cultural Revolution, can illuminate how the dichotomy between civic and noncivic activism shaped the dynamics of popular contention in Mao's era. Such protests started when Mao called for the masses to rebel against "revisionist" authorities. Although those protesters also labeled their organizations with revolutionary names such as "red rebels," they were not interested in political issues. As Perry (2002: 260) noted, "Dubbed 'economistic' because of their relative disinterest in the political debates of the day, these organizations were not centrally concerned with the issue of attacking or defending party leaders. Their focus was directed instead on improving their own material lot." Such protests were staged mainly by two types of people. The first was workers with an inferior status in factories, such as temporary workers (*linshi gong*), contract workers (*hetong gong*), and outside contract laborers (*waibao gong*). They had no access to welfare benefits available to permanent workers, such as job security, pensions, health insurance for their dependents, and so forth. The second group comprised of former city residents who wanted to come back to the cities. Those people left their city for a variety of reasons. Some of them were mobilized to return to their native places as a result of the retrenchment campaign of the early 1960s or were arranged to help out with construction in the interior. Others were young people relocated in the "up to the mountains down to the countryside" and "support agriculture, support the frontiers" campaigns of the 1960s.

Many protesters from across the country staged protests in Beijing because clearly many policies were ultimately made or certified by the central government. At least in the first a few weeks such protests were tolerated. Eager to agitate mass participation in the Cultural Revolution, Mao and his associates were reluctant to crack down on protests of "economism" even though such protesters' goals clearly diverged from the goals of the Cultural Revolution. Mao's wife, Jiang Qing, in particular, showed her sympathy for protesters. The toleration and occasional sympathy from Beijing encouraged the protesters across the country. Shanghai witnessed especially vigorous mobilization. Perry (2002) identified about 354 such protest groups. Other provinces, such as Guizhou and Hunan, also witnessed strong mobilization. Their forceful protests created enough pressure on Beijing and local governments to secure a few temporary but substantive concessions. As a writer remarked, however, workers' struggles were doomed because their claims to particularistic interests pointed to a different direction from the Cultural Revolution, which was a great political revolution with lofty goals of preventing and fighting revisionism (Yang 2016: ch. 11).

Indeed, after a few weeks of toleration, Beijing changed its attitude early in 1967. The government began to ban protesters' organizations and later easily crushed the protests with the imprisonment of a few protest leaders. The CCP Central Committee issued a stern directive on January 11, 1967 (available at https://ccradb.appspot.com/post/100). As it declared, "A small groups of capitalist road-runners were determined to sabotage the Cultural Revolution and distract us from our struggle targets. They agitated a small number of deceived people to struggle with the socialist state under proletariat dictatorship. They lured those masses toward the vicious direction of economism so that the masses disregarded the national, collective, and long-term interests, and single-mindedly pursued personal and temporary interest." This directive illuminated a dilemma the party faced when cracking down on noncivic popular collective action. Because protesters were technically counted as among "the people" rather the enemy, the party had to justify its repression by framing the protests as orchestrated by class enemies, labeled as capitalist road-runners.

The case of economistic protests in 1966–1967 illuminates how the relationship between civic and noncivic activism helps account for the dynamics of popular contention in Mao's era. The main claims of such protests were both materialist and noncivic. Although the government's "economism" label seems to suggest the importance of the materialist claims, the opening and closing of the opportunity for the protests, as well as the methods of state repression, underscore the importance of their noncivic nature. The political opportunity for such noncivic collective action can be attributed to the CCP's facilitation of political and ideological activism. To boost people's motivation to participate in the Cultural Revolution, the regime was initially tolerant toward collective protests for particularistic interests. Exactly because noncivic claims of the protests deviated from the direction of the Cultural Revolution, however, the window of opportunity was soon closed. When the CCP decided to crack down on the protests, its repression on ordinary protesters was constrained because the protests on private interests, while undesirable, still belonged to nonantagonist "contradictions among the people."

PRE-XI REFORM ERA

Mao's death was followed by a rapid regime transformation from totalitarianism to a post-totalitarianism in China. Such transitions, as Linz and Stepan (1996: 42–51) suggest, typically involved the loss of interest by leaders and nonleaders in organizing mobilization and the recognition of a certain degree of social, cultural and economic pluralism. In China the decline of leaders' penchant for mass mobilization was accompanied with a dramatic decrease of the regime's propensity and capacity for repression. The transition to a market economy led to an extensive retreat of the state from many social and economic areas and, therefore, weakened the state's capacity for containing collective action. Many social institutions, such as the work-unit system, which were instrumental for containing popular collective action, severely declined or even entirely collapsed. The state also substantially reduced its use of mass campaigns for coercive purposes. Last but not the least, the state launched a massive campaign for legal reforms since the end of the 1970s. Despite all their limits, legal reforms provided a degree of much needed protection for citizens.

As illustrated by figure 4.2, both civic and noncivic activism began to enjoy considerably more tolerant political environment. It should be noted, however, that the change was not linear, and the toleration had its limits. Howell (2015) observes a cyclical pattern between heavy-handed state repression and muted tolerance for civic activism in the reform era. Whether for civic or noncivic activism, moreover, state toleration was often de facto rather than de jure. Millions of unregistered NGOs technically were illegal and supposed to be banned. However, the government often dealt with them with a so-called three-no policy: no recognition, no banning, and no intervention (Deng 2010). For noncivic activism, similarly, government officials often condoned collective petitions or protests, such as those staged by peasants against excessive taxation or SOE retirees against pension nonpayment, even when they did not strictly abide by the law.

Besides the impact of the regime's general tendencies that had similar effects on all kinds of popular contention, civic and noncivic activism experienced different effects of the regime transformation. The regime continued to take a more polarized approach toward civic activism than noncivic activism. Despite the regime's decreased interests in mass campaigns for ideological purposes, it still found good reason for facilitating certain types of civic activism. Local governments were particularly interested in civic activism that could provide social services and remedy the scarcity of government resources. Many local officials regarded civic activism as important resources to deal with their governance problems. They therefore often adopted a strategy of "welfarist incorporation": The state relaxed its registration regulations for social organizations and encouraged them to provide social services rather than advocating for rights or representing interests (Howell 2015). The state began to establish mutually beneficial partnerships with NGOs (Spires 2011; Hildebrandt 2013), and NGOs often played an active role as policy entrepreneurs (Mertha 2009; Steinhardt and Wu 2016). The regime is even dubbed consultative authoritarianism because of its remarkable accommodation of civil society (Teets 2013). In the meantime, for civic activism perceived by state leaders as directly threatening to the political system, the state remained extremely repressive. The massacre in Tiananmen Square in 1989 is a case in point.

One of the most remarkable changes in the reform era was that noncivic activism started to enjoy a degree of state facilitation, even though such facilitation was merely de facto. In principle, the state still forbade citizens' noncivic collective actions. It nevertheless began to facilitate popular protests through a process of institutional conversion (Chen 2012). To a large extent, state facilitation can be attributed to the increased importance of the functions that popular contention fulfilled for the political system. The CCP in the reform era continued to manage its relationship with the society with mass line, which valued citizen complaints and petitions as an important instrument for political responsiveness and accountability. While the CCP in Mao's era had the capacity to largely confine such forms of claim making to individualized actions, it lost such an ability in the reform era due to the decline of a variety of institutions for social control, such as work units. At the same time, accommodation of collective claim making became more important for two reasons. The transition to a market economy led to the growth of a wide range of group interests while the political system still lacked mechanisms for interest articulation and aggregation. Second, the market reform also increased decentralization and the divergence between central and local government made it both more difficult and more important to hold local officials accountable. When petitions and protests were regarded as an indispensable instrument to attain such goals, the political system created pressure for local officials to be responsive to such claims and also constrained their repression. Under such circumstances, petitioners and protesters are often tempted to appropriate state institutions to stage collective action to defend their interests.

The Rise of Feminist Activism in China

The rise of feminism in China is a good example to illustrate how the transformation of regime characters opened political space for civic activism in the reform era. It was hardly surprising that feminist activism did not develop in China before the reform era. An essential feature of Mao's rule was the absence of ideological pluralism. The dominant state ideology assumed that "sexual equality is an expression of class inequality and private ownership is at the root of women's oppression." It therefore emphasized that sexual inequality should be solved in the production process under public ownership (Wang and Zhang 2010: 41–42). The terminology of "feminism" was rejected as being "Western, narrow, and bourgeois." Also, there was no room for relatively autonomous organizations to promote gender- or sex-related issues. A state corporatist organization, All-China Women's Federation (ACWF), was designated as the sole agency to speak for Chinese women.

Feminist activism began to develop slowly after the reform started in the late 1970s. Although China still witnessed ideological struggles and purges periodically in the 1980s, state repression mainly focused on politically motivated activism. Feminist activists therefore found a little breathing space. However, there was no breakthrough until the Chinese government hosted the fourth World Conference on Women (FWCW) in 1995. Eager to ease international criticism and isolation in the aftermath of Tiananmen incident in 1989, the CCP enthusiastically embraced the opportunity to host the FWCW (Wesoky 2013; Braeuer 2016). This event provided much needed access to resources for feminist activism. Funds from external organizations, such as Ford Foundation, became available. More important, to some extent the state began to recognize the legitimacy of feminist ideology and organizations that were relatively independent from the state. As Wang and Zhang noted, Chinese feminists seized the opportunity and published many articles in the official media, especially in the Women's Federation's newspaper, *Chinese Women's Daily*, introducing women's NGOs from around the world and carefully putting forth the argument that NGOs are not antigovernment organizations (Wang and Zhang 2010: 41). Such efforts helped the Chinese government to accept the legitimacy of NGOs. Indeed, the United Nations conference was a turning point not just for feminist activism but for civic activism in general. As Deng (2010: 186) remarks, "It was not until 1995 that the first wave of true NGOs, established from the bottom up, began to appear in China."

The state's embrace of feminist activism, however, had its limitations. The Chinese government and the ACWF's understanding of the functions of feminist activism remained narrow and utilitarian. They clearly favored organizations that could provide social services and tended to be skeptical of activism for other purposes. As a lesbian activist recounted, "Someone from the ACWF once said to me, 'Why do lesbian groups need to fight for their rights? You are not the ones who get AIDs (compared to gays). How come you have a problem?'" (Zhou 2017: 5).

Even in the moments when the Chinese government was especially friendly toward feminist activism, its suspicion of feminism as an ideological threat never disappeared. This is hardly surprising. After all, even some Western scholars agreed that the focus of civic activism on topics such as feminism is "deeply ideologically charged." Its rise in non-Western countries, to some extent, can be attributed to Western governments' active promotion of global activism concerning human rights and gender issues in those countries (Hemment 2007). In China, most feminist activists had no intention to change the political system or challenge government policies, and many of them were not even interested in engaging in any direct relationship to the government. One activist, for example, claimed that what they were doing was "social" movement and lobbying the government was not "their thing" (Zhou 2017). Their tendency toward independent ideology and autonomous organizations was nevertheless disturbing to a government that was obsessed with social control. Many feminist organizations' reliance on foreign funds, and activists' fondness of Western-styled discourse, such as rights, freedom, and civil society, only exacerbated such suspicions.

The government was sometimes also concerned about the actions taken by activists. Understandably, feminist activists were interested in organizing public events, which were necessary for them to influence the culture and society. A case in point is performance art advocacy, which centers on live performance in public spaces for a public audience (Guo, Fu, and Liu 2013). Anti-domestic violence (ADV) organizations in Beijing, among other feminist organizations, have adopted this form of activism since 2011 (Braeuer 2016). Such actions were not particularly disruptive but often had the ability to create considerable publicity.

Given the tensions between the state and feminist activists, it is no wonder that state toleration of such activism was limited and fragile. Many feminist groups could not fulfill the requirement to find government sponsors to register in the government. They either registered as private business or simply worked underground. Even those registered organizations had to endure police intrusion and even harassment every so often.

SOE Workers' Protests during the Industrial Restructuring

The changing space for noncivic activism is illustrated here with the experience of SOE employees during a dramatic campaign launched by the Chinese government to restructure enterprises in the mid-1990s. The campaign is often described as "grasping the large and releasing the small" (*zhuada fangxiao*), meaning that the Chinese government retained large SOEs while privatizing small- and medium-sized ones. With massive layoffs and firm closings, the restructuring dealt a fatal blow to a great many workers in SOEs. The majority of small- and medium-sized enterprises in the public sector across the country were either closed, allowed to go bankrupt, or had all or part of their assets leased or sold to private entrepreneurs. In response, SOE employees staged numerous collective protests. Their claims concerned a variety of grievances specific to particular groups, factories, or individuals, such as nonpayment or arrears of pensions and salaries.

Compared to protesters of "economism" in the Cultural Revolution, worker protesters in the reform era faced a much more benign regime. State officials, from central leaders to local cadres, often expressed sympathy for workers' grievances. Workers' protests were no longer described by the authorities as narrow-minded pursuit of private interests that were agitated by class enemies. Protesters' main problem, from the government's point of view, was their violation of law and regulations and not their pursuit of private interests.

The sympathy from central leaders is clearly indicated by a speech made by Premier Zhu Rongji to the *xinfang* system, which is in charge of dealing with citizen complaints and petitions, on February 5, 1999. When he discussed the rising popular contention in urban areas that were triggered by industrial restructuring, Zhu pointed out that pensioners were particularly contentious because they had especially strong grievances. He then cited a doggerel circulated among SOE retirees: "Our youth was dedicated to the Party, but no one cares about us when we get old. We are asked to rely on our children, yet all of them lost their job. He expressed not only his deep sympathy but also his determination to solve workers' problems (Renminwang 2013).

Such an attitude not only provided SOE employees with spiritual support but also an effective frame for their mobilization. In this authoritarian system, few justifications were more powerful than statements made by national leaders. Like rightful resisters in the countryside studied by O'Brien and Li (2006), SOE employees often effectively demonstrated their rightfulness by citing leaders' speeches or policy statements. The central government also designed and adjusted a variety of legal and administrative procedures to ensure the responsiveness to petitions and protests. Such institutional mechanisms were instrumental for workers' mobilization.

To be sure, the government's accommodation and facilitation of SOE employees' claim making was not merely driven by state leaders' sympathy but also based on their recognition of the important functions that petitions and protests can fulfill for the political system. The same speech by Premier

Zhu nicely summarized the main benefits of popular contention. He pointed out that the xinfang system designed for responding to petitions and protests is essential to the regime because "normal channels" between the masses and the party might not work (Renminwang 2013). Such an institution provided SOE employees and other ordinary people a perfect cover to gather together and make claims to the government. SOE workers did not hesitate to take advantage of such a system. They were aware that if they fully followed the rules and only delivered their complaints and petitions moderately, they could go nowhere. They therefore often employed a variety of "troublemaking" tactics to create bargaining leverage against the government. By blocking highways, sitting in inside or around government compounds, marching on the street with banners of slogans, and employing other troublemaking tactics, SOE workers often generated strong pressure on local governments to make concessions. Even large and highly disruptive protests were always framed by them as inevitable extension or reasonable escalation of orderly petitions. Since petitions were not allowed to be delivered by more than five people, most of such activities technically violated law or regulations. Although local officials had good reason to crack down on them, their repression was often severely constrained because upper authorities did not want to block the channels of petitions and protests. Indeed, local officials were often under pressure to make expedient concessions. Although SOE employees won few substantive policy victories, it was far from rare for them to obtain expedient concessions from the government, which encouraged more protests and petitions.

A comparison of feminist activism with SOE workers' mobilization suggests that they were perceived by the authorities as two social forces with quite different functions. Accommodating feminist NGOs helped to enhance the Chinese government's reputation and legitimacy in the world. Some NGOs also helped the government to solved social problems, such as AIDS prevention among homosexuals or gender equality in employment. By contrast, the government accommodated SOE workers' collective actions mainly because they provided important feedback to government policy and also helped the government to hold government officials accountable.

Feminist activists and SOE protests also posed quite different threats. Feminism was often viewed as ideologically threatening and described as an issue of national security partly because many feminist organizations had connections to international civil society or foreign governments. Meanwhile, the actions taken by feminist activists were usually too peaceful to be considered endangering social stability. In contrast, SOE workers' protests and other noncivic activism were sometimes perceived threatening to social stability. Indeed, SOE workers' protests during industrial restructuring and peasants' protests against excessive and arbitrary extraction of taxes and levies since the 1990s created a deep sense of crisis to Chinese leaders. Worried about social stability, Chinese leaders expanded and strengthened its stability-maintenance apparatus. Importantly, national security framing and social stability framing had somewhat different effects. When civic activism was viewed as threats to national security, the government usually strengthened its surveillance and repression on such activism. By contrast, the concern about social instability did not simply motivate the government to become more repressive. Instead, one of the government's primary strategies was to demobilize popular contention with expedient concessions. It should be noted that the government's willingness to bargain with peasants or workers was not primarily due to protesters' materialist claims. Labor NGOs and activists who assisted migrant workers to raise wages or obtain injury compensations rarely enjoyed such opportunities, even though they also focused on economic issues. Fighting for public interests rather than their own particularistic interests, they tended to arouse strong suspicion from the government.

SOCIAL ACTIVISM UNDER XI

After Xi Jinping came to power in 2012, China witnessed another remarkable regime transformation. One of the most noticeable changes was the increased repressiveness of the state. To a large extent this can be attributed to the state's improved capacity for coercion. The Chinese state made great efforts to recover the social and economic space it gave up when economic reforms started. The party diligently built branches and tried to repenetrate nonstate institutions and organizations, such as NGOs and private enterprises, which became increasingly dependent on the state for resources and recognition. The state also strengthened the infrastructures for monitoring and controlling in urban space, where population mobility and spatial ineligibility posed great challenges to social control. For example, a grid system (*wanggehua guanli*) enabled the state to reach deeply into almost every neighborhood in most cities. The Chinese state has been adept at using modern technology for surveillance and repression.

Although the enhanced state coercive capacity has shrunk the space for both civic and noncivic activism, the change in state propensity has had uneven effects. The regime's repressiveness of noncivic activism only moderately increased, while repression of civic activism increased dramatically. Some studies show that the Chinese government became more repressive toward noncivic protests under Xi's rule (Chen 2017). The regime's basic approach, however, hardly changed. As discussed, the Chinese government's toleration and de facto facilitation of such activism was primarily based on its recognition of the functions that such claim-making activities could fulfill for the political system, which did not change after Xi came to power. An instruction issued by Xi in July 2017 can nicely illustrate the basic position of the CCP. In this instruction to the eighth national conference on xinfang work Xi pointed out that the government's primary goals for handling petitions and protests should be "to understand people's feelings, use people's wisdom, defend people's interests, and boost people's support." Government officials should focus on the problems raised in popular claim making (Xinhua News 2011). Local governments were still required to contain popular contention, but they should do it mainly by solving people's problems. To be sure, repression was often necessary for coping with collective protests, most of which were still technically illegal. Due to the emphasis on the responsiveness to petitions and protests, however, government repression often remained considerably constrained.

For civic activism, by contrast, Xi's administration raised the intensity of ideological struggles to a new level. In what is described by Lubman (2016) as a neo-Maoist ideological campaign, the CCP declared civil society as one of the seven main perils from the West. The heightened alert to civic activism can partly be attributed to international background. The CCP has long been wary about "peaceful transformation" of the regime. A series of color revolutions in Georgia, Ukraine, and Kyrgyzstan, followed by the Arab Spring revolutions, alarmed Chinese leaders about the threats from outside, including international NGOs. The dramatically intensified repression on civic activism, however, was also accompanied with considerably stronger support of civic organizations by local governments than the pre-Xi era. The number of social organizations, many of which were relatively autonomous, increased substantially in many localities. In Shenzhen, for example, there were 5,019 registered social organizations in 2012, and the number increased to 13,180 in 2018. Unlike in Mao's era when the regime facilitated civic activism with top-down mass campaigns, in Xi's era, the dynamics mainly came from local governments with pragmatic objectives. The government's approach toward civic activism in Xi's era was even more polarized than the earlier reform era.

Feminism under Xi

Even before Xi's rule, feminist activists often experienced harassment and repression from the authorities: Their social media accounts were sometimes closed, their public events were often canceled, and so forth. Yet the repression on feminist activism was remarkably escalated after 2012. One of the most well-known events was the arrest of the "feminist five." Shortly before

International Women's Day on March 8, 2015, five young feminists were detained in China. The police accused them of "picking quarrels and provoking trouble" because they were planning to distribute leaflets in several cities to raise awareness of sexual harassment on public transport. The arrests shocked international society. After all, the planned activities were neither political nor disruptive, and the turnout was expected to be small.

Many NGOs that focused on advocacy on women's rights and other gender- or sex-related issues were banned or forced to close. One of the most famous victims was Zhongze Women's Legal Counseling Service Center, which was founded by a public interest lawyer, Guo Jianmei. It was one of many NGOs that were established right after the FWCW in Beijing. When legal assistance to women was regarded as a relatively safe issue, this NGO received strong support from Beijing University and some government agencies. It was also well recognized by the international society. Like many other NGOs, Zhongze suffered repression before Xi's era. It was forced to cut off from its sponsor, Peking University, in 2010. None of such measures, however, was as harsh as its forced closure in 2016. Similar to most other cases of crackdown in that period, the NGO's linkage to foreign funders was cited as a main reason (Cao 2016). On the other hand, the government became remarkably more supportive of social organizations that could provide social services and did not have connections to foreign countries. In Shenzhen, for example, the government-sponsored Women's Federation worked as an incubator to actively nurture and support social organizations that provided assistance to various women groups, such as single moms and unemployed women.

Labor Activism under Xi

Unlike civic activism, noncivic activism under Xi did not witness a dramatic escalation of repression. Workers' struggles for their private interests were seldom regarded as direct threats to national security unless civic activists from outside got involved. Even though state repressiveness may have somewhat increased in recent years, the government did not try to shut down the channel of contentious bargaining. Workers and other subordinate groups still got the opportunity to mobilize collective actions to elicit relatively favorable response from local governments.

China Labor Bulletin, a Hong Kong-based NGO, has monitored labor activism in China in the past two decades. From 2015 to 2017, it finds that labor collective actions were still frequent and kept growing in that period (China Labor Bulletin 2018). About 80 percent of the 6,694 incidents were focused on salary-related claims. To press the management or the authorities to solve the problems of nonpayment and arrears of salaries, workers resorted to demonstration, sit-in, highway blockade, strike, and other troublemaking tactics. Clearly, workers under Xi did not become more quiescent. Nor did they become more radical or violent. Another finding of the China Labor Bulletin report is that workers were rather rational and their bargaining with the management or the authorities became even more orderly than before. Despite the increased state repressiveness, the space for workers to stage collective action has not dramatically shrunk.

Nevertheless, there were quite a few cases of harsh crackdown on labor activists in recent years, especially a massive crackdown on labor NGOs and activists since around 2015. In Guangdong, where labor NGOs were particularly active in recent two decades, the government almost wiped out labor NGOs with links to Hong Kong or foreign countries. In most of such cases, the government primarily targeted labor NGOs or Marxist college students who came to agitate or support workers' struggles. One of the most famous cases was workers' protests in Jasic Inc. in 2018 in which a few Marxist activists, especially some university students, who offered their support to workers struggling for better working conditions and other related goals, were ruthlessly crushed. In such cases, although outsider activists mostly focused on economic issues, they suffered much harsher repression than worker protesters who struggled for their own particularistic issues. When it comes to the government's response, whether the protesters focus on materialist or nonmaterialist claims is less important than whether the activists were struggling for public or private interests.

CONCLUSION

This study elucidates how the Chinese state coped with civic and noncivic activism according to substantially different logic in all three periods: Mao's era, pre-Xi reform era, and Xi's era. The state was often tempted to take advantage of civic activism to achieve their political or ideological goals or to solve problems in governance. Yet it was also wary of the subversive potential of civic activism. As Nathan (2003) remarks, authoritarian regimes are inherently fragile because of weak legitimacy. It is therefore not surprising that the Chinese government has been anxious about domestic and international challenges to its legitimacy via civic activism. By comparison, noncivic activism was treated with a less polarized approach. The regime relies on citizen complaints and petitions to ensure government responsiveness and political accountability. Although collective protests with troublemaking tactics are formally outlawed, they have often been condoned to a degree, especially when government repression has become more difficult and costly. To some extent the functions and threats of each type of popular collective action changed when the regime transformed. Political space thus evolved accordingly for them.

A clear understanding of the difference between civic and noncivic activism is important not only for academic research but also for strategic decisions by protesters and activists. The Chinese government's willingness to negotiate with workers or peasants in their noncivic activism sometimes created unrealistic and dangerous expectations for civic activists. For noncivic activism, contentious bargaining in the reform era often followed the logic of "small troublemaking leads to small concessions, big troublemaking leads to big concessions." For civic activism, by contrast, aggressive protest tactics usually only prompted harsh repression.

This is not to suggest, however, that political opportunities for civic activism are unrelated to those for noncivic activism. Many structural conditions, such as basic regime characters, have a similar impact on civic and noncivic activism alike. Moreover, the opportunity opened for one type of activism can be taken advantage of by the other type of activism. In 1966, for example, contract or temporary workers seized the momentum created by Mao for revolutionary mass campaigns to stage their protests to press their private issues.

This study of social activism in China raises important questions about the general relationship between authoritarian states and popular collective action. The conventional understanding of state strategies as either repression or concessions proved too narrow or conceptualizing such a relationship. State facilitation of popular collective action is not only common in authoritarian regimes, but it also sometimes even defines the basic nature of the regime. Just like in China, civic and noncivic activism in other authoritarian regimes can fulfill different functions for the political system. Either type of popular collective action can also help to bring down the regime, albeit through somewhat different mechanisms and processes. Only by taking into account different configurations of such functions and threats can we explain the variations and changes in the political environment for civic and noncivic activism in the context of authoritarianism.

REFERENCES

Braeuer, Stephanie. 2016. "Becoming Public: Tactical Innovation in the Beijing Anti-Domestic Violence Movement." *Voluntas* 27 (5): 2106–30.

Cao, Yaxue. 2016. "Guo Jianmei, Zhongze, and the Empowerment of Women in China." *Chinachange.org*, February 14. Accessed February 1, 2020. https://

chinachange.org/2016/02/14/guo-jianmei-zhongze-and-the-empowerment-of-women-in-china/.

Chen, Jay Chi-Jou. 2017. "Youxiao Zhili De Zhiku: Dangdai Zhongguo Jiti Kangzheng Yu Guojia Fanying" [Shackles of Effective Governance: Collective Resistance and State Response in Contemporary China]. *Taiwan Sociology* 33: 113–64.

Chen, Xi. 2012. *Social Protest and Contentious Authoritarianism in China*. New York: Cambridge University Press.

China Labor Bulletin. 2018. "Zhongguo Gongren Yundong Guancha Baogao, 2015–2017" [Report on Chinese Labor Movement, 2015–2017]. *China Labor Bulletin*.

Deng, Guosheng. 2010. "The Hidden Rules Governing China's Unregistered NGOs: Management and Consequences." *China Review* 10 (1): 183–206.

Fritzsche, Peter, and Jochen Hellbeck. 2009. "The New Man in Stalinist Russia and Nazi Germany." In Michael Geyer and Sheila Fitzpatrick, eds., *Beyond Totalitarianism: Stalinism and Nazism Compared*, 302–41. New York: Cambridge University Press.

Fu, Diana, and Greg Distelhorst. 2017. "Grassroots Participation and Repression under Hu Jintao and Xi Jinping." *The China Journal* 79(1): 100–22.

Giugni, Mario. 2004. *Social Protest and Policy Change: Ecology, Antinuclear, and Peace Movements in Comparative Perspective*. Lanham, MD: Rowman & Littlefield.

Guo, Ting, Tao Fu, and Haiying Liu. 2013. *A CDB Special Report: The Diversification of Public Advocacy in China*. Beijing: The China Development Brief.

Hemment, Julie. 2007. *Empowering Women in Russia: Activism, Aid, and NGOs*. Bloomington: Indiana University Press.

———. 2015. *Youth Politics in Putin's Russia: Producing Patriots and Entrepreneurs*. Bloomington, IN: Indiana University Press.

Hildebrandt, Timothy. 2013. *Social Organizations and the Authoritarian State in China*. New York: Cambridge University Press.

Howell, Jude. 2015. "Shall We Dance? Welfarist Incorporation and the Politics of State–Labour NGO Relations." *The China Quarterly* 223: 702–23.

Johnston, Hank. 2011. *States and Social Movements*. Cambridge, UK: Polity.

Kitschelt, Herbert. 1986. "Political Opportunity Structures and Political Protest: Anti-Nuclear Movements in Four Democracies." *British Journal of Political Science* 16: 57–85.

Kriesi, Hanspeter. 2005. "Political Context and Opportunity." In David A. Snow, Sarah A Soule, and Hanspeter Kriesi, eds., *The Blackwell Companion to Social Movements*, 67–90. Oxford: Blackwell.

Lee, Ching Kwan, and You-tien Hsing. 2010. "Social Activism in China: Agency and Possibility." In You-tien Hsing and Ching Kwan Lee, eds., *Reclaiming Chinese Society: The New Social Activism*, 1–13. New York: Routledge.

Lieberthal, Kenneth. 2003. *Governing China: From Revolution through Reform*. New York, W. W. Norton.

Linz, Juan. 2000. *Totalitarian and Authoritarian Regimes*. Boulder, CO: Lynne Rienner.

Linz, Juan, and Alfred Stepan. 1996. *Problems of Democratic Transition and Consolidation: Southern Europe, South America, and Post-Communist Europe.* Baltimore, MD: Johns Hopkins University Press.

Long, Yan. 2018. "The Contradictory Impact of Transnational AIDS Institutions on State Repression in China, 1989–2013." *American Journal of Sociology* 124(2): 309–66.

Lubman, Stanley. 2016. "China's New Law on International NGOs and Questions about Legal Reform." *Wall Street Journal*, May 25.

Mao, Zedong. 1971. *Selected Readings from the Works of Mao Tsetung.* Beijing: Foreign Languages Press.

McAdam, Doug, Sidney Tarrow, and Charles Tilly. 2001. *Dynamics of Contention.* New York: Cambridge University Press.

Mertha, Andrew. 2009. "'Fragmented Authoritarianism 2.0': Political Pluralization in the Chinese Policy Process." *The China Quarterly* 200: 995–1012.

Minzner, Carl. 2015. "China After the Reform Era." *Journal of Democracy* 26 (3): 129–43.

Nathan, Andrew. 2003. "Authoritarian Resilience in China." *Journal of Democracy* 14(1): 6–17.

O'Brien, Kevin, and Lianjiang Li. 2006. *Rightful Resistance in Rural China.* New York: Cambridge.

Perry, Elizabeth. 2002. *Challenging the Mandate of Heaven: Social Protest and State Power in China.* Armonk: NY, M. E. Sharpe.

Renminwang. 2013. "Zhu Rongji Shicha Gongzuo Zaoyu Nongxu Zuojia" [Zhu Rongji Encountered Deceptions in His Inspection Work]. *People.cn.* August 7. Accessed February 1, 2020. http:// book.people.com.cn/n/2013/0807/c367728 -22472291.html.

Spires, Anthony. 2011. "Contingent Symbiosis and Civil Society in an Authoritarian State: Understanding the Survival of China's Grassroots NGOs." *American Journal of Sociology* 117(1): 1–45.

Steinhardt, Christoph, and Fengshi Wu. 2016. "In the Name of the Public: Environmental Protest and the Changing Landscape of Popular Contention in China." *The China Journal* 75: 61–82.

Teets, Jessica. 2013. "Let Many Civil Societies Bloom: The Rise of Consultative Authoritarianism in China." *The China Quarterly* 213: 19–38.

Tilly, Charles. 1978. *From Mobilization to Revolution.* Reading, MA: Addison-Wesley.

Walder, Andrew. 1986. *Communist Neo-Traditionalism: Work and Authority in Chinese Industry.* Berkeley: University of California Press.

Wang, Zheng, and Ying Zhang. 2010. "Global Concepts, Local Practices: Chinese Feminism since the Fourth UN Conference on Women." *Feminist Studies* 36 (1): 40–71.

Wesoky, Sharon. 2013. *Chinese Feminism Faces Globalization.* London: Routledge.

Xinhua News. 2011. "Xi Jinping: Qianfang Baiji Wei Qunzhong Paiyou Jienan, Buduan Kaichuang Xinfang Gongzuo Xinjumian" [Xi Jinping: Try Every Way to

Help the Masses Solve Their Problems, Continuously Move Xinfang Work to a Higher Level]. *Xinhuanet.com*, July 19. Accessed February 1, 2020. http://www.xinhuanet.com//politics/2017-07/19/c_1121346653.htm.

Yang, Jiesheng. 2016. Tianfan Difu: *Zhongguo Wenhua Dageming Shi* [The World Turned Upside Down: A History of the Cultural Revolution]. Hong Kong: Tiandi Tushu.

Zeng, Jinyan. 2015. "China's Feminist Five: 'This Is the Worst Crackdown on Lawyers, Activists and Scholars in Decades.'" *The Guardian*. April 17.

Zhou, Wei. 2017. *From Street Arts to Online Campaigns: How Do Organized Chinese Feminists Deal with Repression in Xi Jinping Era?* Honors thesis, University of North Carolina, Chapel Hill.

Chapter Five

Bureaucrat-Assisted Contention in China

Kevin J. O'Brien (University of California, Berkeley),
Lianjiang Li (Chinese University of Hong Kong),
and *Mingxing Liu* (Peking University)

Most popular contention starts in society. It emerges when people are dissatisfied with the status quo and frustrated that their grievances are being ignored (Marx and Wood 1975; Smelser 1962). In places such as China, disgruntled individuals may be infuriated about excessive taxation (Bernstein and Lü 2000; Chen 2012; Zhang 2015a), alarmed about unbreathable air (Deng and Yang 2013; Steinhardt and Wu 2016), angry about jobs lost and pensions withheld (Hurst and O'Brien 2002; Hurst et al. 2009; Chen and Tang 2013), furious about land expropriation (Sargeson 2013; Chuang 2014; Mattingly 2016), or disappointed that military service remains unrecognized and unappreciated (Diamant and O'Brien 2015; O'Brien and Diamant 2015; Hu, Wu, and Fei 2018). Then, some number of the aggrieved make a decision: Routine institutional means to gain a hearing are wanting and quiescence is no longer an option. The best choice is to take to the streets or agitate online (Li and O'Brien 2008; Cai and Sheng 2013; Zhang 2015b; Yang 2009). Savvy protesters may exploit divisions within the government (Tarrow 1994) and succeed in locating "institutional activists" (Santoro and McGuire 1997; Zhang 2018; Ma 2019) or other insiders who are sympathetic to their cause (Lipsky 1968; O'Brien and Li 2006). But in the end, collective action usually depends on the initiative of people on the society side of the state-society ledger: disgruntled citizens who are ready to take a stand, band together, and set out to right a wrong.

But what if the impetus for contention also lies partly within the state? What if, for example, native-born officials in China help local elites launch or sustain popular action against outsider party secretaries by leaking information and sabotaging repression? And what if the officials who offer this assistance are neither elite allies nor institutional activists (cf., Zhang

2018), but instead seek to use the mobilized citizenry as a weapon in an internal power struggle?

Drawing on archival sources and interviews, this chapter explains how tensions between frequently rotated superiors and their locally born underlings can inspire social mobilization. Our argument hinges on an alliance that homegrown, midlevel bureaucrats in China form with community elites, who are encouraged to stir up collective action against outsiders who are interfering with cozy relationships and opportunities to engage in rent seeking. We show that popular grievances are tapped into and provide kindling to ignite, but that the decision to mount or support a petition drive, demonstration, or a dramatic rescue sometimes originates with native-born officials and socioeconomic elites who have their own personal and community-minded reasons to incite collective action. In the course of examining bureaucrat-assisted contention, we will show how overlapping interests and collusion between bureaucrats and entrepreneurs, retired officials and other local influentials can provoke contention and sometimes scuttle the plans (or careers) of leaders as highly placed as county or even provincial party secretaries.

Bureaucrat-inspired contention has taken place on a number of issues in China over the last few decades, including administrative mergers, land appropriation, wastewater removal, privatization of schools, and the location of trash incinerators, dams, and power plants. Rather than focusing on any particular episode we will rely on data from a number of cases to explain how and why Chinese bureaucrats assist local elites in unleashing the masses on party secretaries who are brought in to rule a district, county, municipality, or province. Then, we will examine how ambitious, heavy-handed, or corrupt secretaries inspire bureaucrat-assisted contention and what this says about several underexplored aspects of political opportunity, framing, and mobilizing structures. We conclude the chapter with a discussion of the implications for theory and China of intrabureaucratic conflicts spilling over into collective action and the impetus for contention being shared among local officials, socioeconomic elites, and members of the wider public.

BUREAUCRAT-ASSISTED CONTENTION

Bureaucrat-assisted contention occurs in China when native-born officials assist local elites in launching or sustaining popular action. Instead of doing their superiors' bidding and co-opting, demobilizing, or suppressing protest (Cai 2010; Chuang 2014; Deng and O'Brien 2013; Ong 2018; Chen 2017), disaffected officials aid disgruntled elites by leaking information and sabotaging repression. The targets of bureaucrat-assisted contention in China are invariably outsider party secretaries, who are rotated in and out frequently and serve as the ranking representative of the party-state in a locality.

The defining feature of bureaucrat-assisted contention is that officials facilitate challenges to state authority, sparking collective action that otherwise might not have happened or helping sustain dissent that would otherwise have swiftly been put to an end. Leaking information about useful government policies in general and a party secretary's wrongdoing in particular, can embolden discontented community elites to mobilize popular action. In Gangu county, Gansu Province, for example, a county party secretary in 2006 planned to recruit underqualified relatives of his political cronies to teach in the local schools. A bureaucrat in the county general office leaked the secretary's plan to elders of a lineage whom the secretary had offended three years before. The elders began to mobilize opposition to the plan. Within two days, hundreds of young unemployed college graduates and their relatives gathered at the county government compound, demanding open and fair teacher recruitment. During the demonstration, several officials, who were allies of the leaker, led the protesters to the party secretary's office and pretended they were trying to stop the protesters from forcing their way in, when in reality they were urging them to do just that. The demonstration drew the attention of the municipal leadership and the party secretary was soon transferred out of the county (interview 1).

Undermining repression of a petition can also jump-start collective action. In Jianli county, Hubei Province, a county party secretary alienated his subordinates and local elites by selling the management rights for the county's best high school to a private firm in 2005. After the sale, the management firm refused to enroll underperforming children of local bureaucrats and community leaders. Irate local officials immediately began to apply pressure on the secretary. In a highly unusual and confrontational move, the county people's congress rejected the government budget at its annual session, reportedly citing the education expenditures as a justification, despite the secretary's strong endorsement of the spending plan. Still, the party secretary refused to give in and the management company went a step further by firing some weak teachers. An episode of bureaucrat-assisted contention then broke out. Several retired officials and local businesspeople whose children or grandchildren had been rejected by the high school encouraged the dismissed teachers to lodge a collective complaint. When three of the teachers were intercepted on their way to the municipal government, local officials who opposed the secretary instructed the guards at the detention center to turn a blind eye to rules that ban detainees from making contact with anyone on the outside. The detained teachers were allowed to use their mobile phones to call their favorite students, who then mobilized other students to come to their rescue. As hundreds of students marched to the government compound to demand the release of the teachers, concerned parents rushed to the area, too. A large and boisterous crowd assembled. Worried that they would fail their annual performance review on the make-or-break criterion of maintaining social stability (Zhou and Yan 2014), municipal leaders put the county secretary under investigation and eventually he was removed (Yang 2011; interview 2).

Officials involved in bureaucrat-assisted contention sometimes only seek to have a measure they oppose reversed. At other times, they go further and deploy contention to topple their superiors. One sign of this latter strategy is offering assistance that officials seldom provide. In Yunnan Province, a former deputy chairman of the provincial people's political consultative conference became famous in 2012 for championing villagers who had been lodging collective complaints to stop their land from being expropriated. He regularly received phone calls from community elites throughout the province, including businesspeople, lineage elders, and "peasant leaders" (Li and O'Brien 2008; Zhang 2015a), begging him for help. But he declined to act on a large majority of the pleas because the cases lacked "political height" (*zhengzhi gaodu*), meaning they did not implicate the outsider provincial party secretary whom he was seeking to unseat (interview 3).

The presence of bureaucrat-assisted contention in China suggests a number of questions. In more open societies, opposition parties and politicians often play a role in staging demonstrations to achieve their own ends. Recent cases include the red-shirt army movement in Thailand (Forsyth 2010), the occupy-central movement in Hong Kong (Ortmann 2015), and the Sunflower Movement in Taiwan (Rowen 2015). China, however, is a relatively closed and order-obsessed authoritarian regime, where assisting popular contention is a high-risk venture for any bureaucrat (Ma 2019: 5). Only during the Cultural Revolution, when "it is right to rebel" became part of the ideology of the day, did officials sometimes organize mass demonstrations against each other, though even then this was always done for the purpose of "defending Chairman Mao" (Dittmer 2001). Throughout the reform era, the central leadership has been much more committed to party unity and vigilant about prohibiting insiders from drawing on popular support and disruption to improve their position in power struggles. What then motivates local officials to support collective action against party secretaries?

INSTITUTIONAL TENSIONS

Like most forms of collective action, bureaucrat-assisted contention has historical precedents. When an emperor attempted to force members of the gentry to contribute more to state coffers, local officials and community elites sometimes colluded to instigate protests against stepped-up extraction (Wakeman 1975; Faure and Siu 1995; Siu 1992; Wong 1997; also see Zhou 2016). Contemporary bureaucrat-assisted contention in China can be traced to two institutional tensions, one between native-born officials and outsider party secretaries and the other between outsider secretaries and local socioeconomic elites. As the "number one in charge" (*yibashou*) in every jurisdiction, party secretaries enjoy far more decision-making power than any other official but are unaccountable to the people they govern, unlike government heads who at least are formally elected by local people's congresses (Manion 2008). Since the 1990s, increasingly strict enforcement of the rule that secretaries must come from a different locality has deepened their detachment from the people they rule (Zhou 2016). Party secretaries are also rotated frequently, most often serving short terms of three to five years in a locality (Landry 2008). Operating under these institutions, secretaries sometimes ignore the interests of their subordinates as well as local elites when ordered to enforce decisions from above (Mei and Pearson 2014). At the same time, eager to score impressive "political achievements" (*zhengji*) that will enhance the likelihood of promotion, many secretaries are tempted to initiate eye-catching but often poorly conceived development projects (O'Brien and Li 1999). Worst of all, secretaries who find themselves "ceilinged" (Kou and Tsai 2014), because they have little hope of promotion owing to age, education, or lack of patrons, may behave like "roving bandits" (Olson 1993) and try to pocket as much as fast as they can before they must retire (Liu 2018).

Officials who assist popular contention, on the other hand, are typically "ordinary leadership cadres" (*putong lingdao ganbu*). This includes chairs and deputy chairs of people's congresses and political consultative conferences, heads of the public security bureau and the court, and directors of government bureaus. Although no less prone to corruption than their adversaries, native-born officials usually have a somewhat longer-term perspective than outsider secretaries on issues such as economic development and environmental protection. They also prefer to nurture and take advantage of opportunities for activities such as bribe taking, shady real-estate deals, and nepotism over many years, while newcomers are inclined to engage in out-and-out plunder by "drying up the pond for fishing" or even "killing the chicken to get the eggs" (see Zhou 2016).

The term "local socioeconomic elites" refers to a stratum that includes individuals such as businesspeople, retired officials, clan elders, retired school principals, and even local "rights activists" (Benney 2013). The core group, however, is made up of private entrepreneurs, who need to cultivate patrons in officialdom, when, for instance, seeking a business license or a tax reduction (Ma 2019: 15–16). Local influentials typically have deep ties with "ordinary leadership cadres," nearly all of whom have made their careers in their hometown. Both groups have an interest in maintaining privileged access to scarce resources such as investment opportunities, good schools, and natural resources and farmland and find themselves on the same side when party secretaries initiate or acquiesce to a decision to pursue an administrative merger, privatize a school, or place a trash incinerator in the community. Outsiders often threaten the cozy relationship that native-born bureaucrats and local elites have built up and can disrupt the ability of both parties to secure advantages they have grown to expect.

Bureaucrat-assisted contention is usually averted because the institutional tensions among native-born officials and outsider secretaries are contained within the bureaucracy. Although they do not always work overly hard to cultivate loyalty among their subordinates, party secretaries typically try to avoid alienating them. Acting on the centuries-old proverb that "even a strong dragon does not trifle with resident snakes" (*qianglong buya ditoushe*), secretaries may refrain from impinging on the interests of underlings or encroaching on their turf. After taking up a new post, they may make conciliatory gestures to soothe anxious subordinates. They, for instance, may announce that they have no desire to reshuffle directors of local government bureaus. Even ambitious or domineering secretaries often test the water first, size up potential rivals, and back off when they "touch the needle hidden in the ball of cotton" (*chajue mianhuatuan zhong you zhen*). For their part, underlings tend to tread carefully and avoid confronting superiors. They accommodate as much as they can and issue warnings only when their "core interests" (*hexin liyi*) are threatened. For instance, they may signal unhappiness about a secretary's "recklessness" or "lack of commitment to the long-term interests of the people" by voting against or abstaining in party committee meetings. Such warnings are usually enough to ward off further incursions. Even when the two sides do not get along well, tension usually simmers at a low level and then disappears because secretaries are rotated so often. As a result, outsider secretaries and native-born officials in most circumstances maintain an uneasy truce that is characterized by under-the-table deals, negotiations, and constant, small tugs-of-war (Mertha 2009).

Tension turns into bureaucrat-assisted contention when secretaries either go too far with a new initiative or experience significant pressure from above. Facing a runaway leader, locally born officials have little effective recourse. The Leninist principle of democratic centralism does not empower subordinates to challenge superiors through institutional channels. In theory, officials can report wrongdoing through the disciplinary inspection system. But in practice, the system seldom can do much if a secretary has powerful patrons or is enforcing a decision from above (Li and Deng 2016; Manion 2016). When conflict reaches this point, local officials may become desperate and willing to take a gamble. They may turn to "nonorganizational activities" (*fei zuzhi huodong*) (interviews 4, 5, 6), by working with disaffected local elites and using mass mobilization to ratchet up pressure on a common enemy. Bureaucrat-assisted contention is a high-risk, high-gain strategy, borne out of dissatisfaction felt by midlevel officials and local influentials who cannot see another, better way to rein in ambitious, grasping, or highhanded party secretaries.

METHODS AND VARIATION

This study was a long-term project that combined ethnography with concept formation. In both the 1990s and the early 2010s, Liu conducted dozens of open-ended interviews with officials in Gansu, Hebei, Hubei, and Zhejiang and observed that native-born officials sometimes deployed popular contention as a means to oust their party bosses. Then Liu and Li engaged in discussions about several cases of what we now call bureaucrat-assisted contention. Next, Li took the lead, after a 2012 conversation with O'Brien, in identifying the features of this type of collective action, its characteristic process of mobilization, and the interaction among the various parties. Liu and Li then conducted additional fieldwork in Hunan, Shandong, Yunnan, Shanghai, Guangdong, and Zhejiang to confirm that the episodes we had located were not idiosyncratic local political dramas but shared certain institutional roots. Meanwhile, we collected accounts of bureaucrat-assisted contention on the internet from Henan, Jiangsu, and Sichuan. Finally, O'Brien wrote the introduction and conclusion and worked with Li to sharpen the concept and incorporate the findings into the field of contentious politics. Throughout the research, we sought to achieve a "fusion of horizons" (Gadamer 1975) with our informants, while identifying themes in the empirics that clarified what was distinctive (and interesting) about bureaucrat-assisted contention.

Owing to the limited number of full cases we have in hand, it is difficult to speak about regional or temporal variation. Nevertheless, our hunch is that bureaucrat-assisted contention is more common in coastal areas where private enterprise has taken off and political loyalty has lost some if its luster, as well as in counties or provinces with a history of factionalism. There may also be an inverse U-shaped relationship, where this type of collective action is uncommon when party secretaries throughout the system are extremely weak or strong and most common where ambitious outsiders fall in the middle: domineering yet vulnerable, not strong enough to lead local-born underlings to give up and resign (Li 2019), and not weak enough so that bureaucrat-assisted contention is unnecessary.

OPPORTUNITIES

From the perspective of protest leaders, divisions within a state are an important component of a political opportunity structure (Tarrow 1994; Meyer 2004; Li and O'Brien 2008; Zhang 2015b). For disaffected bureaucrats in China, opportunities often emerge when party secretaries irritate local socioeconomic elites, people who typically have the moral and financial resources to mobilize collective action. Secretaries are particularly likely to generate openings for bureaucrat-assisted contention when they seek to enforce higher-level decisions that both subordinates and local influentials strongly oppose. In Pingjiang county, Hunan Province, a new party secretary decided in 2014 to go ahead with a controversial plan to build a thermal power plant that would emit considerable pollution. Locally born bureaucrats had accused his predecessor, also a non-native, of "recklessly promoting the project." The new secretary found himself subject to heightened pressure from the provincial party committee and the company that would build the plant, which was run by a former premier's daughter. More ambitious than cautious, he attempted to force the plan through in the face of opposition from local business owners who were concerned about property values and the effect polluted air and water would have on tourism. To forestall possible collusion between his underlings and local influentials, the secretary called an emergency meeting of county officials, at which he announced his decision and issued a stern warning forbidding local cadres and their families from joining any protests against the plant (cf. O'Brien and Deng 2017). Native-born officials, however, did exactly what the secretary feared most. They seized the opportunity he had unwittingly created and leaked the secretary's decision to entrepreneurs who had invested in local real estate and ecotourism. The businesspeople immediately launched a mass campaign, cleverly framing their opposition in terms President Xi Jinping himself had used to preserve "clear waters" and "green mountains" for future generations. Seven demonstrations were staged in three days, drawing in hundreds of people. This led the county secretary to resign and the provincial party committee to shelve the plan (Zhou 2014; Li and Liu 2016). Angry that he had been outmaneuvered, the secretary posted an open letter on the internet, accusing his subordinates of being "unreasonable," "irresponsible," and "indecent" (Tian 2014). He did not appear to realize that he had created the opportunity for popular action and the threat to himself by simultaneously alienating his underlings and harming the investments of local businesspeople.

Party secretaries may also be implicated when opponents use their political allies against them. In Yunnan Province, a provincial party secretary was tripped up by an opportunity generated by his own greed and a follower who could be attacked easier than he could be. In the 2000s, the provincial party secretary, who was from Shaanxi and had made most of his career elsewhere, set out to amass a fortune before reaching retirement age. He took large bribes from local mine owners and promotion seekers and dismissed many officials without good reason, angering a powerful group of native-born officials known as the Qujing Gang. The secretary's misdeeds also drew the attention of Yang Weijun, a former leader of the local consultative conference who had long been working to combat high-level corruption in Yunnan (Wang 2014; H. Zhang 2014; L. Zhang 2014). The Qujing Gang struck back at the secretary by reporting his corruption to the Central Discipline Inspection Commission and by giving Yang evidence of the bribe taking to hand-carry to Beijing. But the Qujing Gang's disclosures failed to have any effect because the secretary had close ties with a member of the Politburo Standing Committee. The secretary, after learning of the campaign being waged against him, retaliated by subjecting his opponents to anticorruption investigations, which landed some of them in prison. The Qujing Gang appeared to be defeated but then discovered an opening that they could exploit. Protests against land appropriation were underway near the provincial capital that were targeting several of the secretary's loyal followers. The Qujing Gang linked up with Yang Weijun and community leaders who were leading the contention to get to the party secretary. Yang then led a group of "rights-defense representatives" (*weiquan daibiao*) to the office of the provincial consultative conference to deliver a petition about the wrongdoing of the secretary's allies. Later, he gave a long speech at a mass meeting outside the capital, criticizing the county officials who mishandled the protest and naming their patron in the provincial government (Wang 2014; Zhu 2015; Liu 2014; interview 3). Although a clear opportunity to challenge the provincial secretary had not existed, actions deep in the bureaucracy made him vulnerable to bureaucrat-assisted contention.

FRAMING

Framing, broadly speaking, consists of defining grievances as an injustice, attributing them to a target or system, and convincing the aggrieved they need not accept their plight and have a realistic chance of prevailing and having justice served (Benford and Snow 2000). An essential element of framing is aligning competing claims of groups or factions of a movement into a commonly accepted framework (Snow et al. 1986, 2014), in part by striking a balance between minimizing risks for participants and maximizing mobilization. Framing in bureaucrat-assisted contention is distinctive in that it involves frame alignment between officials and elites who share a common enemy but not always common goals. Frames for bureaucrat-assisted contention possess two noteworthy features. For one, framing typically has a strongly localist flavor, which helps it resonate with the audience to be mobilized (Noakes and Johnston 2005: 2) and fortifies the identity component of the frame (Gamson 1992). Beyond conjuring a group of the aggrieved into being, "working for the locality" also disguises that elites and officials often have unspoken motives and that addressing public grievances is usually far from the first thing on their minds. Second, frames are unusually precise in pinpointing the source of a grievance and exploiting the vulnerabilities of a target. Thanks to information leaked by officials, local elites know exactly what wrongdoing secretaries have committed and have hard evidence of their excesses or misbehavior. In the Gangu county case discussed previously, the party secretary denied that he had a secret recruitment plan. Protest leaders silenced him by displaying his name list of preferred candidates (interview 1). An even more dramatic episode of framing with devastating accuracy occurred in Gaoping County, Jiangxi Province in 2015. Eager to attract investment to boost his career prospects, a county secretary reached an agreement with a developer who wanted to build resort villas near a scenic lake. The secretary ordered the leaders of the township where the lake was located to carry out the construction plan. Local lineage elders, however, strongly opposed the project because it entailed the relocation of their clan's ancestral tombs. A township official who had poor relations with the township secretary saw an opportunity to stop the construction by using the secretary's words against him. After adjourning a closed-door meeting about the construction project, the secretary walked out of the room and was stunned to see dozens of agitated villagers gathered outside. Confronted by "the masses," the secretary insisted that the meeting was about other, unrelated government business. A young villager then began to play back a recording of the secretary explaining the plan to build the villas during the meeting that had just ended. It turned out that the locally born official had told lineage elders about the meeting beforehand. The clan leaders then mobilized lineage members who shared their belief that ancestral graves should not be tampered with and ill fortune would result if they were. During the meeting, the disaffected official had secretly recorded the secretary's speech and sent the audio clips to the young man's mobile phone (interview 12). Incriminating information, persuasively communicated, made all the difference. The audio clips not only proved that the secretary was plainly lying, but they also provided incontrovertible evidence that a misdeed had occurred and pinpointed the culprit. Naming (Felstiner, Abel, and Sarat 1980–1981), this case reminds us, is often the easy part of framing because everyone can complain that they have been wronged in some way. Information made available to protesters by insiders can do much to help shape an effective, "adversarial" claim by assigning blame for an injustice to a particular person (Gamson 1992).

Beyond precisely identifying the vulnerabilities of a target, the framing of bureaucrat-assisted contention often has a strong localist flavor, with all residents of an area identified as "us" and outsider secretaries labeled as "them." Most party secretaries are outsiders in every sense of the term. Many do not even have their families living with them (interviews 7 and 16). Relying on information concerning where secretaries hail from and where their families remain, the frames that back up bureaucrat-assisted contention invariably feed suspicions that secretaries do not care about the long-term welfare of the local population. In Songjiang District, Shanghai, a university area, the party secretary approved the construction of a lithium battery factory in 2013. Many residents worried that the plant would pose a substantial environmental hazard. Officials who opposed the secretary let word out that his original work unit was a central ministry and that he had been sent down to a lowly district only to gain leadership experience. Furthermore, they made known that he was so confident about a pending promotion to Beijing that he left his family in the capital, more than one thousand kilometers away. Community elites, particularly leaders of homeowners' associations, college professors who had bought homes in the area, and owners of property management companies, used the leaks to mobilize local residents, who were outraged that the secretary was seeking to burnish his record at the expense of the health of thousands of university students and the local property market. A mass demonstration was organized, which alarmed Shanghai's party secretary, who was being considered for promotion to a vice premiership. Eager to maintain a sterling record in "stability maintenance" (*weiwen*), the Shanghai secretary immediately stepped in and terminated the project (D. Liu 2013; interviews 10 and 11).

A "protect our hometown" (*baowei jiaxiang*) frame is an effective way to mobilize residents and expose outsiders as compromised by conflicting loyalties, careerism or greed. In Qidong County, Jiangsu Province, activists in 2012 distilled localism down to its purest form. They spurred residents to join bureaucrat-assisted contention against a wastewater pipeline project a party secretary refused to oppose by simply asking: "Are you a Qidonger?" (interviews 8 and 9). The same frame was adopted to draw local officials, elites, and ordinary citizens together against an outsider who was promoting a mining project in Shifang County, Sichuan in 2012 (Yan 2014; interview 9).

The "protect our hometown" discourse is particularly useful in framing bureaucrat-assisted contention against administrative mergers (Ma 2019: 11). Since the early 1990s, turning counties into municipal districts has drawn the ire of many local officials who are worried about losing autonomy and control over their budgets (Ma 2019: 9–10), as well as experiencing a reduction in rents they can extract from local businesses. Being absorbed into a city is also seen as a threat by many local elites, who stand to lose influence over new, more distant officials and who would have more difficulty gaining access to land, natural resources, licenses, and other benefits that local cadres had been willing to provide (Ma 2005; Zhan 2017). To mobilize collective action against mergers, native-born officials and community leaders often seek to kindle a sense of pride in their hometown. This claim, even when somewhat far-fetched, can be effective in stirring a public that otherwise has little to gain (or lose) from an administrative reorganization. In 2005, for example, the party secretary of Hubei Province decided to merge Daye County into Huangshi City. The change directly threatened the interests of local officials who held shares in several local mining firms. To stop the merger, they leaked the plan to owners of the companies, who immediately began to worry about losing their business licenses after the reorganization. Daye's secretary did not stand up to defend the entrepreneurs because a decision to promote him to deputy mayor was in the offing. Instead, he sought to reassure them and calm them down. The mine owners, however, were unmoved. They mobilized a large petition drive that eventually led to dozens of protesters breaking into government offices and ransacking them. Knowing that most of Daye's residents were indifferent about the merger, the mine owners hired hundreds of local toughs, paid them handsomely, and put them up in high-end hotels. On the day the petition was delivered, the mine owners hired bus companies to give the protesters free rides from the county to Huangshi City. At the urging of local officials, the mine owners also called on all of Daye's residents to defend the county's glorious history as the birthplace of China's metallurgy industry ("Daye" literally means "great smelting"). Should there be a merger, they argued, the city of Huangshi, which was only established in the 1950s, should instead be renamed after the county (interview 15). A localist frame had transformed real (and manufactured) popular pride into group solidarity, while cloaking the self-interest of bureaucrats and entrepreneurs with claims that they were simply pursuing justice and protecting the rights of Daye residents.

A localist frame is a recurring feature in Chinese bureaucrat-assisted contention. It also was adopted in Lingbao County, Henan Province, which is the hometown of the philosopher Lao Tzu, the legendary founder of Taoism. In 2010, many local cadres opposed the Sanmenxia party committee's decision to transform the county into a city district. Like their counterparts in Daye, they feared that they would lose opportunities to extract unwarranted payments, in their case, ones derived from mining, tobacco cultivation, and apple orchards. So they leaked the merger plan to a group of retired officials, including a respected former chairman of the county people's congress. They also made the proposal known to dozens of businesspeople in the county congress and political consultative conference, who began to worry that their products might lose a well-known brand name. Again, the general public had little at stake in the merger. As had happened in Daye, officials and businesspeople in Lingbao appealed to hometown pride to mobilize a series of demonstrations. Officials did their part by releasing information that revealed how the municipal government had been siphoning off the county's natural resources since the 1980s. The businesspeople used this knowledge to rile up the public, comparing the municipal government to a colonial power (Liu 2010). Precise, localist framing that appealed in different ways to local bureaucrats, elites, and the broader populace generated enough pressure that the municipal authorities put off the merger. The county secretary who acquiesced to the reorganization was left discredited and disgraced. In short order, he was shuffled off to a position in the municipal people's congress and quietly went into semi-retirement at the age of fifty-one.

MOBILIZING STRUCTURES

How bureaucrat-assisted contention is mounted also has several notable features. In social movement theory, mobilizing structures are normally located within society (McAdam, McCarthy, and Zeld 1996: 143–44; Munson 2010). Bureaucrat-assisted contention does rely on social networks and organizations such as lineage groups, internet chat groups, nongovernmental organizations (NGOs), and business associations. Interestingly, however, it can also turn the government hierarchy itself into a mobilizing structure. In Changxing County, Zhejiang Province, contention broke out after the Huzhou City party committee decided to turn a county into a municipal district. Changxing's outsider party secretary accepted the merger, but local officials and local elites did not. To underscore its opposition, the county business association applied for permission to organize a demonstration against the merger (J. Liu 2013). In an even bolder move, the association called for its members to go on strike and keep their businesses closed until the decision was reversed (interview 13). What many people did not know is that county officials had used the bureaucracy to help stir the association into action and assemble the opposition. At the encouragement of locally born officials, several township heads announced their collective resignation as a protest against the reorganization. To dramatize their resolve, they posted their resignation letter on the internet (J. Liu 2013). It turned out that the township officials' daring gesture originated with a guarantee from a senior leader of the county people's congress, who assured them that they would not lose their jobs if they joined the contention (interview 13). The government hierarchy has also been relied on elsewhere to encourage officials to boycott or sabotage repression. In Yuhang district, Hangzhou, for example, several county officials opposed the construction of a trash incinerator. At their behest, every township head suddenly went missing when the city police came to look for help in halting a protest involving hundreds of villagers (Heng 2014; interview 14).

With officials refusing to take part in repression or even undermining it, bureaucrat-assisted contention can be remarkably resilient. In Hunan Province, resistance to excessive taxation in the 1990s and early 2000s was spirited and persistent, in part owing to bureaucrats who tipped off protest leaders when party secretaries dispatched the police to arrest them (Li and O'Brien 2008; Zhang 2015a, 2015b). The resistance to land appropriation in Jinning County, Yunnan Province lasted from 2012 to 2014. It continued for so long in large part because of the support of a provincial official and other cadres who provided the local elites who led the protest with evidence of the provincial secretary's corruption (Liu 2014; interview 3). That the bureaucracy itself could be used as a mobilizing structure reminds us of the opportunities provided by a far-flung, multilevel state where officials are not always on the same page and that movement entrepreneurs can be located both within the bureaucracy and in society.

SOME CONSEQUENCES AND IMPLICATIONS FOR THEORY

As the episodes discussed in this chapter have made clear, bureaucrat-assisted contention is difficult to pull off but often works. A coalition of convenience between native-born officials and local elites can generate enough pressure, when coupled with social mobilization, to get the better of a party secretary in a district, county, or even a province. Ironically, in a regime obsessed with "harmony" (*hexie*) and stability, the disruptiveness that makes bureaucrat-assisted contention relatively uncommon can also make it effective, by showing officials at higher levels that something is seriously awry. This echoes the popular Chinese saying that "big disturbances lead to big solutions, small disturbances lead to small solutions, and no disturbance leads to no solution,"

(Cai 2010: 234)[1] and suggests that although mobilizing the disaffected and making a commotion is risky in an authoritarian setting, drawing together a range of aggrieved parties, crossing the state-society border, and creating a spectacle (O'Brien and Deng 2015: 470) can produce results.

Bureaucrat-assisted contention is of course not always successful, and more research is needed to understand when and where it fails. Still, repeated recourse to this type of collective action can have lasting consequences by reconfiguring the relationship among secretaries, local officials, and socioeconomic elites. Once they force concessions or drive a secretary away, native-born bureaucrats are inclined to revive their cooperation with local influentials and launch contention again against a secretary's successor. Aware of what happened last time, new appointees are often more cautious and work harder to avoid simultaneously alienating local officials and elites. Over time, bureaucrat-assisted contention may not even need to be unleashed to have an effect. After more than a decade when maintaining stability has been the regime's top priority (Zhou and Yan 2014), a credible threat is often sufficient to check a secretary's power, ambitions, or avarice.

At the same time, it should be noted that although bureaucrat-assisted contention is invariably carried out in the name of a locality, success does not always benefit local residents or even the people who were mobilized to take part. In Shifang County, Sichuan Province, for example, a group of mine owners joined forces with native-born officials to stage a noisy antipollution protest that halted the construction of a large, new smelting operation. But the bureaucrats and businesspeople had colluded simply to drive out a competitor who the mine owners feared would be a more efficient and cleaner competitor and who the officials worried would be more difficult to shake down. The contention and its reputation for instability turned the county into an "orphan" (*guer*) that was out of favor with higher levels of government and investors. The collective action had succeeded in blocking the new plant, but the county lost out on a 13.7 billion yuan (US$2.2 billion) investment that would have boosted local incomes, while the mine operators continued to pollute as much as they had before (Yan 2014; interview 9).

For students of social movements, bureaucrat-assisted contention draws attention to some less-appreciated aspects of three concepts that have been at the heart of the field for decades. First, it says something unexpected about divisions within the state and defections that provide openings for social forces. Opportunities can arise when a leader pushes subordinates into the arms of local elites who have their own complaints about the leader. Institutional tensions and alienating decisions can generate a rough-and-ready partnership that unites middle-level bureaucrats and influential members of society who have the wherewithal to mobilize the public. Second, like everything associated with bureaucratic-assisted contention, frame alignment cuts across the state-society divide. Local elites use leaked information to turn broad grievances (e.g., dissatisfaction with the environment) into actionable demands. With crucial assistance from within the state, claims home in on a named culprit and specified offenses, and bureaucrats and local elites draw on hometown pride to package their charges in a discourse that emphasizes protecting local interests. Last, as with opportunities and framing, mobilizing structures span state and society. Leaders antagonize local influentials and subordinates within the government. Although local elites deploy social networks and other means to pull the public into contention, what stands out is how much of the impetus for protest lies within the state and how actions by leaders and their subordinates both fuel collective action.

Bureaucrat-assisted contention also reminds us that familiar concepts such as opportunity and mobilizing structures must be contextualized when they travel to illiberal countries that lack active intermediary organizations. This type of collective action arises in China not because social movement organizations exploit splits within the state, as is often seen in more open societies, but because disaffected officials inside a divided state look outward and cobble together an alliance with societal forces. China's dearth of social movement organizations, in this sense, is a structural feature of its authoritarian system that draws three aggrieved parties together and leads native-born officials to a build a makeshift, informal mobilizing structure that, to some degree, takes the place of a conventional SMO, and makes coordination and collective action possible. In this challenging opportunity structure, what appears to be a strength of the state (i.e., its ability to suppress civil society organizations) can create a vulnerability, and what appears reckless for officials (i.e., mobilizing elites and fomenting contention) can be an effective way to confront one's superiors.

Bureaucrat-assisted contention neither fits snugly in state-society ways of thinking nor with imagining that a thick, black line exists between members of the state and challengers. Instead, it highlights two actors (bureaucrats and local elites) in a four-party game that also includes leaders and the public. Contention originates in the middle reaches of the government and is energized by a bureaucratic power struggle that draws in aggrieved people from the higher reaches of society. The impetus for protest is shared and midlevel officials are full-fledged participants in contention, not just champions, elite allies, or "institutional activists" (Santoro and McGuire 1997; Yang 2017; Ma 2019). Bureaucrat-assisted contention is mutually constituted and hinges on parties working across the state-society divide. Disaffected bureaucrats and elites both play a critical role, as each pursues a common target for their own reasons, with the public brought in as a supporting player to ratchet the pressure up one final notch.

INTERVIEWEE LIST

1. Government official, 2014, Lanzhou.
2. Government official, 2016, Wuhan.
3. Government official, 2015, Kunming.
4. Policy researcher, 2014, Guangzhou.
5. Policy researcher, 2018, Shanghai.
6. Government official, 2009, Shanghai.
7. Policy researcher, 2016, Beijing.
8. Policy researcher, 2016, Beijing.
9. Policy researcher, 2016, Beijing.
10. Policy researcher, 2017, Shanghai.
11. Policy researcher, 2017, Shanghai.
12. Policy researcher, 2017, Guangzhou.
13. Government official, 2015, Hangzhou.
14. Policy researcher, 2017, Hangzhou.
15. Government official, 2009, Wuhan.
16. Policy researcher, 2014, Beijing.

NOTE

1. The case for the effectiveness of disruptive tactics in democracies reaches back at least as far as Gamson (1975), Piven and Cloward (1979), and McAdam (1982). For more on the debate over "disruption vs. moderation," see Giugni (1999: xvi–xviii) and McAdam and Su (2002). In China, the evidence is mixed, with some scholars arguing that tactical escalation in the wake of policing mistakes can generate leverage and concessions (O'Brien and Deng 2015), while others find that "troublemaking but not disruptive tactics" are most effective (Chen 2012: 182–84). Overall, evidence from China on "the power of disruptive collective action" (Cai 2010, chapter 6) shows that a "supportive regime" and "level of democratization" (Amenta, Caren, Chiarello, and Su 2010: 299) may not be as crucial as some political mediation models suggest.

REFERENCES

Amenta, Edwin, Neal Caren, Elizabeth Chiarello, and Yang Su. 2010. "The Political Consequences of Social Movements." *Annual Review of Sociology* 36: 287–307.

Benford, Robert D., and David Snow. 2000. "Framing Processes and Social Movements: An Overview and Assessment." *Annual Review of Sociology* 26: 611–39.

Benney, Jonathan. 2013. *Defending Rights in Contemporary China*. London: Routledge.

Bernstein, Thomas P., and Xiaobo Lü. 2000. "Taxation without Representation: Peasants, the Central and the Local States in Reform China." *The China Quarterly* 163: 742–63.

Cai, Yongshun. 2010. "Local Governments and the Suppression of Popular Resistance in China." *The China Quarterly* 193: 24–42.

Cai, Yongshun, and Zhiming Sheng. 2013. "Homeowners' Activism in Beijing: Leaders with Mixed Motivations." *The China Quarterly* 215: 513–32.

Chen, Feng, and Mengxiao Tang. 2013. "Labor Conflicts in China: Typologies and Their Implications." *Asian Survey* 53(3): 559–83.

Chen, Xi. 2012. *Social Protest and Contentious Authoritarianism in China*. New York: Cambridge University Press.

———. 2017. "Origins of Informal Coercion in China." *Politics & Society* 45(1): 67–89.

Chuang, Julia. 2014. "China's Rural Land Politics: Bureaucratic Absorption and the Muting of Rightful Resistance." *China Quarterly* 219: 649–69.

Deng, Yanhua, and Guobin Yang. 2013. "Pollution and Protest in China: Environmental Mobilization in Context." *China Quarterly* 214: 321–36.

Deng, Yanhua, and Kevin J. O'Brien. 2013. "Relational Repression in China: Using Social Ties to De-mobilize Protesters." *The China Quarterly* 215: 533–52.

Diamant, Neil J., and Kevin J. O'Brien. 2015. "Veteran's Political Activism in China." *Modern China* 41(3): 278–312.

Dittmer, Lowell. 2001. "The Changing Shape of Elite Power Politics." *China Journal* 45: 53–67.

Faure, David, and Helen F. Siu, eds. 1995. *Down to Earth*. Stanford, CA: Stanford University Press.

Felstiner, William L. F., Richard L. Abel, and Austin Sarat. 1980–1981. "The Emergence and Transformation of Disputes: Naming, Blaming, Claiming...." *Law and Society Review* 15: 631–54.

Forsyth, Tim. 2010. "Thailand's Red Shirt Protests: Popular Movement or Dangerous Street Theatre?" *Social Movement Studies* 9(4): 461–67.

Gadamer, Hans-Georg. 1975. *Truth and Method*, trans. and ed., Garrett Barden and John Cumming. NY: The Seabury Press.

Gamson, William A. 1975. *The Strategy of Social Protest*. Homewood, IL: The Dorsey Press.

———. 1992. *Talking Politics*. New York: Cambridge University Press.

Giugni, Marco. 1999. "How Social Movements Matter: Past Research, Present Problems, Future Developments." In Marco Giugni, Doug McAdam, and Charles Tilly, eds., *How Social Movements Matter*, xiii–xxxii. Minneapolis: University of Minnesota Press.

Heng, Lu. 2014. "Hangzhou Garbage Incinerator Project Forced to Postpone by Violent Protest" [in Chinese]. Accessed March 13, 2019. https://www.bbc.com/zhongwen/simp/china/2014/05/140511_hangzhou_incenerator.

Hu, Jieren, Tong Wu, and Jingyan Fei. 2018. "Flexible Governance in China: Affective Care, Petition Social Workers, and Multi-Pronged Means of Dispute Resolution." *Asian Survey* 58(4): 679–703.

Hurst, William, Thomas B. Gold, and Jaeyoun Won. 2009. "Introduction." In Thomas B. Gold, Thomas B., William J. Hurst, Jaeyoun Won, and Li Qiang, eds. *Unemployment with Chinese Characteristics*, 1–16. New York: Palgrave Macmillan.

Hurst, William, and Kevin J. O'Brien. 2002. "China's Contentious Pensioners." *The China Quarterly* 170: 345–60.

Kou, Chien-wen, and Wen-Hsuan Tsai. 2014. "'Sprinting with Small Steps Towards Promotion': Solutions for the Age Dilemma in the CCP Cadre Appointment System." *China Journal* 71: 153–71.

Landry, Pierre. 2008. *Decentralized Authoritarianism in China*. New York: Cambridge University Press.

Li, Fenfei, and Jinting Deng. 2016. "The Limits of Arbitrariness in Anticorruption by China's Local Party Discipline Inspection Committees." *Journal of Contemporary China* 25(97): 75–90.

Li, Lianjiang. 2019. "The Cadre Resignation Tide in the Wake of the 18th Party Congress." *China: An International Journal* 17(3): 188–99.

Li, Lianjiang, and Liu Mingxing. 2016. "Collusion between Government Officials and Socioeconomic Elites: An Invisible Hand in Chinese Contentious Politics" [in Chinese]. *Twentieth Century* 157: 57–67.

Li, Lianjiang, and Kevin J. O'Brien. 2008. "Protest Leadership in Rural China." *China Quarterly* 193: 1–23.

Lipsky, Michael. 1968. "Protest as a Political Resource." *American Political Science Review* 62(4): 1144–58.

Liu, Dan. 2013. "Behind the Crash of the Songjiang Battery Factory Project" [in Chinese]. Accessed on 13 March 2019. http://finance.sina.com.cn/china/dfjj/20130617/163515814490.shtml.

Liu, Derek Tai-wei. 2018. "The Effects of Institutionalization in China: A Difference-in-Differences Analysis of the Mandatory Retirement Age." *China Economic Review* 52: 192–203.

Liu, Jinsong. 2010. "Unrest Caused by the Plan to Merge Lingbao as a District" [in Chinese[. *Economic Observation Newspaper*, October 29. Accessed March 13, 2019. http://www.eeo.com.cn/eobserve/eeo/jjgcb/2010/11/01/ 184289.shtml.

Liu, Jun. 2013. "Converting a County into a District: Changxing Is Unhappy" [in Chinese]. *Southern Weekend*, May 16. Accessed March 13, 2019. http://www.infzm.com/content/90408.

Liu, Yanxun. 2014. "Yang Weijun: A Non-Party High Official Who Reported on Bai Enpei" [in Chinese]. *Southern Weekend*, September 4, 2014. Accessed February 25, 2019. http://www.infzm.com/content/103901.

Ma, Laurence J. C. 2005. "Urban Administrative Restructuring, Changing Scale Relations and Local Economic Development in China." *Political Geography* 24(4): 477–97.

Ma, Xiao. 2019. "Consent to Contend: The Power of the Masses in China's Local Elite Bargain." *China Review* 19(1): 1–29.

McAdam, Doug. 1982. *Political Process and the Development of Black Insurgency, 1930–1970*. Chicago: University of Chicago Press.

McAdam, Doug, and Yang Su. 2002. "The War at Home: Antiwar Protests and Congressional Voting, 1965–1973." *American Sociological Review* 67(5): 696–721.

McAdam, Doug, John D. McCarthy, and Mayer N. Zald, eds. 1996. *Comparative Perspectives on Social Movements: Political Opportunities, Mobilizing Structures, and Cultural Framings*. New York: Cambridge University Press.

Manion, Melanie. 2008. "When Communist Party Candidates Can Lose, Who Wins? Assessing the Role of Local People's Congresses in the Selection of Leaders in China." *China Quarterly* 195: 607–30.

———. 2016. "Taking China's Anticorruption Campaign Seriously." *Economic and Political Studies* 4(1): 3–18.

Marx, Gary T., and James L. Wood. 1975. "Strands of Theory and Research in Collective Behavior." *Annual Review of Sociology* 1: 363–428.

Mattingly, Daniel C. 2016. "Elite Capture: How Decentralization and Informal Institutions Weaken Property Rights in China." *World Politics* 68(3): 383–412.

Mei, Ciqi, and Margaret M. Pearson. 2014. "Killing a Chicken to Scare the Monkeys? Deterrence Failure and Local Defiance in China." *China Journal* 72: 75–97.

Mertha, Andrew. 2009. "Fragmented Authoritarianism 2.0: Political Pluralization in the Chinese Policy Process." *The China Quarterly* 200: 995–1012.

Meyer, David. 2004. "Protest and Political Opportunities." *Annual Review of Sociology* 30: 125–45.

Munson, Ziad W. 2010. *The Making of Pro-life Activists*. Chicago: University of Chicago Press.

Noakes, John A., and Hank Johnston. 2005. "Frames of Protest: A Roadmap to a Perspective." In Hank Johnston and John A. Noakes, eds., *Frames of Protest: Social Movements and the Framing Perspective*, 1–32. Lanham, MD: Rowman and Littlefield.

O'Brien, Kevin J., and Yanhua Deng. 2015. "Repression Backfires: Tactical Radicalization and Protest Spectacle in Rural China." *Journal of Contemporary China* 24(93): 457–70.

O'Brien, Kevin J., and Yanhua Deng. 2017. "Preventing Protest One Person at a Time: Psychological Coercion and Relational Repression in China." *China Review* 17(2): 179–201.

O'Brien, Kevin J., and Neil J. Diamant. 2015. "Contentious Veterans: China's Retired Officers Speak Out." *Armed Forces & Society* 41(3): 563–81.

O'Brien, Kevin J., and Lianjiang Li. 1999. "Selective Policy Implementation in Rural China." *Comparative Politics* 31(2): 167–86.

———. 2006. *Rightful Resistance in Rural China*. New York: Cambridge University Press.

Olson, Mancur. 1993. "Dictatorship, Democracy, and Development." *American Political Science Review* 87(3): 567–76.

Ong, Lynette H. 2018. "Thugs and Outsourcing of State Repression in China." *China Journal* 80: 94–110.

Ortmann, Stephan. 2015. "The Umbrella Movement and Hong Kong's Protracted Democratization Process." *Asian Affairs* 46(1): 32–50.

Piven, Frances Fox, and Richard A. Cloward. 1979. *Poor People's Movements: Why They Succeed and How They Fail*. New York: Vintage Books.

Rowen, Ian. 2015. "Inside Taiwan's Sunflower Movement: Twenty-Four Days in a Student-Occupied Parliament, and the Future of the Region." *Journal of Asian Studies* 74(1): 5–21.

Santoro, Wayne A., and Gail M. McGuire. 1997. "Social Movement Insiders: The Impact of Institutional Activists on Affirmative Action and Comparable Worth Policies." *Social Problems* 44(4): 503–19.

Sargeson, Sally. 2013. "Violence as Development: Land Expropriation and China's Urbanization." *Journal of Peasant Studies* 40(6): 1063–85.

Siu, Helen F. 1992. *Agents and Victims in South China*. New Haven, CT: Yale University Press.

Smelser, Neil J. 1962. *Theory of Collective Behavior*. New York: Routledge and Kegan Paul.

Snow, David A., E. Burke Rochford, Jr., Steven K. Worden, and Robert D. Benford. 1986. "Framing Processes, Micromobilization, and Movement Participation." *American Sociological Review* 51(4): 464–81.

Snow, David, Robert Benford, Holly McCammon, Lyndi Hewitt, and Scott Fitzgerald. 2014. "The Emergence, Development, and Future of the Framing Perspective: 25+ Years Since 'Frame Alignment.'" *Mobilization: An International Quarterly* 19(1): 23–46.

Steinhardt, H. Christoph, and Fengshi Wu. 2016. "In the Name of the Public: Environmental Protest and the Changing Landscape of Popular Contention in China." *China Journal* 75: 61–82.

Tarrow, Sidney. 1994. *Power in Movement*. New York: Cambridge University Press.

Tian, Zili. 2014. "Farewell to Pingjiang" [in Chinese]. Accessed March 30, 2019. http://www.360doc.com/content/14/1115/ 13/14303931_425288520.shtml.

Wakeman, Frederic E. 1975. *The Fall of Imperial China*. New York: Free Press.

Wang, Quyu. 2014. "Yang Weijun Reported on Two Incumbent Provincial Party Secretaries in a Row" [in Chinese]. Accessed March 13, 2019. http://news.takungpao.com.hk/mainland/focus/2014-12/2857617_4.html.

Wong, Bin. 1997. *China Transformed*. Ithaca, NY: Cornell University Press.

Yan, Dingfei. 2014. "The Shifang Post-Protest Syndrome: A Dilemma for the Whole Country" [in Chinese]. *Southern Weekend* October 30. Accessed February 25, 2019. http://www.infzm.com/content/105194.

Yang, Dali. 2017. "China's Troubled Quest for Order: Leadership, Organization, and the Contradictions of the Stability Maintenance Regime." *Journal of Contemporary China* 26(203): 35–53.

Yang, Guobin. 2009. *The Power of the Internet in China*. New York: Columbia University Press.

Yang, Lanxi. 2011. "Tragedies Under the Free Mandatory Education System" [in Chinese]. Accessed February 27, 2019. http://bbs.tianya.cn/post-free-2261517-3.shtml#213_85393957.

Zhan, Jing Vivian. 2017. "Do Natural Resources Breed Corruption? Evidence from China." *Environmental and Resource Economics* 66(2): 237–59.

Zhang, Huan. 2014. "92-Year-Old Yang Weijun: Combating Corruption for over a Decade" [in Chinese]. *People's Net*, September 9. http://yuqing.people.com.cn/n/2014/0909/c383249-25627639.html.

Zhang, Liuchang. 2014. "Exposing Bai Enpei" [in Chinese]. *First Finance Net*, August 30. https:// www.yicai.com/news/4013708.html.

Zhang, Wu. 2015a. "Protest Leadership and State Boundaries: Protest Diffusion in Contemporary China." *The China Quarterly* 222: 360–79.

———. 2015b. "Leadership, Organization and Moral Authority: Explaining Peasant Militancy in Contemporary China." *China Journal* 73: 59–83.

Zhang, Yang. 2018. "Allies in Action: Institutional Actors and Grassroots Environmental Activism in China." In Patrick G. Coy, ed., *Research in Social Movements, Conflicts and Change 42*, 9–38. Bingley, UK: Emerald Publishing Limited.

Zhou, Kai, and Xiaojun Yan. 2014. "The Quest for Stability." *Problems of Post-Communism* 61(3): 3–17.

Zhou, Qingshu. 2014. "Behind the Resignation of the Pingjiang County Party Secretary in Hunan" [in Chinese]. *New Beijing Daily*, November 24: A16–17. Accessed March 13, 2019. http://www.chinanews.com/gn/2014/11-24/6805533_2.shtml.

Zhou, Xueguang. 2016. "The Separation of Officials from Local Staff: The Logic of the Empire and Personnel Management in the Chinese Bureaucracy." *Chinese Journal of Sociology* 2(2): 259–99.

Zhu, Zheng. 2015. "The Three Choices of Yang Weijun" [in Chinese]. *Southern Weekends*, February 6. Accessed February 25, 2019. http://www.infzm.com/content/107729.

Chapter Six

"Lawyering Repression" and Protest Demobilization Under Rule of Law Authoritarianism

Yue Xie (Shanghai Jiao Tong University)

Scholars who study the protest-coercion relationship have concisely categorized repression into hard and soft types according to coercive forms and severity of sanctions (della Porta and Reiter 1998; Ferree 2005; Linden and Klandermans 2006). To maintain law and order or defend the ruling power, hard repression typically operates violently and often results in material losses, physical damage, widespread arrests, and sometimes death. Hard repression in democracies, although sometimes present, is generally less evident than under authoritarian systems (Carey 2009: 16–18). It is "costly, rude, and potentially dangerous for authorities" (McCarthy, Britt, and Wolfson 1991: 49) because excessive reliance on hard repression can lead to a backlash in the short term and reduce the ruling party's legitimacy in the long term (Brockett 1993; Lichbach 1987; Loveman 1998; Goldstone and Tilly 2001; Francisco 2005).

Considering the social and political risks of hard repression, states often develop tactics in a soft repressive repertoire that includes stigmatization (Linden and Klandermans 2006), ridicule, and silence (Ferree 2005). However, scholarship on soft repression under democracy and authoritarianism has theoretical gaps. Studies of soft repression in democracies outnumber those in authoritarian systems, and regarding the agents of soft repression, nonstate actors in democracies received more attention than those in authoritarian regimes (Earl 2003; Ferree 2005). This study attempts to fill these gaps and deepen our understanding of soft repression by focusing on a particular type of soft repression in the People's Republic of China that uses lawyers and their dependence of state institutions to limit collective action.

In communist China, rule-of-law reforms since 1980 have fueled the large number of individual and collective challenges, which often are directed against local governments violating laws. Citizens defend their interests and rights by using the courts, petitioning offices, and collective protest actions, often in combination (Diamant, Lubman, and O'Brien 2005; O'Brien and Li 2006). To defuse tense disputes, the regime actively mobilizes lawyers who ostensibly draw on their professional training and independence from state authority to assist in dispute-resolution processes to settle citizen grievances through mediation rather than judicial decisions. Yet using a mix of political pressure and material rewards, the state inclines lawyers to moderate disputes in a manner that wavers between legality and illegality, forcing people with grievances to accept the lawyers' mediation offers (*tiaojie*), often at the expense of the claimants' interests and rights. Thus, this kind of repression operates in a hidden and nonviolent manner in the name of abiding by the law, and claimants may not be conscious of their own losses with respect to interests, rights, or both. In exchange, claimants who receive redress must make a credible commitment to settlement and withdrawal of their challenges. In the study of contentious politics, soft repression is an understudied dimension of state repression, especially in authoritarian states. These "soft" tactics that work through the legal system are compelling and fascinating in their creative ways to dampen collective challenges to the Chinese party-state.

I call these tactics "lawyering repression," and discuss them here as an innovative strategy invented within rule-of-law authoritarianism to demobilize groups with grievances by means of nonstate actors. The strategy involves the interaction of the state, society, and third parties (e.g., lawyers), and was made possible by reforms that originally favored legal mobilization (Burstein 1991). Few studies of contentious politics have focused on why and how nonstate actors implement repressive policies, how an authoritarian regime can successfully demobilize aggrieved citizens legally, peacefully, and "softly," and why aggrieved citizens may switch from a strategy of mobilization to demobilization. By analyzing the tactics of lawyering repression, this chapter describes the causal relationship between soft repression enforced by nonstate actors and demobilization. This is a perspective that differs from most studies of contentious politics that prioritize the causal relationship between hard repression and demobilization.

To explain these relationships I draw on the process-mechanism language characteristic of the dynamics of contention (DOC) approach (McAdam, Tarrow, and Tilly 1997, 2001; Tilly 2008; McAdam and Tarrow 2011). The authors of DOC advocated for a dynamic and interactive approach that simultaneously considers the roles of structural, rationalist, and cultural elements to seek causal explanations for collective contention. Introduced more than twenty years ago, the goal was to move beyond static theories of political process and mobilization structures toward a more dynamic and processual understanding of the field. An original DOC goal was to specify the "big" fundamental processes of contentious politics and then identify the intervening mechanisms at work within these field-defining processes.

Mechanisms are "delimited changes that alter relations among specified sets of elements in identical or closely similar ways over a variety of situations," and processes are "regular sequences of such mechanisms that produce similar (generally more complex and contingent) transformations of those elements" (McAdam, Tarrow, and Tilly 2001: 24). In the process-mechanism approach, mobilization is considered a dependent variable caused by several recurring mechanisms.[1] In contrast, the process of demobilization—especially soft repressive elements—has received much less attention in the scholarly community in terms of its conditions and dynamics (Tilly and Tarrow 2015: 127). Later, Tilly (2005: 225) defined demobilization as a process in which people stop making contentious claims and cease engaging in contentious politics. Thus, this study focuses on the general process of demobilization and offers a close analysis of the soft mechanisms of lawyering repression in the hope of contributing to our understanding of how authoritarian states limit and repress contentious politics.

NONSTATE ACTORS, SOFT REPRESSION, AND DEMOBILIZATION

Studies of soft repression in democracies have demonstrated that nonstate actors are less likely to be linked to coercive repression than state actors. Rulers bear high political risk in cases of excessive and explicit violence, particularly large-scale massacres (McCarthy et al. 1991: 49) because violence can induce backlash, which leads to escalating violence and stronger antiregime mobilization (Lichbach 1987; Brockett 1993; Loveman 1998; Goldstone and Tilly 2001; Francisco 2005). Ferree (2005) conceptualized the soft repression tactics exerted by private agents in the American feminist movement in terms of ridicule, stigma, and silence. She noted that soft repression could demobilize movements by preventing the formation of collective identities and ideas that support cognitive liberation or oppositional consciousness (Ferree 2005: 141). Linden and Klandermans (2006) expanded on Ferree's findings by discussing the interactive relationship between soft and hard repression enforced by private agents and state actors. They concluded that media "stigmatization" primed public sentiment for the harsh repression of extreme-right groups in democratic Germany. Soft repression laid the foundation for hard repression because of the media's negative characterization of the movement.

The rationale by which private agents engage in coercive activities is sometimes identical in authoritarian regimes and democracies. Dictators prefer soft repression by private agents to avoid backlash and protest escalation (Brockett 1993). In developing countries such as Kenya and Rwanda, rulers used private agents not formally linked to state security forces to provide cover regarding international opinion (Roessler 2005). In the Middle East, the Jordanian government used third parties such as thugs, media, and tribal heads to repress challengers in a soft manner (Moss 2014: 270). They did this because reformers included members of the royal family and some tribal elites, and they wanted to protect them from hard repression. In communist China, local governments tend to use various soft methods to defuse contention and repress claim making, such as "informal repression" (Chen 2017; Fu 2017; Ong 2018) and "relational repression" (Deng and O'Brien 2013). Contradictory directives from the central government—such as requiring local agencies to refrain from violent repression while simultaneously requiring that they achieve prioritized targets in security, economic growth, and environmental protection (Xie 2012)—encourage local governments to repress protests as softly as possible by means of thugs, contracted laborers, and bureaucrats.

I see three shortcomings or omissions that run through this literature on soft repression. First, case studies of repression under authoritarianism tend to draw clear boundaries between independent and dependent private agents, ignoring variations in degree of dependence. For example, using thugs to quiet dissent—in Jordan (Moss 2014) and in China (Ong 2018)—means employing actors with weaker links to the regime than, say, using state-run media or grassroots bureaucrats (Deng and O'Brien 2013; Chen 2017). The two are not comparable because the latter's institutional connections to the state are stronger. Second, many of the cases of soft repression occur at local levels and are not generalizable nationally as state policy. These first two points mean that much of the soft repression literature is not helpful for comparative research among different state systems. Third, few studies explicitly connect soft repression by nonstate agents to the institutional structures of authoritarianism. Most studies assess authoritarianism only in the abstract, rather than specifying the factors of a regime that influence and organize repressive activities. Consequently, macrolevel political institutions appear unrelated to microlevel actions. Lawyering repression in communist China, as I define it here, is conducted by lawyers who are organized by the regime, and who ostensibly represent ordinary citizens, mostly petitioners whose interests and rights—while protected by law—have been violated by local officials and government agencies. Chinese lawyers constitute a group that is institutionalized but independent of the regime. They are legally distinguished from authority as well as from society. The mechanism of lawyering repression is distinct from other forms of soft repression because in China it is a national policy consistently exercised, rather than a local and temporary tactic, occurring in the context of the Chinese Communist Party's (CCP) dedication to rule-of-law reform. This makes it a significant strategy of demobilization of contentious politics in contemporary China. Following Earl (2003: 59), it holds the potential to tell us more about the structure of political opportunities of soft repression than cases of nonstate-actor soft repression in democracies.

THE MECHANISM OF LAWYERING REPRESSION

In China, legal collective action occurs in the context or the regime's initiation of rule-of-law reforms, particularly in terms of rights protection, citizenship, and power restriction. Legal collective action includes various contentious strategies, such as collective or individual litigation, petitioning upward ("lettering and visiting" or *xinfang* in Chinese), and street protests. Sometimes all three are used in combination by aggrieved groups of citizens. Legal mobilization in China can be ascribed to this extension of rights to which citizens are entitled. Urban residents can learn about their rights and how to defend their interests and rights by legal means, and the regime attempts to subject its citizens to its laws through consistent education about laws (Gallagher 2006, 2017). For example, with the help of nongovernmental organizations, migrant workers can sue employers who have not abided by labor laws (Fu 2017). The increase of either "rule consciousness" or "rights consciousness" was accompanied with the extension of the petitioning practices of xinfang (Li 2010). Inspired by intellectuals, the media, and lawyers, petitioners understand not only the law but also judicial procedures.

Citizens often resort to petitioning upward to higher levels of administration. Xinfang is rooted in the historical tradition of Confucianism, and is an institution that embodies the principle of populism and ultimately serves communist rule. By petitioning, the populace can directly voice their grievances by writing and visiting higher-level divisions of the party-state apparatus, including the central government in Beijing. In addition, xinfang functions as a means to monitor the numerous principal political agents (Townsend 1969; O'Brien and Li 2006; Lorentzen 2013). The central government does not allow its subordinate agencies to violently crack down on lawful petitioning and instead advocates settling disputes through soft methods. However, petitioning upward occasionally escalates into contentious action and even collective violence (Li and O'Brien 2008), which undermines the party and state's image image, and thus threatens their legitimacy their legitimacy (O'Brien and Li 2006). In these cases, the regime often mobilizes lawyers to defuse disputes through mediation of claims and grievances.[2]

Episodes of "lawyering repression" involve interactions among petitioners, lawyers, and the regime. These interactions enable the demobilization of xinfang petitions and collective actions through a combination of three crucial submechanisms.

First, there is the informal dependence of lawyers on the regime. Although formally independent of the state, lawyers and their firms tend to establish informal dependencies with authorities. Lawyers may be fearful of punishments because of the cases they take. They may seek political protection by developing beneficial personal relationships with officials. Finally, the judicial system can easily manipulate lawyers by monopolizing resources and intervening in case investigations.

The second submechanism constitutes a cultural construction and reinforcement of fundamental principles that most lawyers in China readily agree on, such as rule of law and social harmony. It is a type of counterframing by the regime that disposes lawyers to cooperate to mitigate contentious litigation and encourages them to manage petitioning disputes through mediation. In the minds of many legal professionals, this might be considered inconsistent with the principles of the protection of rights and the rule of law, but authorities have managed to construct a new narrative that everyone can agree to—a new "legal consensus," which encourages mediation rather than litigation. This new consensus functions as a submechanism of soft repression and is based on the social construction of a counterframe that limits collective action and favors the regime's goals rather than petitioners.

The third submechanism of legal demobilization I label "citizenship bargaining." Petitioners often emphasize the rights and collective identity entailed in citizenship and use constitutionally guaranteed rights as a weapon to pressure local governments in petitions. Lawyers tend to defuse this collective identity by focusing on individual settlements. Both the regime and the lawyers understand the demobilizing effect when collective identity among petitioners is undermined. Although lawyers often sympathize with and stand by the victims they represent, they also may ignore or even criticize their collective claims of human rights abuses engendered in citizenship.

In the next sections, I analyze these three submechanisms of lawyering repression. I base my analysis on data gathered during three years of fieldwork conducted mainly in the megacities of Shanghai, Beijing, and Nanjing. I interviewed twenty-four lawyers employed by eleven law firms. I also interviewed twenty-six petitioners whose legal claims and petitioning activities were "softly repressed" by lawyers. A third group of interviewees consisted of thirty local cadres who were directly responsible for judicial affairs involving lawyering management. All the interview participants were involved in a nationwide policy targeted at defusing disputes between petitioners and officials regarding urban household demolitions.

LAWYERS INFORMALLY DEPENDENT ON POLITICS

Between 1980 and 2007, rule of law reforms focused on formally separating lawyers from overt control by political institutions. Chinese lawyers and their firms were gradually liberated from the monolithic political control of the CCP.[3] According to a new Lawyers' Law in 1996, lawyers became financially independent of the official legal organs and could provide professional services for all clients. Based on Western legal professionalism, the regime established the Chinese Lawyers' Society (CLS), a national association to protect its members' rights. As the practice of law became institutionalized, aggrieved citizens seized on the political opportunities created by these reforms. In particular, ordinary citizens, through lawyers, gained the right to sue local governments. Yet, collective action through legal channels, sometimes involving lawyers joining with their clients to file lawsuits, placed pressure on the state and has led to backlash. Crackdowns have escalated recently to subjugate lawyers to the regime, and political opportunities have contracted slightly.

Personal Incentives for Dependence

The Lawyers' Law, while officially cutting ties between local cadres and lawyers, did not prohibit active personal relations among them (Michelson 2007). Most lawyers I interviewed for this study acknowledged that maintaining private connections with officials holding power in the judiciary system was overwhelmingly vital for client business (Lo and Snape 2005). Such reciprocal relationships have been conceptualized as a "symbiotic exchange" process (Liu 2011). Lawyers exchange social and material help with officials who monopolize the administration of justice and distribution of key resources, and in return, officials give case referrals, allocate projects, and make payments from the state and judicial agencies. Although this symbiotic exchange represents a key dimension of lawyering politics in China, my research reveals that it ignores several equally crucial points.

The first incentive for lawyers to approach legal officials and establish personal relationships entails the expectation of gaining more traction in the lucrative lawyering market. Increasing financial investment in public legal services has expanded the market and increased competition. Figure 6.1 indicates that financial investment in 2010 was as much as 958 million yuan,

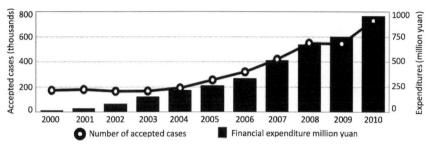

Figure 6.1. Financial Expenditures and Number of Cases Accepted by Courts 2000–2010
Source: *The Yearbook of Chinese Laws, 2001–2011*. Beijing: The Yearbook Press of Chinese Laws

more than fifty times that in 2001 (18.7 million yuan), and the number of cases accepted by courts was 727,401 in 2010, nearly six times that in 2001 (132,097 cases). The large financial investment indicates that the state exerts significant leverage in the lawyering market. By manipulating the allocation of these expenditures, official judicial agencies can easily make lawyers rely on them financially. A prominent lawyer interviewed for this study confirmed this reality and opined that small bars rely more heavily on the judicial system than large ones do (NJ2019001).[4] Additionally, maintaining close ties with officials helps enhance competitiveness in the lawyering market, even though the benefits could be limited (Gelatt 1991). Clients have high regard for lawyers with government connections because they are perceived to have more lawyering capacity (SH2019003). Unsurprisingly, both lawyers and firms greatly respect honors awarded by the justice system. All interviewed lawyers confirmed this, claiming that the regime's assessment is more valuable than how much will be charged.

Second, the dynamics that encourage lawyers to extend their social ties can reduce the costs of defending cases. In situations in which public security, courts, and procuratorates combine to dominate the full process of investigating a lawsuit, lawyers commonly must consider whether and to what extent these departments open investigations to them. When clients are criminal suspects, lawyers often face difficulties in collecting evidence, meeting their clients, and reading case files (Wang 2004). One survey indicated that meeting criminal suspects during police investigations remains the most problematic procedural hurdle. Nearly 70 percent of the respondents reported it to be one of the most difficult problems, and 57 percent reported difficulty in collecting evidence (Liu and Halliday 2016: 50–51).

Third, considering their personal safety, lawyers expect to be protected under the umbrella of justice agencies against being illegally punished through actions such as being beaten, detained, or imprisoned (Michelson 2007). A CLS's report found that, in reality, lawyers' rights were increasingly violated between 2015 and 2017, with 109 cases in 2015, 136 in 2016, and 422 in 2017 (September 3, 2018). Moreover, lawyers with criminals as clients are illegally punished because the procuracy acts as both the prosecutor and the supervisor. This power imbalance leads procurators to often abuse Article 306 of the Criminal Law as a tool of vengeance against uncooperative lawyers. Cited under Article 306, most accused lawyers were wrongly prosecuted and imprisoned for evidence fraud. An unpublished survey revealed that between 1997 and 2002, more than 500 lawyers were convicted under Article 306 (Lynch 2010).

Political Dynamics of Lawyering Dependence

By taking advantage of political opportunities generated by legal reforms to organize judicial resistance within or outside courts, both those with grievances and lawyer groups ultimately exasperate the single-party regime (Brockett 2005: 230; Lynch 2010), which no longer tolerates these activist lawyers and has ruthlessly repressed legal mobilization (Clarke 2009; Pils 2014). Moreover, provoked by a couple of transformative events (Pils 2014), the regime has used aggressive measures to "domesticate" all lawyers. The first event involved thirty-five rights lawyers publishing a collective open letter challenging the legitimacy of Beijing's CLS and calling for democratic elections. The other was related to the Charter '08 movement, which was primarily organized by Liu Xiaobo, a renowned Chinese dissident and 2010 winner of the Nobel Peace Prize. Most of the radical rights lawyers signed on in support of Liu's advocacy. The regime's aggressive measures mainly consisted of, first, directly intervening in internal lawyering affairs and, second, politicizing lawyers by absorbing them into the CCP.

Sectors of justice management, namely the Ministry of Justice (MOJ) at the national level and its subsidiary agencies, have emphasized administrative intervention in the lawyering business since 2008. The CLS in affiliation with the MOJ has made efforts to implement the will of the state (Lynch 2010) and promulgate policies that force lawyers to abstain from representing lawsuits that frequently involve or accompany collective contentions such as xinfang. Acceptance of these types of lawsuits, which are defined as highly sensitive, is tightly controlled through various rules: (a) all agency decisions must be made collectively by a law firm instead of by individual lawyers, (b) before accepting such cases, any firm's decision must be endorsed by the local justice agency, and (c) any firm disobeying these rules is to be held fully accountable for any negative consequences. These methods are unofficial but are nevertheless put into practice to punish defiant lawyers and their affiliated firms. The most influential punishment is delicensing of troublesome lawyers and firms, which sometimes takes the form of preventing lawyers from passing the annual licensing renewal (Clarke 2009). In 2013 alone in Beijing, approximately ten law firms and more than ten "rights lawyers" failed to be relicensed, thus effectively becoming disqualified to practice law and closing their businesses (Yang 2013). Sometimes authorities intimidate law firms with the threat of relicensing failure to pressure them into firing lawyers who disregard the MOJ regulations (Liu 2014). These punitive measures contribute to increasing deference to the authority of MOJ and CLS among lawyers and law firms and have created a sense among all law professionals that they must comply with and depend on the authorities (SH2009002).

As part of the project to "domesticate" lawyers, by the mid-2000s, the regime had systematically co-opted elite lawyers into the party-state apparatus. Local communist party committees directly installed branches in law firms and recruited lawyers as members. By the end of 2016, all provincial divisions of the CLS had established party committees. Of more than 26,000 law firms, 16,500 had established party branches, and among more than 340,000 qualified lawyers, more than 100,000 were party members, accounting for 31 percent of lawyers nationwide (Shao 2017). Additionally, numerous politically loyal lawyers have been assigned by the CCP to serve as delegates of the People's Congress at various levels in forms parallel to those of a parliament in democracies. In 2018 alone, a record twenty-two lawyers attended the Thirteenth National People's Congress. At the grassroots level, political cooption involves many more lawyers. Even among the interviewed firms, no one was excluded from the party's branches. At least half of the lawyers had been members of the party, and three directors were or are members of the local People's Congress. They confirmed the positive role such political identities play in encouraging lawyers to be subject to the state's will (SH2019A001, SH2019A003, SH2019006).

CONSTRUCTION OF LEGAL CONSENSUS

In addition to the incentives—personal, political, and material—the regime has constructed a cultural narrative to encourage the cooperation of lawyers. It uses a concise slogan, *yifa zhiguo* (governing the country by law, or hereafter, GCBL), as a discursive construction that functions as a counterframe (Snow and Benford 1992) to limit collective action and facilitate soft repression.

GCBL is both ambiguous and flexible. It can be understood as either "rule of law" or "rule by law," with important distinctions between the two. For example, dissenting citizens and activist lawyers have launched rights-defending challenges in the past under the rule-of-law constitutional framework. In contrast, a rule-by-law interpretation provides the state with a lawful basis for constraining contentious action by emphasizing the interests of the whole society and the overall ruling order over individual rights and interests. The result is that, on the one hand, GCBL corresponds with the principle of the rule of law and sends a strong signal to lawyers that constitutionalism in China is acceptable. This possibility resonates with lawyers' ideals of fairness and justice. On the other hand, lawyers draw on the cultural tradition of Chinese law by conceding that mediation is a supplementary function that lawyers have always performed. In sum, this two-pronged interpretation of GCBL postulates that collectivism and the supremacy of the state's interests should guide legal settlements.

Inventing Constitutional Discourses

In the post-Mao era, legal reform was triggered by several factors, such as the consolidation of institutional capacity, a desire for increased political legitimacy (Moustafa 2007: 39), as well as the opening to foreign direct investment (Wang 2015). Early reforms progressed on the basis of rule-of-law rhetoric. First, the Constitution was rewritten in the early 1980s and articles concerning the protection of human rights and checks on authority were added in 1982 (and remain unchanged to this day). In 1987, the Congress dominated under the CCP passed the rule that "any organization cannot exercise power beyond laws." Party General Secretary Jiang Zemin (1989 to 2002) and his successors Hu Jingtao and Xi Jinping continued this policy, embracing the legal discourse of "rule of law," "rule by law," and "governing the country by law," as measured by their frequent usage in public speeches during the party conferences (see figure 6.2). Thus, the construction of the GCBL constitutional discourse continued, even though the spirit of the rule of law has degenerated recently (Minzner 2018).

Strikingly, on July 9, 2015, the Ministry of Public Security organized a nationwide repressive crackdown, resulting in the arrest of more than three hundred rights lawyers, some of whom have been imprisoned (Fu 2018). Since then, the regime has attempted to placate lawyers through discursive strategies. In 2016, the party-state apparatus confirmed the centrality of lawyering institutions in not only protecting human rights but also enacting the GCBL strategy (Xinhua Agency 2016). In addition, lawyers are portrayed as mediators who can help the CCP maintain social order, educate citizens, and manage disputes. Lawyers' participation in xinfang mediation is praised as an innovation in legal reform. In official documents, the regime makes clear that lawyers are required to participate in mediation, abide by laws in reaching settlements, and to prioritize the rights and interests of petitioners. According to my interviews with

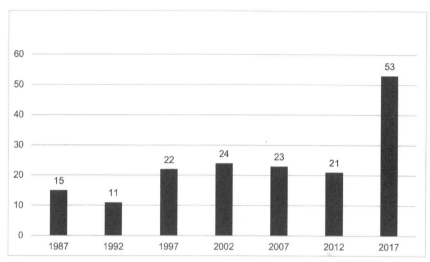

Figure 6.2. Frequency of Legal Discourse in Speeches of CCP General Secretaries, 1987–2017.

Note: The General Secretary of the Communist Party was Zhao Ziyang, who was politically purged because of his sympathy with the student movement of 1989.

the lawyers, such discursive proclamations were received positively. If officials invoked such a rule of law discourse, respondents admitted the impossibility of refusing local government's requests to participate in mediation (NJ2018B009, SH2019B008). Other interviewees viewed these discourses as idealistic but pragmatic in establishing the rule of law (SH2019A0011).

Rule of Law with Chinese Characteristics

Another discursive strategy is to draw on traditional cultural resources to emphasize mediation rather that litigation, encouraging a rule of law system with Chinese characteristics. My respondents often mentioned that Chinese judicial reform should not entirely be modeled after the West but should draw from the long history of traditional Chinese culture. Tiaojie (mediation) represents a traditional Chinese practice evolved from Confucianism that has been developed by the CCP into an out-of-court dispute resolution system. Mediation, not litigation, is considered to be preferable insofar because it emphasizes a stability-based morality that prioritizes the role of emotion over law to defuse disputes. The advantages of mediation over litigation include fewer hurt feelings among the involved parties, less time consumed, and quick resolution of disputes (Lubman 1967, 1997).The CCP has succeeded in revising the institution of tiaojie to fit its needs in maintaining an orderly and harmonious society.

During the Maoist era, mediation was widely employed to serve political purposes. Mediation organizations and policy enforcement were dominated by communist cadres at the grassroots level (Cohen 1966; Lubman 1967). Unlike its counterpart in the West, Chinese mediation is operated and manipulated by judges or officials, and sometimes participants are forced to accept negotiated positions that undermine their own interests and rights (Huang 2006). Post-Maoist legal reform accentuated legal professionalism and de-emphasized mediation in dispute resolution. However, since the mid-2000s the CCP has reemphasized tiaojie by opening it to more disputes than before and extending it beyond the judicial system. Numerous people such as retired cadres are recruited to assist in mediation processes, and grassroots courts are allowed to legalize bargained-for deals reached through mediation to guarantee higher efficiency (Xie 2012). Because lawyers are seen as more professional than amateur mediators, they have been increasingly mobilized into mediation[5]

Several interviewed lawyers and petitioners agreed with officials on the comparative advantages of using more lawyers (SH2019A002, SH2019C001, SH2019C003, SH2019C0015). They argued that governmental officials and judges represent state authority and, therefore, cannot be impartial. Most amateur mediators are perceived to act on behalf of local governments' interests. Interviewees also mentioned the practical advantages of mediation over litigation (SH2019A008, SH2019A010). They said mediation is simpler, less restrictive, and thus more efficient. Mediated disputes must be closed within thirty days, whereas the litigation process has no time restriction.[6]

Lawyering in Collectivism

Another discursive construction that draws on Chinese culture is collectivism, a perspective that has prevailed in Chinese society for more than two thousand years and is, of course, reflected in communist ideology. It is engrained by the CCP in lawyering culture and has been widely accepted by lawyers. The core principle of collectivism is that lawyers should prioritize collective interests over private interests, although at times, the protection of private interests better protects collective interests (Liebman 1999). One lawyer that I interviewed observed that he did not engage in public mediation service to maximize business because it was time consuming and paid little (SH2019A007). He continued by stating that only by recognizing the supremacy of collective interests would a lawyer sacrifice his individual interests this way. In practice, the primacy of collective interests typically blends with those of the CCP. Recently, the MOJ (2019) asked lawyers to serve the people as their utmost mission.

To reinforce collectivism, lawyers who are perceived to lack the spirit of public service are publicly criticized. A former MOJ minister (Zhang 2014) denounced lawyers' tendency to focus on clients and ignore public legal services. A spirit of public service has become a key element by which the CCP mobilizes lawyers to participate in xinfang mediation. However, I close this section by pointing out that in addition to collectivist appeals, the MOJ recruits lawyers through practical means mentioned previously, for example, by promoting mediation as an opportunity to enhance social reputation and to expand a firm's market share (MOJ 2019). Several interviewees affirmed these private incentives and acknowledged that practicing mediation would create opportunities to maintain ties with local governments, accumulate social credits, and increase their lawyering competitiveness (SH2019A002, SH2019A008, BJ2018A002).

CITIZENSHIP BARGAINING

McAdam (2004) discusses a mechanism for mobilization whereby third-party sympathizers support and collectively identify with protesters. I suggest that there is a corresponding mechanism of soft repression by which a third party demobilizes protesters by dampening and fragmenting their collective identity. Regarding lawyering repression, I will discuss in this section how third-party lawyers (or brokers) inhibit the collective identity of petitioners by drawing on different elements in the concept of citizenship (*gongmin*). Notably, gongmin has been actively confirmed and institutionalized by the single-party regime in China. In this section I will analyze how officially mobilized lawyers engage in "citizenship bargaining" by playing upon two distinct interpretations—"rights consciousness" versus "rules consciousness"—with the effect of inhibiting the mobilization function of collective identity formation and encouraging claimants to relinquish their collective rights.

Gongmin was introduced in the first Constitution in 1954 but was not used to designate people of Chinese nationality in the 1982 Constitution. In a 2004 constitutional amendment, the first connection between gongmin and human rights was established, replacing the concept of the "people" (*renmin*), which was used to exclude those who were considered enemies of the state (Goldman and Perry 2002: 7). However, as in other authoritarian regimes, the CCP has adopted a distinct definition of citizenship, which emphasizes obligations more than rights (Ginsburg and Moustafa 2008). Additionally, the current party strategy is to reinforce the practice of social rights and the basic well-being of all but to provide fewer civil and political rights (Dickson 2002: 258–59). Because political participation is a particularly crucial dimension of measuring citizenship, the CCP has incrementally opened its political system to civil society since the 1980s. However, this opening was achieved selectively, allowing certain voices into the process while excluding others (Goldman 2005). Activists who sought political reform were persecuted, detained, and even imprisoned for their actions, without exception.

In a period of rapid social change, and to guide an emergent understanding of citizenship that synchronizes with the regime's definition, the CCP has instituted a series of policies for "law popularization" (*pufa* in Chinese) and "law aids" (*fayuan* in Chinese). Beginning in the 1980s, these have been the most influential policy initiatives among numerous top-down citizen-education projects that the regime sponsors. Both sets of policies have the political mission of molding citizens according to the regime's criteria, to not only obsequiously follow the state's laws but also actively protect law and order for the state. The discursive resources derive from the party's ideology predicated on the principles of socialism, collectivism, and patriotism. The key point is that these projects of citizenship-related education are fundamentally conducive to disaggregating the collective identity that all citizens should share (Chen 2018: 14) and promoting rule consciousness instead of rights consciousness (Li 2010). Consequently, contentious collective actions based on citizens' rights are difficult to initiate and sustain in a coordinated manner.

Citizen education has become an increasing concern of the regime, and lawyers have become major participants because of their professional advantages. Using appeals to the spirit of public service mentioned previously, the regime mobilizes lawyers to educate citizens on judicial policies and how to make legal claims for their interests. Regardless of the service they provide (pufa, fayuan, or tiaojie), lawyers have no autonomy to deviate from the rule-by-law framework. In other words, although citizens enjoy human rights on paper as written in the Constitution, lawyers cannot emphasize them in practice. The interviewed lawyers who had engaged in pufa, fayuan, and tiaojie all indicated that their interactions with individual citizens never exceeded the regime's definition of citizenship. Participation in citizen-education projects is compulsory for lawyers and their firms. All interviewed firms routinely performed legal services such as mediation in accordance with local judicial agencies' assignments. Several interviewed lawyers affirmed the positive function of the mediation process whereby petitioners can learn more about law and behave in a more law-abiding manner (SH2019A002, SHA2019A004, SH2019A006, NJ2018A001).

Table 6.1 shows that these citizen-education policies appear to have successfully imparted an understanding of the law as a basis to defend rights and interests. All thirty-four petitioners who I had interviewed were

Table 6.1. Profiles of Thirty-Four Petitioners on House-Demolition Disputes

Stated claim	Rights (23)	Illegal actions of government (29)	Redress (33)	Unemployed (1)	Mixed (26)
Channels for learning laws	Pufa (14)	Fayuan (0)	Taiojie (8)	Self-collection (16)	Mixed (13)
Defense strategy	Litigation (34)	Petitioning (34)	Violent action (0)	Accessing media (15)	Mixed (34)
Understanding of citizenship	Private rights above collective interests (5)	Collective rights over private interests (17)	Equally important (4)	Conditionally important (6)	No response (2)

Note: Totals add up to more than 34 because respondents reported in multiple categories.

involved in disputes concerning household demolition. The top row of "Stated Claims" lists that twenty-three petitioners based their claims on an understanding of rights and twenty-nine on an understanding of legality. Line 2, "Channels for learning laws" shows that more than half of the petitioners benefited from projects such as pufa and tiaojie (see also Gallagher 2006; Whiting 2017). Although most respondents received guidance from lawyers, the second row shows that a considerable number also acquired legal knowledge by themselves. With improved understanding of rights and laws, petitioners were able to report the wrongdoings of local governments (in table 6.1 regarding forced household removals) and to demand that their rights be respected and protected. Petitioners sued local governments and officials for violating related laws.

However, these interviews also revealed that citizen-education campaigns contributed to mitigating these challenges. According to the bottom row in table 6.1, "Understanding of Citizenship," seventeen respondents placed "collective responsibility above private rights"—identical to the regime's definition. Although twenty-three respondents reported claims for rights (column two, top), most were also concerned to negotiate for economic redress with government officials (column four, top: thirty-three). A pattern that emerged in the interviews was that, when petitioning upward, respondents tended to file grievances based on rights violations by local officials, but when bargaining with lawyers, they strategically altered their claims to focus on economic redress. Rights were used as a weapon initially, but this strategy changed when the lawyers entered the scene.

My interviews revealed that shifting from rights claims to financial claims was easy for some petitioners but difficult for others. Under the lawyers' repeated persuasion, a majority of the interviewed petitioners agreed to abandon demands that the government be held accountable. Only two respondents did not accept this recommendation, saying that their desire for justice was more meaningful than economic redress. Typically, a major condition of dispute settlement was that petitioners must stop petitioning upward to higher levels of government agencies, particularly to the central government in Beijing. Almost no one accepted this condition at first because, in their perspective, giving up the tool of skip-level petitions meant relinquishing a powerful weapon to force local governments to negotiate. Many respondents reported doubts about the promises made by local governments. Ultimately, the lawyers helped to allay these doubts, several being persuaded by the lawyers' admonishment that petitioning Beijing brought shame on the party and the state. Several petitioners reported that, in the end, they even regretted their contentious actions.

Transforming Collective Rights into Individual Interests

Based on interviews with both lawyers and petitioners, I identified four tactical patterns that were used to encourage petitioners to accept economic compensation through mediation rather than pursuing investigation of officials responsible for their grievances and claims. Broadly speaking, all four strategies focus on citizenship. One lawyer stated that both rights and interests of citizenship were equally indispensable for petitioners: rights relate to their face or respect and interests relate to their potential gain (BJ2019A003). Few interviewed petitioners made claims based only on rights, namely, seeking compensation without a rights claim, and only two respondents from my sample did not withdraw their rights claims. The challenge for lawyers was to maintain a balance between rights and interests in mediation, while simultaneously getting petitioners to withdraw their claim for rights and settle only for compensations.

Petitioners who experienced hardships and cumulative suffering often showed intense anger toward local cadres. The first tactic lawyers used was to quickly pacify petitioners by responding affirmatively to their claims for rights in a high-profile way. Lawyers, unlike local cadres, explicitly confirmed the legality of petitioners' claims and sometimes even of petitioning actions. The reasoning often heard was, "No one and no organization has power to refute or deny your claims because your rights are protected by the Constitution" (SH2018A002, SH2019A004; NJ2018A001). This tactic was often effective in appeasing angry petitioners who experienced deep and lasting disputes with cadres (SH2019A002).

When confirming the legality of petitioners' claims, lawyers often mitigated anger by a second tactic. They criticized radical actions by using the rhetoric of national interest and collectivism. During mediation, petitioners often reverted to disruptive repertoires when the amount of redress was unsatisfactory. Typically, lawyers appealed to collective interests to warn against and deter such actions. One lawyer warned a petitioner that his radical actions had broken normal social order and resulted in the loss of collective interests (SH2019A006). Another lawyer seriously denounced a petitioner who had been interviewed by Voice of America to discuss his suffering. In the lawyer's view, revealing his victimhood and injustices to a foreign organization not only humiliated the central government but also caused the entire Chinese population to lose face globally (SH2019A003). Both of these lawyers stated that the petitioners ultimately apologized for these actions and expressed satisfaction with redress.

A third tactic was related to pragmatism. In their mediation activities, lawyers frequently encouraged petitioners not to sacrifice their pressing material needs. Nearly all interviewed petitioners lived in poverty with little dignity. For many, long-term petitioning led to unemployment, divorce, and homelessness. Some petitioners made many trips between Beijing and their home cities, while enduring local governments' ridicule and labeling as social pariahs. Pursuing their claims had driven many petitioners into destitution and social isolation. One lawyer attributed his successful mediation to his insights into petitioners' predicaments (SH2019A008). A petitioner's household was removed fifteen years ago, and he lost his job two years later. Within ten months, his wife divorced him and left their daughter behind. Because his long-term petitioning efforts had exerted heavy pressure on his daughter, she grew to hate him and left him one year ago. The lawyer seized on this petitioner's vulnerabilities and persuaded him to accept redress. He was finally moved when the lawyer ensured he would have a bright future and a normal happy life if he withdrew the rights claim and accepted redress. In his interview, the petitioner acknowledged that "being as rich as others" was the most crucial aspect for ending his dispute with the local government (SH2019C005).

Finally, regarding collective contentions lawyers appear to have learned from the regime a final tactic: creating divisions among petitioners. In a collective petition, those who obtain redress typically must swear to not reveal the compensation amount to their counterparts. To pay as little as possible, local governments usually "divide and conquer" to separate the collective rights claims from material interests, even when petitioners have a strong collective consciousness and similar claims. For individual petitioners, accepting this condition is easy because lawyers tend to exaggerate the redress amounts. Although lawyers guarantee claimants that their redress is maximized, they often warn that redress may fail if the amount is revealed. An illegal demolition case involved 505 households in one location. Under consistent contentious pressure, the local government agreed to mediate the dispute through lawyers. The lawyers isolated claimants from each other to ensure that no one knew how much their neighbors received in the negotiation process. However, nearly all individual households with the same background and similar claims were compensated differently.

CONCLUSION

Lawyering repression is an innovative repertoire in the toolkit of authoritarian coercion that has never been addressed in scholarship on contentious politics. It has emerged from citizens taking advantage of political opportunities created by rule of law reform to participate in legal mobilization and subsequent contentious actions, individually or collectively, to challenge authoritarian rule. Lawyering repression as a type of soft repression makes practical contributions to authoritarian rule because soft repression by private actors, at least temporarily, can more effectively deescalate state-citizen disputes and sustain political legitimacy than can hard repression by state actors. Authoritarian responses to social challenges by means of lawyering repression alter conventional understandings of state repression. Specifically, soft repression is typically linked to democratic regimes, whereas autocracies are thought to be inclined to use coercive hard repression. This study's conceptualization of lawyering repression contributes to research on the mobilization-repression nexus. It focuses on the rarely addressed field of soft repression practiced by nonstate actors under authoritarianism. I believe lawyering repression offers more political opportunities as well as threats under authoritarianism than it does under a democracy.

To explain the causal relationship between lawyering repression and demobilization, this study drew on the process-mechanism approach developed by McAdam et al. (2001) and moved beyond theories of political process, mobilization structure, and cultural framing. Findings revealed the workings of the mechanism of lawyering repression—a soft strategy in the process of demobilization. My analysis identified several submechanisms in the interactions of three parties: the regime's agents, lawyers, and petitioners. Unlike causal explanations of mobilization by activists, these submechanisms describe the causes of demobilization by the regime. Such an exploration has rarely been undertaken in studies of demobilization under authoritarianism (McAdam 2004). A full relational analysis of contentious politics must consider the processes of demobilization as well as the processes of mobilization. Both are part of the contentious episodes that form cycles of protest (Tarrow 1994).

Finally, whether the three submechanisms identified here are applicable in various settings out of China should be investigated. According to the principles of DOC, empirically identified mechanisms are considered robust if they operate similarly under disparate conditions. The mechanisms identified here may feasibly be applied in various settings to demobilize contentious action regardless of the authoritarian or democratic context. However, the case of China suggests that such a process-mechanism explanation between demobilization and lawyering repression most likely applies to single-party authoritarian states that resemble communist China. Single-party authoritarian regimes, relative to other types of authoritarianism, are more inclined to concentrate attention on rule of law construction (Moustafa 2007) and respond to various grievances through softer means because they are more susceptible to challenges to their political legitimacy (Geddes 1999). Episodes of lawyering repression have not occurred under other political conditions, such as personal and military authoritarianism. Undoubtedly, further research to test the possibility and the degree to which these mechanisms operate would be valuable.

NOTES

1. These mechanisms are attribution of threat and opportunity, social appropriation, and social construction (McAdam, Tarrow, and Tilly 2001: 44–48).

2. This is an approach to professional law agency that contrasts with the prevailing model in the West of litigation through the court system.

3. The altered relationship between politics and lawyering is reflected in the shift in the official definition of lawyers from "workers of the state" in 1980 to "professionals" in 1996. According to the Lawyers' Law of 1996, which was the first to regulate lawyers and lawyering, lawyers were no longer legal cadres, could establish their own bar associations, were financially independent of the original legal organs, and could provide professional services for all clients.

4. These citations identify the anonymous interviews, distinguished by location (NJ: Nanjing, SH: Shanghai, and P: Peking), year, and sequence.

5. A top CLS official (Wang 2017) argued that lawyer mediation is more professional, independent, and efficient compared with that by cadres and judges.

6. It was also mentioned that mediation is more advantageous than litigation as local governments and cadres can escape administrative accountability as well as save face (SH2019A001, SH2019A005, NJ2018A001). Rational cadres are only concerned about their positions, and no one desires reprimand by higher-level leaders.

REFERENCES

Brockett, Charles.1993. "A Protest-Cycle Resolution of the Repression/Popular-Protest Paradox." *Social Science History* 17(3): 457–84.

———. 2005. *Political Movements and Violence in Central America*. Cambridge, UK: Cambridge University Press.

Burstein, Paul. 1991. "Legal Mobilization as a Social Movement Tactic: The Struggle for Equal Employment Opportunity." *American Journal of Sociology* 96(5): 1201–25.

Carey, Sabine C. 2009. *Protest, Repression and Political Regimes: An Empirical Analysis of Latin America and Sub-Saharan Africa*. New York: Routledge.

Chen, Sicong. 2018. *The Meaning of Citizenship in Contemporary Chinese Society: An Empirical Study through Western Lens*. Singapore: Springer.

Chen, Xi. 2017. "Origins of Informal Coercion in China." *Politics & Society* 45(1): 67–89.

Clarke, Donald. 2009. "Lawyers and the State in China: Recent Developments." Testimony before the Congressional-Executive Commission on China. Accessed January 16, 2021. https://www.cecc.gov/sites/chinacommission.house.gov/files/documents/hearings/2009/CECC%20Hearing%20Testimony%20-%20Donald%20Clarke%20-%2010.7.09.pdf.

Chinese Lawyer Society (CLS). *Statistic and Analysis on the Defending Rights of Lawyers in Half 2018*. Retrieved April 26, 2019. http://www.acla.org.cn/article/page/detailById/23923.

Cohen, Jerome A. 1966. "Chinese Mediation on the Eve of Modernization." *California Law Review* 54(3): 1201–26.

Della Porta, Donatella, and Herbert Reiter. 1998. "Introduction: The Policing of Protest in Western Democracies." In Donatella della Porta and Herbert Reiter, eds., *Policing Protest: The Control of Mass Demonstrations in Western Democracies*, 1–32. Minneapolis: University of Minnesota Press.

Deng, Yanhua, and Kevin J. O'Brien. 2013. "Relational Repression in China: Using Social Ties to Demobilize Protesters." *The China Quarterly* 215(3): 533–52.

Diamant, Neil Jeffrey, Stanley B. Lubman, and Kevin J. O'Brien. 2005. *Engaging the Law in China: State, Society, and Possibilities for Justice*. Stanford, CA: Stanford University Press.

Dickson, Bruce. 2002. "Do Good Businessmen Make Good Citizens?" In Merle Goldman and Elizabeth J. Perry, eds., *Changing the Meanings of Citizenship in Modern China*, 255–87. Cambridge, MA: Harvard University Press.

Earl, Jennifer. 2003. "Tanks, Tear Gas, and Tax: Toward a Theory of Movement Repression." *Sociological Theory* 21(1): 44–68.

Ferree, Myra Marx. 2005. "Soft Repression: Ridicule, Stigma, and Silencing in Gender-Based Movements." In Christian Davenport, Hank Johnston, and Carol Mueller, eds., *Repression and Mobilization*, 138–58. Minneapolis: University of Minnesota Press.

Francisco, Ronald. 2005. "The Dictator's Dilemma." In Christian Davenport, Hank Johnston, and Carol Mueller, eds., *Repression and Mobilization*, 58–84. Minneapolis: University of Minnesota Press.

Fu, Diana. 2017. *Mobilizing without the Masses: Control and Contention in China*. Cambridge, UK: Cambridge University Press.

Fu, Hualing. 2018. "The July 9th (709) Crackdown on Human Rights Lawyers: Legal Advocacy in an Authoritarian State." *Journal of Contemporary China* 27(112): 554–68.

Gallagher, Mary E. 2006. "Mobilizing the Law in China: 'Informed Disenchantment' and the Development of Legal Consciousness." *Law & Society Review* 40(4): 783–816.

———. 2017. *Authoritarian Legality in China: Law, Workers, and the State*. Cambridge, UK: Cambridge University Press.

Gelatt, Timothy A. 1991. "Lawyers in China: The Past Decade and Beyond." *New York University Journal of International Law and Politics* 23: 751–99.

Geddes, Barbara. 1999. "What Do We Know about Democratization after Twenty Years?" *Annual Review of Political Science* 2: 115–44.

Ginsburg, Tom, and Tamir Moustafa, eds. 2008. *Rule by Law: The Politics of Courts in Authoritarian Regimes*. Cambridge, UK: Cambridge University Press.

Goldman, Merle. 2005. *From Comrade to Citizen: The Struggle for Political Rights in China*. Cambridge, MA: Harvard University Press.

Goldman, Merle, and Elizabeth J. Perry. 2002. "Introduction: Political Citizenship in Modern China." In Merle Goldman and Elizabeth J. Perry, eds., *Changing the Meanings of Citizenship in Modern China*, 1–19. Cambridge, MA: Harvard University Press.

Goldstone, Jack A., and Charles Tilly. 2001. "Threat (and Opportunity): Popular Action and State Response in the Dynamics of Contentious Action." In Ronald R. Aminzade, Jack A. Goldstone, Doug McAdam, Elizabeth Perry, William H. Sewell, Jr., Sidney Tarrow, and Charles Tilly, eds., *Silence and Voice in the Study of Contentious Politics*, 179–94. New York: Cambridge University Press.

Huang, Philip. C. C. 2006. "Court Mediation in China, Past and Present." *Modern China* 32(3): 275–314.

Linden, Annette, and Bert Klandermans. 2006. "Stigmatization and Repression of Extreme-Right Activism in the Netherlands." *Mobilization: An International Journal* 11(2): 213–22.

Li, Lianjiang. 2010. "Rights Consciousness and Rules Consciousness in Contemporary China." *The China Journal* 64: 47–68.

Li, Lianjiang, and Kevin J. O'Brien. 2008. "Protest Leadership in Rural China." *The China Quarterly* 193(1): 1–23.

Lichbach, Mark Irving. 1987. "Deterrence or Escalation? The Puzzle of Aggregate Studies of Repression and Dissent." *Journal of Conflict Resolution* 31(2): 266–97.

Liu, Sida. 2011. "Lawyers, State Officials and Significant Others: Symbiotic Exchange in the Chinese Legal Services Market." *The China Quarterly* 206(2): 276–93.

———. 2014. "When Would Stop Re-Licensing Lawyers?" [Lvshi Nianjian Heshi Xiu]. *Caijing* [*Finance*]. March 23.

Liu, Sida, and Terence Halliday. 2016. *Criminal Defense in China: The Politics of Lawyers at Work*. New York: Cambridge University Press.

Lo, Carlos, and Ed Snape. 2005. "Lawyers in the People's Republic of China: A Study of Commitment and Professionalization." *The American Journal of Comparative Law* 53(2): 433–55.

Lorentzen, Peter L. 2013. "Regularizing Rioting: Permitting Public Protest in An Authoritarian Regime." *Quarterly Journal of Political Science* 8(2): 127–58.

Loveman, Mara. 1998. "High-Risk Collective Action: Defending Human Rights in Chile, Uruguay, and Argentina." *American Journal of Sociology* 104(2): 477–525.

Lubman, Stanley. 1967. "Mao and Mediation: Politics and Dispute Resolution in Communist China." *California Law Review* 55(5): 1284–359.

———. 1997. "Dispute Resolution in China after Deng Xiaoping: Mao and Mediation' Revisited." *Columbia Journal of Asian Law* 11(2): 229–391.

Lynch, Elizabeth M. 2010. "China's Rule of Law Mirage: The Regression of the Legal Profession since the Adoption of the 2007 Lawyers Law." *The George Washington International Law Review* 42: 536–85.

McAdam, Doug. 2004. "Revisiting the U.S. Civil Rights Movement: Toward a More Synthetic Understanding of the Origins of Contention." In Jeff Goodwin and James M. Jasper, eds., *Rethinking Social Movements: Structure, Meaning, and Emotion*, 201–32. New York: Rowman & Littlefield.

McAdam, Doug, and Sidney Tarrow. 2011. "The Dynamics of Contention Ten Years On." *Mobilization: An International Quarterly* 16(1): 1–10.

McAdam, Doug, Sidney Tarrow, and Charles Tilly. 1997. "Toward an Integrated Perspective Politics." In Mark Lichbach and Alan Zuckerman, eds., *Comparative Politics: Rationality, Culture, and Structure*, 142–73. Cambridge, UK: Cambridge University Press.

———. 2001. *Dynamics of Contention*. New York: Cambridge University Press.

McCarthy, John D., David W. Britt, and Mark Wolfson. 1991. "The Institutional Channeling of Social Movements by the State in the United States." *Research in Social Movements Conflicts, and Change* 13(2): 45–76.

Michelson, Ethan. 2007. "Lawyers, Political Embeddedness, and Institutional Continuity in China's Transition from Socialism." *American Journal of Sociology* 113(2): 352–414.

Minzner, Carl. 2018. *End of An Era: How China's Authoritarian Revival is Undermining Its Rise*. New York: Oxford University Press.

MOJ. 2019. "guanyu zhengqiu dui 'sifabu guanyu chujin lvshi canyu gongyi falv fuwu de yijian'de gonggao" [The Note on the Consultation on 'MOJ's Advice for Promoting Lawyers' Engagement in Public Law Service']. Retrieved May 16, 2019. http://www.moj.gov.cn/government_public/content/2019-04/24/gggs_233758.html.

Moss, Dana M. 2014. "Repression, Response, and Contained Escalation under Liberalized Authoritarianism in Jordan." *Mobilization: An International Quarterly* 19(3): 261–86.

Moustafa, Tamir. 2007. *The Struggle for Constitutional Power: Law, Politics and Economic Development in Egypt*. New York: Cambridge University Press.

O'Brien, Kevin J., and Lianjiang Li. 2006. *Rightful Resistance in Rural China*. New York: Cambridge University Press.

Ong, Lynette H. 2018. "Thugs and Outsourcing of State Repression in China." *China Journal* 80(1): 94–110.

Pils, Eva. 2014. *China's Human Rights Lawyers: Advocacy and Resistance.* New York: Routledge.

Roessler, Philip G. 2005. "Donor-Induced Democratization and the Privatization of State Violence in Kenya and Rwanda." *Comparative Politics* 37(2): 207–25.

Shao, Ke. 2017. "quanguo lvshi hangye dangwei chengli" [The Establishment of the Party's Commission in Lawyering Industry], October 31. Retrieved September 23, 2019. https://www.thepaper.cn/newsDetail_forward_1844494.

Snow, David, and Robert Benford. 1992. "Master Frames and Cycles of Protest." In Aldon Morris and Carol McClurg Mueller, eds., *Frontiers in Social Movement Theory*, 133–55. New Haven, CT: Yale University Press.

Tarrow, Sidney. 1994. *Power in Movement.* New York: Cambridge University Press.

Tilly, Charles. 2005. "Repression, Mobilization, and Explanation." In Christian Davenport, Hank Johnston, and Carol Mueller, eds., *Repression and Mobilization*, 211–26. Minneapolis: University of Minnesota Press.

———. 2008. *Explaining Social Processes.* Boulder, CO: Paradigm.

Tilly, Charles, and Sidney Tarrow. 2015. *Contentious Politics.* New York: Oxford University Press.

Townsend, James R. 1969. *Political Participation in Communist China.* Berkeley: University of California Press.

Wang, Chun. 2017. "lvshi xin juese: cong susong dailiren dao zhiye tiaojieren" [The New Role of Lawyers: From Agent to Mediator]. *Renmin zhoukan* [*The People Weekly*] 21: 18–19.

Wang, Chunbo. 2004. "lvshi zhiye fengxian xianzhuang de fenxi" [The Analyzing the Risky Situation in Lawyers' Career]. *Qiushi* [*Seeking the Truth*] 11(4): 82–83.

Wang, Yuhua. 2015. *Tying the Autocrat's Hands: The Rise of the Rule of Law.* Cambridge, UK: Cambridge University Press.

Whiting, Susan H. 2017. "Authoritarian 'Rule of Law' and Regime Legitimacy. *Comparative Political Studies*, 50(14): 1907–1940.

Xie, Yue. 2012. "The Political Logic of *Weiwen* in Contemporary China." *Issues & Studies* 48(3): 1–41.

Xinhua Agency. 2016. "zhonggong zhongyang bangongting guowuyuan guanyu shenhua lvshi zhidu gaige de yijian" [The Advice on Further Reforming Lawyering Institution by Office of the CCP's Center and Office of State Department], issued on June 13. Accessed May 9, 2019. http://www.gov.cn/xinwen/2016-06/13/content_5081785.htm.

Yang, Ming. 2013. "Beijing Tongguo 'Nianjian' Poshi Weiquan LvshiJiufan" [Beijing Forcing the Subordination of Weiquan Lawyers Through 'Annual Relicensing'], June 10. Retrieved April 28, 2019. https://www.voachinese.com/a/beijing-uses-annual-license-renewals-20130610/1678752.html.

Zhang, Fusen. 2014. "lvshi zhidu de gaige yu wanshan" [To Reform and Improve Lawyers' Institution]. *Zhongguo falv pinglun* [*China's Law Review*] 3: 25–31.

Part III
ENVIRONMENTAL PROTEST

Chapter Seven

State Elites and Movement Alliances against the Nu River Dam

Setsuko Matsuzawa (The College of Wooster)

Social movement scholars have focused on the ways that movements in democratic contexts create public pressure, lobby for public interests, and acquire state elite allies to influence public policy (McAdam 1996). In authoritarian regimes, political opportunity structures are not as open as those in democracies, leading to more challenges to movements when they attempt to influence policies. State elites in authoritarian regimes may not be as responsive to movements as their counterparts in democracies, either. However, the unresponsiveness of state elites does not entirely prevent state-movement alliances from coalescing in nondemocratic contexts, especially when state elites perceive movements as potential allies in advancing their own agendas (Zhang 2018; Tong 2005; O'Donnell and Schmitter 1986). Social movements have also exploited cleavages among state elites for their own benefits (Suh 2011). In democracies, elite allies are generally considered key to social movement success (Amenta, Caren, and Olasky 2005; Andrews and Gaby 2015), but to what extent is this true in the authoritarian context?

China provides an interesting case for the exploration of state elites and movements collaboration. In its contemporary history, major political leaders, such as Mao Zedong and Deng Xiaoping, created or supported social movements to enlist popular support to enhance their own political bases. For example, Chairman Mao was known for masterminding numerous campaigns with staged public performances (Perry 2002) to obtain the people's support for the advancement of his policies. Deng's initial acquiesces toward the Democracy Wall movement (1978–1979) in the Xidan district in Beijing were intended to garner popular support to compete against Hua Guofeng, Mao's hand-picked successor. Deng's strategy led him to successfully oust Hua Guofeng and consolidate his leadership position in the Chinese Communist Party (CCP) during a period of political uncertainty after Mao's death (Perry

2018; Goldman 2002). These historical events represent interesting intersections between state elites and movements. Although movement success heavily depends on support from state elites in the authoritarian context, the motivations and strategies of state elites who offer the support are understudied.

Why and how do state elites ally with movements or other actors? This chapter focuses on state elites and movement collaboration by using a case study on environmental activism against the controversial Nu River hydropower dam project in Yunnan, a southwest province in China. It explores, over the period of 2003–2005, the ways in which alliances were formed, mainly among scientists, nongovernmental organizations (NGOs,) the media, and environmental ministry officials and to lesser extent with transnational actors. The Nu River anti-hydropower dam case was the first and still only successful transnational anti-dam movement in China. It led to the temporary suspension of the hydropower dam project in 2004.

The thematic framework that I employ with the Chinese case is the political mediation model. The model was developed to understand political contexts that may mediate the relationships between social movements and their influence on policy outcomes (Amenta et al. 2010). In the model, nonmovement actors, such as state elites, play key mediator roles able to influence relationships in various ways, depending on their calculated responses to a movement (Amenta et al. 2005; Amenta 2006: Andrews and Gaby 2015). With the focus on the motivations and strategies of state elites in the Chinese context, this chapter provides comparative insights on state-movement interactions within an authoritarian state.

As Magee and McDonald (2006: 42) have pointed out, the Nu River hydropower dam project became a point of contention when China's hydropower industry was decentralized, which destabilized China's traditional top-down decision-making channels. This change opened a window of opportunity for collaboration between state elites and the movement to create popular support and strengthen their respective positions. The Nu River hydropower dam project also became the first test case for the State Environmental Protection Administration (SEPA), a ministerial-status agency from 2003 to 2008, to enforce Environmental Impact Assessment (EIA), based on a newly enacted law.

In the case of anti-dam activism against the planned construction of Nu River hydropower dams, the key state elite ally of the movement actors was the SEPA. The SEPA's willingness to ally with environmental NGOs heightened after the enactment of China's EIA Law on September 1, 2003. The law gave the SEPA a gatekeeper role in approving environmental impact assessment reviews. The environmental ministry's primary concern was to enforce a strict and unbiased EIA of the planned construction of the Nu River hydropower dams, whereas movement collaborators sought to halt the planned construction. Although their end goals were different, they collaborated to gain public support for their causes. State elites and movement actors formed an alliance of the SEPA, scientists, the media, and environmental NGOs, so that they could develop public discourse favorable to their causes. Public participation by scientists and environmental NGOs was justified based on the EIA law, which stipulates public participation in environmental decision-making.

This case study presents the first case of state-led alliance between state elites and movement actors in China's environmental campaigns. Drawing data from fieldwork in China, as well as newspaper archive research between 2003 and 2005, this chapter describes how movement actors as well as state elites from the SEPA interacted with each other and created movement dynamics in different stages of mobilization to halt the construction of the hydropower dam project.

There were two main stages of mobilization against the planned construction. The first stage was from the initiation of the planned dam project to its temporary suspension by Premier Wen Jiabao in 2004. The second stage was after the 2004 suspension. This chapter focuses heavily on the first stage and explores the strategic formation of an alliance among the SEPA, scientists, environmental NGOs, and the media.

STATE-MOVEMENT INTERACTION IN ENVIRONMENTAL ACTIVISM

Environmental movements in China have been driven by Chinese environmental NGOs, which emerged around the mid-1990s. Their first nationally publicized environmental campaign was against a local county government in Yunnan in 1995 to protect the habitat of the snub-nosed monkey from deforestation caused by excess logging. It led to a logging ban at the locality. For the rest of the twentieth century, NGO environmental activism centered on relatively benign topics, such as animal protection and recycling. Environmental NGOs often engaged with the media to advocate their cause. During this period, environmental NGOs established a pattern of interacting with the state in environmental campaigns.

Environmental NGOs expose environmental injustice and often ask sympathetic state actors to intervene and remedy the situation. Major environmental NGOs in China are often led by Chinese intellectuals who are "organizational entrepreneurs with professional expertise and international connections" (Yang 2005: 61). Historical Confucius thoughts legitimize the roles of intellectuals as advisers to the rulers to help them to govern. By urging the state to do the right thing, Chinese environmental NGOs have played the role of concerned intellectuals. The elite nature of Chinese environmental NGOs in comparison to other types of NGOs has helped them to ally with environmentally conscious political and policy elites (Matsuzawa 2012).

In the twenty-first century, environmental activism shifted to more controversial topics, including SARS, HIV/AIDS, hydropower dams, waste incinerators, and industrial facilities (Bondes and Johnson 2017; Hildebrandt 2013; Huang and Yip 2012; Matsuzawa 2011; Mertha 2008; Steinhardt and Wu 2016; Sun and Zhao 2008; Wong 2015, 2016; Zhu 2017). When the Nu River hydropower dam controversy arose, environmental NGOs in China had been in existence for about a decade and had accumulated experience in leading successful environmental campaigns that included the cooperation of the media. As Yang and Calhoun argue, there were "the interactive dynamics of civil society and different types of media in the [Nu River anti-dam] campaign" (2007: 226). The interactive dynamics of nonstate actors can be extended to include state actors.

The existing research in Chinese studies shows how interactive dynamics between state actors and nonstate actors may develop. Cleavages among state elites in the context of an authoritarian regime open up opportunities for movement actors (Chen 2014; Shi and Cai, 2006; Sun and Zhao, 2008). In rural China, movement actors skillfully exploited opportunities or loopholes within the authoritarian state and made their protests be perceived as "rightful resistance" (O'Brien and Li 2006).

Movement alliances form among movement actors as well as between state and movement actors. These latter alliances tend formed when state actors reach out to movement actors who share common interests or goals (Li and Liu 2016) and when state actors want to advance their own agenda (Tong 2005). Such state-movement alliances can be open alliances (thus, they are public knowledge) or hidden alliances, especially from the rest of the state (Zhang 2018).

In the case of anti-dam activism against the Nu River hydropower dam project, a small group of SEPA elites[1] who shared favorable views on the activism of environmental NGOs decided to collaborate with nonstate actors, including environmental NGOs and the media (Tong 2005, Xie and Mol 2006; Xie 2009; Zhang and Barr 2013). However, why and how the SEPA officials collaborated with nonstate actors has not been well explored.

THE POLITICAL MEDIATION MODEL IN THE AUTHORITARIAN CONTEXT

The political mediation model has provided a useful analytical framework for understanding the relationship between movements and their policy impacts in democracies. Scholars have argued that a movement generally becomes influential if state actors see it as potentially helping or hampering their own goals. However, the actual processes through which social movements influence policy outcomes remain unclear (Amenta et al. 2010). To add clarity to the political mediation argument, some works focus on specific mechanisms (e.g., Andrews 2001; Kolb 2007; Basseches 2019), on the influence of different strategies at different points in the political process (McAdam and Su 2002; Cornwall et al. 2007; Olzak and Soule 2009), or within different political contexts (Kriesi et al. 1995; Linders 2004). This chapter adds a concrete example of political mediation processes in an authoritarian state.

In both democracies and nondemocracies, political elites are considered as key decision makers. Thus, social movements attempt to influence elites by creating public pressure via the media (Amenta et al. 2009; Andrews and Caren 2010) and via protests. Protests and public opinion interact with each other to influence policy outcomes (Olzak and Soule 2009). In the authoritarian context, however, protests may cause the defection of political and policy elites by increasing their perceived risk of being colored as social movement allies (Zhang 2018). Even in democracies, political elites who are regarded as social movement allies or "activist legislators" may also be stigmatized, reducing their influence on legislative outcomes (Olzak et al. 2016). Especially in the authoritarian context, state elites are more likely to be motivated to collaborate with movements if the benefits clearly outweigh the risks. Hidden state-movement alliances in China, for example, are one of the strategies of state elites who wish to manage their potential risks.

State-led alliances between state elites and movement actors are also observed in China. In the case of state-led alliances, state elites identify common ground with movements to advance their own agendas, serving as key mediators. They work as friends of movements to help yield mutual benefits by providing movements with opportunities. In democracies, social movement-led alliances are more common. Movements attempt to identify potential political elite allies sympathetic to their causes. However, they may end up identifying political elites who are not as committed as desired.

THE NU RIVER HYDROPOWER DAM PROJECT

On June 14, 2003, the Yunnan provincial government and the China Huadian Group Company, a state-owned electric enterprise, announced their agreement on the Nujiang hydropower dam project with construction to begin in September of that year. Eight of the project's thirteen dams were to be built across the middle reaches of Nujiang (the Nu River) in the Nujiang Lisu Autonomous Prefecture (Lisu-minority prefecture) in Yunnan. Given the impetus of the central government's Western Development Campaign in Western provinces since 1999, the proposed construction of the dams was expected to move ahead swiftly or at least that was what many within the Nujiang prefectural government believed.

SEPA's Mediation

The SEPA's mediation began by providing concerned scientists with a forum to discuss the proposed dam construction project. After the enactment of China's EIA law, the SEPA's cooperation with the media and NGOs intensified. All of the movement actors were enlisted to create favorable public discourse on the need for an environmental impact assessment.

Pre-EIA Law

After the announcement on the construction agreement in June 2003, the SEPA and the Yunnan Environmental Protection Bureau (YEPB) moved quickly in their campaign against the Nu River hydropower dam plan. In the same month, the YEPB organized two conferences in Kunming, the capital city of Yunnan. Both shared a common theme: "Dams and their Ecological Impacts." The conference organizers intended to publicize the project and its ecological impacts to as many people as possible. The conferences were well attended. Nearly fifty various experts and representatives from Yunnan and outside the province participated in each conference (*China Water Transport Newspaper* 2003). The conferences provided concerned scientists with a forum where they could express their views. One of the scientists was Professor He Damin, a local expert on rivers, from the Asian International Rivers Center of Yunnan University. Since 2001, Professor He had been advocating for the protection of China's last two pristine rivers, including the Nu River. At the conference, he expressed his opposition to the construction of the Nu River hydropower dam project. He became an initial forceful voice against the project, but his was a minority voice among local experts in Yunnan.

Despite its initial cooperation with the SEPA, the YEPB had to defect from the campaign by October 2003 due to pressure from the Yunnan Provincial Governor's Office. Meanwhile, Professor He had also been threatened to keep quiet by the provincial branch of the CCP[2] as the Yunnan provincial government and the CCP had teamed up together to support the dam. Professor He could no longer speak his views to reporters or researchers.

On August 12–14, 2003, the National Development and Reform Commission (NDRC) organized a meeting to evaluate a report: "Planning of Electricity Exploration in Middle and Lower Stream of Nu River." More than

140 people attended, including representatives from the SEPA and relevant bureaucracies (*Yunnan Daily* 2003a). The SEPA expressed reservations about the report because the report suggested that the NDRC had ignored the SEPA's prior request for a strict environmental impact assessment of the planned project, conducted by neutral institutions.[3] Despite the SEPA's reservations, the report was approved at the meeting and was delivered to the State Council for final approval (Xie and Mol 2006).

In the past, the NDRC's approval would have ended further policy discussions on the dam project among relevant bureaucracies. However, the SEPA continued to show clear opposition to the planned Nu River hydropower dam project to influence the State Council. This attitude of the SEPA was new and significantly differed from its attitude toward another dam controversy at the time—the proposed construction of the Yangliuhu dam at Dujiangyan in Sichuan Province. In the case of the Yangliuhu hydropower dam project, the SEPA was not an active participant in the controversy and, in fact, officially supported the project, whereas local offices in Dujiangyan, such as the Dujiangyan World Heritage Office, the Dujiangyan Cultural Relics Bureau, and the Dujiangyan Environmental Protection Bureau, were key opponents to the planned dam project.

In the Yangliuhu hydropower dam project, the media played a significant role in publicizing the planned dam's potentially adverse impacts on the Dujiangyan irrigation system, a UNESCO World Heritage cultural site.[4] The project was halted in late August 2003 (Mertha and Lowry 2006).

Post-EIA Law

On September 1, 2003, the SEPA's persistent concerns with the Nu River hydropower dam project were encouraged and justified by the enactment of China's EIA law. The law requires environmental reviews and public consultation in the planning stages of major public and private development projects. The new law gave the SEPA a gatekeeper role in enforcing environmental reviews. The SEPA had anticipated that the law's enactment would provide it with an opportunity to justify and legitimize its opposition to the Nu River hydropower dam project. Thus, the planned project became a test case for the SEPA to exercise its newly granted administrative power. Yet, the SEPA was facing an uphill battle against a pro-dam coalition, including the powerful NDRC, the Yunnan provincial government, the state-owned Huadian Group, and the Nu River prefectural government. Therefore, the SEPA had a good reason to ally with potential movement actors, including concerned anti-dam scientists and the media, especially via environmental journalists, with the hope of placing EIA and the Nu River project into public discourse and mobilizing popular support to strengthen its own position as the gate keeper of the EIA law.

On September 3, 2003, only two days after the enactment of China's EIA law, the SEPA held an expert forum in Beijing, titled, "The Expert Forum on Protection of the Ecological Environment in the Hydroelectric Development on the Nu River Basin." The forum provided concerned scientists with an opportunity to participate in the debate over the proposed Nu River hydropower dam project. As with the prior two conferences held in Kunming the previous June, the forum in Beijing provided concerned scientists with a venue. However, unlike the prior conferences, the purpose of the forum in Beijing was no longer just to publicize the project and its ecological impacts. Rather, the SEPA had a clear intention to showcase the oppositional voices of the experts at the conference.[5]

At the Beijing forum, more than thirty scholars and researchers exchanged opinions on the dam project. A strong oppositional voice belonged to Professor He Damin who had come from Yunnan to attend the forum. It was more comfortable for him to voice his opposition to the dam project in Beijing without being observed or pressured by the Yunnan provincial government and the provincial branch of the CCP. By this time, Professor He no longer attended local conferences on the dam controversy because his oppositional views were not appreciated in Yunnan (*China Water Transport Newspaper* 2003). Representatives from the NDRC and water electricity-related bureaucracies were also at the forum. These pro-dam bureaucracies contended that "constructing the Nu River dam will effectively alleviate poverty" and that "the Nu River dam will not contradict a designation of the World Heritage natural site" (*China Water Transport Newspaper* 2003), but they constituted the minority voice at the expert forum. The majority of the participants—about thirty experts in the fields of ecology, agriculture, forests, and geology—all opposed the dam. The opposition argued that "It should be decided based on EIA" and that "Poverty alleviation can be achieved via ecological tourism, like Lijiang." Whereas scientists opposed to the dam project based their concerns on its ecological and geological impacts, a director-level SEPA official and forum organizer brought up the social impacts of the proposed dam on local populations by raising the question of resettlement.[6] The SEPA official stated that if resettlement was ill handled, people would be further impoverished (*China Water Transport Newspaper* 2003). The comment challenged the contention of dam supporters that the dam would alleviate local poverty. Also, by mentioning the issue of resettlement, the SEPA implied the importance of public participation and public access to information as stipulated in the EIA law.

In addition to governmental representatives and concerned scientists, other key actors at the forum included the media and NGOs. Probably, the participation of these two latter groups was most important of all. This was the first time that the media and NGOs participated in government-organized forums on river development (*Science News* 2009).

Since the forum was a high-level government-organized event, involving representatives from the NDRC and water- and electricity-related bureaucracies, it is likely that the SEPA, the forum's organizer, encouraged (or perhaps invited) the media and NGOs to be present. Wang Yongchen, the representative of the Green Earth Volunteers, a Beijing-based NGO, and a journalist herself with the Beijing People's Radio, rendered her voice against the dam project at the forum. She brought journalist groups from a dozen media outlets to the forum (*Science News* 2009).[7] These journalists later published newspaper articles describing the majority view of the experts at the forum opposing the dam plan.

Since the 1990s, environmental reporting by journalists has increased in China. The commercialization of media and the development of alternative media, especially on the internet, have also create spaces for (environmental) journalists to engage in investigative journalism rather than act as a government mouthpiece (Yang and Calhoun 2007; Yang 2009; Jiang 2011; Lei 2016, 2018). Yang and Calhoun (2007) argue that public responses to environmental reporting has helped to create China's Green sphere. As mentioned previously, the media played a significant role in framing the debate over the construction of the Yanglihu dam in Sichuan. The success of the Yanglihu anti-dam campaign not only provided the media with lessons on how to inform the public to influence the government's decision-making process but also made the SEPA aware that potential movement actors, such as the media and NGOs, could make a strong ally in gaining popular support from the public for the enforcement of the EIA law, even regarding sensitive environmental issues, such as the construction of a hydropower dam.

Key Political Mediators Inside the SEPA

The SEPA's willingness to ally with the media, scientists, and domestic environmental NGOs owes to the existence of key political mediators inside the organization.[8] Pan Yue, who came to be known as China's "environmental tsar," was the highest-ranking and most powerful political mediator inside the SEPA. He became the senior deputy director of the SEPA in 2003. During his thirteen-year tenure as deputy environmental minister (2003–2016),[9] he launched numerous high-profile campaigns against industrial polluters.[10] Prior to his ascendancy on China's political ladder, he had been an environmental journalist, one of China's first, beginning in the 1980s (Ma 2016). From 1982 to 1986, he was the chief editor of *China Environmental Journal* and from 1989 to 1993 the deputy chief editor of *China Youth Daily*, the official newspaper of the Communist Youth League of China (CYL). He had caused *China Youth Daily* to be active in reporting on environmental issues. His environmental journalism background likely caused him to feel close to fellow journalists and to join forces with the media as he launched his quest for environmental protection from within the SEPA. He was also part of the environmentalist circle in Beijing and, thus, had a personal and occupational proximity to environmental journalists.

MOBILIZING THE EIA LAW

A small group of environmental mediators inside the SEPA, including Pan Yue, not only organized forums, but they also began promoting the EIA law. Not surprisingly, on the day when China's EIA law was enacted, *China Environmental News* (CEN), the official newspaper of the SEPA, along with other popular newspapers, featured an article on the EIA law. The SEPA's article included an interview with Mr. Zhu, the director of the (environmental) Supervision and Monitoring Bureau of the SEPA, charged with supervising and monitoring the enforcement of the EIA law. The law was described as the most important piece of environmental legislation in China over the previous ten years. (There were twenty-two environmental laws passed from 1993 to 2002.) The article also described that the EIA law encouraged public participation (individuals, experts, and work units) and transparency.

On September 5, 2003, the SEPA featured an article on the planned construction of the Nu River hydropower dam project, titled, "The Pristine Environment of the Nu River Should Be Preserved." The article was positioned under the headline of "Based on the Law, Carry out *Environmental Impact Assessment.* Secure National Ecological Safety" (emphasis mine). The article detailed six reasons why the Nu river should be preserved. They were: (1) The Nu River was a pristine river with ecological diversity and a World Heritage Ecological Site; (2) the planned dam would not solve issues of local poverty because the project was not cost effective; (3) the area was unsafe for the construction of a dam due to a weak plateau; (4) the planned dam would upset the ecological balance, and a loss of diversity would prevent China from becoming the leader in the field of life sciences in the twenty-first century; (5) the dam would cause water pollution and irreversible damage to the river and its ecology and diversity. Because of the adverse effects of the dams, many countries had given up on them and have not built new ones; and (6) the Nu River was the last pristine river and very special to China. Although the article did not mention it, these six reasons had originated from the expert opinions expressed at the Expert Forum in Beijing, organized by the SEPA two days before. After raising these six points, the article criticized the dam construction plan for employing a "traditional mindset," "deciding a project first, then assess it later," and "implementing a policy first, then discuss proof." Last, the article called for securing the ecology of the nation as well as instituting *sustainable development* with *scientific* proof (emphases mine) via EIA.

During the era of Hu Jintao and Wen Jiabao's leadership (2003–2013), scientific development (*Kexue fazhan*) was emphasized and frequently conflated with sustainable development. Although "the marriage of the discourse of science and sustainability" was used to justify large development projects (Magee and McDonald 2006: 51), I argue that it also benefited the SEPA and its efforts to add EIA to scientific and sustainable development discourses. For example, from September 2003 to May 2004, a key word search of "EIA" and "EIA law" in the *China Environmental News* showed that EIA, science, and sustainable development were discussed together 70 percent of the time. EIA was always discussed with either science or sustainable development. By blending EIA with these concepts, the SEPA wanted to secure the importance of EIA when large-scale development projects are planned.

On the other hand, my content analysis of pro-dam newspapers, such as *China Electric Power News*, the official newspaper of the National Energy Bureau under the NDRC, and *Yunnan Daily*, revealed that the proponents for the Nu River hydropower dam project use the discourses on poverty alleviation in addition to the discourses on science and sustainable development to justify their support for the project.

SEPA ELITES-MOVEMENT ALLIANCE

The 2003 EIA law (clauses 6, 11, and 21) encourages public participation in decision-making and information disclosure to the public. As the official government enforcer of the EIA law, the SEPA's public outreach to gain popular support for assessing the environmental impacts of planned projects was a legitimate step. The proposed construction of the Nu River hydropower dam became the first vehicle for the SEPA to advocate for the newly enacted EIA law. Although the SEPA could present its views against the planned dam project in the form of an article in its official newspaper, the readership was too limited to reach a wide audience. The SEPA needed to mobilize media outlets to sway public opinion.

Some political mediators inside the SEPA had personal ties with environmental journalists and NGO members. As social movements scholarship has shown, such personal and social ties contribute to successful mobilization (Friedman and McAdam 1992; Marwell, Oliver, and Prahl 1988; Diani 1995). In the case of Nu River anti-dam activism, one of the key environmental journalists was Wang Yongchen. Wang had personal connections with Mr. Mu, then vice director of the (Environmental) Supervision and Monitoring Bureau of the SEPA. According to Pan Yue, a small group of top leaders in the SEPA quietly approved Mr. Mu's willingness to collaborate with environmental NGOs. During the policy process and the Nu River anti-dam campaign, Mr. Mu provided Wang and her NGO with substantial environmental and policy information (Xie 2009). Therefore, the anti-dam campaign, particularly before the temporary suspension in February 2004, was a coordinated effort of the SEPA and movement actors, such as environmental journalists and environmental NGOs.

Both Wang and Zhang Kejia, another journalist from *China Youth Daily*, had become notable figures due to their successful media campaigns against the planned Yangliuhu hydropower dam project. They emerged again as initial key movement actors in the case of the planned Nu River hydropower dam project. They began their media campaigns right after the NDRC approved the report on "Planning of Electricity Exploration in Middle and Lower Stream of Nu River" in mid-August of 2003. On August 19, 2003, Zhang (2003a) published her article with *China Youth Daily*, titled, "Dam Building on Nu River is Planned. Construction is Opposed." Despite the NDRC's approval of the plan, Zhang's article focused on opponents' (the SEPA) voices. It appears that Zhang knew the SEPA's reservations on the report at the meeting. Wang's article, "Please Keep the Last River that Has Ecological Significance," first appeared in *Southern City News* on August 20, 2003. It was reprinted in *People's Political Consultative Daily*, the official newspaper of the Chinese People's Political Consultative Conference (CPPCC),[11] on August 26, 2003.

As mentioned previously, Wang and her fellow journalist groups attended "The Expert Forum on Protection of the Ecological Environment in the Hydroelectric Development on the Nu River Basin," organized by the SEPA in Beijing on September 3, 2003. Zhang was the first journalist to publish on the expert meeting. Her article, "13 Dams to Be Built on the Last Ecological River, Experts Vehemently Oppose the Development of the Nu River" (Zhang 2003b), came out on September 5, 2003, or four days before the SEPA's article on the expert meeting published in *China Environmental News*. Other newspaper articles followed. For example, on September 11, 2003, the *People's Daily,* a state-run newspaper, also featured the Nu River dam controversy in "Preserve an Ecological River for the Next Generation." The media's frames on the planned project at that time centered on the experts' (scientific) reservations concerning the project and made emotional pleas to the public.

"Emotion work" (Hochschild 1979) is an accepted strategy in mobilization (Goodwin, Jasper and Polletta 2001; Goodwin and Pfaff 2001) and has effectively transformed grievance into action in contemporary Chinese mobilizations. Such examples range from the Communist Revolution (Perry 2002; Liu 2010) to the 1989 Chinese student movement (Yang 2000). The dam controversy's major media coverages widened public attention and ignited public debate.

By allying with movement actors, such as scientists, the media, and NGOs, the SEPA intended to systematically place EIA into public discourse. First, science was mobilized. The SEPA invited scientists to attend forums. Scientists supplied credibility and scientific information to anti-dam discourse, emphasizing the importance of the scientific data in the decision-making process, which justified the application of EIA to dam projects. The media, led by environmental journalists, informed the public of the scientific information as well as EIA. Environmental NGOs mobilized to raise public awareness of, and sentiment toward, both the Nu River and the people whose lives would be affected by the planned construction of the dam project. As "the discourse-producing publics of the green sphere" (Yang and Calhoun 2007: 217), environmental NGOs picked up the scientific information and produced science-based discourses. NGOs also engaged in movement activities with citizens, through which science-based discourses were diffused to a wider audience.

SEPA'S MEDIATION

The SEPA continued its mediation via its newspaper and forums. On September 9, 2003, the environmental ministry published the article, "Experts Call for Preserving the Nu River" (*China Environmental News* 2003a), which described that five academicians and twenty-two scholars at the "Expert Forum on Protection of the Ecological Environment in the Hydroelectric Development on the Nu River Basin" in Beijing had issued a statement against the planned construction of the Nu River hydropower dam project. The article also stated that because the Nu River is an international river, the world had been paying attention to the issue, which implied that China should not take the issue lightly. The article argued that without EIA, the planned project would become *unscientific* (emphasis mine). It also called for the participation of the dam-affected ethnic minority (Lisu ethnic minority).

During October 20–21, 2003, the SEPA conducted the fourth expert meeting in Kunming, Yunnan.[12] Dam opponents and supporters exchanged heated discussions. Dam opponents were mostly experts from Beijing, whereas dam supporters included representatives from relevant agencies of the Nu River prefectural government and the Yunnan provincial government, local scientists, and scholars (*China Water Transport Newspaper* 2003).

Prior to the meeting (October 14–19, 2003), the SEPA conducted fieldwork in Yunnan with experts from Beijing. On October 19, one day before the expert meeting began in Kunming, *Yunnan Daily* (2003b) ran an article titled, "Nujiang (Nu River) County should develop Nu River hydropower source" to express its support for the planned dam project. The article emphasized that the production of the report, "Planning of Electricity Exploration in Middle and Lower Stream of Nu River," which had been approved by the NDRC that August, had taken almost three years of effort. It also stated that, by 2020, the Nu River prefectural government would help the Yunnan provincial government to achieve three goals: (1) constructing a national base for hydropower and minerals; (2) creating a world tourism brand under "Three Parallel Rivers" (a UNESCO World Heritage natural site); and (3) reaching a provincial GDP of 80 billion yuan (*Yunnan Daily* 2003b). Three weeks after the fourth expert meeting, the SEPA conducted more fieldwork. Its primary purpose was to listen to the opinions of the local government (the Nu River prefectural government) and the Yunnan provincial government. This time, the SEPA did not bring experts with them. Perhaps, the SEPA wanted to engage in a dialogue with local governments, and this might not have been possible if anti-dam experts had been present.

THE INFLUENCE OF ENVIRONMENTAL NGOs

Environmental NGOs began mobilizing inside China and beyond its borders. Some collected petition signatures opposing the planned Nu River dam project. Some organized forums. Some used an international venue to issue a joint statement opposing the Nu River dam project. It was signed by representatives from more than sixty countries (Sun and Zhao 2008). These mobilizations were sometimes coordinated via *guanxi*, personal connections among environmental NGO leaders (Xie and Mol 2006).[13] SEPA-NGO collaboration was also observed. The SEPA provided an NGO with an opportunity to collect petition signatures. In October, 2003, during China's first "Green Forum," a public relations event in Beijing organized by the SEPA, Wang Yongchen circulated a petition letter, which called for *the enforcement of the EIA law* (emphasis mine). Sixty-two signatures were collected from Chinese music and film stars on a petition to protect the Nu River (Yardley 2005). Also, Wang spread the petition via email, reaching environmentalists outside China. The Nu River dam controversy seemed to create a dichotomy, a "nation-wide environmental world versus Yunnan" mentality (*China Water Transport Newspaper* 2003).

Dam supporters typically criticized dam opponents for not having visited the Nu River area and, thus, for not being concerned with local poverty. In response to the criticism, twenty journalists, researchers, and environmentalists from Beijing and Yunnan conducted a study tour along the Nu River, from February 16 to 24. During the tour, Premier Wen Jiabao commented in Beijing:

> We should carefully study and make a *science-based* strategic decision in regard to such a large-scale hydroelectric project that attracts a high degree of attention in society and involves different opinions in terms of environmental protection." (*Science News* 2009, emphasis added).

Wen's comment suggested that the state-movement alliance had influenced policy outcomes. His comment had a reassuring effect on the SEPA, implying that an EIA should be treated seriously. Yet, movement actors were not entirely optimistic because the hydropower project had not been canceled. Environmental NGOs, in particular, continued their efforts by holding photo exhibitions on the Nu River inside and outside China and by creating the Nu River website, which was partially funded by international NGOs. Chinese environmental NGOs continued to reach out to transnational actors and arenas. They collaborated with a transnational corporation and international NGOs, in both domestic and transnational venues, adopted campaign rhetoric intended for both global and local consumption, and pressured UNESCO as well as foreign governments (Matsuzawa 2011, 2019).

SEPA'S MEDIATION AFTER PREMIER WEN'S COMMENT

Premier Wen's comment caused a de facto suspension of the project. However, both sides of the Nu River dam project debate continued their campaigns through the media. Pro-dam official newspapers, including *Yunnan Daily* and *China Electric Power News*, continued to justify the need for a dam by framing it from the perspective of poverty alleviation. On the other hand, the SEPA's discourse on the Nu River dam controversy shifted from the need for EIA to how to conduct proper EIA so as to "make a science-based strategic decision" in Wen's words.

At a policy meeting back in August 2003, when relevant bureaucracies discussed the report, "Planning of Electricity Exploration in Middle and

Lower Stream of Nu River," the SEPA's concern had been that the NDRC had not followed through on the SEPA's request to conduct a rigorous EIA for the planned dam construction. Thus, the SEPA did not trust that the NDRC would select suitable EIA professionals unattached to the NDRC and capable of conducting impartial and rigorous EIA. EIA-related articles that were published in *China Environmental News* after Wen's comment showed the SEPA's lingering concerns, including the need for neutral parties in conducting EIA, the qualifications of, and training for, EIA engineers, and the importance of public participation.

The Nu River dam project was officially suspended in April 2004. The SEPA continued to feature articles on the EIA law in *China Environmental News*. The SEPA's willingness to continue to ally with the media and environmental NGOs to promote the EIA law and encourage public participation was still evident in these articles. One article mentioned the roles that the media could play in exposing environmental wrongdoings.[14] Another discussed case studies on how citizens rallied around the EIA law and effectively protected the environment with a successful example of subway construction in Beijing.[15]

On May 11, 2004, the SEPA's official newspaper, *China Environmental News*, published a lengthy article based on a discussion held among the three well-known environmental NGO leaders in Beijing. The title of the article was "Call of Famous Environmentalists: Listen to NGOs' Voice." These leaders were Liang Congjie of the Friends of Nature, Wang Yongchen of the Green Earth Volunteers, and Liao Xiaoyi of the Global Village of Beijing. Their talk centered on how Chinese environmental NGOs have contributed to environmental protection via facilitating public participation. They also discussed the "Green Alliance" between environmental NGOs and the media. The Nu River hydropower dam project was mentioned as a good example of how the media impacted the policy-making process. They concluded that both NGOs and the state share the same purpose of achieving sustainable development (*China Environmental News* 2004a).

The Nu River hydropower dam controversy was briefly resurrected in July 2005 when Premier Wen requested the relevant agencies—including the NDRC, the SEPA, and the Ministry of Water Resources—to further conduct studies on the project after he returned from his visit to Yunnan. In response to this new development, sixty-one Chinese social organizations, the majority of which were environmental NGOs, along with ninety-nine Chinese citizens, submitted a petition in August 2005. They requested of the Chinese central government public disclosure of the EIA report on the Nu River hydropower dam project.

On August 30, 2005, the *China Environmental News* published two lengthy articles. Pan Yue penned one of the articles titled, "Strategic EIA and Sustainable Development." It described in detail the relationship between EIA and sustainable development. The other article featured the Eighth Green China Forum speech held in Beijing on August 28, 2005. The theme of the forum was also "Strategic EIA and Sustainable Development" (China Environmental News 2004b).

Since then, the dam plan has been scaled back, and China's most recent Thirteenth Five-Year Plan (2016–2020) no longer expects to generate electricity from the planned dam during that period. Thus, the Nu River hydropower dam plan appears to be de facto permanently suspended.

CONCLUSION

This chapter explored why and how state elites ally with movements. It focused on a state-movement alliance—involving the SEPA, scientists, the media, and environmental NGOs—during presuspension mobilization against the proposed Nu River hydropower dam project. As the gate keeper of the EIA law, the SEPA elites saw a clear benefit from collaborating with movement actors: to augment its power to enforce strict EIA.

In the process of state-movement interaction, the SEPA emerged as the key mediator, aiming to blend EIA with the discourses on science and sustainability so that EIA would be placed firmly in the public discourse. The SEPA first mobilized scientists. Scientists emphasized the importance of the collection of scientific data, which helped EIA to be added to the discourses on science and sustainability. The media was mobilized to publicize to a wide audience scientific reasons to oppose the proposed dam project. Environmental NGOs also mobilized to join the forces demanding EIA with the hope of halting the dam project.

The state-movement alliance here may not have been possible without the existence of prior personal ties among state elites and movement actors (e.g., between Pan Yue and Wang Yongchen). Although previous works have emphasized the importance of preexisting personal ties in participation in a movement (e.g., Snow, Zurcher and Ekland-Olson 1980), such personal ties are especially important to consider when actors engage in high-risk activities in authoritarian contexts. The existence of personal ties may also reduce uncertainty in political mediation processes. In this case study, state elites saw mutual benefits based on their collaboration with movement actors. Although their end goals were somewhat different, state elites and movement actors collaborated to gain public support for their causes. The enactment of the EIA law also helped the SEPA to justify the public participation of scientists and environmental NGOs in the environmental decision-making process. Thus, state elites may decide to ally with movement actors to create popular support for their policy goals (in this case, the enforcement of EIA), which, in turn, may increase the influence of movement actors on policy outcomes (in this case, halting the dam project).

This study presents the first case of a state-led alliance between state elites and movement actors in China's environmental campaigns. Future research should continue to explore more cases of state-movement alliances to highlight and differentiate the motivations and behavioral patterns of state elites as key mediators in authoritarian contexts. For example, state-movement alliances have been observed in regard to other social issues in China, including access to public schools by migrant children in cities (Hsu and Hasmath 2014; Hsu 2012) and controversial land appropriation (Lin 2009; Van Rooij 2007). As for movement actors, in the time since the research for this article focused on its anti-dam case, scientists have more fully emerged as one of the key movement actors in environmental issues. It would be interesting to explore other cases to examine the likelihood of the formation of state-movement alliances when other types of movement actors, including lawyers, doctors, religious figures, etc., are involved.

NOTES

1. They are also CCP members.
2. Telephone interview in Kunming in October 2003.
3. The NDRC was in charge of environmental impact assessment on the planned Nu River dam project.
4. Mount Qingcheng and the Dujangyan Irrigation System were inscribed as a World Heritage site in 2000. See https:// whc.unesco.org/en/list/1001.
5. Interview with an informant in Beijing in August 2004.
6. Fifty thousand people were estimated to be resettled if the dam were to be built as planned.
7. Since 1997, she has hosted environmental salons for journalists. The salon helped to mobilize journalists (Yang and Calhoun 2007).
8. I use the term, "political mediators." Because most of these key SEPA elites are CCP members, they are technically both political and policy elites.
9. In 2008, the SEPA was renamed as the Ministry of Environmental Protection. Pan Yue's position became Vice Minister of the Ministry of Environmental Protection.
10. He was sidelined for a few years prior to his retirement from the ministry.
11. The CPPCC is a political advisory legislative body in China, two-thirds of whose members belong to the CCP. The CPPCC also includes the United Front (a CCP-approved party) and independent members.

12. The first and second expert forums were held in Kunming in June 2003. The third forum was held in Beijing in September 2003.
13. Xie and Mol (2006) describe that Wang Yongchen, in particular, had personal ties with the SEPA, the media, and environmental NGOs.
14. *China Environmental News*, 2004d
15. *China Environmental News*, 2004c.

REFERENCES

Amenta, Edwin, 2006. *When Movements Matter: The Impact of the Townsend Plan and US Social Spending Challengers*. Cambridge, MA: Russell Sage Foundation.

Amenta, Edwin, Neal Caren, and Sheera Joy Olasky. 2005. "Age for Leisure? Political Mediation and the Impact of the Pension Movement on U.S. Old-Age Policy." *American Sociological Review* 70(3): 516–38.

Amenta, Edwin, Neal Caren, Sheera Joy Olasky, and James E. Stobaugh. 2009. "All the Movements Fit to Print: Who, What, When, Where, and Why SMO Families Appeared in the *New York Times* in the Twentieth Century." *American Sociological Review* 74: 636–56.

Amenta, Edwin, Neal Caren, Elizabeth Chiarello, and Yang Su. 2010. "The Political Consequences of Social Movements." *Annual Review of Sociology* 36(1): 287–307.

Andrews, Kenneth T. 2001. "Social Movements and Policy Implementation: The Mississippi Civil Rights Movement and the War on Poverty, 1965 to 1971." *American Sociological Review* 66: 71–95.

Andrews, Kenneth T., and Neal Caren. 2010. "Making the News: Movement Organizations, Media Attention, and the Public Agenda." *American Sociological Review* 75(6): 841–66.

Andrews, Kenneth T., and Sarah Gaby. 2015. "Local Protest and Federal Policy: The Impact of the Civil Rights Movement on the 1964 Civil Rights Act." *Sociological Forum* 30(1): 509–27.

Basseches, Joshua A. 2019. "'It Happened behind Closed Doors': Legislative Buffering as an Informal Mechanism of Political Mediation." *Mobilization* 24(3): 365–88.

Bondes, Maria, and Thomas Johnson. 2017. "Beyond Localized Environmental Contention: Horizontal and Vertical Diffusion in a Chinese Anti-Incinerator Campaign." *Journal of Contemporary China* 26: 504–20.

Chen, Xi. 2014. *Social Protest and Contentious Authoritarianism in China*. New York: Cambridge University Press.

China Environmental News. 2003a. "Experts Call for Preserving the Nu River." September 9.

———. 2003b. "Interview with Mr. Zhu Xingyan, the Director of the Supervision and Monitoring Bureau of the SEPA with regard to the Implementation of the EIA Law." September 1.

———. 2003c. "The Pristine Environment of the Nu River Should Be Preserved." September 5.

———. 2004a. "Call of Famous Environmentalists: Listen to NGOs' Voice." May 11.

———. 2004b. "Green China: The Eighth Forum Speech" August 30.
———. 2004c. "Speech by Mr. Wu Bo, the Vice Director of the EIA Bureau of the SEPA at the Board Meeting of China Environmental News." April 29.
———. 2004d. "Take Advantage of the Opportunity and Create New EIA Monitoring Work." April 21.
China Water Transport Newspaper. 2003. "Does Nujiang (Nu River) County Still Need to Build Dams?" December 15.
Cornwall, Marie, Brayden G. King, Elizabeth Legerski, and Kendra Schiffman. 2007. "Signals or Mixed Signals? Why Opportunities for Mobilization are not Opportunities for Policy Reform." *Mobilization* 12(3): 239–54.
Diani, Mario. 1995. *Green Networks: A Structural Analysis of the Italian Environmental Movement*. Edinburgh: Edinburgh University Press.
Friedman, Debra, and Doug McAdam. 1992. "Collective Identity and Activism: Networks, Choices, and the Life of a Social Movement." In Aldon D. Morris and Carol McClurg Mueller, eds., *Frontiers in Social Movement Theory*, 156–73. New Haven, CT: Yale University Press.
Goldman, Merle. 2002. "The Reassertion of Political Citizenship in the Post-Mao Era: The Democracy Wall Movement." In Merle Goldman and Elizabeth J. Perry, eds., *Changing Meanings of Citizenship in Modern China*, 159–86. Cambridge, MA: Harvard University Press.
Goodwin, Jeff, and Steven Pfaff. 2001. "Emotion Work in High-Risk Social Movements." In Jeff Goodwin, James M. Jasper, and Francesca Polletta, eds., *Passionate Politics: Emotions and Social Movements*, 282–302. Chicago: University of Chicago Press.
Goodwin, Jeff, James M. Jasper, and Francesca Polletta. 2001. "Why Emotions Matter." In Jeff Goodwin, James M. Jasper, and Francesca Polletta, eds., *Passionate Politics: Emotions and Social Movements*, 1–26. Chicago: University of Chicago Press.
Hildebrandt, Timothy. 2013. *Social Organizations and the Authoritarian State in China*. New York: Cambridge University Press.
Hochschild, Arlie R. 1979. "Emotion Work, Feeling Rules and Social Structure." *American Journal of Sociology* 85: 551–75.
Hsu, Jennifer. 2012. "Layers of the Urban State: Migrant Organisations and the Chinese State." *Urban Studies* 49(16): 3513–30.
Hsu, Jennifer, and Hasmath Reza. 2014. "The Local Corporatist State and NGO Relations in China." *Journal of Contemporary China* 23(87): 516–34.
Huang, Ronggui, and Ngai-Ming Yip. 2012. "Internet and Activism in Urban China: A Case Study of Protests in Xiamen and Panyu." *Journal of Comparative Asian Development* 11: 201–23.
Jiang, Zhan. 2011. "Environmental Journalism in China." In Susan Shirk, ed., *Changing Media, Changing China*, 115–27. Oxford: Oxford University Press.
Kolb, Felix. 2007. *Protest and Opportunities: The Political Outcomes of Social Movements*. Frankfurt am Main, Germany: Campus Verl.
Kriesi, Hanspeter, Ruud Koopmans, Jan W. Duyvendak, and Marco G. Guigni. 1995. *New Social Movements in Western Europe: A Comparative Analysis*. Minneapolis: University of Minnesota Press.

Lei, Ya-Wen. 2016. "Freeing the Press: How Field Environment Explains Critical News Reporting in China." *American Journal of Sociology* 122: 1–48.

———. 2018. *The Contentious Public Sphere: Law, Media, Authoritarian Rule in China.* Princeton, NJ: Princeton University Press.

Li, Lianjiang, and Minxing Liu. 2016. "The Collusion of Clerks and Gentry: A Hidden Hand in China's Contentious Politics" [Lishen gongmou: Zhongguo kangzheng zhengzhi zhong yizhi yinbi de shou]. *The Twenty-First Century* 157: 57–67.

Lin, George C. S. 2009. *Developing China: Land, Politics and Social Conditions.* New York: Routledge.

Linders, Annula. 2004. "Victory and Beyond: A Historical Comparative Analysis of the Outcomes of the Abortion Movements in Sweden and the United States." *Sociological Forum* 19: 371–404.

Liu, Yu. 2010. "Maoist Discourse and the Mobilization of Emotions in Revolutionary China." *Modern China* 36(3): 329–62.

Ma, Tianjie. 2016. "Pan Yue's Vision of Green China." *China Dialogue Online Article*, August 3, 2016. Retrieved October 22, 2017. https://www.chinadialogue.net/article/show/single/en/8695-Pan-Yue-s-vision-of-green-China.

Magee, Darrin, and Kristen McDonald. 2006. "Beyond Three Gorges: Nu River Hydropower and Energy Decision Politics in China." *Asian Geographer* 25(1–2): 39–60.

Marwell Gerald, Pamela Oliver, and Ralph Prahl. 1988. "Social Networks and Collective Action: A Theory of the Critical Mass." *American Journal of Sociology* 94: 502–34.

Matsuzawa, Setsuko. 2011. "Horizontal Dynamics in Transnational Activism: The Case of Nu River Anti-dam Activism in China." *Mobilization* 16(3): 369–87.

———. 2012. "Citizen Environmental Activism in China: Legitimacy, Alliances, and Rights-based Discourses." *ASIANetwork Exchange: A Journal for Asian Studies in the Liberal Arts* 19(10): 81–91.

———. 2019. *Activating China: Local Actors, Foreign Influence, and State Response.* New York: Routledge.

McAdam, Doug. 1996. "Conceptual Origins, Current Problems, Future directions." In Doug McAdam, John D. McCarthy, and Meyer N. Zald, eds., *Comparative Perspectives on Social Movements*, 23–40. Cambridge: Cambridge University Press.

McAdam, Doug, and Yang Su. 2002. "The War at Home: Antiwar Protests and Congressional Voting, 1965 to 1973." *American Sociological Review* 67: 696–721.

McCormick, Sabrina. 2009. *Mobilizing Science: Movements, Participation, and the Remaking of Knowledge.* Philadelphia: Temple University Press.

Mertha, Andrew C. 2008. *China's Water Warriors: Citizen Action and Policy Change*, Ithaca, NY: Cornell University Press.

Mertha, Andrew C., and William R. Lowry 2006. "Unbuilt Dams: Seminal Events and Policy Change in China, Australia, and the United States." *Comparative Politics* 39(1): 1–20.

O'Brien, Kevin J., and Lianjiang Li. 2006. *Rightful Resistance in Rural China.* Cambridge: Cambridge University Press.

O'Donnell, Guillermo, and Philippe C. Schmitter. 1986. *Transitions from Authoritarian Rule: Tentative Conclusions about Uncertain Democracies.* Baltimore, MD: Johns Hopkins University, 1986.

Olzak, Susan, and Sarah A. Soule. 2009. "Cross-Cutting Influences of Environmental Protest and Legislation." *Social Forces* 88(1): 201–25.

Olzak, Susan, Sarah Soule, Marion Coddou, and John Muñoz 2016. "Friends or Foes? How Social Movement Allies Affect the Passage of Legislation in the U.S. Congress." *Mobilization* 21(2): 213–30.

Pan, Yue. 2005. "Strategic EIA and Sustainable Development." *China Environmental News.* August 30.

Perry, Elizabeth J. 2002. "Moving the Masses: Emotion Work in the Chinese Revolution." *Mobilization: The International Quarterly Review of Social Movement Research* 7(2): 111–28.

———. 2018. "Casting a Chinese 'Democracy' Movement: The Roles of Students, Workers, and Entrepreneurs." In Jeffrey N. Wasserstrom and Elizabeth J. Perry, eds., *Popular Protest and Political Culture in Modern China*, 19–31. New York: Routledge.

Science News. 2009. "China's Media Power Evidenced in 'Anti-Dam' Movement." October 2009.

Shi, Fayong, and Cai, Yongshun. 2006. "Disaggregating the State: Networks and Collective Resistance in Shanghai." *China Quarterly* 186: 314–32.

Snow, David A., Louis A. Zurcher, and Sheldon Ekland-Olson. 1980. "Social Network and Social Movements: A Microstructural Approach to Differential Recruitment." *American Sociological Review* 45(5): 787–801.

Steinhardt, H. Christoph, and Fengshi Wu. 2016. "In the Name of the Public: Environmental Protest and the Changing Landscape of Popular Contention in China." *The China Journal* 75: 61–82.

Suh, Doowon. 2011. "Institutionalizing Social Movements: The Dual Strategy of the Korean Women's Movement." *Sociological Quarterly* 52(3): 442–71.

Sun, Yanfei, and Dingxin Zhao. 2008. "Environmental Campaign." In Kevin O'Brien, ed., *Popular Protest in China*, 144–62. Cambridge, MA: Harvard University Press.

Tong, Yanqi. 2005. "Environmental Movements in Transitional Societies: A Comparative Study of Taiwan and China." *Comparative Politics* 37:167–88.

Van Rooij, Benjamin. 2007. "The Return of the Landlord: Chinese Land Acquisition Conflicts as Illustrated by Peri-Urban Kunming." *The Journal of Legal Pluralism and Unofficial Law* 39(55): 211–44.

Wang, Yongchen. 2003. "Please Keep the Last River that Has Ecological Significance." *Southern City News.* August 20. Guangzhou.

Wong, Natalie W. 2015. "Advocacy Coalitions and Policy Change in China: A Case Study of Anti-Incinerator Protest in Guangzhou." *Voluntas* 27: 2037–54.

Wong, Natalie W. M. 2016. "Environmental Protests and NIMBY Activism: Local Politics and Waste Management in Beijing and Guangzhou." *China Information* 30:143–64.

Xie, Lei. 2009. *Environmental Activism in China.* London: Routledge.

Xie, Lei, and Arthur P. Mol 2006. "The Role of Guanxi in the Emerging Environmental Movement in China." In Aaron M. McCright, Terry N. Clark, and Anders P. Moller, eds., *Community and Ecology: Dynamics of Place, Sustainability and Politics*, 269–92. Bingley: Emerald.

Yang, Guobin. 2000. "Achieving Emotions in Collective Action: Emotional Processes and Movement Mobilization in the 1989 Chinese Student Movement." *The Sociological Quarterly* 41(4): 593–614.

———. 2005. "Environmental NGOs and Institutional Dynamics in China." *China Quarterly* 181: 46–66.

———. 2009. *The Power of the Internet in China: Citizen Activism Online*. New York: Columbia University Press.

Yang, Guobin, and Craig Calhoun. 2007. "Media, Civil Society, and the Rise of a Green Public Sphere in China." *China Information* 21(2): 211–36.

Yardley, Jim. 2005. "Vast Dam Proposal Is a Test for China." *The New York Times*. December 23.

Yunnan Daily. 2003a. "The Report on Planning of Electricity Exploration in Middle and Lower Stream of Nu River Passed the Review in Beijing." Kunming. August 15.

———. 2003b. "Nujiang (Nu River) County Should Develop Nu River Hydropower Source." Kunming. October 19.

Zhang, J. Y., and Barr, M. 2013. *Green Politics in China: Environmental Governance and State-Society Relations*. London: Pluto Press.

Zhang, Kejia. 2003a. "Dam Building on Nu River Is Planned. Construction Is Opposed." *China Youth Daily*. August 19. Beijing.

———. 2003b. "13 Dams to Be Built on the Last Ecological River, Experts Vehemently Oppose the Development of the Nu River." *China Youth Daily*. Beijing. September 5.

Zhang, Yang. 2018 "Allies in Action: Institutional Actors and Grassroots Environmental Activism in China." *Research in Social Movements, Conflicts and Change* 42: 9–38.

Zhu, Zi. 2017. "Backfired Government Action and the Spillover Effect of Contention: A Case Study of the Anti-PX Protests in Maoming, China." *Journal of Contemporary China* 26: 521–35.

Chapter Eight

Relational Mechanisms of NGOs in Environmental Protests

Yang Zhang (American University)

In social movement research, institutional allies are broadly regarded as one form of political opportunity structure (POS) for grassroots protesters (Gamson 1975; McAdam 1996; Tarrow 1994), but how their partnership emerges and endures has not been sufficiently addressed.[1] Institutional and insurgent actors often have different identities and interests and thus adopt distinctive agendas and repertoires. Their relationship becomes even more tenuous in authoritarian regimes with strong state power because institutional actors risk severe consequences for coordinating with protesters (Chen and Moss 2018). Using nongovernmental organizations (NGOs) as an example, this chapter investigates whether, how, and why institutional actors participate in popular protests despite these obvious constraints.

The relationship between NGO environmentalism and grassroots environmental protest is a case in point. Environmental NGOs (ENGOs) and grassroots activists represent two characteristic types of environmental activism. ENGOs are often formal, routinized, and well-funded organizations comprised of professionals that work for broad environmental protection outside of the government but through institutional channels. By comparison, grassroots environmental activists—sometimes associated with NIMBYism (not in my backyard)—are temporarily mobilized to oppose specific projects, often in proximity to their homes, which may have adverse effects on their health, community, or quality of life (Dokshin 2016; Michaud, Carlisle, and Smith 2008). Given their contrasting missions, institutional levels, organizational modes, and operational methods, these two groups typically follow separate paths toward environmental goals, which themselves are only tangentially related.

Their relationship is even more subtle in "liberalized authoritarian" contexts (Moss 2014), given the state's hybrid means to control civil society and social protests (Fu 2017; Heurlin 2010). In China, for instance, NGOs occupy a precarious space and tend to avoid organizing mass action because of government suspicion of their ability to mobilize the public. Meanwhile, grassroots activists may spontaneously mobilize through residential neighborhood networks, social media, and online forums to stage large-scale demonstrations that directly object to proposed projects close in proximity. The state may allow the incidental resistance of grassroots protesters against potentially hazardous projects but not tolerate their alliance with social organizations that might disturb "social stability." Furthermore, with its corporatist ruling style, the Chinese state and NGOs are not entirely confrontational but often symbiotic: the state needs NGOs to deliver various social services, while NGOs rely on abundant material, political, and symbolic resources from the state (Heurlin 2010; Hildebrandt 2013; Spires 2011).

Given the complexities outlined, have NGOs been absent in environmental protests? If not, how does such institutional partnership emerge and evolve in the authoritarian context? In this chapter, I examine and explain the variations of ENGO participation in four nationally renowned popular protests in four cities of China: anti-PX chemical plant protests in Xiamen (2007) and Kunming (2013),[2] and anti-waste incinerator protests in Beijing (2007) and Guangzhou (2009). Notably, all four protests are broadly regarded as major events in China's environmental activism (Steinhardt and Wu 2016; Sun, Huang, and Yip 2017; Zhang 2018).

Yet, there were notable variations regarding NGO partnership in the four protests. In Xiamen, the local ENGO was only willing to provide scientific knowledge about PX to citizens, while national NGOs in Beijing were unable to offer support. In the Beijing case, a few NGOs participated in the campaign with information provision and policy advocacy, yet in an invisible way. In Guangzhou, activists of national NGOs not only provided information and advocated policy change but also helped local activists create their own NGO. Finally, the Kunming case witnessed full-scale partnership of both local and national ENGOs, including policy advocacy, coalition building, and even protest mobilization. For simplification, NGO engagement in each of the four protests is called: minimal presence (Xiamen), invisible involvement (Beijing), creative coordination (Guangzhou), and pervasive participation (Kunming).

Why did ENGOs participate in similar kinds of environmental protests to varying degrees? I find that the variation in participation cannot be explained by organizational resources, civic communities, or political environment; rather, it hinges on the strength of skillful agencies to broker otherwise disconnected actors and resources and to buffer political pressure for their partners. The best scenario for synergy occurs when brokers at different levels and localities are bound together to produce robust coordinated action and durable alliance. It is thus not internal properties of the organizations or their structural environments but NGOs' relationships with each other and with other actors (e.g., the state and grassroots activists) that largely determines NGOs' incentives and capacities to participate in popular protests.

This research contributes to a few theoretical agendas. Within the social movement literature, it specifies whether and how institutional alliances emerge and endure amid authoritarian control. Additionally, the chapter not only exemplifies the relational model in explaining social movement dynamics (Fligstein and McAdam 2011; McAdam, Tarrow, and Tilly 2001) but also shows how the buffering mechanism, together with the well-studied brokering mechanism, sustains and secures institutional involvement in contentious movements in nondemocratic contexts. Finally, it contributes to the emerging literature on the nuanced triangular relationship among social movements, NGOs, and the authoritarian state (Brass 2016; Heurlin 2010; Long 2018).

INSTITUTIONAL ALLIANCE WITH PROTESTS: A RELATIONAL APPROACH

Institutional activists are considered vital allies for social movement actors by facilitating movement mobilization and favorable outcomes (Amenta et al. 2010; McAdam 1996; Meyer and Minkoff 2004; Tarrow 1994). However, the literature has not sufficiently addressed the genesis and variations of institutional alliance: How does such partnership emerge and endure and why does it vary across similar cases? These questions are important for both institutional activists within the state (Banaszak 2010; Santoro and McGuire 1997; Stearns and Almeida 2004; Suh 2011) and nonstate institutional actors such as NGOs, labor unions, and the media (Böhm 2015; Schock 2005).

This theoretical gap becomes significant in nondemocratic contexts where institutional support of protests is monitored, restricted, and suppressed (Chen and Moss 2018). More than incentives and resources, institutional activists need to offset political pressure to give support for popular protests. As such, institutional activism in social movements should not be taken for granted, as it remains a puzzle to be solved. NGOs, for example, present an interesting case, considering their tense but symbiotic relationship with the authoritarian state (Brass 2016; Spires 2011). Although authoritarian governments such as those in Kenya, Jordan, and China were historically skeptical of NGOs and adopted repressive and exclusionary policies, they have moved to a more sophisticated, corporatist model to effectively control NGOs while using them to deliver social services (Heurlin 2010). However, NGOs' involvement in social protests remains perceived as subversive activity, threatening the stability and legitimacy of the ruling regime (Moss 2014). Despite that, interestingly, NGOs are found to be involved in contentious politics with different levels and tactics (Mische 2008; Schock 2005; Suh 2011).

How, then, does NGO partnership with protests emerge and endure? Such partnership cannot exist without certain attributes, such as organizational strengths and resources, civic communities, and political environments (Gamson 1975; McAdam 1982; McCarthy and Zald 1977; Tarrow 1994). Large and eminent organizations have resources and reputations to contribute; robust civic communities breed frequent and sustainable collaboration among multiple actors; and open political environments allow more institutional involvement in contentious politics. Despite being preconditions, these structural or organizational attributes are insufficient to ensure the onset and endurance of institutional participation in contentions (Fligstein and McAdam 2011:21; McAdam et al. 2001). Institutional alliance will not automatically come into existence even when those conditions are present, and it varies greatly across similar cases.

In this chapter, I adopt a relational approach that emphasizes relational actors and corresponding relational mechanisms, such as brokerage (Fligstein and McAdam 2011; Gould 1995; McAdam et al. 2001; Tilly 2005).[3] Such key relational actors are "coalition brokers," "bridge builders," or "bridging leaders" in social movements (Diani 2003; Mische 2008; Obach 2004: 24; Rose 2000: 143). Successful partnership hinges on the brokerage that facilitates resource sharing and durable coordinated action. For example, brokerage is a key to facilitating coordination in the transnational advocacy network of climate politics (Hadden 2015).

Given the authoritarian control of civil society, partnership between institutional actors and grassroots protesters is often an eventful, emergent, and ephemeral process of assemblage (Sewell 2005; Snow and Moss 2014). Without a durable organizational framework, informal and interpersonal brokerage becomes even more critical. This process relies on temporary but skillful assemblage of otherwise disconnected actors and elements—national institutions, grassroots protesters, resources, opportunities, and knowledge—by brokers who are locally embedded but who also have translocal connections or who have nationwide influence but also closely connect with a particular locality. Precisely because this is a process of assemblage across locations and organizations, the variation of institutional participation in protests cannot be explained by mere area- or organization-specific factors as "independent" variables.

Two vital mechanisms—brokering and buffering—contribute to institutional involvement in popular protests. The brokering mechanism specifically indicates a catalytic process of coordination for collective goods rather than brokering to benefit the brokers themselves (Stovel and Shaw 2012:146). These catalyst brokers do not adopt the *tertius gaudens* strategy to control and take advantage of the only passage between the brokered parties (Burt 1992; Gould and Fernandez 1989; Simmel 1950); they rather use the *tertius iungens* strategy to facilitate direct contact and exchanges between the brokered parties so as to enable coordinated and innovative collective actions (Obstfeld 2005; Quintane and Carnabuci 2016; Stovel and Shaw 2012). Under authoritarian regimes, only by this way can unconnected resources be assembled to sustain risky contentions (Osa 2003).

An equally important mechanism is buffering, especially given that all relevant parties in social movements face great pressure and threats from the authoritarian state. The social network literature notes different kinds of brokerage, including gatekeeping (Fernandez and Gould 1994; Friedman and Podolny 1992; Gould and Fernandez 1989; Hillmann 2008). Gatekeepers may broker ties from rather than toward their opponents and act as a counterweight against powerful outside actors (Stovel and Shaw 2012:142; Kellogg 2014). This sociological insight has great implications for social movement studies: Skillful actors not only broker to assemble resources and increase advantages for their allies but also buffer to reduce risks and lessen political pressures for their partners. Previous research found that reform-minded state actors buffer pressure for their movement allies (Banaszak 2010; Stearns and Almeida 2004; Suh 2011), and international organizations give domestic NGOs and activists leverage over their state, producing transnational boomerang effects (Frank, Hironaka, and Schofer 2000; Keck and Sikkink 1998: 12–13). Likewise, we may well expect that domestic social actors shoulder risks and threats for each other, especially in nondemocratic settings. In summary, both brokering and buffering mechanisms are indispensable to break barriers for institutional participation in popular protests.

The best scenario of synergy appears when brokers at different levels or areas are binding together to produce durable, mutually supportive alliances. Given authoritarian states' vigilance against cross-regional and cross-sectional alliances, an alliance endures when brokers are not only connected but also embedded in each other's professional or regional communities (Gould 1995). In so doing, they share information and resources and coordinate collective actions without unilateral dependence, thus avoiding the dilemma of centralization and overinstitutionalization of grassroots activism (Gamson 1975; Piven and Cloward 1979). Such embedded but symmetric relationships between brokers further ensure the aforementioned tertius iungens brokering for collective goods and mutual buffering of the pressure so as to share political risks. In this way, for example, national organizations are able to penetrate local communities and deliver support to citizen activists while local organizations are able to access the national policy community. Furthermore, they buffer political pressure for each other and for grassroots protesters, greatly reducing the risk associated with confrontational movements in authoritarian regimes. Bound brokers thus make partnership durable and robust.

This relational approach offers insights to the puzzle of NGO participation in popular protests in China. Notably, several recent studies of Chinese environmental activism have also noticed this institutional partnership and often use certain organizational or area-specific attributes to explain such partnership (Bondes and Johnson 2017; Steinhardt and Wu 2016; Sun et al. 2017; Wong 2016). By focusing on exceptionally successful cases with robust synergy, however, these works tend to overestimate the level of NGO participation in protests. This selection bias may further result in the fallacy of causal speculation; such case studies tend to offer idiosyncratic organizational or structural factors to account for success, but these factors are often insufficient to produce institutional alliance. Furthermore, by using area- and organization-specific factors, these works cannot account for the different activities of the same organizations in similar cases. My relational approach, as will be shown, offers clues to such nuanced questions.

METHODS AND DATA

This chapter investigates the variations of ENGO participation in four environmental protests (figure 8.1 maps the four cases). These four cases are chosen from the two most visible movement sectors in China—anti-PX and anti-waste incinerator protests—and are among the most well-known protests in the last decade. Meanwhile, the four cities also represent open political spaces and vibrant civic communities in China: Beijing houses the headquarters of national NGOs and regional offices for international NGOs; Xiamen, a coastal city, is famous for its civil society and community organizations; Guangzhou is a politically open city with vigorous media market; and Kunming has hosted a large number of international NGOs for nearly three decades. Despite these similarities across the cases and cities, there are great variations regarding the form and level of NGO participation in the protests. Furthermore, my study not only features subnational comparisons but also examines the disjuncture and connections between each locality and the national policy community (Diani 2015).

In 2008, 2012, and 2018, I conducted fifty in-depth interviews with individuals involved in the four protests.[4] Employing the "sequential interviewing" method, I interviewed environmental officials, citizen protesters, and

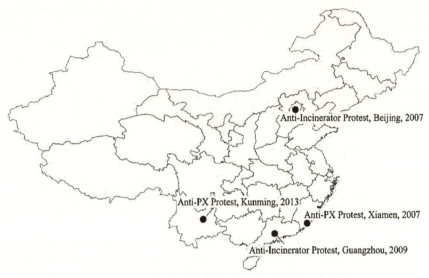

Figure 8.1. Four Cases of Anti-PX and Anti-Incinerator Protests in China

NGO leaders and activists, with the objective to saturate information for my questions (Small 2009: 24–25). These interviews offer inside knowledge and diverse perspectives about the relationship between ENGOs and environmental protesters. In addition, I draw on newspaper coverage, government publications and reports, NGO newsletters, social surveys conducted by national NGOs, and other secondary sources. This mix of data makes my analysis both accurate and novel because I use the second sources to reconstruct the process of these events while relying on the firsthand interview data to answer key analytic questions.

NGOs AND POPULAR PROTESTS IN CHINA'S ENVIRONMENTAL ACTIVISM

Environmental activism in China has been constituted by a complex network of actors, including environmental protection agencies, especially the national agency—State Environmental Protection Agency (SEPA, 1998–2008) and Ministry of Environmental Protection (MEP, 2008–2018)—ENGOs, journalists, lawyers, scientists, and citizen activists (Economy 2010; Sun and Zhao 2008; Zhang 2018). Until 2007, the defining feature of Chinese environmentalism was institutional activism in environmental campaigns without street confrontations (Ho and Edmonds 2007; Sun and Zhao 2008).

In particular, since the founding of China's first domestic ENGO—Friends of Nature—in Beijing in 1994, ENGOs have been increasing in number and influence and have become the most vigorous advocates for environmental protection (Economy 2010; Yang 2005). As of 2005, there were 2,768 environmental social organizations in China, further increasing to 3,539 in 2008, and 6,636 in 2013 when the Kunming anti-PX Protest occurred (Shapiro 2016: 124). During the 1990s and the early 2000s, ENGOs actively participated in a number of environmental campaigns, such as the Golden Snubnosed Monkey Protection Movement (1995–1996) and the anti-dam campaigns to protect the Dujiangyan World Heritage Site (2003) and the Nu River (2003–2006) (Mertha 2008; Sun and Zhao 2008). Together with reformist officials, reporters, and scientists, ENGOs achieved favorable outcomes and increased their spaces in environmental governance without engaging in contentious collective actions. As such, their relationship with popular protests was tenuous because they tended to keep distance from open confrontation with the state.

During the last decade (2007–2016), however, Chinese environmental activism witnessed a populace increasingly aware of environmental health hazards and a wave of large-scale, grassroots protests (Steinhardt and Wu 2016). This wave of protests started in 2007 with the two landmark unrests over the PX chemical plant in Xiamen and the waste incinerator in Beijing. Within a few years, dozens of sizable popular protests arose in several cities of China, contesting targets such as subway construction in Nanjing (2011), a copper alloy plant in Shifang (2012), and a coal power plant in Heyuan (2015). The most visible cases, nevertheless, were still anti-PX and anti-incinerator protests in dozens of cities from coastal and interior areas (Liu 2016; Steinhardt and Wu 2016). The four cases examined here represent the typical scale and scenario of such protests (see table 8.1 for a summary).

This new wave of grassroots protests shows features of NIMBYism: Protests were led by middle-class residents concerned about the potential negative health impacts of chemical pollutants infiltrating their neighborhoods and harming health. Residents were also concerned about the potential decrease

Table 8.1. A Summary of the Four Cases

City	Movement Period	Protest Dates	Protest Repertories	Protest Size	Direct Outcomes
Xiamen, Fujian	March–December, 2007	June 1–2, 2007	March and demonstration	10,000–20,000	Cancellation and relocation
Haidian, Beijing	2007–2011	June 5, 2007	Demonstration	1,000–3,000	Suspension and cancellation
Guangzhou, Guangdong	2009–2012	November 23, 2009	Demonstration	1,000	Relocation
Kunming, Yunnan	2013	May 4 and 16, 2013	March and demonstration	1,000–3,000	Suspension

in property value due to pollution, odor, and noise from nearby plants. By using internet forums and social media to share information and organize protests, these citizens attempted to shape decision-making favorably. These protests often surpassed community boundaries, involved a critical mass of protesters, and engaged in policy advocacy. As shown in table 8.1, all four cases achieved substantive movement outcomes. This chapter, nevertheless, focuses on procedural outcomes or organizational outcomes that were directly related to institutional activism (Amenta, Andrews, and Caren 2018). Specifically, although NGOs have been reported to be present in these protests, it is still unclear how such institutional support emerged and why their engagement varied. It is this gap that draws me to conduct the subsequent analysis.

VARYING NGO PARTICIPATIONS IN POPULAR PROTESTS

To analyze ENGO participation in the four cases, I refer to four tactics: information provision,[5] policy advocacy,[6] coalition building,[7] and protest participation.[8] This is not an exhaustive list,[9] but it does capture the most commonplace and effective tactics and demonstrates the variations of ENGO participation across the four cases (see table 8.2 for a summary). Information provision, the least risky form, occurred in each of the four cases. Policy advocacy was present in Beijing, Guangzhou, and Kunming. Coalition building occurred in Kunming and Guangzhou, albeit with different features: In Kunming, national and local ENGOs were linked for coordinated actions; in Guangzhou, national ENGOs helped grassroots activists create their own organization and cofounded with the latter a national advocacy coalition. Protest participation of NGOs occurred only in Kunming, whereas ENGOs deliberately distanced themselves from the protests elsewhere.

Table 8.2. A Summary of NGO Partnership in the Four Protests

Cases	Information Provision	Policy Advocacy	Coalition Building	Protest Participation
Xiamen: Minimal presence	+	–	–	–
Beijing: Invisible involvement	+	+	–	–
Guangzhou: Creative coordination	+	+	+	–
Kunming: Pervasive participation	+	+	+	+

NGO, nongovernmental organization.

Given their varying levels, tactics, and features of ENGO participation, I characterize the participation in the four cases as follows: minimal presence (Xiamen), invisible involvement (Beijing), creative coordination (Guangzhou), and pervasive participation (Kunming, see table 8.2). I will briefly introduce the basics of each case, starting with Xiamen and ending with Kunming, and then discuss NGOs' participation in each.

Xiamen: Minimal Presence

In the 2007 Xiamen anti-PX campaign, citizen activists carried the protest from street mobilization through successfully halting the PX plant while the local ENGO Green Cross was merely willing to provide scientific knowledge. The citizen activists began to issue petitions as early as 2005, but the mobilization only gained citywide momentum after a few scientists submitted a joint proposal objecting to the PX plant in the annual Chinese People's Political Consultative Conference in March 2007. Although the motion failed, media coverage of the controversy triggered grassroots mobilization of Xiamen citizens, which led to a large-scale march and demonstration on June 1 and 2, 2007. The public outcry encouraged SEPA to intervene in this project by conducting another Environmental Impact Assessment (EIA). After a public hearing, authorities announced in December 2007 that the project would be halted and relocated (Johnson 2010; Zhang 2018).

The Xiamen protest saw minimal ENGO involvement in the form of information provision. Green Cross only interacted with protesters during the initial petition period by providing basic scientific information about the PX chemical (interviews with petition organizers, 2008). This type of information provision was neutral because the information could have been used by protesters to fuel their protests but could also have been used by the government to show that they were taking appropriate safety and environmental protection measures. When asked by Xiamen citizens to assist in organizing a march, however, Green Cross refused outright with the well-known "Three No" principle: "Our attitude on the march is straightforward: no support, no opposition, no organizing" (interview with the leader of Green Cross, Ms. Ma, 2008). Green Cross had good reason for concern—the local Environmental Protection Bureau (EPB) made it clear that even sharing protest-related information would be deemed unacceptable, threatening to shut down the organization (interviews with volunteers of Green Cross, 2008). In the postprotest period, Green Cross was involved in policy making when channels for institutional participation were open, but it largely served as a policy consultant for the Xiamen municipal government rather than working with citizen activists. In other words, it partnered with the state and not with activists. Xiamen citizen activists, protesters, reporters, and scholars all complained of the betrayal of their once-trusted NGO even after the conclusion of this event (interviews with Mr. Li, Mr. Mo, Mr. Huang, and Ms. Yuan, 2008).

Meanwhile, national ENGOs in Beijing were unable to offer effective support to the grassroots activists in Xiamen despite their attempt to do so. At that time, China's environmental activism was in its golden age, thanks primarily to a triangular network of reformist officials, ENGOs, and reporters under the coordination of SEPA, especially its Deputy Director Pan Yue (Ho and Edmonds 2007; Sun and Zhao 2008). As such, Beijing NGOs were eager to participate in this event and sent delegates to Xiamen, but they were unable to find local accommodations as Green Cross declined to collaborate (interviews with Mr. Ye in 2008, Ms. Wang in 2012, and Mr. Zhang in 2018). Without significant NGO participation, the success of this movement largely hinged on the tacit coordination between grassroots activists on the street and institutional activists within the state (Zhang 2018).

Beijing: Invisible Involvement

Like Xiamen, the campaign to halt construction of a waste incinerator in Beijing succeeded mainly through citizen activism. Also starting in 2005, residents in the Haidian District self-organized to contest the proposed nearby incinerator plant. On World Environmental Protection Day (June 5) of 2007—only three days after the Xiamen anti-PX protest—thousands of residents demonstrated in front of the SEPA building. Two days later, SEPA Deputy Director Pan Yue announced that the project (and the Xiamen PX plant) would be suspended until comprehensive EIAs were completed. After a series of subsequent advocacy and petitions, the government eventually decided to move the plant site to a more remote location in 2011.

During this process, a few Beijing-based NGOs provided information and resources to grassroots activists, yet largely in an invisible way. They stayed away when residents petitioned and protested the proposed incinerator. Like Green Cross in Xiamen, they refused to engage in the outright protest when they were approached by the residents (interviews with NGO leaders Mr. Chen in 2008, Ms. Wang and Mr. Huo in 2012, and Liulitun activists in 2008). After the protest was over, however, NGOs such as Friends of Nature and Green Beagle came forward to provide scientific information, help residents create community programs around waste management, teach citizens how to implement proper waste management in their neighborhoods, and connect grassroots activists to media to make their voice heard (Lang and Xu

2013). For example, Mao Da, then a staff member of Green Beagle, continued offering knowledge and suggestions about waste management by sending emails to grassroots activists (focus group discussion with NGO practitioners and researchers, Beijing, 2012). Likewise, when approached by Liulitun residents in 2009, Friends of Nature invisibly offered help. As commented by a member of Friends of Nature,

> We had great involvement in Liulitun [anti-incinerator campaign]. . . . But we had kept low profile in public. . . . We tried to be behind the scenes as much as possible. For example, when the residents of Liulitun were unable to speak out, we helped them to appear in CCTV through a series of professional operations. In the TV programs, they appeared as [affected] homeowners of the neighborhood, while we were called environmental volunteers (interview with Mr. Bo, 2018).

Guangzhou: Creative Coordination

The anti-incinerator movement in Guangzhou was similar to Beijing in scale and repertoire, but the residents self-organized into a formal NGO after the protests. In September 2009, residents in the Panyu District of Guangzhou began speaking out against a nearby waste incinerator by signing petitions and hanging banners on their buildings expressing concern about pollution and health issues. They further protested in front of the Guangzhou municipal government building in November 2009. The district party secretary promised to halt construction of the plant, but protesters wanted to cancel construction outright rather than move the plant to a more remote location.

Beijing NGOs such as Friends of Nature and Green Beagle stepped in to support the Panyu activists with mentorship and training. The local branch of Friends of Nature contacted the grassroots activists as early as during their public events to collect petition signatures, but neither side collaborated further at that time (interview with activist Mr. Ming, 2018). After local residents had suspended the incinerator project, they wanted to create a group (called "Green Family") for continuing advocacy for green waste management practices. After hearing that Friends of Nature had helped the Liulitun protesters set up community recycling projects, the Panyu activists came to learn more about these experiences during workshops organized by Friends of Nature. Thanks to this interaction, in spring 2012 they eventually developed a formal NGO—Eco-Canton—to continue to advocate for alternative waste treatment options (Bondes and Johnson 2017; Wong 2016). Since its founding, Eco-Canton has closely collaborated with ENGOs in Beijing, and it immediately joined the Zero Waste Alliance—a national advocacy network founded in December 2011 (Wong 2016).

Beijing ENGOs, according to a Guangzhou-based NGO activist and researcher, played three roles in the creation of Eco-Canton: "They increased the visibility of the issue, . . . delivered social movement experience and know-how, [and] provided external resources [that were] not just money" (interview with Mr. Chen, 2018). They participated through the following means:

> [We] gave them suggestions regarding the NGO management capacity: how to register the organization, build a board of council, and organize the core team. . . . I also provided a few external opportunities, such as external awards [which] provided start-up funding. (Interview with Mr. Ju of Friends of Nature, 2018)

This experience of partnership was transformative for both grassroots activists and ENGO practitioners. For local activists, they successfully transformed their localized NIMBYism into environmentalism, or "NIABYism"—"not-in-anyone's-backyard" (Boudet 2011). For members in Beijing NGOs, they were impressed by local activists' "civic temperament" and their determination to move beyond NIMBYism from the beginning (interviews with Mr. Huo and Ms. Ran, 2012, and Mr. Ju, 2018). Together with other events, this experience pushed sixteen NGOs—including Friends of Nature and Green Beagle in Beijing—to move forward by creating the Zero Waste Alliance, whose founding members also included several grassroots activists, such as those in the Guangzhou campaign (focus group discussion with NGO practitioners and researchers, Beijing, 2012). This durable alliance was made through continuous partnership between institutional and grassroots activists.

Kunming: Pervasive Participation

The Kunming anti-PX protest saw perhaps the greatest ENGO involvement, including information provision, policy advocacy, coalition making, and certain forms of protest participation. On May 4, 2013, about three thousand people gathered in the Kunming city center to protest against a petrochemical plant planned by the China National Petroleum Corporation (PetroChina). Citizens expressed concerns over the project and its potential chemical consequences, but the local government downplayed the risks while emphasizing the economic benefits. Around this time, two Kunming-based local ENGOs—Green Watershed and Green Kunming—sought ways to gain information and organize the public in criticism of this project. However, not only did the local government prevent disclosure of the EIA, but it also warned the two ENGOs to cease involvement in the case. Later, the local government agreed to release the EIA report for the plant. The two local ENGOs then worked with national ENGOs to create a coalition to reassess the siting of the plant. This combination of local and national pressure succeeded in stopping the PX project in 2015 (Steinhardt and Wu 2016; Sun et al. 2017).

NGO participation in the Kunming protest features several tactics. Above all, NGOs at Kunming and Beijing used policy advocacy to change the siting decision of the PX project, increase transparency of this project, and include more public participation in the decision-making process. After the protests in May 2013, the local government agreed to halt the project on June 2, released the EIA on June 28, 2013, and then put the project on hold for further consultation. At this point local ENGOs entered the conversation by working as partners of both the grassroots protesters and the local government authorities. Together with a few national ENGOs—Friends of Nature, Nature University, and the Institute of Public and Environmental Affairs (IPE)—they actively advocated against the plant during public hearings and consultation meetings (interview with Mr. Fei of the Green Kunming and Mr. Gang and Mr. Yang of the Green Watershed, 2018). In July 2013, NGOs from Yunnan and Beijing made a joint statement to the MEP and requested it retrieve the EIA approval for this project. As a follow-up, Friends of Nature and Nature University in Beijing held a press conference to speak directly to the public and to PetroChina, raising the profile of the protest while pressuring both PetroChina and the Yunnan provincial government to halt construction and review the project's siting decision. Then, in November 2013, when a refinery plant in Qingdao, Shandong Province, exploded and caused sixty-three deaths, Friends of Nature was able to link the accident to the Kunming plant. Subsequent investigations, conducted by Green Watershed, revealed that a lack of transparency around the decision-making process had led to public distrust of the government and made space for potentially illegal behavior to occur (interview with Mr. Yang, the principal of this investigation, 2018). Overall, the local and national ENGOs were able to use their expert knowledge, organizational powers, and network of connections to advocate for policy change based on the local Kunming conflict.

In addition, coalition work was a salient feature of this campaign. Before the protests, two local NGOs—Green Kunming and Green Watershed—jointly visited the PX plant site to investigate the potential environmental problems of this project; after the two protests, Green Watershed and Green Kunming solicited residents to sign petitions for the local government to release the EIA (interviews with members of the two ENGOs, 2018). More critically, the coalition work between national ENGOs and local ENGOs, especially Green Watershed, became pronounced after the initial protests. Friends of Nature, Nature University, and IPE joined the investigation and training exercises in Kunming and networked with local ENGOs to share information and strategize against the PX plant. In addition, IPE provided its pollution data regarding petrochemical enterprises; Natural University provided two detectors for monitoring PM 2.5;[10] Friends of Nature connected Green Watershed with environmental litigation lawyers to file lawsuits against the local government and MEP for malfeasance or nonfeasance and also jointly supported residents to file suits for government malfeasance;[11] and a few philanthropic foundations offered funding to conduct the nationwide investigation about PX-related controversies (interviews with Mr. Gang, Mr. Yang, and Mr. Zhang, 2018). Additionally, national ENGOs used their media connections to publicize the PX conflict in Kunming to the wider public.

Last but not least, the Kunming case saw (albeit limited) protest participation on the part of local ENGOs. Despite receiving warnings from the government, Green Watershed organized two workshops to train citizens to resist "rationally" before the second protest. These workshops became crucial sites for mobilization until they were prohibited. One organizer described:

> Before the second protest, we intended to do something. The first was to train citizens to fight for their rights rationally. There were about 100–200 participants in our first workshop. . . . [The government] maintained that these workshops mobilized citizens to protest, although we told citizens not to do so but to use other means (interview with Mr. Xiao, 2018).

In conclusion, ENGOs in Kunming had a clear interest in ensuring the government reversed its decision and persisted in their actions despite the government's warnings and surveillance. Despite the dangers from involvement with demonstrations, the ENGOs and their activists still joined or supported the citizen-led protests to convince the government to heed their concerns. In this way, grassroots protesters and local and national NGOs formed a coherent alliance, working together to expand the reach of their influence and create opportunities to bargain with the government. This durable alliance was key to the landslide success of the campaign.

BROKER AND BUFFER: EXPLAINING VARIATIONS OF NGO PARTICIPATION

Why did ENGOs participate in these grassroots environmental protests to varying degrees? Although organizational and area-specific attributes are important preconditions, I find that they are not sufficient to activate and sustain NGO participation. Instead, I find the key is the brokering and buffering efforts of skillful agencies and the binding of such brokers at different levels or localities. This relational explanation offers critical clues for answering the preceding question.

The Attributional Explanations

Several area- or organization-specific attributes have been raised to explain ENGO partnership. The first pertains to the organizational strength and resources of certain NGOs (Hsu, Hsu, and Hasmath 2017); for example, ENGOs in Beijing possess the resources and reputation to supervise local governments and collaborate with local ENGOs, and arguably, "they are implicitly endorsed by the central government to disclose the malfeasance of local governments" (Sun et al. 2017:4). However, these same Beijing ENGOs merely invisibly partnered with the campaign in Beijing and were unable to function in the Xiamen case, even if they sought to. Furthermore, this explanation overstates the relationship between the central government and national NGOs since the central government is, first and foremost, the backer of local governments in China's unitary political system, despite its internal fragmentation.

Alternatively, NGO participation may be related to the number (rather than the size) of NGOs, and the overall level of civic community engagement, such as the case of Kunming (Hildebrandt 2013; Teets 2015; Wu 2013). The unusual success of the anti-PX movement in Kunming is said to be related to its vibrant civil society, including the ENGO community in Yunnan (Steinhardt and Wu 2016; Sun et al. 2017). However, these factors should not be overestimated in this case. According to several informants in Kunming (interviews with Mr. Fei, Mr. Mo, Mr. Yang, and Mr. Gang, 2018), Yunnan's ENGO community had been greatly weakened by new NGO registration policies and stricter regulation since 2009 (see also, Teets 2015).[12] Furthermore, the similarly rich civic community tradition in Xiamen did not ensure an equivalent level of ENGO partnership, despite its effects in mobilizing a large number of citizens into the protests. Likewise, Beijing's dense NGO networks did not lead to equivalent robust participation in the anti-incinerator protests in Beijing.

Finally, open political environments are argued to be critical for facilitating institutional activism, especially in an overall authoritarian regime (Wong 2016; Wu 2013). In Guangdong, for example, greater political openness and more participatory governance mechanisms were in place (Wong 2016: 2048). This factor may explain why the governments in Guangdong were generally more tolerant with popular protests and more willing to encourage citizens' political participation; but we should remember that the Guangzhou anti-incinerator protest ran its course with the partnership of national ENGOs in Beijing rather than any existing local NGOs.[13]

In other words, although these attributes are important, they have not pinpointed the variations of NGO participation in these environmental protests. Furthermore, a good explanation should be able to account for even subtler variations, such as the differences in participation levels of the same national NGO in similar cases. Why were the same Beijing ENGOs able to be active and effective in Guangzhou and Kunming but only invisibly participated in Beijing and were unable to offer partnership in Xiamen? I find the relational approach also offers analytical leverage for addressing such nuanced variations.

The Relational Explanation

The key to explaining variation in ENGO participation in grassroots protests is the capacity of certain brokers for bridging resources and for buffering risks for each other. This process occurs when local or national ENGOs act as intermediaries between grassroots activists and government authorities, participating in both policy advocacy and grassroots protests (even if tacitly) or linking local residential communities with the national policy community. Successful brokers are either embedded in the locality while having translocal connections or possess nationwide networks while having close connections to a particular locality. In addition to brokerage, they also buffer political pressure for each other by partaking in risky tasks. The best scenario for synergy occurs when such brokerage at the local and national levels are bound. In such cases, the partnership becomes robust and durable without unilateral dependence, as already well-connected actors are further embedded in each other's community. I illustrate this argument in a reverse order by revisiting the Kunming case first because it provides a full-fledged illustration of these mechanisms.

The Kunming protest is an example of brokerage and their interconnectedness. First, the two local ENGOs in Kunming played a vital role in linking grassroots communities and the municipal government. They worked with citizen activists but were also expected by the government to resolve tension between the state and the protesters, partly because they maintained good relationships with the government (interview with Mr. Yang, 2018). For example, Green Watershed held workshops and invited citizen activists, environmental officials, and PetroChina representatives to join in conversation. When the EIA report was released, the two ENGOs acted as brokers of a deal between the local government and residents by discussing and gathering information from government offices they had access to and sharing this information with residents.

Second, several activists within national ENGOs served as bridges for Kunming citizens and the national policy and NGO community in Beijing. Among the most active were a few native Yunnanese professionals in ENGOs and philanthropic foundations in Beijing, such as Mr. Li Bo, former director-general (January 2009–May 2012) of Friends of Nature. Mr. Li alerted Beijing ENGOs to the initial protest events in Kunming. As put by an NGO leader, "There were many Yunnanese in the entire environmental protection field, not only NGOs but also media and other professionals such as environmental consulting firms. . . . In the process of this incident, those Yunnanese thought they shouldn't let it go, but should participate" (interview with Mr. Bo, 2018). Those Beijing ENGO activists were mediators between their home province and their professional communities, spreading information and facilitating collective action and policy consultation.

Most critically, the binding of brokerage at the local and national levels proved key to the favorable substantive outcomes and many procedural reforms that did not occur in other similar cases. Specifically, Kunming ENGO leaders such as Mr. Yu Xiaogang of Green Watershed served as brokers among local communities and national NGOs, and national ENGO leaders such as Li Bo mediated Kunming ENGOs and resources in Beijing. Unknown to the public, Mr. Yu was born and had lived in Beijing during his childhood before moving to Yunnan and had built broad connections with Beijing ENGOs in several early campaigns. As such, Mr. Yu was able to use his national network of partnerships to pull in national NGOs and form a successful movement coalition, and he was also willing to offer national partners necessary information and assistance that enabled them to get deeply involved in local events. Meanwhile, by using their expert knowledge and large networks, national ENGOs granted credibility to the Kunming NGOs and raised the profile of the conflict. One example of such mutual brokerage is that Li Bo helped Yu Xiaogang navigate administrative and legal channels in Beijing, while Yu accompanied Li to visit provincial and municipal offices in Kunming (interview with Mr. Gang, 2018). Not only did they share resources, but they also coordinated actions in environmental litigation and policy consultation (interview with Mr. Gang of Green Watershed and Mr. Huo in Beijing, 2018).

This partnership proved to be critical also because of the buffering mechanism. National ENGOs supported the local groups to conduct contentious activities on the ground, while they exercised their abilities to pressure the government indirectly and to advocate for transparent policies as the events in Kunming unfolded. As put by a leader of Beijing ENGO,

> Those organizations in the front line—either Mr. Yu's [Green Watershed] or the Green Kunming—had greater pressure, because the incident occurred where they operated. Therefore, it would be better if we could share some of their pressures and support by coordinated action, restraining them from exposure to great pressure (interview with Mr. Bo, 2018).

In short, the Kunming case is (almost) a social movement. The role of NGOs involved more than just partnership with grassroots activists; it was closer to a social movement organization, linking with other institutional activists such as lawyers, experts, foundations, and reporters. The key of its success is thus not area- or organization-specific attributes but how those attributes were linked up to become effective and low-risk in the authoritarian system.

In Guangzhou, no local NGO played the same brokerage role seen in Kunming, but the links among national brokers and leaders of citizen activists facilitated partnership. In particular, when grassroots activists such as Mr. Ming sought to transform their activism from momentary mobilization to a momentous movement, their connection with national ENGOs in Beijing played a critical role. As early as 2009, Mr. Ming met Mr. Zhang of Friends of Nature in a telecast program and has since then received continuous suggestion from Mr. Zhang (interview with Mr. Ming, 2018). But Zhang brought more than just a suggestion: "what we have done is the linkage of resources, such as linking of scholars and professionals in Guangzhou with them" (interview with Mr. Zhang, 2018). Although political opportunities, resources, and knowledge were available in Guangzhou, it was skilled agency to bridge these dispersed elements together to sustain an extended and expanding agenda.

Mr. Ming became an individual member of the newly established national advocacy coalition—Zero Waste Alliance—in December 2011. He later established his own organization Eco-Canton in 2012, partly because he continued to learn from existing NGOs with which he maintained connections (interview with Mr. Ming, 2018). The interpersonal brokerage eventually turned into institutional outcomes. Not surprisingly, a number of ENGO leaders became members of Eco-Canton's founding council.

Furthermore, this loosely linked coalition began to buffer risks for each other. First, building alliance increased solidarity against political pressures: "[The alliance] makes everyone 'jointly hold together for warmth.' According to one commentator of our city, 'We are not fighting alone'" (interview with NGO activist, Mr. Yun, 2018). Second, NGOs reduced political pressure for each other by using the strategy of "supervising government from outside" (*yidi jiandu*), partly because China's multifold and often fragmented control of civil society resulted in the lack of coordinated state actions across jurisdictions (Chen 2012; Fu 2017; Mertha 2008; O'Brien and Li 2006). An NGO practitioner and researcher in Guangzhou commented:

> When local NGOs cannot advance certain sensitive jobs in their home areas, other members of the alliance can do so. . . . Requesting government for information disclosure, for instance, can be taken over by external organizations.

... Like 'supervising government by outside media' (*meiti yidi jiandu*),[14] this is [the practice of] "supervising government by outside NGOs" (NGO *yidi jiandu*) (interview with Mr. Chen, 2018).

In the Beijing case, national ENGOs were unable to be too active in protests occurring in the national capital. There, "national" NGOs were also "local" ENGOs and, hence, have to directly confront the municipal government if they are involved in contentious activities. As such, they served at most brokers behind the scenes. Additionally, in Beijing there was a lack of "local" ENGOs acting as buffers between local authorities and national ENGOs. In particular, the absence of the buffering mechanism made those otherwise resourceful and renowned national NGOs vulnerable to government surveillance if they were involved. One NGO leader explains:

> In the political and social environment of China, the surveillance system [of Beijing] is strict, especially when it is related to "mass disturbances" (*quntixing shijian*). If we participate [in such incidents] in a high-profile, public, and direct way, we would offer some local administrator an excuse: "You see, NGOs join them" (interview with Mr. Wang, 2012).

Finally, the Xiamen ENGOs did not bridge Xiamen's vibrant civic community with national ENGOs and SEPA activists in the anti-PX movement. Although SEPA activists and national ENGOs sought to support grassroots activists, they were unable to find local partners because Xiamen's local NGOs, such as Green Cross, declined to partner with national ENGOs in Beijing when the latter made the request. One Xiamen activist said: "several Beijing NGOs dispatched their representatives to Xiamen, but Ms. Ma was not willing to offer any local accommodation and assistance. So they had to go back to Beijing after staying a few days" (interview with Mr. Ye in Xiamen, 2008). A Beijing ENGO leader commented, "How could we do anything if the Xiamen NGO did nothing?" (interview with Ms. Mu in Beijing, 2012). Overall, it was not ENGO partnership but the coordination between policy makers within SEPA and grassroots protesters that made the Xiamen movement successful (Zhang 2018).

Table 8.3 summarizes three attributional explanations and the relational explanation across the four cases. In particular, it is also informative to summarize the specific roles of Beijing NGOs within these explanations: Simply put, neither their resources nor reputations but their varying relationships with local partners made them initiative in Kunming, inspiring in Guangzhou, invisible in their home city (Beijing), and ineffective in Xiamen.

Table 8.3. Alternative Explanations of NGO Participation in the Four Protests

Cases	NGO Participation	Alternative Explanations			
		Organizational Strength	Political Openness	Civic Communities	Relational Ties
Xiamen	Minimal presence	Median	Median	High	No brokering or buffering
Beijing	Invisible involvement	High	Low	Median	Brokering but no buffering
Guangzhou	Creative coordination	Median	High	High	Brokering and buffering
Kunming	Pervasive participation	Median	Median	Median	Brokering, buffering, and binding of brokers

NGO, nongovernmental organization.

CONCLUSION

Contentious politics is politics of possibility, especially in nondemocratic contexts. Given the dangers associated with contentious movements, why did environmental organizations participate in popular protests in China? And when they did so, why did they participate in similar cases to varying degrees, ranging from minimal presence of information provision to pervasive and pro-active participation? This chapter finds that the variations of NGO participation in popular protests mostly hinged on the efforts of certain agencies to link recourses and reduce risks through the mechanisms of brokering and buffering. When brokers at different levels are bound together, protest campaigns see robust coordinated actions and durable partnerships, as well as favorable procedural outcomes such as public hearings, stricter environmental regulations, and deliberative participation mechanisms.

Are there alternative explanations? One option is the diffusion model and imitation mechanism over a cycle of contentions over time (Tarrow 1994). The difference of NGO partnership, according to this explanation, is that in Beijing and Xiamen both NGOs and grassroots activists had no precedent examples and were inexperienced, while Guangzhou and Kunming activists can learn from those preceding cases. Furthermore, the key mechanism might not be relational ties, but rather nonrelational imitation and learning through mass media and the internet (e.g., Liu 2016). This alternative explanation may apply to unorganized grassroots activists who did learn from precedent protests via the internet, but it is less useful in explaining the variations of NGO involvement. First, although the anti-PX and anti-incinerator movements in Xiamen and Beijing were the first of their kind, there were ample precedents of NGO participation in other environmental campaigns, such as the antidam movements. Furthermore, 2007 was often regarded as the best moment of environmental activism in China, while the period of 2008–2014 saw an adverse trend of environmental governance due to an anti-reform power reshuffle within MEP (Zhang 2018). As such, we cannot assume that NGOs would be increasingly involved in the later protests. On the contrary, NGOs did not play a role in most other environmental protests during this period; in effect, at nearly the same time of the Kunming protest, another anti-PX protest in Chengdu (at a neighboring province) was thwarted and did not witness NGO participations (SCMP 2013).

This research makes new contributions to the study of brokerage in social movements. While previous studies have often emphasized how bridge builders link otherwise disconnected actors and resources (Obach 2004; Rose 2000), I contend that another mechanism, the buffering mechanism, is also vital, especially in authoritarian regimes, given the political pressures for each party related to the contention. The buffering agents may be powerful reformist officials (Banaszak 2010) and prominent international organizations (Keck and Sikkink 1998: 12–13), but they could also be domestic social actors who need to break severe political barriers by building informal relations with each other. Additionally, this chapter demonstrates that the binding of brokers can reinforce the brokering and buffering mechanisms without unilateral dependence. This finding echoes Roger Gould's (1995) classical study about the Paris Commune: The linkage of the neighborhood and organizational networks might increase militia morale because those militias served as information conduits between their community and organizations. In the case of Yunnan, similarly, Kunming NGOs became even more devoted once they saw the involvement of Beijing NGOs via the conduit of Yunnan-born NGO activists in Beijing. Finally, this research echoes a processual relational take: Although successful movement alliance often depends on preexisting ties, such as that among leaders of Kunming NGOs and national NGOs, the ties and brokerage may emerge in dynamic interactions of multiple actors (McAdam et al. 2001; Tilly 2005). For example, the relational tie in the Guangzhou case was formed in the process of, rather than before, this movement.

The effects of relational ties and brokerage in social movements are certainly not limited to authoritarian contexts (Hadden 2015), but their roles in nondemocratic societies are indeed more significant. Given that social relations are often fluid and rules are unclear in authoritarian societies, the social skills of strategic actors become vital (Moss 2014; Osa 2003). Those actors can serve as brokers between policy makers and protesters when they conceive of their relationships with the state as constantly in flux and, thus, gauge their goals and actions against those of state actors, even when working in partnership with them. Their success or failure to carve out contentious political space depends on whether the organizational, spatial, and temporal positions they inhabit enables them to assemble favorable opportunities, resources, and actors together and reduce political pressures for each other to sustain robust coordinated actions.

To conclude, social organizations and grassroots activists are the most vital actors in the emerging civil society of China. They strive to expand civic space, break through political constraints, and navigate new terrains of transgressive activism. Though durable social movements are still controlled,[15] uncommon forms of coordination between NGOs and grassroots protesters—as documented here—open up possibilities for exceptional cases of activism. Expanding the public space, after all, is not given but collectively created from the bottom up through both every day and eventful resistance.

NOTES

1. This chapter uses the terms "institutional allies," "elite allies," and "institutional activists" interchangeably (McAdam 1996; Santoro and McGuire 1997; Tarrow 1994).

2. PX is the abbreviation for paraxylene, which is broadly used in the petrochemical industry.

3. Brokerage may be generally defined as "the process of connecting actors in systems of social, economic, or political relations in order to facilitate access to valued resources" (Stovel and Shaw 2012:141).

4. Following other studies on China's environmental protests (Steinhardt and Wu 2016; Sun et al. 2017; Wong 2016), I have anonymized all individual informants while using real names of their organizations, unless otherwise specified.

5. Social organizations provide neutral information and knowledge sharing about controversies to an audience without intending to provoke protest. In this minimal level of participation, the boundary between the two sets of actors is clear and purposively maintained by the institutional actors to distance themselves from open confrontation with the state.

6. Social organizations influence policy making to favor grassroots activists by bargaining with state actors, providing expert consultation, and increasing media coverage. This is not regular policy participation in nonconfrontational issues but purposeful coordinated action for grassroots protesters on sensitive issues.

7. Social organizations make alliances with each other to support grassroots movements or help grassroots activists institutionalize the activism (McCammon and Campbell 2002; Meyer and Corrigall-Brown 2005). In authoritarian societies, coalition making is relatively risky because it may be interpreted as an "organizational weapon" against the state.

8. Social organizations participate in the protest by mobilizing and organizing citizens, joining in street-level demonstrations, or providing material or moral resources to sustain the protest and support protesters. For institutional actors, these activities are risky under an authoritarian state.

9. For example, another tactic is (environmental) public interest litigation: Social organizations issue lawsuits against government, corporations, or other interest groups on behalf of citizens whose interests are impaired. Public interest litigation is rightful but considered confrontational in many authoritarian systems (Stern 2013).

10. PM 2.5 is the abbreviation for particulate matter 2.5, a microscopic air pollutant.

11. Most of these lawsuits, however, were declined by the court. In China, environmental organizations had not been allowed to the plaintiff of environmental public interest lawsuits until the passing of the new environmental law in 2015. Before that, only one exceptional case was put on record by a municipal court in Yunnan in 2011 (Shapiro 2016: 137; Stern 2013: 120).

12. For example, the registered international NGOs in Yunnan dropped from more than two hundred in 2007 to fewer than forty as of 2012 (interview with Mr. Mo, 2018).

13. The movement organizer recalled that local ENGOs seldom joined citizen activism (interview with Mr. Ming, 2018).

14. For the study of "supervising government by outside [media]" in China, see Lei 2017.

15. Since 2013, China has witnessed an adverse political climate and a downward trend of NGO participation in popular protests (Fu and Distelhorst 2018). Nevertheless, there has been greater emphasis of environmental governance during the same period (Dai and Spires 2018). Another study is needed to offer a full account of such mixed signals.

REFERENCES

Amenta, Edwin, Kenneth T. Andrews, and Neal Caren. 2018. "The Political Institutions, Processes, and Outcomes Movements Seek to Influence." In David A. Snow, Sarah A. Soule, Hanspeter Kriesi, and Holly J. McCammon, eds., *The Wiley Blackwell Companion to Social Movements*, 2nd ed., 447–65. Hoboken, NJ: Wiley Blackwell.

Amenta, Edwin, Neal Caren, Elizabeth Chiarello, and Yang Su. 2010. "The Political Consequences of Social Movements." *Annual Review of Sociology* 36: 287–307.

Banaszak, Lee Ann. 2010 *The Women's Movement Inside and Outside the State*. New York: Cambridge University Press.

Böhm, Timo. 2015. "Activists in Politics: The Influence of Embedded Activists on the Success of Social Movements." *Social Problems* 62(4): 477–98.

Bondes, Maria, and Thomas Johnson. 2017. "Beyond Localized Environmental Contention: Horizontal and Vertical Diffusion in a Chinese Anti-Incinerator Campaign." *Journal of Contemporary China* 26(106): 504–20.

Boudet, Hilary. 2011. "From NIMBY to NIABY: Regional Mobilization against Liquefied Natural Gas in the United States." *Environmental Politics* 20(6): 786–806.

Brass, Jennifer N. 2016. *Allies or Adversaries: NGOs and the State in Africa*. New York: Cambridge University Press.

Burt, Ronald. 1992. *Structural Holes: The Social Structure of Competition.* Cambridge, MA: Harvard University Press.

Chen, Xi. 2012. *Social Protest and Contentious Authoritarianism in China*. Cambridge: Cambridge University Press.

Chen, Xi, and Dana M. Moss. 2018. "Authoritarian Regimes and Social Movements." In David A. Snow, Sarah A. Soule, Hanspeter Kriesi, and Holly J. McCammon, eds., *The Wiley Blackwell Companion to Social Movements*, 2nd ed., 666–81. Hoboken, NJ: Wiley Blackwell.

Dai, Jingyun, and Anthony J. Spires. 2018. "Advocacy in an Authoritarian State: How Grassroots Environmental NGOs Influence Local Governments in China." *The China Journal* 79(1): 62–83.

Diani, Mario. 2003. "'Leaders' or Brokers? Positions and Influence in Social Movement Networks." In Mario Diani and Doug McAdam, eds., *Social Movements and Networks: Relational Approaches to Collective Action*, 105–22. Oxford: Oxford University Press.

———. 2015. *The Cement of Civil Society: Studying Networks in Localities*. New York: Cambridge University Press.

Dokshin, Fedor A. 2016. "Whose Backyard and What's at Issue? Spatial and Ideological Dynamics of Local Opposition to Fracking in New York State, 2010–2013." *American Sociological Review* 81(5): 921–48.

Economy, Elizabeth. 2010. *The River Runs Black: The Environmental Challenge to China's Future*. Ithaca, NY: Cornell University Press.

Fernandez, Roberto M., and Roger V. Gould. 1994. "A Dilemma of State Power: Brokerage and Influence in the National Health Policy Domain." *American Journal of Sociology* 99(6): 1455–91.

Fligstein, Neil, and Doug McAdam. 2011. *A Theory of Fields*. New York: Oxford University Press.

Frank, David John, Ann Hironaka, and Evan Schofer. 2000. "The Nation-State and the Natural Environment over the Twentieth Century." *American Sociological Review* 65(1): 96–116.

Friedman, Ray, and Joel M. Podolny. 1992. "Differentiation of Boundary Spanning Roles: Labor Negotiations and Implications for Role Conflict." *Administrative Science Quarterly* 37(1): 28–47.

Fu, Diana. 2017. "Fragmented Control: Governing Contentious Labor Organizations in China." *Governance* 30(3): 445–62.

Fu, Diana, and Greg Distelhorst. 2018. "Grassroots Participation and Repression under Hu Jintao and Xi Jinping." *The China Journal* 79(1): 100–22.

Gamson, William A. 1975. *The Strategy of Social Protest*. Belmont, CA: The Dorsey Press.

Gould, Roger V. 1995. *Insurgent Identities: Class, Community, and Protest in Paris from 1848 to the Commune*. Chicago: University of Chicago Press.

Gould, Roger V., and Roberto M. Fernandez. 1989. "Structures of Mediation: A Formal Approach to Brokerage in Transaction Networks." *Sociological Methodology* 19: 89–126.

Hadden, Jennifer. 2015. *Networks in Contention: The Divisive Politics of Climate Change.* New York: Cambridge University Press.

Heurlin, Christopher. 2010. "Governing Civil Society: The Political Logic of NGO-State Relations under Dictatorship." *Voluntas* 21(2): 220–39.

Hildebrandt, Timothy. 2013. *Social Organizations and the Authoritarian State in China.* New York: Cambridge University Press.

Hillmann, Henning. 2008. "Localism and the Limits of Political Brokerage: Evidence from Revolutionary Vermont." *American Journal of Sociology* 114(2): 287–331.

Ho, Peter, and Richard Edmonds, eds. 2007. *China's Embedded Activism: Opportunities and Constraints of a Social Movement.* New York: Routledge.

Hsu, Jennifer Y. J., Carolyn L. Hsu, and Reza Hasmath. 2017. "NGO Strategies in an Authoritarian Context, and Their Implications for Citizenship: The Case of the People's Republic of China." *Voluntas* 28(3): 1157–79.

Johnson, Thomas. 2010. "Environmentalism and NIMBYism in China: Promoting a Rules-Based Approach to Public Participation." *Environmental Politics* 19(3): 430–48.

Keck, Margaret E., and Kathryn Sikkink. 1998. *Activists Beyond Borders: Advocacy Networks in International Politics.* Ithaca, NY: Cornell University Press.

Kellogg, Katherine C. 2014. "Brokerage Professions and Implementing Reform in an Age of Experts." *American Sociological Review* 79(5): 912–41.

Lang, Graeme, and Ying Xu. 2013. "Anti-Incinerator Campaigns and the Evolution of Protest Politics in China." *Environmental Politics* 22(5): 832–48.

Lei, Ya-Wen. 2017. *The Contentious Public Sphere: Law, Media, and Authoritarian Rule in China.* Princeton, NJ: Princeton University Press.

Liu, Jun. 2016. "Digital Media, Cycle of Contention, and Sustainability of Environmental Activism: The Case of Anti-PX Protests in China." *Mass Communication and Society* 19(5): 604–25.

Long, Yan. 2018. "The Contradictory Impact of Transnational AIDS Institutions on State Repression in China, 1989–2013." *American Journal of Sociology* 124(2): 309–66.

McAdam, Doug. 1982. *Political Process and the Development of Black Insurgency, 1930–1970.* Chicago: University of Chicago Press.

———. 1996. "Conceptual Origins, Current Problems, Future Directions." In Doug McAdam, John D. McCarthy, and Mayer N. Zald, eds., *Comparative Perspectives on Social Movements*, 23–40. Cambridge, UK: Cambridge University Press.

McAdam, Doug, Sidney Tarrow, and Charles Tilly. 2001. *Dynamics of Contention.* New York: Cambridge University Press.

McCammon, Holly, and Campbell, Karen. 2002. "Allies on the Road to Victory: Coalition Formation between the Suffragists and the Woman's Christian Temperance Union." *Mobilization* 7(3): 231–51.

McCarthy, John D., and Mayer N. Zald. 1977. "Resource Mobilization and Social Movements: A Partial Theory." *American Journal of Sociology* 82(6): 1212–41.

Mertha, Andrew C. 2008. *China's Water Warriors: Citizen Action and Policy Change*. Ithaca, NY: Cornell University Press.

Meyer, David S., and Catherine Corrigall-Brown. 2005. "Coalitions and Political Context: US Movements against Wars in Iraq." *Mobilization* 10(3): 327–44.

Meyer, David S., and Debra C. Minkoff. 2004. "Conceptualizing Political Opportunity." *Social Forces* 82(4): 1457–92.

Michaud, Kristy, Juliet Carlisle, and Eric Smith. 2008. "Nimbyism vs. Environmentalism in Attitudes toward Energy Development." *Environmental Politics* 17(1): 20–39.

Mische, Ann. 2008. *Partisan Publics: Communication and Contention across Brazilian Youth Activist Networks*. Princeton, NJ: Princeton University Press.

Moss, Dana. 2014. "Repression, Response, and Contained Escalation Under 'Liberalized' Authoritarianism in Jordan." *Mobilization* 19(3): 261–86.

Obach, Brian K. 2004. *Labor and the Environmental Movement: The Quest for Common Ground*. Cambridge, MA: MIT Press.

O'Brien, Kevin J., and Lianjiang Li. 2006. *Rightful Resistance in Rural China*. New York: Cambridge University Press.

Obstfeld, David. 2005. "Social Networks, the *Tertius Iungens* Orientation, and Involvement in Innovation." *Administrative Science Quarterly* 50(1): 100–30.

Osa, Maryjane. 2003. "Networks in Opposition: Linking Organizations through Activists in the Polish People's Republic." In Mario Diani and Doug McAdam, eds., *Social Movements and Networks: Relational Approaches to Collective Action*, 77–104. Oxford: Oxford University Press.

Quintane, Eric, and Gianluca Carnabuci. 2016. "How Do Brokers Broker? *Tertius Gaudens*, *Tertius Iungens*, and the Temporality of Structural Holes." *Organization Science* 27(6): 1343–60.

Piven, Frances Fox, and Richard A. Cloward. 1979. *Poor People's Movements: Why They Succeed, How They Fail*. New York: Vintage.

Rose, Fred. 2000. *Coalitions across the Class Divide: Lessons from the Labor, Peace, and Environmental Movements*. Ithaca, NY: Cornell University Press.

Santoro, Wayne, and Gail McGuire. 1997. "Social Movement Insiders: The Impact of Institutional Activists on Affirmative Action and Comparable Worth Policies." *Social Problems* 44(4): 503–20.

Schock, Kurt. 2005. *Unarmed Insurrections: People Power Movements in Nondemocracies*. Minneapolis: University of Minnesota Press.

Sewell, William H. 2005. *Logics of History: Social Theory and Social Transformation*. Chicago: University of Chicago Press.

Shapiro, Judith. 2016. *China's Environmental Challenges*, 2nd ed. Cambridge: Polity Press.

Simmel, Georg. 1950. *The Sociology of Georg Simmel*, trans. Kurt H. Wolff. Chicago: Free Press.

Small, Mario L. 2009. "'How Many Cases Do I Need?' On Science and the Logic of Case Selection in Field-Based Research." *Ethnography* 10(1): 5–38.

SCMP. 2013. "Kunming Residents Rally against Chemical Plant." *South China Morning Post* May 4. https://www.scmp.com/news/china/article/1230117/kunming-residents-rally-against-chemical-plant.

Snow, David, and Dana Moss. 2014. "Protest on the Fly: Toward a Theory of Spontaneity in the Dynamics of Protest and Social Movements." *American Sociological Review* 79(6): 1122–43.

Spires, Anthony J. 2011. "Contingent Symbiosis and Civil Society in an Authoritarian State: Understanding the Survival of China's Grassroots NGOs." *American Journal of Sociology* 117(1): 1–45.

Stearns, Linda Brewster, and Paul D. Almeida. 2004. "The Formation of State Actor-Social Movement Coalitions and Favorable Policy Outcomes." *Social Problems* 51(4): 478–504.

Steinhardt, H. Christopher, and Fengshi Wu. 2016. "In the Name of the Public: Environmental Protest and the Changing Landscape of Popular Contention in China." *The China Journal* 75(1): 61–82.

Stern, Rachel E. 2013. *Environmental Litigation in China: A Study in Political Ambivalence*. New York: Cambridge University Press.

Stovel, Katherine, and Lynette Shaw. 2012. "Brokerage." *Annual Review of Sociology* 38: 139–58.

Suh, Doowon. 2011. "Institutionalizing Social Movements: The Dual Strategy of the Korean Women's Movement." *Sociological Quarterly* 52(3): 442–71.

Sun, Xiaoyi, Ronggui Huang, and Ngai-Ming Yip. 2017. "Dynamic Political Opportunities and Environmental Forces Linking up: A Case Study of Anti-PX Contention in Kunming." *Journal of Contemporary China* 26: 1–13.

Sun, Yanfei, and Dingxin Zhao. 2008. "Environmental Campaign." In Kevin O'Brien, ed., *Popular Protest in China*, 144–62. Cambridge, MA: Harvard University Press.

Tarrow, Sidney. 1994. *Power in Movement: Social Movements and Contentious Politics*. New York: Cambridge University Press.

Teets, Jessica C. 2015. "The Evolution of Civil Society in Yunnan Province: Contending Models of Civil Society Management in China." *Journal of Contemporary China* 24(91): 158–75.

Tilly, Charles. 2005. *Identities, Boundaries and Social Ties*. New York: Routledge.

Wong, Natalie W. M. 2016. "Advocacy Coalitions and Policy Change in China: A Case Study of Anti-Incinerator Protest in Guangzhou." *Voluntas* 27(5): 2037–54.

Wu, Fengshi. 2013. "Environmental Activism in Provincial China." *Journal of Environmental Policy & Planning* 15(1): 89–108.

Yang, Guobin. 2005. "Environmental NGOs and Institutional Dynamics in China." *China Quarterly* 181: 46–66.

Zhang, Yang. 2018. "Allies in Action: Institutional Actors and Grassroots Environmental Activism in China." *Research in Social Movements, Conflicts and Change* 42: 9–38.

Part IV

HONG KONG

Chapter Nine

How Protests Evolve

The Umbrella Legacy of the Anti-Extradition Movement

Ming-sho Ho (National Taiwan University)

> We need to keep evolving, improving, and outrunning the enormous machine that confronts us.
>
> —Denise Ho

The ability to critically examine one's past conduct and to revise subsequent decisions accordingly—or what social scientists generally refer to as "reflexivity"—has been seen as a core component of human agency. Although we exercise such capacity routinely in our everyday lives, less attention has been paid to how collective actors learn from their own campaigns and devise a new strategy to achieve their goals.

Social movements essentially involve a "cognitive praxis" because they produce knowledge about desired changes, and "interactions between contemporary social movements and the 'old' ones" are an important source of such social learning (Eyerman and Jamison 1991: 55, 58). Protest diffusion, or the so-called demonstration effect, is no less than a successful effort by movement activists who have taken stock of what has happened in their culturally, politically, and geographically proximate regions and deployed similar tactics. The East European revolutions of 1989 (Ash 1990; della Porta 2014; Kumar 2001), the "Color Revolutions" in the first few years of this century (Bunce and Wolchik 2011), and the Arab Spring of 2011 (Alimi, Sela, and Sznajder 2016; Bayat 2017; Lawson 2015) are among the best-known cases of such cross-fertilization. While learning from neighboring cases has been thoroughly reviewed in the existing literature, less scholarly attention has been devoted to the question of how protesters reflect on their prior engagement and thereby set forth a novel campaign. How the lessons learned from previous protests influence newer ones is the main research question of this study.

This chapter looks at Hong Kong's anti-extradition movement of 2019 and how it took cues from the umbrella movement that erupted five years earlier and, thus, evolved into a more powerful challenge to the authorities. The 2019 campaign erupted over an amendment bill introduced by Hong Kong Special Administrative Region Government that would allow the transfer of fugitives wanted by the judiciary in the People's Republic of China, be they Hong Kong residents, expats in the territory, or international passengers transferring at the airport. From the time the government announced the revision draft in February 2019, it immediately became controversial as foreign governments, the local business community, lawyers, opposition politicians, and students voiced their concerns. Opponents perceived the amendment as a sinister attempt to undermine Hong Kong's autonomy, which had hitherto maintained its colonial heritage of rule of law and judicial independence—in contrast to mainland China where judges are answerable to the communist leadership and law is no more than a political instrument to silence dissidents. As such, the fear of being arbitrarily extradited to China was the initial impetus for this movement.

In June, the dispute flared up as two major peaceful demonstrations attracted 1 million and 2 million participants, respectively. In a city of 7.5 million permanent residents, the participation ratio was unprecedented, and yet it garnered only a cold response from officials. The government announced a temporary suspension of the amendment on June 15, 2019, but adopted a repressive strategy toward protesters with police crackdowns, mass arrests, and criminal prosecution. Although the fear of being sent to China was not lifted, the brutal use of police force and contrived violence from pro-government gangsters further fanned popular fury. During the summer months, the anti-extradition movement grew into territory-wide resistance of such an extent that the Chinese media once hinted at a Tiananmen-style military solution to what they called "sprouts of terrorism."

While peaceful protests persisted in the form of rallies, demonstrations, general strikes, class boycotts, human chains, boycotting pro-government shops, posting on so-called Lennon Walls, and collective singing, frontline protesters escalated their use of force over the months. Initially they built barricades to block traffic only, after some time they increasingly threw bricks and Molotov cocktails, vandalized subway stations and pro-government stores, and practiced vigilantism against pro-government assaulters. On September 4, the government finally announced the formal withdrawal of the amendment; nevertheless, such a belated concession failed to subdue the movement, which had grown to a full-blown pro-democracy campaign that demanded suffrage election for top leadership and full direct elections for the legislative body.

One month later, the government invoked emergency powers to ban wearing masks in public spaces, which again backfired by inciting protests throughout the eighteen districts, leading to the suspension of services on all subway lines on the evening of October 4. At the anniversary of its flare-up (June 2020), there have been more than 9,000 arrests, including 1,808 arrestees who faced criminal charges, more than 300 refuges taking shelter in other countries, more than ten politically related suicides, and several injuries that had resulted in permanent physical impairment. Rumors circulated widely that police killed some young protesters and disguised the murders as suicides, and the government was not able to demonstrate convincing evidence to counter those conjectures. The same went with the accusation that policemen raped female arrestees repeatedly. Over the months, the anger over police brutality emerged as a more salient concern for participants (Lee, Yuen et al. 2019: 22). The landslide victory for pro-democracy camp in the district council election on November 24 signified the unwavering popular support for the protesters, even though they have increasingly stepped up the use of force and the city's economy went into a recession.

At the time of writing (July 2020), the movement still maintained its momentum after one year of intensive mobilization, although large-scale and intense confrontations became more infrequent after the eruption of COVID-19 crisis in January 2020 and the draconian national security law imposed in July. Its participants diverted their attention to newer arenas, including organizing new labor unions, using newly gained district councils to pressure the government, promoting alternative pro-movement economy (the so-called yellow economic sphere), protesting the government's clumsy efforts to deal with the coronavirus epidemic (the reluctance to close the China border and the hasty plan to set up quarantine facilities).

How do we explain the extraordinary tenacity of the Hong Kong protesters? Why have they been capable of deploying such a varied protest repertoire, ranging from hand-in-hand human chains by high school students in uniform to the destruction of subway stations by masked firebrands? What are the sources of such resilience that have enabled protesters to carry on despite attempts by police and mobsters[1] to repress them? These questions are certainly of vital interest to Hong Kong and Beijing incumbents, who have repeatedly alluded to so-called foreign forces lurking behind the scenes.

In place of such paranoia, this chapter maintains that the solution to these puzzles lies in how the activists appropriated the lessons of the 2014 umbrella movement. In the following, I will argue (1) the occupation zones in the previous movement functioned as incubators for new ideas that were deemed as experimental and unorthodox at the time but were later put into practice in the newer movement, (2) the flourishing of postoccupy organizations laid the foundation for mobilizing networks, and finally (3) the bitter ending of the exhausted occupy protest was a painful lesson for participants who had no choice but to pursue a decentralized and disruptive course. In short, Hong Kong's protesters evolved into a more powerful challenger because they became more resourceful, more connected, and more courageous as a result of critical reflection on their previous experiences.

Research data have come from many sources. For journalistic reports, I rely extensively on online media outlets, particularly the Stand News (https://thestandnews.com/). I have been based in Boston and Taipei since the eruption of the anti-extradition movement, and I flew to Hong Kong three times for short-term field observation. Until February 2020, I conducted twenty-three in-depth interviews with participants, including students, union staff, nongovernmental organization (NGO) volunteers, opposition politicians, and academics.

THE UMBRELLA LEGACY: SPILLOVER, PROTEST CYCLE, OR ABEYANCE?

On the afternoon of September 28, 2014, policemen launched tear gas to disperse a crowd that had gathered for nearly two days outside the Legislative Council. Prior to that, police used pepper spray to attack protesters who had nothing but plastic wrap, goggles, and umbrellas for self-protection. The crowd fled once tear gas canisters were launched; yet they kept coming back. The escalated use of police force shocked and angered many Hongkongers who had not been previously concerned about the political reform that had been the subject of intense discussion for more than one year. Three noncontiguous occupation zones in Admiralty, Causeway Bay, and Mong Kok immediately came into being. Knowing that their eviction efforts had backfired, the police stopped using tear gas and had to tolerate the defiant presence of thousands of protesters. As what have been seen in Cairo's Tahrir Square, Madrid's Puerta del Sol, and New York's Zuccotti Park, spontaneous and creative activities sprouted in the encampment areas and became a symbol of popular defiance (Gitlin 2012; MacDonald 2002; Maeckelbergh 2011).

What was later dubbed the umbrella movement involved a seventy-nine-day occupy protest to demand genuine suffrage of the top leader. Three weeks later, a televised dialogue between student delegates and officials took place without reaching a consensus that was acceptable to both sides. Afterward, the movement was torn by multiple centrifugal tendencies including moderates who intended to end the confrontation as quickly as possible, radicals who agitated for more disruptive initiatives, and student leaders who struggled to prolong the precarious status quo. Amid pro-government mob violence, court orders, and police eviction, the umbrella movement ran out of steam and finally collapsed without achieving its goal.

The umbrella movement was the largest incident of popular contention since Hong Kong's handover to China in 1997. Students took up the unfinished democratization project left behind by their senior political leaders. The movement shared many characteristics with other contemporary occupy protests, such as reliance on digital media, the predominance of youthful participants, and the near absence of preexisting organizations. Given its significance, the umbrella movement has generated a wealth of research literature (Cai 2017; Cheng and Chan 2017; Jones 2017; Lee 2017; Ma and Cheng 2019; Ng and Wong 2017). For social movement students, the umbrella movement raised a number of research questions regarding its genesis. Why did an East Asian city that apparently lacked the political tradition of civil disobedience and took pride in being a world city excelling in expediting the flow of money and goods generate a longer occupy protest than Cairo, Madrid, and New York? Ho (2019) examines Beijing's ill-attempted control strategies and how Taiwan's sunflower movement of the same year provided a template for Hong Kong's students to initiate their own action. Lee and Sing (2019) pointed at how the Chinese rule brought about the triple dispossessions, economic, political, and cultural, sowing the seed for the mass revolt.

How is the umbrella movement related to the anti-extradition movement five years later? Scholars have long recognized that social movements are not distinct happenings but, rather, interconnected events in the cascading sequence of social change. The existing literature provides three conceptual approaches to understand the relationship between preceding movements and subsequent ones. The first approach to analyze movement-to-movement influence can be subsumed under the notion of "spillover" (Meyer and Whittier 1994), or the phenomenon where a preceding movement's tactics or slogans incidentally inspire a subsequent one. Previous activism bequeaths a legacy of personalized politics in that former participants continue their commitment to change the world in their everyday lives (Ando 2014; Lichterman 1996). Spillover can also be found in some seemingly conservative organizations, such as the Catholic church and the military (Katzenstein 1990) or state bureaucracy (Banaszak 2005). Spillover can occur in an adversarial milieu, a paradigmatic case being how U.S. feminism was born in the endemic sexual discrimination of the 1960s New Left movements and yet shared the latter's ethos of personal liberation (Evans 1979). In short, the spillover notion highlights the fact that a social movement has the potential to ignite new rounds of mobilization in the least expected areas or about completely different issues.

Second, the protest cycle approach starts with the premise of a rise-and-fall pattern because intensive protest participation is not easily sustained.

Students of the political opportunity structure generally assume opportunity expansion and contraction shapes the dynamic of contention because of the shifting cost of collective action (Chang 2015; McAdam 1982; Meyer 1990; Tarrow 1989), whereas the social psychological approach emphasizes the declining subjective satisfaction in prolonged movement involvement (Hirschman 1982). The protest cycle literature typically considers early-rising movements as innovators who demonstrate the effectiveness of protests, whereas latecomers are more constrained by their predecessors (Snow and Benford 1992: 145–150; Tarrow 1989: 60).

The protest cycle literature marks a significant improvement over the previous "natural history" approach, which implies a more or less mechanic and regular understanding of the ebb and flow of protest activities. Koopmans (2004) contends "protest wave" should be a more appropriate term because it does not carry the connotation of inevitable recurrence. Moreover, the decline of protest activism does not necessarily follow the paths of institutionalization, marginalization, or radicalization because there are more possible scenarios. Della Porta (2013) also argues against the danger of generalization from few select historical cases. Protest waves can be concluded in more open-ended manners.

Finally, the third perspective focuses on how movement activists tide themselves over against political headwinds and sustain their ideological commitment to wait for the next round of resurgence. Taylor (1989) famously coined the term "structure of abeyance" to make sense of how U.S. feminist veterans survived the conservative backlash of the 1950s by building an intimate community among participants. Abeyance highlighted the fact that the talk about movement "birth" or "death" was potentially misleading since a movement could "contract and hibernate" in the face of a hostile environment (Taylor 1989: 772). As such, successfully managing the lessons of defeat turns out to be the key to later participation. If a "fortifying myth" exists that can maintain the allegiance of participants, it is more likely to encourage them to become engaged in future confrontations (Einwohner 2002; Voss 1998).

Although spillover, protest cycles, and abeyance explain certain aspects of subsequent dynamics, none of them can adequately account for the linkage between the umbrella movement and the anti-extradition movement. The conclusion of the umbrella movement stimulated a number of campaigns, including a plethora of community-based or profession-based organizations (the so-called post-Umbrella organizations), some new protests (the "fishball revolution" of 2016 being the most prominent),[2] young participants' electioneering in the 2015 District Council election and the 2016 elections to the Legislative Council, and localism—advocating independence or self-determination—as political demands (Lam and Cooper 2018). On the surface, the flourishing of these postoccupy activisms lent support to the protest cycle/wave thesis (the umbrella movement itself being an event in a series of contentions including the 2019 movement) and the spillover thesis (participation being diverted into other arenas). Nevertheless, with the ratcheting-up of government repression since 2016, including disqualifying movement activists from joining the election, not seating six opposition Legislative Council members, disbanding pro-independence organizations, and imprisoning movement leaders, the participation wave unleashed by the umbrella movement appeared a spent force.

Elsewhere, Hong Kong's pro-democracy camp sustained a series of setbacks, such as a revision to the legislature's house rule outlawing filibusters from opposition lawmakers (December 2017), immigration preclearance in the high-speed rail station that allowed mainland officials to exercise authority in the territory (June 2018), and the second reading of a law that would punish disrespectful behaviors during national anthem singing up to three years in jail (January 2019). The pro-democracy camp was defeated in two consecutive single-seat by-elections in 2018, which they used to enjoy the upper hand. Clearly, the opposition movement was stuck in the doldrums, which probably in turn enticed the government to propose the controversial extradition amendment without regard for potential domestic and international criticism.

The abeyance explanation mostly applies to the post-Umbrella community and professional organizations because they were formed to address the political situation after the occupy protest. However, these organizations were originally intended to play a proactive role, rather than becoming inward-looking and self-contained communities. At first, they were confident that they could either spread pro-democracy messages to different sectors or localities, or pressure functional constituency lawmakers who had generally adopted a pro-Beijing stand. As movement activism receded, these organizations became less active as a result. Moreover, the abeyance structure as depicted in Taylor (1989) lasted over a decade as the U.S. feminists were forced to sustain the postwar conservative backlash, which is also different from Hong Kong's protesters who only experienced around two years of low tide prior to their next resuscitation.

Spillover, protest cycles, and abeyance only provide partial answers to the rise of the anti-extradition movement. Implicit in the three approaches is an understanding of knowledgeable and reflective agency, which is capable of applying movement tactics in the unexplored arenas (spillover), imitating a novel and successful predecessor (protest cycles), and ensuring survival in a hostile environment (abeyance). The following sections will look at the agency issue by identifying mechanisms by which Hong Kong participants took stock of the umbrella movement.

OCCUPATION ZONES AS A SOCIAL INCUBATOR

The emergence of occupation zones in the recent protests—where people usurped public spaces in their confrontation with the authorities—has become more widespread. Some observers use the term "prefigurative politics" to understand the explosion of spontaneous activities like independent media, soup kitchens, people's libraries, environmentally friendly gardening, and so on because they intend to emphasize that participants literally enacted the vision of their ideal society (Graeber 2013). Nevertheless, not all these spontaneous activities were only for self-expressive purposes; some were adopted for practical purposes. Food provisioning and garbage collection was a necessity for a sustained confrontation, and these activities also created a community of solidarity and sharing symbolically. Moreover, I contend that the occupation zones emerged as an incubator for new strategic ideas that had the potential to be more widely adopted. One participant described her personal experience during the umbrella movement as follows:

> While we were in the occupation zones, we were fantasizing about what we could do. There were some things we wanted to do, but did not put into practice then. We also initiated some campaigns on a small scale. For instance, we often screened documentaries on worldwide protests in the occupation zone, but we did not have the similar screening and discussion elsewhere. There has been talk about "letting flowers blossom everywhere" (*biandi kaihua*) at that time, but the truth is we failed to bring the movement momentum to different communities. We tried different things and found some ideas were workable. After the Umbrella occupation, we did not have a main battlefield, and that was why each of us had to find his/her own one.

A novel idea born in this social laboratory was that protesters should not constrain themselves to the occupation zones but rather spread demands for democracy to different communities. Particularly when the umbrella movement entered its second month, participants found themselves increasingly on the defensive because they had to fill in the occupation zones with enough people to maintain pressure on the government. In so doing, occupy protesters actually limited their impact on certain urban areas and forfeited the opportunity to involve more citizens. Recognizing this problem, students launched an "umbrella community day" on the day fifty-seven by setting up flyer distribution booths. However, these community outreach initiatives were not successful because they came too late and easily became the target of pro-government mobsters. After the end of umbrella movement, there emerged a spin-off campaign to organize neighborhoods with the slogan "support the umbrella movement by going down to communities" (*chengsan luoqu*). Its proponents maintained that activists should go beyond occupying the streets to "reoccupy our communities." Many of these activities were parts of the post-Umbrella movements (see below), but clearly there existed an implicit and shared understanding the previous campaign was not successful because its strength was contained in the occupation zones only.

Once the anti-extradition movement emerged, protesters took heed of the need to disperse the protest more evenly across geographic areas. Starting in July, campaigners have launched demonstration in suburban towns, including Tuen Mun, Sheung Shui, Sha Tin, Yuen Long, Wong Tai Sin, Tin Shui Wai, Sham Shui Po, Tsuen Wan, To Kwa Wan, and so on. In the past, political protests tended to be concentrated on Hong Kong Island, particularly in the political and financial hub, Central and Admiralty (see figure 9.1). A more spatially scattered movement not only made police preparation more difficult but also facilitated the participation of suburban citizens.

Campaigners took care to align their demonstrations closely with distinctive local community grievances. For instance, a demonstration in Tuen Mun (July 6) was framed as a protest against lewd interaction by mainland women in exchange for cash in a local park,[3] and a demonstration in To Kwa Wan

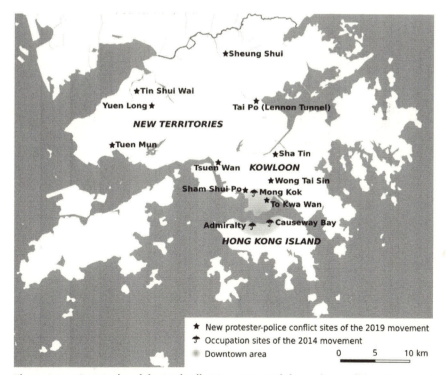

Figure 9.1. Geography of the Umbrella Movement and the Anti-extradition Movement

(August 17) emphasized the nuisance posed to local residents due to traffic problems associated with busing of mainland visitor groups. Moreover, since the police was rather indiscriminate in using force, the decentralized pattern of protest mobilization was able to spread out the brunt of police force so as to create a more broad-based participation. Fear of policemen has become an everyday reality even for nonpartisan citizens (Choi 2020), and the brutality left traumatized experiences for many underage children (Cheng 2020). There have been numerous cases in which the police arbitrarily arrested young people and used tear gas in densely populated areas, which has galvanized neighborhood opposition. After the November election, a journalistic report found that the districts that sustained police tear gas assault tended to vote for pro-democracy candidates more than those districts without similar experience—a clear evidence of citizen backlash over police repression.[4]

During the umbrella movement, Lennon Wall referred to a section of a concrete staircase in the government complex that was covered with handwritten sticky notes. Because students made up the majority of participants, it was not a surprise that they used such stationery to decorate the occupation zone. It soon evolved into a space for spontaneous expression as well as a powerful artistic project because of the colorful mosaic.

In tandem with the decentralizing trend, Lennon Walls popped up in many localities, particularly in the pedestrian corridors connecting with a metro station. The underpass in Tai Po, a suburban town in New Territories, became famous for its spectacular "Lennon Tunnel." While there were still handwritten sticky notes, the new Lennon Walls were decorated more with designed posters that were prepared by professional visual artists and downloaded and printed by local volunteers. Localized Lennon Walls served many functions. They became the community bulletin boards constantly updated with the movement's progress. For returning frontline protesters, they symbolized a warm welcome after a bruising engagement with the police. Lennon Walls were manned daily by neighborhood activists, who were vulnerable to assault by pro-government supporters. Over the weeks, Lennon Wall volunteers learned the art of not confronting assaulters directly nor physically subduing them for the police because they were usually released afterward; as such, an "if-you-destroy-one-we-will-post-a-hundred" strategy was later widely adopted so as to minimize the casualties.

As an occupy protest, the umbrella movement was sustained by those participants who were willing to spend time in the occupation zones day and night. Many activities emerged such as street lectures, concerts, sing-alongs, and film screenings so as to transform those seemingly idle hours into a more rewarding time. After the conclusion of the occupy protest, many post-Umbrella organizations held community film-screening activities to continue the activism. The anti-extradition movement inherited this tradition by spreading it more broadly. Previously, it was *Ten Years*, a 2015 award-winning film about Hong Kong's political future that was the most popular choice; later, the screening broadened to include *Lost in Fumes*, a biodocumentary of Edward Leung, a young pro-independence leader, *1987: When the Day Comes*, a South Korean film on the pro-democracy student movement, and *Winter on Fire*, a documentary about the Ukrainian revolution. The widened film selection indicated that participants had become more resourceful in mobilizing video materials.

Like other social movements, umbrella movement participants sang together to demonstrate their solidarity and commitment. In the occupation zone, they sang the Cantonese version of "Do You Hear the People Sing," "Raising an Umbrella" (a movement song created by professional artists), and other Cantonese pop songs. In the first three months of the anti-extradition movement, participants still sang existing songs. With the advent of "Glory to Hong Kong," an anonymously created song widely perceived as the territory's "national anthem," in late August, a "singing revolution" surged throughout the territory. The song was a battle hymn that glorified Hongkongers' courageous pursuit of liberty, and it instantly went viral. People sang the song collectively in schools, churches, a football stadium, and on the ferry. A decentralized movement encouraged the participants to take advantage of the local shopping malls connected to metro stations. The atriums in these buildings became a ready-to-use arena theater for movement supporters to sing "Glory to Hong Kong" together. The spectacle of hundreds of people gathering on different floors, facing each other, and singing in unison with the knowledge that other Hongkongers were doing the same simultaneously throughout the territory powerfully dramatized their determination. And this would not have been possible if the new campaign had proceeded as another occupy protest.

Another innovative idea that emerged from the occupation experience was that protesters should go beyond the guiding principle of civil disobedience by masking their identity, fighting back against police, disrupting governmental organs, and challenging the symbols of Beijing's sovereignty over Hong Kong. Supporters of this strategy were identified as "militants" (*yong wupai*) during the umbrella movement, and they remained marginalized then. In 2014, spontaneous initiatives to interrupt the National Day ceremony (October 1), to blockade public servants from entering their offices (October 3), to storm into the Legislative Council (November 19), and so on were forcibly intercepted by the movement leaders, who denounced these tactics as "irresponsible hit-and-run." Security team members threatened to arrest them and hand them over to the police, and there were some pro-movement lawyers who announced their refusal to defend these radicals in court. Vandalism of public property was strictly prohibited then. Militants were seen then as unwelcome troublemakers, if not suspected as disguised agent provocateurs.

The militants represented a radical tendency beyond the philosophy of civil disobedience that undergirded the umbrella movement. In the 2016 fishball revolution, a young pro-independence leader Edward Leung advocated a more proactive strategy of "the edge of violence" (*baoli bianyuan*) to entice the authorities into indiscriminate repression by provocative actions so as to awaken popular resistance. Leung paid his personal price by being sentenced to six years in prison, but his ideas was apparently picked up later. The willingness to accept, support, or even engage in disruptive tactics on the part of more moderate participants has been identified as "an ethics of solidarity" (Lee 2019), which represented a clear breakthrough of the tolerable scope of action.

These ideas were heterodox and embryonic in 2014 and came into fruition in 2019. In the first few weeks of the anti-extradition movement, participants quickly adopted the black-bloc tactic by fully covering their faces with facial masks, gas masks, goggles, and helmets and dressing themselves fully in black to avoid identification. Protesters avoided using their identity cards when taking public transportation because of the risk of exposing themselves. As a frontline student described, he always prepared different clothing for rallies and demonstrations. When intense confrontations took place, there were always volunteers who distributed masks to other unprotected participants. Free clothing was sometimes provided at metro stations to facilitate protesters fleeing from the scenes of engagement. Another young interviewee mentioned,

> I have experienced the umbrella movement when I was a student then. And we knew that it was useless if you just aimed at an appealing picture for being peaceful and orderly. We took the lesson that we should not demarcate ourselves from those militant protesters because we shared the same goal. So there are still some voices of denunciation against certain violent acts of protesters, but it has been much toned down, unlike what we have seen back in 2014.

The anti-extradition movement relied more extensively on encrypted internet platforms such as Telegram and LIHKG, where anonymous users proposed actions and the most popular ones were pushed to the top of the chatroom by the algorithm of responses (Lai and Wu 2019).[5] Such decision-making and coordination mechanisms proceeded without the need for a centralized coordinator, which was generally referred to as the "main stage" during the umbrella movement because of the physical presence of a podium in the occupation zone in Admiralty. Then Hong Kong Federation of Students, representing the territory's university student unions, was widely seen as the movement leadership, and Alex Chow and Lester Shum emerged as its public faces. A movement without a main stage turned out to be more flexible and adaptive in tactics, and more accommodating to disruptive protests.

As such, more daring actions have been taken in the anti-extradition movement. On the evening of July 1, protesters stormed the Legislative Council by smashing the glass door at the entrance. There they read a pro-democracy declaration before retreating to safety. Sovereignty symbols such as the national emblems and national flag have been defiled in many events, and Beijing's representative presences in Hong Kong, including the Liaison Office, the Bank of China, China Travel Service, Xinhua News Agency, and other pro-Beijing organizations have typically been the targets of vandalism. Such acts of radical defiance were certainly frowned on by moderates, but they were rarely disapproved of in public by the pro-movement camp.

In sum, the ideas of more evenly spreading the campaign spatially and escalating the confrontation physically and symbolically were already brewing during the umbrella movement, but they were constrained at that time. These suggestions emerged naturally from the participants from their own experiences in the occupation zones and were only half-heartedly attempted. One might further argue that many protest repertoires in the anti-extradition movement originated from some seminal ideas from the 2014 movement. Participation from high school students in the form of class boycott, human chains, and collective singing dated back to the famous Study Corner in the Admiralty occupation zone, where high school students were encouraged to join and enjoy the free tutoring. The 2019 movement generated a form of "economic warfare" in which protesters profusely patronized pro-movement stores and boycotted pro-government ones. This represented a further elaboration of the "supporting small stores" operation whereby umbrella movement participants encouraged shopping at the stores whose business was devastated by the occupation in Mong Kok. In this way, the umbrella movement functioned as a social laboratory to generate newer movement ideas to be implemented later on.

THE USES OF POST-UMBRELLA ORGANIZATIONS

One notable feature of the anti-extradition movement has been the involvement of different categories of people, arguably one source of its remarkable endurance. Prior to the flare-up in mid-June, students and lawyers launched their protests against the amendment. Mainland migrants, journalists, artists, social workers, schoolteachers, designers, and Christians joined the ranks by announcing their opposition. There has been a persistent attempt to present the movement as an inclusive and broad-based campaign characterized by participants of multiple identities and multiple professions from early on.

Since the government has adopted a shock-and-awe strategy, the unbridled use of police force incidentally created new victims that enlarged the ranks of the anti-extradition movement. People with visual impairments complained about police treating their white canes as assault weapons (June 14). Thousands of mothers held rallies to protest the police brutality of young protesters (June 14 and July 5). Gender activists denounced sexual violence by the police against female participants and organized a Hong Kong #Metoo rally (June 29). Journalists (July 14) and social workers (June 21) held their own silent marches because they were also assaulted by the police. A sit-in by medical doctors and nurses took place on July 26 because police attempts to arrest the injured in hospitals violated their professional creed.

On July 21, hundreds of baton-wielding gangsters stormed into the Yuen Long metro station and assaulted protesters who had just returned from a clash with the police in the city center. For more than half hour, police conveniently allowed the mobsters to reign the station with terror, and many innocent passengers were severely injured. There had been many previous episodes in which the police were suspected of clandestinely collaborating with pro-government triads; however, the Yuen Long Incident lent undeniable evidence to such conjecture, which in turn stimulated a newer wave of mobilization with more participants. The Hong Kong General Chamber of Commerce and thirty-four retired high-ranking officials announced their support for establishing an independent inquiry committee to look into police violence—one of the five major demands of the anti-extradition movement. Book publishers, film directors and screenplay writers, aviation industry workers, professional athletes, performance artists, financial industry workers, and football umpires released their own statements or held protest events.

Government employees were the most unexpected entrant into the movement because they were legally required to uphold the principle of political neutrality and duly execute government decisions. An internet campaign emerged in which different categories or divisions of government employees jointly published open letters that denounced wrongdoing by the police and supported the movement's demands. The endorsement came with a display of photographs of government employee identification cards with the holders' names being covered. Hundreds of administrative officers and executive officers, the two top grades in the government structure, initiated this campaign, and they were followed by employees at the Fire Services Department, the West Kowloon Cultural District, the Information Services

Department, and Radio Television Hong Kong. More surprisingly, dissident public servants also came from the Department of Justice and Security Bureau, which supervises the police. The unprecedented activism within the government led to a rally of public servants on August 2, which purportedly attracted forty thousand participants.

How can we explain the exceptional scope and reach of protest mobilization? True, the indignation at ever-increasing police brutality was the main psychological thrust that motivated participation from various professions. But for this psychological motive to be channeled into protest actions, preexisting organizations usually played a facilitative role. In major contemporary worldwide protests, a preexisting network of interconnected activists has been a critical key to movement emergence (Clarke 2014; Flesher Fominaya 2014; Gerbaudo 2012: 61; Gunning and Baron 2014: 165–66). What appeared to be a spontaneous outburst might be more accurately described as a preplanned outcome.

As noted previously, in the wake of the umbrella movement, profession-based organizations mushroomed to carry on the unfinished democratization project. Over the years, the intensity of their engagement declined, but on the outbreak of anti-extradition movement, these post-Umbrella organizations became active again. These movement veterans provided an infrastructural network to undergird the newer rounds of protest.

Twenty-three organizations based on professions, including accountants, insurance workers, medical doctors, IT workers, and so on, jointly produced a statement to protest the Yuen Long incident. There were cases in which post-Umbrella activists decided not to use their original organizational name but joined the new Telegram groups or Facebook fan pages that sponsored protest events. For instance, activists from Umbrella Parents, which as the name suggests consisted of mother and father participants in the 2014 movement, joined the organizing team of the mothers' rallies in June and July. Since Umbrella Parents was generally seen as partisan because of its previous participation in the election, they decided to shelve the organizational name to attract more neutral mothers. There was another reason why these post-Umbrella organizations chose to participate anonymously. Many of them were registered and their leaders were publicly known. Transparency and openness had been intended to enhance the credibility of these organizations when they engaged in policy lobbying or public education. However, such an organizational strategy was emphatically not suitable in 2019 because participants incurred the risk of police arrest or mob violence.

The availability of these preexisting organizations and participants made some protest events possible. In 2014, the umbrella movement leaders called for a general strike but received a weak response from certain sectors. In

2019, the strike on August 5, which brought about the cancellation of more than 150 flights and claimed to have attracted 350,000 participants, was a significant milestone. How did a political strike emerge in highly capitalistic Hong Kong? According to a Confederation of Trade Unions staff, union leaders were initially skeptical.

> We know many of our rank-and-file members are angry at the government. But we are a union federation with more than two hundred thousand members. If we initiate a general strike, people would expect us to mobilize at least more than ten thousand people. But we are not sure whether we can meet that expectation.

While union leaders showed hesitancy, young workers who had the personal experience of the umbrella movement agitated for a general strike via the internet platform, and their initiation received enthusiastic responses. In the end, union leaders and staff also joined the campaign without mobilizing their constituencies. The success of August 5 strike was apparently a major breakthrough in that many workers later decided to organize new unions. As of January 2020, more than forty labor unions have emerged, injecting a new impetus to Hong Kong's labor movement. In early February, in a protest against the Hong Kong government's reluctance to close the border during the coronavirus outbreak, Hospital Authorities Employee Alliance, one of the new unions, launched a five-day strike.

In addition, the involvement of different professionals provided vital logistic support to the ongoing movement. Spark Alliance, a legal aid organization formed to support the 2016 fishball revolution arrestees, was active in sending out lawyers to different police stations to negotiate the release or bailout of the arrested demonstrators. Field Social Workers were a group of professional social workers who attempted to maintain a buffer zone at the conflict sites so as to moderate the use of force by the police as much as they could.

Professionals were able to open new zones of engagement so as to increase pressure on the government. More than two hundred visual artists and designers joined a Telegram channel that freely circulated their pro-movement creative works, and as many as 150 pieces a day could be easily downloaded for communication purposes. Bank workers with insider knowledge of their industry launched a financial noncooperation movement that encouraged the deposit holders of China-owned banks to withdraw their money and close their accounts. Although there have been no reported incidents of a bank run, Hong Kong's financial regulator was forcibly put on alert for having to monitor the daily cash flow of banks.

In short, despite its seeming failure, the umbrella movement bequeathed a wealth of manpower resources scattered across different strata and professions. The anti-extradition movement was able to mount a more powerful and broadly based challenge partly because it successfully activated these legacies.

DECENTRALIZATION AND UNITY: THE LESSONS OF THE FAILURE

In an interview, one umbrella movement veteran shared his complex reflections on the previous round of intense movement participation. On the one hand, there was a feeling of self-blame because they had missed a valuable opportunity.

> Over the past five years, we have tried many ways to do it again. We are constantly thinking of the question: if we were given the chance to do it over again what would be a better way to proceed? This question has been deeply in the minds of many people.

On the other hand, there was a pervasive sense of defeatism because the outcome of the umbrella movement was not a more democratic Hong Kong, but arguably the opposite, if one took the series of repressions into consideration. Similarly a former vice-chair of Labour Party, a pro-democracy party, revealed:

> My friends in the pro-democracy movement circle believed Hong Kong was not likely to witness a serious movement over the next five to ten years. It was in the low tide, and we were at a loss as to what to do next. I also know many young students in the localist camp shared the same pessimism. Regardless their ideological differences (leftwing, localist, or pan-democratic), the younger generation was particularly saddened and frustrated.

Many umbrella movement leaders and followers underwent a deeply traumatic experience and much soul-searching afterward. What emerged later was a shared conviction that they should pursue a different strategy to avoid making the same "mistake." Since the umbrella movement proceeded as student-led civil disobedience, its alternative was no less than a decentralized and militant movement. A participant interviewed by *South China Morning Post* contended, "Occupy is like a mirror . . . . We are actually doing the opposite of what we did five years ago" (Ibrahim and Lam 2020: 60).

During the umbrella movement, the "main stage" in the Admiralty occupation zone was managed daily by NGO activists in close collaboration with students, thus symbolizing the leadership. Yet, as the movement became increasingly stuck in a quagmire, students could not obtain satisfactory concessions from the government, or contain the growing restiveness among participants. Toward the later period, several episodes of protest emerged against the main stage and these in-fights further weakened the movement as it was rapidly losing steam. The painful lesson of ineffectual leadership that ended in indecision and distrust was clearly heeded. As a former student leader acknowledged in an interview, a main stage was liable to make mistakes because it assumed too many responsibilities. "Now there is no main stage, the responsibility is on everyone."

On the surface, the anti-extradition movement shared the same skepticism of leadership with the contemporary global protests, such as the Spanish Indignados movement and the Occupy Wall Street in New York. There existed an unmistakable ethos of decentralization, spontaneity, and bottom-up creativity. However, Hong Kong's protesters came to adopt this strategic response largely out of their personal reflections of the previous experience. Throughout the confrontation, there was barely any reference to the international cases. Participants often cited Edward Leung, a charismatic young political prisoner, for the rejection of peaceful civil disobedience, rather than foreign movement gurus who advocated for "leaderless movements." Moreover, the use of "main stage" as a shorthand for leaders, leading organizations, and a commanding center in the rally carries a distinctive local flavor because it refers to the dysfunctional podium erected in Admiralty during the 2014 umbrella movement. The same goes for the "be water" philosophy, which maintains protesters should be flexible and fluid to outsmart, rather than "out-force" the police. The idea originates from Bruce Lee, a beloved local kung fu movie star, who used to characterize the essence of martial art as "be shapeless, formless, like water."

Therefore, the anti-extradition movement emerged with the understanding that no individuals or groups could claim the moral authority over others, and participants were given greater latitude in choosing their actions as they saw fit. In the June 12 besiegement of the Legislative Council that forcibly postponed the extradition amendment, such a pattern of decentralized collaboration had already surfaced. While opposition lawmakers were using legislative tactics to delay the session, a number of independent actions emerged simultaneously on the street. Motorists manufactured minor incidents to create de facto road blockage and Christians sang religious hymns continuously for hours, while masked protesters attempted to storm the Legislative Council.

Hong Kong's demonstrators used the phrase "as brothers climb the mountain, each has to make an effort" to describe the decentralized pattern. Essentially this involved adaptation to new roles for movement organizations and politicians, who were no longer automatically seen as leaders. Activists of Demosisto, a political party led by Joshua Wong, held a number of events to publicize the danger of the extradition amendment before June. Once the movement gained its own momentum, they found it no longer necessary to "initiate events or rallies," and instead, they readjusted to an auxiliary role, focusing on issues such as provision of resources to frontline protesters or creating video clips to highlight police brutality.

Joshua Wong adjusted to the new role quickly. He was released from jail after a two-month sentence on the morning of July 17, the second prison term for his involvement in the umbrella movement, and in the afternoon he made his appearance in the Legislative Council and spoke to the protesters there. On July 23, as protesters gathered outside of the Legislative Council, he used a microphone to direct the crowd to besiege the police headquarters in Wan Chai, and later on the protest evolved into a spontaneous action to paralyze the neighboring government agencies, including Revenue Tower and immigration headquarters. Wong was then severely criticized for this attempt to take charge. As such, he learned not to assume such a high-profile role in subsequent gatherings but concentrated on an international lobbying campaign in Taiwan, Germany, and the U.S.

In the umbrella movement, opposition lawmakers represented a moderate wing that urged students to end the occupation quickly so as to minimize inconveniences. As such, they incurred resentment from younger participants who later voted for candidates advocating localism or self-determination (the latter represented by Demosisto) in the 2016 legislative election, thus suffering a loss in the number of seats. Taking stock of the lesson, opposition politicians firmly stood behind the demonstrators, even on some occasions when the government deliberately made use of disruptive incidents to change public opinion, such as storming and vandalizing the Legislative Council (July 1) and blocking the airport (August 12 and 13). Even when the government finally rescinded the controversial amendment, opposition lawmakers still criticized the concession as not enough (September 4). Younger opposition politicians often appeared at the sites of confrontation; while they sought to reduce tension by negotiating with the police, they largely refrained from preventing protesters from taking more assertive action. A number of them were physically attacked by the police or by mobsters, which undoubtedly drew politicians and militant protesters closer.

The changing roles of politicians and celebrity activists underscored a newly formed consensus of solidarity or ethos of "no division" among moderates and radicals, which essentially entailed a greater tolerance for disruptive action and protesters increasingly resorting to violence. In the wake of the umbrella movement, the advocates of civil disobedience were convicted and jailed one after another, which appeared to indicate the futility of relying on peaceful measures only. At the onset of the anti-extradition movement, the consensus of unity was quickly established because it was patently clear that two peaceful demonstrations of millions of participants were still not enough to change the minds of incumbents. Poll data show evidence that tolerance of radical protests was increasing over the course of events. According to an on-site survey, the proportion of protest participants who agreed or agreed very much with the statement "radical protests will antagonize other people" was steadily declining: 54.4 percent in June, 36.8 percent in July, and 34.8 percent in August (Lee, Tang et al. 2019: 25; author's calculation), a clear indication of increasing tolerance of disruptive acts.

In the first two months, protesters largely refrained from using disruptive force. On August 5, Chief Executive Carry Lam held a press conference to condemn a list of episodes of what she called "extreme violence," including blockading traffic, besiegement of police stations, destruction of public properties, brick-throwing, setting fires, and producing Molotov cocktails and firebombs.[6] After her denunciation, protesters used more aggressive force, such as vigilantism against mobster assaulters (since late August), vandalism of metro station facilities (since early September), and destruction of pro-government stores (since early October). Yet, despite the continuing official censure, there has been no visible reversal in public support for the movement—an indication of the enduring consensus of unity. The clearest evidence for popular support comes from the result of district council election on November 24. It represents a resounding victory for the pro-democracy camp, which secured 389 seats (86 percent) and took control of seventeen district councils (out of eighteen). Previously, the pro-government politicians even though voters would punish the pro-democracy forces for their support for "violence." Afterward, it was clear they became the target of public ire, with their seats decimated from 289 to 59.

CONCLUSION

One of the most iconic figures of the 2019 movement is the so-called firemen who skillfully used traffic cones and bottled water to neutralize tear gas canisters. Hongkongers jokingly claimed that chemical weapons had become a part of their everyday reality so that it has become a rare privilege to enjoy a weekend without the toxic gas in the long summer of 2019. Such bravery and stoicism stood in striking contrast to the mass panic and indignation that arose when police officers shot eighty-seven tear gas canisters on September 28, 2014, which gave rise to the umbrella movement. Ironically, in the following seventy-nine days of occupation, police did not fire tear gas, yet the movement ended in exhaustion and a growing schism without achieving its goals.

How do Hongkong's protesters evolve? Why do they rise from the previous defeat? This chapter sought to identify the linkage from the umbrella movement to the anti-extradition movement. The existing theoretical approaches of protest cycles, spillover, and abeyance provide insufficient answers to the puzzle of the spectacular rebirth of Hong Kong's pro-democracy movement five years on. In addition, social movement researchers have found that a campaign loss is not necessarily the end of the story because it can be reinterpreted as a "positive experience of collective identity" to sustain later mobilization (Beckwith 2016: 62). Rather than forging a collective identity, I maintain that Hong Kong protesters internalized the lesson of defeat and thereby became capable of launching a more daring challenge to the authorities.

More specifically, this chapter identified three main mechanisms of learning: (1) the occupation zones were an incubator for new and experimental tactics which were later adopted, (2) the postoccupy organizations sustained a network of participants scattered across different professions that emerged as the mobilizing infrastructure, and (3) participants recognized the need for more decentralized decision-making and tolerance for radical protests. In a word, protesters became more innovative, connected, fluid, and militant, which became hallmarks of their remarkable strength in the face of unrelenting government repression.

The future of Hongkongers' pursuit for political freedom remains undecided. As of now (July 2020), although the anti-extradition movement has not fulfilled all its demands, it has secured achievements that were unlikely at its onset. The extradition bill has been withdrawn, and more than three hundred activists have been elected as district councilors. Also, the U.S. enacted legal measures to punish Hong Kong officials who violated human rights. These advances appear more significant in light of how China's grip has tightened in other regions under Xi Jinping. However, since the 2020 New Year demonstration, there have not been any large-scale collective actions, and intense confrontations between protesters and police have become infrequent. Most of the neighborhood Lennon Walls have been cleansed, and the authorities appeared to have regained lost territory. True, the movement has shown its fatigue, particularly with more than nine thousand accumulated arrestees and hundreds of activists who fled to Taiwan and other safe areas. The coronavirus epidemic also brought about a lull in the battle. There is certainly no foretelling of the finale of the Hongkongers' struggle, but how they reflected on this history-making episode will affect the trajectory of the next round of contention.

The nimble adaptation on the part of protesters is only one side of the story. For a fuller understanding of the dialectic of contention, it is necessary also to analyze the regime's learning curve. On June 30, Beijing unilaterally imposed a national security law despite international condemnation. The draconian legislation outlawed four vaguely worded crimes of subversion secession, terrorism, and collusion with foreign forces. It also implanted mainland security agents in Hong Kong and threatened to send suspects arrested there to mainland courts. The law has effectively ended the city's semiautonomy and forced activists to flee to other countries or go underground. Yet, Hongkongers remained defiant as evidenced in the larger-than-expected turnout (607,000) in a primary of pro-democracy camp on July 11–12, which the authorities condemned as a violation of the new national security law. It remains to be observed how Hong Kong's protesters can further evolve in response to the more challenging political landscape.

NOTES

1. Hong Kong's criminal organizations, generally known as "triads" in the international media, have long been a persistent feature in the city. Originating from mutual-aid societies among immigrant laborers, the operation of triads evolved from petty crimes such as extortion, gambling, and prostitution into modern profit-making business. Beginning in the 2014 umbrella movement, mobsters have been involved in the pro-government rallies, and their physical assault on peaceful protesters was widely noticed. In the 2019 anti-extradition protest, their escalated use of violence and apparent connivance by the police further fanned the public anger. In mainland China, such police-and-mobster collaboration has been a frequent feature when the authorities attempt to enforce an unpopular order, such as land confiscation.

2. The "fishball revolution" was an overnight protest, originating from a resistance against the government crackdown on street food peddlers during the lunar new year holidays of 2016 and evolved into a severe civil unrest, resulting in a mass arrest and sentencing of the participants, including the charismatic young pro-independence leader Edward Leung, who received a six-year sentence in prison. Fishballs are a popular snack in Hong Kong, and the name carries the implication that Hongkongers will defend their own way of living despite the Chinese encroachment. The fishball revolution marked the transition of Hongkonger resistance from peaceful civil disobedience to a more proactive form, and the sever punishment bequeathed a lesson for future activists to remain anonymous and skeptical of the judiciary system.

3. Hong Kong has traditionally been tolerant on prostitution. The Tuen Mun protest was not about sex for cash payment per se but, rather, that mainland Chinese women enticed local men to dance intimately with them in a local park for tips. The unbecoming scene of groping in the public scandalized neighborhood residents.

4. *Stand News*, November 25, 2019, accessed February 17, 2020, https://bit.ly/2u4H2kS.

5. Hongkongers enjoy greater internet freedom than mainland Chinese because they can access Facebook, YouTube, Twitter, and other digital platforms that are

banned in the mainland. However, after the failure of mask ban in October to curb the protest tide, the government was contemplating the option to shut down some internet media that protesters frequently used. So far such drastic curtailment of internet access has not taken place in Hong Kong.

6. *Stand News,* August 5, 2019, accessed November 5, 2019, https://bit.ly/32ck08x.

REFERENCES

Alimi, Eitan Y., Avraham Sela, and Mario Sznajde, eds. 2016. *Popular Contention, Regime, and Transition: Arab Revolts in Comparative Global Perspective.* Oxford, UK: Oxford University Press.

Ando, Takemasa. 2014. *Japan's New Left Movements: Legacies for Civil Society.* London: Routledge.

Ash, Timothy Garton. 1990. *The Magic Lantern: The Revolution of '89 Witnessed in Warsaw, Budapest, Berlin, and Prague.* New York: Penguin.

Banaszak, Lee Ann. 2005. "Inside and Outside the State: Movement Insider Status, Tactics, and Public Policy Achievements." In David S. Meyer, Valerie Jenness, and Helen Ingram, eds., *Routing the Opposition,* 149–76. Minneapolis: University of Minnesota Press.

Bayat, Asef. 2017. *Revolution without Revolutionaries: Making Sense of the Arab Spring.* Stanford, CA: Stanford University Press.

Beckwith, Karen. 2016. "All Is Not Lost: The 1984–85 British Miners' Strike and Mobilization after Defeat." In Lorenzo Bosi, Marco Giugni, and Katrin Uba, eds., *The Consequences of Social Movements,* 41–65. Cambridge, UK: Cambridge University Press.

Bunce, Valerie, and Sharon Wolchik. 2011. *Defeating Authoritarian Leaders in Post-Communist Countries.* Cambridge, UK: Cambridge University Press.

Cai, Yongshu. 2017. *The Occupy Movement in Hong Kong: Sustaining Decentralized Protest.* London: Routledge.

Chang, Paul Y. 2015. *Protest Dialectics: State Repression and South Korea's Democracy Movement, 1970–1979.* Stanford, CA: Stanford University Press.

Cheng, Edmund W., and Wai-Yin Chan. 2017. "Explaining Spontaneous Occupation: Antecedents, Contingencies and Spaces in the Umbrella Movement." *Social Movement Studies* 16(2): 222–39.

Cheng, Sealing. 2020. "Pikachu's Tears: Children's Perspectives on Violence in Hong Kong." *Feminist Studies* 46(1): 216–25.

Choi, Susanne Y. P. 2020. "When Protests and Daily Life Converge: The Spaces and People of Hong Kong's Anti-extradition Movement." *Critique of Anthropology.* DOI: 10.1177/0308275X20908322.

Clarke, Killian. 2014. "Unexpected Brokers of Mobilization: Contingency and Networks in the 2011 Egyptian Uprising." *Comparative Politics* 46(4): 379–94.

Della Porta, Donatella. 2013. "Protest Cycles and Waves." In David A. Snow, Donatella della Porta, Bert Klandermans, and Doug McAdam, eds., *The Wiley-Blackwell Encyclopedia of Social and Political Movements,* 1014–19. Oxford: Blackwell.

———. 2014. *Mobilizing for Democracy: Comparing 1989 and 2011*. Oxford: Oxford University Press.

Einwohner, Rachel L. 2002. "Motivational Framing and Efficacy Maintenance: Animal Rights Activists' Use of Four Fortifying Strategy." *Sociological Quarterly* 43(4): 509–26.

Evans, Sara. 1979. *Personal Politics: The Roots of Women's Liberation in the Civil Rights Movement and the New Left*. New York: Vintage Books.

Eyerman, Ron, and Andrew Jamison. 1991. *Social Movements: A Cognitive Approach*. Oxford, UK: Polity Press.

Flesher Fominaya, Christina. 2014. "Debunking Spontaneity: Spain's 15-M/Indignados as Autonomous Movement." *Social Movement Studies* 14(2): 142–63.

Gerbaudo, Paolo. 2012. *Tweets and the Streets: Social Media and Contemporary Activism*. New York: Pluto.

Gitlin, Todd. 2012. *Occupy Nation: The Roots, the Spirit, and the Promise of Occupy Wall Street*. New York: Harper Collins.

Graeber, David. 2013. *The Democracy Project: A History, A Crisis, A Movement*. New York: Allen Lane.

Gunning, Jeroen, and Ilan Zyi Baron. 2014. *Why Occupy a Square: People, Protests and Movements in the Egyptian Revolution*. Oxford: Oxford University Press.

Hirschman, Albert O. 1982. *Shifting Involvements: Private Interest and Public Action*. Oxford: Basil Blackwell.

Ho, Ming-sho. 2019. *Challenging Beijing's Mandate of Heaven: Taiwan's Sunflower Movement and Hong Kong's Umbrella Movement*. Philadelphia: Temple University Press.

Ibrahim, Zuraidah, and Jeffie Lam, eds. 2020. *Rebel City: Hong Kong's Year of Water and Fire*. Singapore: World Scientific.

Jones, Brian Christopher, ed. 2017. *Law and Politics of Taiwan Sunflower and Hong Kong Umbrella Movements*. London: Routledge

Katzenstein, Mary Fainsod. 1990. "Feminism within American Institutions: Unobtrusive Mobilization in the 1980s." *Signs* 16(1): 27–54.

Koopmans, Ruud. 2004. "Protest in Time and Space: The Evolution of Waves of Contention." In David A. Snow, Sarah A. Soule, and Hanspeter Kriesi, eds., *The Blackwell Companion to Social Movement*, 19–64. Malden, MA: Blackwell.

Kumar, Krishna. 2001. *1989: Revolutionary Ideas and Ideals*. Minneapolis: University of Minnesota Press.

Lai, K. K. Rebecca, and Jin Wu. 2019. "Protesters in Hong Kong Have Changed Their Playbook." *New York Times*, July 4, 2019. Accessed November 3, 2019. https://nyti.ms/2NGcoE6.

Lam, Wai-man, and Luke Cooper, eds. 2018. *Citizenship, Identity and Social Movements in the New Hong Kong: Localism after Umbrella Movement*. London: Routledge.

Lawson, George. 2015. "Revolution, Nonviolence, and the Arab Springs." *Mobilization* 20(4): 453–70.

Lee, Ching Kwan, and Ming Sing, eds. 2019. *Take Back Our Future: An Eventful Sociology of the Hong Kong Umbrella Movement*. Ithaca, NY: Cornell University Press.

Lee, Francis, ed. 2017. *Media Mobilization and the Umbrella Movement*. London: Routledge.
———. 2019. "Solidarity in the Anti-Extradition Bill Movement in Hong Kong." *Critical Asian Studies*. https://doi.org/10.1080/14672715.2020.1700629.
Lee, Francis, Gary Tang, Samson Yuen, and Edmund Cheng. 2019. *The Report of On-Site Survey of Anti-Extradition Bill Amendment Protest*. Hong Kong: Centre of Communication and Public Opinion Survey Chinese University of Hong Kong.
Lee, Francis, Samson Yuen, Gary Tang, and Edmund W. Cheng. 2019. "Hong Kong's Summer of Uprising: From Anti-Extradition to Anti-Authoritarian Protests." *China Review* 19(4): 1–32.
Lichterman, Paul. 1996. *The Search for Political Community: American Activists Reinventing Commitment*. Cambridge, UK: Cambridge University Press.
Ma, Ngok, and Edmund W. Cheng, eds. 2019. *The Umbrella Movement: Civil Resistance and Contentious Space in Hong Kong*. Amsterdam: Amsterdam University Press.
MacDonald, Kevin. 2002. "From Solidarity to Fluidarity: Social Movements Beyond 'Collective Identity.'" *Social Movement Studies* 1(2): 109–28.
Maeckelbergh, Marianne. 2011. "Doing Is Believing: Prefiguration as Strategic Practice in the Alter-Globalization Movement." *Social Movement Studies* 10(1): 1–20.
McAdam, Doug. 1982. *Political Process and the Development of Black Insurgency 1930–1970*. Chicago: Chicago University Press.
Meyer, David S. 1990. *A Winter of Discontent: The Nuclear Freeze and American Politics*. New York: Praeger.
Meyer, David S., and Nancy Whittier. 1994. "Social Movement Spillover." *Social Problems* 41(2): 277–98.
Ng, Michael H. K., and John D. Wong, eds. 2017. *Civil Unrest and Governance in Hong Kong*. London: Routledge.
Snow, David A., and Robert D. Benford. 1992. "Master Frames and Cycles of Protest." In Aldon D. Morris and Carol McClurg Mueller, eds., *Frontiers in Social Movement Theory*, 133–55. New Haven, CT: Yale University Press.
Tarrow, Sidney. 1989. *Democracy and Disorder*. New York: Clarendon Press.
Taylor, Verta. 1989. "Social Movement Continuity: The Women's Movement in Abeyance." *American Sociological Review* 54(5): 761–75.
Voss, Kim. 1998. "Claim Making and the Framing of Defeats: The Interpretation of Loss by American and British Labor Activists." In Michael Hanagan, Leslie Page Moch, and Wayne Te Brake, eds., *Challenging Authority*, 136–48. Minneapolis: University of Minnesota Press.

Chapter Ten

Memory Making in Hong Kong's Tiananmen Vigils

Edmund W. Cheng and Samson Yuen
(Hong Kong Baptist University)

For thirty years, tens of thousands of people would gather at Hong Kong's Victoria Park on June 4 for a common purpose: to commemorate the day when the Tiananmen movement, a massive student-led, pro-democracy movement in China in 1989, was brutally suppressed by the Chinese authorities. During the poignant ceremony, participants would light candles, sing pro-democracy songs, listen to survivors' testimonies, and perform Chinese funeral rituals to mourn the people killed in the crackdown. Although most mourners did not participate directly in the movement, the ritualistic practices would serve as their annual reminder of the momentous event. Such practices would reopen the repository of history, allowing them to revisit, and possibly preserve and pass on, the painful memories of the crackdown—which have been heavily censored and suppressed in mainland China to the present day (Link 2010; Wasserstrom 2018).

Given its phenomenal scale and resilience, the candlelight vigil is undoubtedly the most important and symbolic commemoration of the Tiananmen movement today and also one of the most resilient commemorations dedicated to political violence. Despite—or because of—its profound political significance, the commemoration has been a fiercely contested event locally. For many years, parallel to the efforts by the organizer—The Hong Kong Alliance in Support of Patriotic Democratic Movements of China (henceforth, the Alliance)—to maintain these memories, pro-regime groups in Hong Kong have tried to discredit the vigil and question its account of the movement—for instance, whether people died, how many died, and whether the crackdown could be justified for the greater good. Despite these challenges, the vigil has survived. One may claim that these memory challenges have unintentionally strengthened the moral weight of the commemoration while mobilizing more people to attend the vigil. It was not until recent years that the nearly indisputable status of the vigil began to come under a more serious challenge. Nativists—a new political force splintered from traditional pro-democracy groups—have challenged the form of the commemoration and its meanings without disputing the factual content of the Tiananmen crackdown. These memory contestations have fueled heated debates among pro-democracy supporters regarding the implications of remembering Tiananmen, leading to the withdrawal of major groups of vigil participants and the emergence of alternative repertoires. Compared with the pro-regime groups, the nativists, despite their support for democracy, have been surprisingly more effective in weakening the moral resonance of the vigil.

What eroded the vigil's resonance? Why does the same collective memory facilitate social mobilization at one point in time but inhibit it at another? We posit that the differential impact of collective memory cannot be solely explained by a changing context. Research is needed to examine the relationship among the memory work process, collective actions, and the context in which they are situated. Although scholars have recognized the role of collective memory in shaping collective identities in movements, little is known about how the contested nature of the collective memory process—the fact that the same memory can be contested by multiple actors—constitutes collective identity building. Even though collective memory may serve as a useful cultural building block to strengthen collective identity and mobilization potential, the recasting of the same memory may destabilize the existing collective identity and disrupt mobilization.

By studying the contestation of memories in Hong Kong's Tiananmen candlelight vigil, we argue that the transformation of collective memory into collective identity does not follow a linear process. Instead, collective identity building is shaped and mediated by the interaction between the memory repositories and the repertoire that expresses them. Although the performative repertoire of the vigil has long consolidated the memory of the Tiananmen crackdown against challenges from its deniers, this repertoire has been contested more successfully by nativist memory challengers with a competing repertoire without disputing the content. Our findings aim to highlight the performative and filtering role of repertoires in reproducing collective memory. By highlighting the mediating factors that govern such a relationship, we hope to reveal a more nuanced relationship between collective memory and collective identity.

THE CULTURAL APPROACH IN SOCIAL MOVEMENTS

Collective memory—a body of symbols, representations, and narratives about the past shared by a group of people—is a powerful resource that gives people a sense of who they are, shapes their social and political preferences, and mobilizes them to take action. Much research has examined how collective memories operate in relation to individual memories (Olick 1999), how they are transmitted via formal and informal institutions (Edy 2006), how they shape political culture (Assmann and Czaplicka 1995; Shevel 2011; Zerubavel 1995), and how they legitimate regimes (Zerubavel 1995). Recently, the relationship between collective memories and contentious politics has also gained increasing scholarly attention (Harris 2006; Meyer 2006; Polletta 2006; Zamponi 2018). As a cultural process that reflects group preferences and shapes the symbolic environment of collective actions, collective memories play a crucial role in strengthening group solidarity, reducing the cost of cooperation among individuals, and providing actors with historically grounded information to make decisions. In this sense, examining the contentious impact of building and contesting collective memories may make a useful contribution to the cultural approach in studying social movements, which has drawn much attention in recent decades (Goodwin and Jasper 1999; Goodwin, Jasper, and Polletta 2001).

Studies on the concept of culture in movement research not only highlight culture as a framework or formative condition of social movements but also emphasize the constitutive role of culture in shaping movements' internal characteristics and dynamics (Baumgarten, Daphi, and Ullrich 2014; Johnston and Klandermans 2013). This perspective has prompted scholars to go beyond traditional focuses on the opportunities and resources that structure the contentious behavior of actors and to instead focus on the meanings and affects that motivate and constitute them. Since then, the "cultural turn" of social movement studies has led to the flourishing of in-depth studies that focus on specific cultural elements, including emotions (Jasper 1997; Juris 2008), symbols (Sawer 2007), rituals (Staggenborg and Lang 2007), frames (Benford and Snow 2000), and narratives (Daphi 2017; Nepstad 2001).

Collective memories provide another important perspective on how culture shapes movements. Existing studies have discussed two ways in which collective memories shape contentious politics. One involves examining how memories facilitate collective actions. Memories of past events and historical figures can be used strategically by political actors to frame grievances and encourage collective actions (Harris 2006; Jansen 2007). By inducing unity among individuals and linking the present to past experiences, collective memories can create and maintain collective identities (Farthing and Kohl 2013; Gabel 2013; Gongaware 2003, 2010), enabling people to mobilize in the absence of resources and political opportunities (Polletta and Jasper 2001; Taylor and Whittier 1992). Furthermore, memories of previous movements may help to channel movement diffusion (Zamponi and Daphi 2014). Nevertheless, collective memories can also have a constraining effect by imposing prescription and proscription on collective actors in the form of taboos, prohibitions, duties, and requirements (Olick and Levy 1997). Such memories can create different types of strategic dilemmas for movement activists. Meanwhile, strong and deeply rooted identities can divide activist groups and undermine their ability to mobilize ordinary participants (Zamponi 2018).

In short, collective memories both facilitate and constrain collective actions. That is, the mere presence of collective memories does not predetermine their participatory consequences. Such indeterminacy is further confounded by the contested nature of the collective memory process. Unlike organizational resources that can be readily mobilized, collective memory is not a "thing" but a contested, interactive, and social process (Halbwachs 1992; Jedlowski 2001). This process involves the participation of multiple actors, who may serve as mnemonic agents and often engage in memory work to compete over how to interpret the past, what should be remembered, and the form remembrance should take (Zerubavel 1996). By making memory a site of struggle, this contested process inevitably involves the selection and exclusion of certain narratives of the past (Jansen 2007). The question, therefore, is not whether memory is distorted but to what extent it is distorted and what mechanisms and actors are responsible.

That collective memories are only partially malleable is well recognized in contemporary memory studies. Contrary to the constructivist view that considers collective memories to be "invented traditions" that instrumentally serve present needs (Halbwachs 1992; Hobsbawm and Ranger 1983), recent works have argued that collective memories cannot be invented from scratch—partly because they are restricted by the available materials from the "actual past" (Brubaker and Feischmidt 2002; Schudson 1989; Wagner-Pacifici and Schwartz 1991) and partly because of the plurality of memories that exist in a modern society (Schudson 1993). Therefore, some scholars have devised a processual view of collective memories, seeing them as a cumulative and constantly evolving process (Zelizer 1995) dependent on previous remembrance (Olick 1999). This process combines both changes and continuities: while they remain stable due to constraints imposed by the "actual past" and previous memory struggles, they also have to adopt changes such that their resonance can be regenerated along with social transformations. In other words, the collective memory process is path dependent but not path determinant. Tensions abound throughout the process; changes always coexist and intermesh with continuities and constraints from the actual past.

The processual nature of collective memories has also informed studies of contentious politics in a theoretical way. Francesca Polletta (1998) looks at how storytelling—narratives about events or the past—helps to create and maintain collective identities that form the basis of mobilization. Her study of U.S. student activism in the 1960s shows that the production of narratives about sit-ins as spontaneous was central to an emerging collective identity among protesters that aimed to signal a break from previous tactics and movement goals. Priska Daphi (2017) similarly examines how narratives of the global justice movement played a role in shaping collective identity of participants: activists from different groups of the movement, or former activists, told different stories about the movement. In contrast with Polletta (1998) and Daphi (2017), Timothy B. Gongaware (2003, 2010) engages more directly with the memory process, focusing on how it forges and maintains collective identity within movement groups. Unlike previous literature that emphasized memory as a "building block" of collective identity (Polletta and Jasper 2001), Gongaware argues that it is the interactive memory process that matters: the creation and maintenance of collective memory are "important means for movement members to develop a unity around movement ends, means, fields of action, [and] networks of relations" (2003: 513). Through the exchange of narratives in the everyday interaction of group members, both processes help to "incorporate old notions of the movement's past with new notions concerning various elements of collective identity" (Gongaware 2003: 513; 2010)—thus enhancing the potential for mobilization.

While the processual nature of collective memory has already gained traction, still little attention has been put on the importance of context in mediating and shaping this process. The neglect of context is partly revealed in that most of the aforementioned studies focus primarily on how processes of collective memory or narrative strengthen movement identity but not otherwise. Context, however, matters in that collective memory can evolve along with changes in the spatial and temporal context. As the context shifts, collective memory can invite contestation from mnemonic agents, which may impose an uncertain impact on collective identity. As Paolo Jedlowski (2001) points out, "relating memory so closely to identity can lead us to forget that memory is also something that can contradict the identity that an individual wishes to adopt at any given moment" (p. 36). In other words, memory does not necessarily serve the identity of a group and its present interests at all times. The key, therefore, is to carefully observe how collective memory processes shape elements of the collective identity of movements in a contingent manner, taking into account the underlying contexts and events that unfold over time (Gillan 2018). Thus, the aim of this research is to shed more light on the role of context in the collective memory process by focusing on the contextually sensitive process in which mnemonic agents sustain and contest collective memories and their impact on protest movements. Specifically, how does memory contestation shape collective identities? Why does the memory process, despite contestation at a certain moment, facilitate collective identity building? Why are mnemonic agents able to contest the memory process at other moments and weaken collective identity or even create counter identities?

A DYNAMIC MODEL OF COLLECTIVE MEMORY

We tackle these questions by proposing a dynamic model that breaks down the collective memory process (the independent variables) and links the components with the construction of collective identity (the dependent variable). Collective identity has been regarded as a key building block of mass mobilization because participants often share certain commonalities when they engage in collective actions. In social movement studies, scholars have conceptualized collective identity in two perspectives: one perspective locates it within the individual, seeing it as "an individual's cognitive, moral and emotional connection with a broader community, category, practice, or institution" (Polletta and Jasper 2001: 285); another perspective situates it on the group level, focusing on the self-understanding of a group as a collective (Daphi 2017; Melucci 1996; Taylor and Whittier 1992;). We side with the latter, because shared meanings, we believe, play a more important role than individual beliefs in shaping collective actions. In this regard, we draw on Alberto Melucci's approach (1996) to collective identity as "an inter-active and shared definition produced by a number of individuals (or groups at a more complex level) concerning the orientations of their action and the field of opportunities and constraints in which such action is to take place" (p. 70). As such, collective identity is not a static reflection of preexisting structural conditions nor an aggregation of individual-level attitude and belief but "a system of relations and representation" (Melucci 1995: 50) regarding the movement's shared interests, motivations to act, and strategic choices. Collective identity is also subject to a continuous process of negotiation and reconstruction through social interactions between actors (Melucci 1996; Taylor and Whittier 1992). Thus, it can be identified through the observable phenomena of action and interaction (Whittier 1995: 16). To capture collective identity analytically, we follow Melucci's (1996) distinction among its cognitive, emotional, and relational dimensions, focusing particularly on the first two for the purposes of this chapter. The cognitive dimension concerns actors' shared definitions about the "ends, means and the field of action," while the emotional dimension focuses on the affective recognition between individuals, sometimes manifested through collective rituals and practices. Analyzing these two dimensions in the process of movements will be helpful for us to delineate changes in participants' collective identity.

We follow Lorenzo Zamponi (2018) to conceptualize the collective memory process as comprising the interaction between two elements: the repository of memory and the repertoire of memory. Defined as "the set of products, both implicit and explicit, formal and informal, symbolic and material that act as objectified carriers of the past" (Zamponi 2018: 7), a repository of memory refers to the contents of memory that provide an account of the events being remembered: what actually happened; who the actors are and what their roles are; how they happened; and what the consequences are. These repositories are "objectified" in that they must be stored in different mediums, such as the mass media; however, they are not objective, since they have undergone selection and exclusion by mnemonic agents. Although we recognize that objectification is necessary for memories to be observed by the public, we differ from Zamponi (2018) and intend to focus on the content of a memory repository rather than its manifestation as a storage facility. For the repertoire of memory, we follow Zamponi (2018) to define it as "the set of mnemonic practices that social actors put in place in reference to the past" (2018: 7). This includes both different forms of remembering, such as ceremony, rituals, museums, and documentaries, and myriad practices, such as songs, poems, eulogies, and silences—all of which involve the active role of mnemonic agents. Compared with a memory repository, which involves passive objects, a memory repertoire is an active process of remembering that enables mnemonic agents to access different memory repositories.

The collective memory process in social movements is thus a process in which the two basic elements—repository and repertoire—interact under the influence of mnemonic agents. Two types of mnemonic agents are involved in the process: memory entrepreneurs and memory challengers. Memory entrepreneurs are those who actively invoke content from memory repositories and express them through repertoire to produce meanings that help to mobilize people. These meanings, expressed through the cognitive ideas concerning the movements' goals, means, and networks of relations (Gongaware 2003) and the emotional investments of participants, provide the building blocks of collective identity, which in turn facilitate collective actions. Memory challengers, on the other hand, are the adversaries who seek to disrupt the same memory process by contesting the account of memory repositories or repertoires. By doing so, memory challengers aim to interfere with the collective identity-building process by disrupting the cognitive and emotional resonance, which in turn weakens any existing identities shared by movement participants or by creating alternative ones that achieve similar effects.

This description merely captures the memory process at a given moment. In fact, the model also moves dynamically across time. Figure 10.1 illustrates this temporal model. At T1, memory repertoires serve a performative role

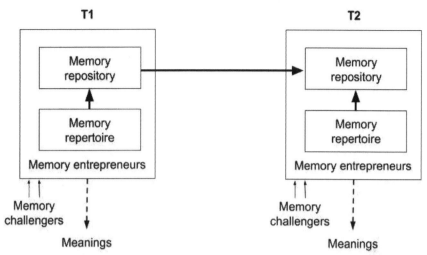

Figure 10.1. A Dynamic Model of the Collective Memory Process

for memory entrepreneurs to highlight and consolidate certain dimensions of the distant past, thus helping to generate meaning and collective identity. During this process, new content may be added to the memory repository, while outdated content may be filtered out. Meanwhile, memory challengers can contest this process by disputing either the actual past or its performative representation. Depending on the outcome of contestation, a renewed memory repository will be invoked by memory entrepreneurs at T2, which will prompt another round of performance and contestation through which a new set of meanings can be produced.

COMMEMORATING THE TIANANMEN MOVEMENT IN HONG KONG

As both a commemoration to mourn the dead and a protest to seek vindication, Hong Kong's Tiananmen candlelight vigil presents a pertinent case study to examine how collective memory processes shape collective identity in movements. The case offers several advantages. First, unlike many other movements where participants often invoke memories of different events (Harris 2006), the candlelight vigil draws on the memories about a single event—the 1989 Tiananmen movement. This context thus allows researchers to isolate the memory process from other noise to focus on the evolution of the same set of memories involving a similar set of mnemonic agents. Second, the thirty-year existence of the vigil provides a long duration to observe the memory process, allowing us to delineate the trajectory of change and continuity along a temporal order. Third, collective identity is a particularly important element for the vigil. Since its stated goals (e.g., to seek vindication from Beijing) are difficult to achieve, the organizer's more realistic objective is to fortify memories about Tiananmen and pass on the collective identity concerning the stated goals to the younger generation. In other words, collective identity is not simply a by-product of the vigil but an intended movement goal. Observing this outcome—not only through turnout but also through participants' solidarity around the stated goals—allows researchers to examine the impact of the memory process.

Despite its empirical richness, few scholars have examined the candlelight vigil in the context of the collective memory process. Most studies have focused on its role and implications in Hong Kong's political activism (Chan and Chan 2014; Cheng 2016: 402; Kuan 2015; Veg 2017: 331–33). The works of Francis Lee and Joseph M. Chan (2013, 2016) are the only exceptions considering the memory aspect of the event. The authors engage with two key dimensions in the collective memory process of the Tiananmen movement: (1) memory transmission, which deals with whether and how collective memories about the movement are passed down to the younger generation who did not experience the event (Lee and Chan 2013), and (2) memory mobilization, a communicative process through which vigil organizers use the news media and schedule their actions to recall people's memory of the movement when the vigil approaches (Lee and Chan 2016). However, while Lee and Chan have provided useful insights on how Tiananmen memories are transmitted and mobilized, questions regarding the role of the vigil in the memory process remain unanswered. There is a further question concerning the relationship between memory contestation and mobilization. Lee and Chan (2016) show that efforts to contest collective memory resulted in the proliferation of discourses upholding the dominant representation of the past. However, what allows this dominant representation of memory to be defended against contestation? Why is memory contestation sometimes successful in challenging the dominant representation despite its dominance?

METHODS AND DATA

Our analysis begins in 1990 when the Alliance conducted the first annual Tiananmen vigil at Victoria Park. To analyze the cultural process of collective memory building and contestation over time, this chapter adopts a mixed method research design. We adopt different methods as not all data sets can cover the study period, which requires the data to be contrasted and verified.

First, our main data source comes from a set of time-series and quantitative data collected from six years of on-site surveys at Victoria Park between 2010 and 2018. At the vigil, the research team divided the park into different zones and routes. was All interviewers were assigned to a specific zone where they would walk in circles and invite every tenth person they saw within the designated route to complete the survey.[1] The interviewers, ranging from twenty to thirty each year, were trained with a set of fieldwork protocols to ensure standardization and to minimize selection bias.

Second, we compared our survey data with qualitative data observed in the protest sites. Over the study period, we conducted participant observation and spoke randomly to the participants at the three-hour-long vigil to confirm our understanding of their stored memories and memory repertoire as well as the degree of their collectiveness. We also examined the official programs distributed and performed at the vigil to trace how memory entrepreneurs have used repertoire to draw on and consolidate their memory of Tiananmen. All thirty years of programs were collected from the Alliance's online archive, except the ones in 1990, 1994, and 1995, which have gone missing in the archive for unknown reasons.

Third, we extended our data collection by conducting six semistructured interviews with the leaders of the Alliance and nativist groups, who are, respectively, the mnemonic agents operating and contesting the vigils and thus have access to firsthand information. They were asked questions regarding their respective role in and solidarity with the vigils, their attempts to preserve or challenge the memories of the Tiananmen, and their emotions and identity associated with the Tiananmen protests.[2] The interviews were conducted between May 2018 and January 2019 in Hong Kong in a designated venue agreed on by both the interviewers and interviewees, and they typically lasted two hours each. We also traced the discursive contestations from both the pro-regime elites and pro-democracy nativists by analyzing their views in six major Chinese-language newspapers one month before and after the annual vigils between 1999 and 2018. These newspapers were often selected by the existing literature for their mass circulation and diverse political spectrum.

THE NEXUS OF COMMEMORATION AND MOBILIZATION

While making meaning of the vigil has been a dynamic process featuring contestations among mnemonic agents, the initial participatory experiences of these agents shaped how and what the Tiananmen event had been remembered for. Established on May 21, 1989, the Alliance regarded itself as "a child of the 1989 pro-democracy movement" (Szeto 2011: 3). In the weeks that followed, the Alliance initiated three mass rallies, each attracting more than 1 million Hong Kong citizens, who were traditionally regarded as apathetic in political affairs, to march on the streets (Lau and Kuan 1988). During the same summer, Hong Kong citizens signed petitions and donated millions to the movement. Meanwhile, elites across the political spectrum smuggled resources to Tiananmen Square and, after the crackdown, rescued the protesters from mass arrests. Even pro-China politicians sided with the majority at that historic moment and condemned the Chinese authorities.

The Mnemonic Agents' Participatory Experience

The deep involvement of Hong Kong citizens within and beyond its border prompted Chinese Communist Party (CCP) leaders to accuse Hong Kong of being "the base for subverting communism" (Lau 2015: 61). However, their support for the Tiananmen movement also had the unintended consequence of inspiring Hong Kong's own pro-democracy movement. The fact that Hong Kong, then a British colony, was shielded from the harsh repression in mainland China amplified the urgency of installing democratic institutions to defend the political enclave's existing freedoms after the transfer of sovereignty in 1997. Previous studies have confirmed that the 1989 protest event produced an enlightening experience to transform Hong Kong's elitist-oriented democracy movement to a mass movement (Lam 2004; Ma 2007).

This collective participatory experience explains why the Alliance has a broad-based representation of the pro-democracy force. At its peak, the Alliance comprised 146 affiliated organizations, including the Democratic Party, Hong Kong Federation of Students, Hong Kong Professional Teachers' Union, and Hong Kong Confederation of Trade Unions. These key players in Hong Kong's democracy movement are also routinely present at the vigil. Indeed, as argued by Albert Ho, chair of the Alliance and a veteran activist, the primary goal of the vigil is to support rather than lead China's democratic movement. In this sense, persistent mass mobilization was the only way to contribute to the democracy movement after it was repressed in 1989. Commemoration and mobilization are thus two sides of a coin:

> Take [the Tiananmen vigil's] most popular slogan, "never want to remember, dare not forget" (*buxianghuiyi, weiganwangji*), as an example. The first half concerns emotion; the second, obligation. Our perseverance in mourning the Tiananmen victims and our commitment to pursuing Hong Kong's democracy came from the same [source of] antecedent and memory. . . . We see no contradiction in the dual objectives (Interview 5).

Figure 10.2 shows the vigil participation and donation patterns, emphasizing the nexus between commemoration and mobilization. While there was

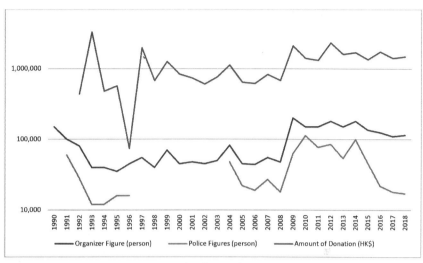

Figure 10.2. Turnout and Donation for the Vigil
Source: The Alliance's annual reports and media report.

a discrepancy between the organizer and police figures, the overall trend is a rising turnout until the post-2014 period.[3] The peaks of mobilization in 1999, 2004, 2009, and 2014 coincided with the five-year or ten-year anniversaries of the Tiananmen movement and partly with critical protest events. For instance, the 2004 vigil preceded the July 1 rally, which later prompted the resignation of the first chief executive. The 2014 vigil took place right before the umbrella movement. On the other hand, the low tide of the vigil in 1995–1998 and post-2015 coincided with the 1997 handover and the rise of nativism in 2015. Despite the ups and downs in turnout, the vigil has continued to rally those with and those without personal experience of June 4. Table 10.1 shows that between 11.6 and 30.4 percent of those who joined the vigil between 2010 and 2018 were newcomers. Stalwart protesters, those who had attended the vigil more than ten times, constituted 20.9 to 37.1 percent of participants. Finally, the donations received by the Alliance during the vigil have been on the rise, reaching a minimum of HK$1.3 million and a maximum of

Table 10.1. History and Frequency of Vigil Participation, 2010–2018

Year/Participation	Newcomers	1–3 Times	4–6 Times	7–9 Times	10 Times or More
2010 (N = 540)	30.4	28.3	14.4	5.9	20.9
2013 (N = 444)	21.8	30.4	20.7	6.1	20.9
2014 (N = 580)	21.0	27.9	20.9	6.7	23.4
2015 (N = 861)	11.6	20.3	24.0	10.0	34.0
2018 (N = 663)	20.1	9.4	22.2	11.3	37.1

HK$2.3 million after its twentieth anniversary in 2009. This proxy indicator confirmed that the vigil has remained resilient and served as an important source of resource mobilization for Hong Kong's pro-democracy force. Comparative population surveys further suggested that respondents tended to slightly over-report their vigil participation, which indicates that "the June-Fourth event has become a socially desirable ritual" (Kuan 2015: 39).

Entries are the percentages of respondents within each group who listed their frequency of participation. The frequency of participation is regrouped as follows for testing other variables in the subsequent tables: casual (0–3 times), regular (4–6 times), and stalwart participants (7 or more times).

Moreover, the collective identity among vigil participants is reflected in their shared interests and motivations to act. Table 10.2 shows that in 2018, regardless of how frequently they participated, participants regarded the preservation of the historical truth of Tiananmen as their top priority and recognized the necessity of continuing the commemoration. In fact, "preserving Hong Kong society's memory of June 4" (72.3 to 77.4 percent) was the greatest common two motivations—"demanding that the Chinese government vindicate June 4" and "struggling for democracy in China," two official Alliance objectives—are significantly correlated with the frequency of participation.[4] This result suggests that the more frequently participants attend the vigil, the more likely they are to endorse the objectives of the movement entrepreneurs. By objective uniting the three groups of casual, regular, and stalwart participants. This was followed by "demanding that Chinese authorities vindicate June 4" (55.7 to 71.2 percent) and "mourning the death from June 4" (59.6 to 66.6 percent). The table also indicates that the other attributing responsibility to the authorities for repressing the peaceful protest and causing civilian casualties, these shared motivations have provided a cohesive glue maintaining the collective identity among vigil participants.

Forging Collective Identity through Memory Repertoire

The memory repertoire that was chosen for the vigil was, in fact, determined not only by the initial participatory experiences of the mnemonic agents but also by their organizational origins. On September 12,1989, the Alliance organized a one-hundred-day sacrificial mass that attracted more than fifty thousand participants. However, nearly half of the participants left in the middle of the ceremony (Pun 2012: 250); most of them found the performance of pop singers inappropriate and disrespectful to the victims. The Alliance reached a consensus that the vigil should resemble "sacrifice as though present," a Confucian tenet (Leys 1997: 3.12) emphasizing that sacrifice must be solemn as if the deceased were present (Interviews 4 and 5). This event

Table 10.2. Perceived Motivations and Participation Frequency, 2018

Participants/ Motivation	Mourn the deaths from 6/4	Demand China government vindicates 6/4	Criticize China's existing human rights condition	Preserve Hong Kong society's memory of 6/4	Protest Hong Kong government's position on 6/4	Struggle for democracy in China	Struggle for democracy in Hong Kong
Casual (n = 193)	59.6	55.7$_a$	45.5	72.3	35.8	34.5	47.2
Regular (n = 146)	63.0	50.3$_b$	44.1	77.4	38.1	31.7$_a$	44.1
Stalwart (n = 320)	66.6	71.2$_{ab}$	47.8	75.9	43.6	42.5$_a$	58.7
F-values	2.196	10.441**	.870	1.702	1.242	3.582*	2.645

Questions: How important are the following motivations in driving you to participate in the June fourth vigil? How often do you participate in the June fourth vigil? Entries are the percentages of respondents within each group who strongly agreed with the statement. The F-values were derived from a one-way analysis of variance (ANOVA) test of differences in the means of the three groups of participants (casual, regular, and stalwart) with the perceived motivations. Entries in the same column sharing the same subscripts a and b differ from each other significantly in post hoc Bonferroni tests.

* $P < .05$.

** $P < .001$.

also helped recruit nearly two hundred volunteers for the Alliance, many of whom are still helping every year. Their commitment explains why the present ritualistic form has been adopted to the present day.

The use of solemn rituals as memory repertoire serves a performative role in encouraging people to remember Tiananmen even if they did not experience it. Traditionally, the Chinese funeral ceremony, known as *shou ling*, is semiprivate and reserved for relatives and friends of the deceased who stand as guards beside the coffin (Chan et al. 2005). When the ceremony is extended to include strangers, it means that the mourning of Tiananmen victims has also become a political manifesto. In fact, the vigil has been routinized to recall the distant past to strengthen the collective identity of the participants. In every vigil, the Goddess of Democracy and a large poster of the Tiananmen Gate were placed on the two sides of Victoria Park, each, respectively, being the symbol of resistance and crackdown in the 1989 movement. The Statue of Condolence engraved with the phrase "martyrs of democracy live in eternity" was placed at the center, which used physical proximity to stage to denote sacrifice and memory of the martyrs. The ceremony would begin with the anthem "River of Sorrow," performed through Chinese *erhu* instrument and coming from a story about struggle and persistence dating back to the Han dynasty. On stage, young and veteran members of the Alliance would read the obituary note, light a torch, lay a wreath, and burn the book of condolences to the victims. Downstage, hundreds of thousands of protesters dressed in white and dark colors would bow three times to the statue, which are standard customs and rituals practiced in Chinese funerals. Subsequently, they would maintain a moment of silence, hold up candles, sing pro-democracy songs, and listen to testimonies.

No concrete concession by the Beijing authorities has ever been offered after the vigil. However, the iconic image of the "candlelight sea" visualizing the collective identity of the hundreds of thousands of mourners, has never failed to create a strong moral criticism of the Communist regime. This collective performance involving both the organizers and participants is a crucial element of maintaining and strengthening the collective identity of vigil participants. For instance, the 2013 vigil was caught in a thunderstorm that damaged all the audio and visual equipment, yet most participants insisted on staying and completing the rituals. This commitment indicates participants' intention to showcase their solidarity and perseverance and demonstrates how the performative power of the repertoire was amplified by participants' enthusiastic feedback.

In addition to serving a performative role, the vigil's memory repertoire fulfills a filtering function by selectively highlighting specific aspects of collective memories such that they can easily be recalled and transmitted beyond the vigil. This is achieved by the nonroutine section of the vigil, typically after the rituals. Over the years, the rule has been to select repertoires that are peaceful, interactive, and easy to participate in. Since the mid-1990s, the Alliance even established a working committee to review feedback from volunteers and participants to adjust the program (Interview 1). This mechanism ensures that the memory repertoires correspond to the Alliance's stated goals and participants' changing expectations (Interviews 4 and 6).

Figure 10.3 traces the activities of the nonroutine section listed in the programs. In the early 1990s, songs, poems, and prose were the main items and were staged to allow participants to express their grief and anger. Since 2001, documentaries and original footage about Tiananmen, as well as survivors' testimonies, have become linchpins. The latter include the Tiananmen Mothers, who lost their children in the crackdown; exiled leaders such as Wang Dan, Fang Zheng, and Xiong Yan; and dissidents such as Teng Biao and Hu Jia. These truth-bearing materials were included because of the growing need to remind participants about the Tiananmen event, which became more distant in time into the 2000s (Interview 2).

This part of the memory repertoire not only helps participants recall the event but also serves to highlight and prioritize what in the memory repository is deemed important to remember. For instance, playing videos of the Tiananmen Mothers emphasizes not only that people died but also that those who died were sons and daughters. Inviting local speakers who witnessed

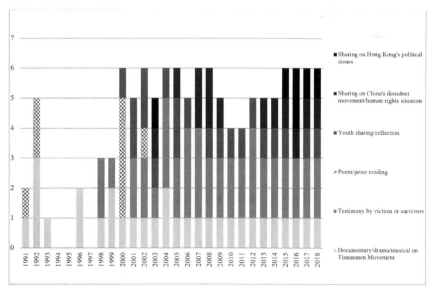

Figure 10.3. Nonroutine Repertoire in the Candlelight Vigil, 1991–2018
Source: Brochures of the candlelight vigil

Table 10.3. Perceived Vividness of Memories and Participation Frequency, 2014

Participants/ Motivation	Student Mourning of Hu Yaobang	Declaration of Upheaval by Li Peng	Site Visit by Zhao Ziyang on May 19	Crackdown on June 4	Mass Rally of Hong Kong Citizens	Hunger Strike by Tiananmen Students
Casual (n = 118)	44.1	51.7	61.0	73.7	69.5	65.3
Regular (n = 82)	48.8	57.3	72.0	81.7	80.5	73.2
Stalwart (n = 169)	71.6	78.7	87.6	94.1	89.9	85.8
X^2	29.551**	29.899**	28.674**	30.601**	20.089*	22.161*

Question: Which of the followings are your most vivid memories of the June fourth vigil? How often do you participate in the June fourth vigil?
Entries are the percentages of respondents within each group who agreed with the statement. The X^2 values were derived from cross-tabulating the tripartite participants (casual, regular, and stalwart) with the deepest memories on a 3-point Likert scale.
*$P < .05$.
**$P < .001$.

the massacre, in turn, highlights the intimate relationship of Hong Kong with the students in 1989. Indeed, table 10.3 shows that the most vivid memories across different groups of participants in the 2014 vigil are "the crackdown on June 4" (73.7 to 94.1 percent), followed by "the mass rally of Hong Kong citizens" (69.5 to 89.9 percent). These most-remembered moments attest to the filtering role of the memory repertoire in highlighting regime atrocities and Hong Kong's popular mobilization for democracy. The frequency of vigil participation is also positively correlated with the intensity of key memories about Tiananmen; such memories are more imprinted in the minds of stalwart participants than in the minds of regular and casual participants.

The filtering role of the vigil's memory repertoire is further illustrated by the inclusion of new speakers and activities, which helps to shift attention to other aspects of the memory repositories that warrant remembering. For instance, since 2000, the slogan "passing on the flame of remembrance" has been emphasized. "Youth representatives" have also been identified and given time to share their views. Over time, more local speakers have been included in the program to speak about Hong Kong's struggle for democracy. Although these activities are only added cautiously, they have nevertheless increased the emphasis on the local significance of Tiananmen. Compared with the routinized rituals that aim to recall and consolidate the Tiananmen memories through rigid and solemn collective performances, these nonroutine, interactive repertoires allow for some degree of flexibility to reorder and filter what is being remembered.

Although this reflects the organizers' strategic use of the memory repertoire, these repertoires are also deemed essential from the participants' per-

Table 10.4. Perceived Importance of Repertoires among Age Groups, 2018

	Light Candle	Observe Silence and Bow	Sing Pro-Democracy Songs	Read Obituary Note	Stage Youth's View	Listen to Witnesses' Testimony	Watch Original Footage
17 and younger (n = 20)	45.0	60.0	15.0	35.0	50.0	55.0	50.0
18–24 (n = 117)	35.0	40.2	12.8	16.2	24.8	48.7	41.0
25–29 (n = 80)	32.5	38.8	16.3	13.8	26.3	42.5	43.8
30–39 (n = 113)	47.8	53.1	21.2	24.8	29.2	51.3	50.4
40–49 (n = 86)	44.2	47.7	16.3	19.8	31.4	48.8	52.3
50–64 (n = 101)	62.4	68.3	38.6	37.6	49.5	48.5	50.5
65 and older (n = 21)	76.2	71.4	57.1	52.4	71.4	76.2	66.7
F-values	5.826**	3.742*	5.195**	6.513**	6.022**	1.002	1.230

Question: Please rank the following repertoires in the June fourth vigil by their importance.
Entries are the percentages of respondents within each age group who strongly agreed with the repertoires on a 5-point Likert scale.
*$P < .05$.
**$P < .001$.

spective. Table 10.4 reveals that the older generation (aged fifty and older) ranked "observing silence and bowing" and "lighting candles" as the two most important components but also recognized the importance of "listening to witnesses' testimonies" and "watching original footage." By contrast, the younger generation (aged twenty-nine and younger) ranked "listening to witnesses' testimonies" and "watching original footage" as the two most important components. The difference between these two groups can be explained by their different degree of possession of the actual past: While youth participants demanded authentic testimonies to recall the historical details and significance of Tiananmen, older participants valued both rituals and testimonies in fulfilling those functions. Overall, these memory repertoires are generally considered important by all participants, but the variation in the perceived importance between the young and old participants also hints at the unfolding memory contestations, which we now discuss.

THE REGIME LOYALISTS' CHALLENGES

Although the vigil has long preserved the actual past and the contemporary subtext of the Tiananmen movement, contestation of the Tiananmen memory from pro-regime loyalists has persisted all along. These challenges come in several ways. A typical one is to try to downplay and censor the discussion of the Tiananmen protests in the public sphere. Partly out of the fear of provoking public outrage, stalwart pro-Beijing politicians often keep quiet and avoid public debate about Tiananmen, while those from business parties occasionally displayed an ambivalent stance—for instance, by calling the incident "a tragedy." But despite their subtle difference in attitudes, these regime loyalists in the legislature have, since 1998, consistently voted down a motion tabled by pro-democracy legislators that demanded the central government vindicate the Tiananmen movement. In 1997 and 1998, the first chief executive, Tung Chee-hwa, even attempted to persuade the founding chair of the Alliance, Szeto Wah, to abandon the vigil and disband the Alliance in exchange for Beijing's greenlight for universal suffrage.

Compared with these actors, other pro-regime elites have engaged the Tiananmen memories more directly by using a consequential lens to justify the crackdown. For instance, various members of the National People's Congress and the Chinese People's Political Consultative Conference—and even Hong Kong's second chief executive Donald Tsang—have advocated that citizens should forget about June 4 and focus their attention on China's economic prosperity, which they said was only possible because of the crackdown. Interestingly, such direct challenges often provoked severe backlashes from the civil society. Tsang's comments on Tiananmen, for instance, immediately prompted protests from pro-democracy legislators. Media responses were also negative, as Tsang was criticized for "lacking conscience" and "not representing Hong Kong people." The enormous public pressure forced Tsang to issue an apology admitting to the use of improper language. The "mistake" was also proactively invoked by the Alliance to amplify the call on people to attend what would become the largest commemoration—in 2009—in its twenty years of history.

A third type of challenge, often used by countermovement groups and senior regime loyalists, attempts to deny existing accounts and memories of Tiananmen; for instance, where the crackdown actually happened, whether the death toll has been exaggerated, or who should share the responsibility. The most symbolic case occurred in 2007, when Lik Ma, chair of the largest pro-regime political party, openly rejected the term "June 4 massacre" and implied that no one was killed by army tanks. These remarks, unsurprisingly, sparked public outrage. Pro-democracy activists and their supporters called Ma's words "whitewashing" and denounced him as "cold-blooded." Although these denial accounts almost disappeared after the incident, the rise of pro-regime countermovement groups in the early 2010s brought them back into the public sphere. Because of their spontaneous and murky background, these groups often strike with transgressive narratives and claims like "soldiers also died," "no one died on Tiananmen Square," or "students should be accountable for their radical claims and actions." On the whole, however, their challenges were not effective. The fact that they did not diffuse to more prominent regime loyalists shows that the reposited memory about Tiananmen remained strongly protected by popular support.

THE NATIVISTS' CHALLENGES

In the mid-2010s, a new set of memory challengers began to emerge, this time from the nativists, an emerging group of pro-democracy activists who distinguish themselves from traditional democrats and advocate a Hong Kong-first approach in fighting for democratization. Vowing to defend local autonomy against the trend of "mainlandization," nativists rallied their support through a series of protests against mainland visitors and began to participate in electoral politics after the umbrella movement (Yuen and Chung 2018). The vigil has also become a major site for nativists to bolster their political influence. They have challenged the Alliance and the vigil in two ways. First, they argue that the candlelight vigil promotes a form of Chinese nationalism that has fallen out of sync with the younger generation. As many young people did not experience the Tiananmen events and tended to have a much stronger local identity than Chinese identity, nativists held that young people should not feel any responsibility for attending the vigil. Even if they choose to commemorate the victims, they should do so out of respect for human rights rather than nationalistic sentiments (Interview 2). Nationalism, they argue, emotionally bonds Hong Kong people to the Chinese nation and diverts attention from the struggle for democracy. As such, Hong Kong people should keep a distance from mainland political affairs and concentrate their efforts on local issues.

Nativists' second critique centers on the form of the vigil: They contend that the vigil has been too ritualistic, banal, and replete with old-fashioned repertoire. As a renowned nativist commentator remarked, "The vigil should introduce something new, like having different booths organizing their own activities; it should not be just singing, shouting slogans, lighting candles . . . and then just leaving the event behind afterwards" (Li 2015). To them, these rituals serve only a symbolic purpose and have no actual impact on either the Chinese government or Hong Kong's democratization progress. Some further argue that both the Alliance and the pro-democracy parties have been taking advantage of the vigil and the Tiananmen victims to gain political currency. Others take issue with the slogan and argue that "seeking vindication" could endorse the Chinese government and legitimize the oppressor of Hong Kong.

Their notion is that the Tiananmen commemoration should not be monopolized by the Alliance. Commemorations can take place at other venues and times—not necessarily in Victoria Park and not always on June 4. New forms of commemoration should be introduced, with more discussion and fewer funeral rituals and with more about Hong Kong and less about China.

Different from the pro-regime elites, the nativists' challenge does not concern the memory repository as much as the repertoire of commemoration. Nativists do not dispute the historical account of the crackdown; they too acknowledge that many innocent people died in the event and condemn the brutality of the Chinese government. They take issue with the importance and meanings that people attach to such memories, particularly the Chinese nationalism invoked in commemorating the victims. For nativists, these meanings are largely attributable to the vigil's repertoire. As such, new repertoires are needed to express the repository of Tiananmen memories such that the nationalistic dimension of their representation can be diluted and expunged. Thus, starting in 2013, nativist groups—including political groups and university student unions—began to organize alternative commemorations while urging their supporters not to attend the Victoria Park vigil.

These alternative commemorations share a common feature: They all reject the core commemorative activities seen in the vigil. In fact, it is inaccurate to call them "commemoration." For instance, in 2013, Hongkongers Priority, a nativist group, held a barbeque on June 4 in front of the Liaison Office, China's official organ in Hong Kong, and called the event "June 4 is none of my business." University student unions also began to organize alternative commemorations since 2015, but they framed these events as forums whose purpose was less to commemorate than to discuss and liberate the meanings of Tiananmen. During these forums held on university campuses, there were no funeral rituals, no songs, no testimonies, and no candles—none of the symbols that constitute the Victoria Park vigil. Instead, these forums adopted a rather academic approach. Speakers were invited to debate what the Tiananmen movement means for contemporary Hong Kong and its political future, which in effect downplayed the emotional and nationalistic resonance of the event. This is perhaps most explicitly illustrated by the theme of the June 4, 2017, forum held by the University of Hong Kong student union: "nationalistic sentiments are over, why keep the candlelight?"

The impact of nativists' memory challenges was profound. Although the vigil attendance maintains consistently above one hundred thousand (which is much higher than the levels in the 1990s until the late 2000s), it has fallen substantially from the peak years around the early 2010s. Organizers particularly noticed the decline of young people in recent years compared with figures from the late 2000s (Interview 6). The shrinking turnout was most evident in the annual rally typically held a week before the vigil; in the early 2010s, there were consistently two to three thousand protesters, but in 2016 and 2017, there were approximately one thousand.

It is unclear to what extent these declining numbers were related to the nativists' memory challenges. What is certain is that the alternative commemorations were effective in weakening the sense of collectiveness emanating from the candlelight vigil, both in terms of the cognitive and emotional dimension. On the one hand, these alternative commemorations produced and amplified competing narratives about what Tiananmen means for Hong Kong—for instance, that Hong Kong people have no responsibility in caring about politics in mainland China. By "commemorating" in a more detached and reflective manner, it dilutes and chips away the emotional resonance—grief, frustration and anger—evoked by the candlelight vigil. Feeling bereaved about the Tiananmen crackdown is no longer the only game in town. One can now be cool-headed and rational in remembering Tiananmen (Interview 3).

On the other hand, even though the vigil managed to maintain a consistently high turnout, key participating groups, such as local universities' student unions, have stopped attending the vigil since 2015. The Hong Kong Federation of Students, which had been a core member of the Alliance and a veteran movement organization, even withdrew its membership in 2016. The withdrawal of these nativist organizations not only precipitated the declining number of young participants but also eroded the vigil's professed commitment to pass on memories to youth. Indeed, participants have shown increasing disagreement with some objectives set by the Alliance. According to our on-site surveys from 2010 to 2018, fewer participants think that Hong Kong people have a responsibility to promote democracy in China, and more participants think they do not. Moreover, as table 10.5 indicates, there have been an increasing number of reports in the media about what nativists think about the Tiananmen commemoration and how they respond to it. These reports provided an alternative cognitive lens for the public to understand the Tiananmen event, reorienting the motive of participation from striving for China's democratization to fighting for Hong Kong's own democracy movement. To a certain extent, these nativists' challenges were also likely to have unintentionally made space for pro-regime groups to promote their own contestation and strengthen their denials of the crackdown.

The Alliance did try to address these memory challenges by updating the repertoire of the vigil. After 2015, the vigils have noticeably more emphasis on local political issues, particularly in response to Hong Kong's democratic retrogression. New songs about freedom and democracy have replaced old songs that had a nationalistic overtone. Young bands have been invited to perform live music and liven up the melancholic ambience. Outside of the

Table 10.5. Hong Kong Media's Reporting on Tiananmen

Year	Reports on June 4 That Do Not Cover Nativism	Reports on June 4 That Cover Nativism	Percentage
2010	335	8	2.39
2011	334	8	2.40
2012	462	8	1.73
2013	512	162	31.64
2014	504	96	19.05
2015	327	167	51.07
2016	346	158	45.66
2017	229	71	31.00

Author synthesis. A summary of the content analysis derived from 3,727 articles published in the WiseNews database between January 1, 2010, and December 31, 2017.

vigil, the Alliance has introduced a range of new activities to attract young people: Internet radio programs and public talks about Tiananmen, outings, a film competition, and art exhibitions. A flyer written in a question-and-answer format was also published in 2015 to address criticisms against the vigil. Nevertheless, these changes did not fundamentally change the funeral-like form of the vigil, and they were introduced only "within bounds" (Interview 6). As an organizer explained:

> We always experiment with new ideas, but we can't change things too radically. Say if we bring in new songs, some people would become uncomfortable and walk out of the vigil. Sometimes I even got called by old friends who asked me to stop. If new things do not work out, then we fall back on our old practices. As the late Szeto Wah used to say, tomb sweeping is tomb sweeping. We don't always need to do it a new way (Interview 6).

Indeed, new additions to the program sometimes backfired. In 2015, three university student union leaders were invited on stage to share their thoughts on Hong Kong's democracy movement. However, after taking the stage, they burned the Basic Law document as an act of protest against the Chinese authorities. Many stalwart participants left early because they found the act disrespectful to the solemn ceremony.

Thus, memory repertoires are also constrained by their past trajectories, similar to how collective memory contents are constrained by the actual past. Since they serve a crucial role in consolidating the memory repositories, their course cannot be altered too radically, or else it might provoke backlash from participants who are used to the established repertoires. Such constraints also mean that memory entrepreneurs are not always capable of responding effectively to memory contestation, which happens when the nativists challenge the vigil through the alternative repertoires. Despite the efforts made to renovate the vigil, the alternative repertories and the competing meanings they produced have been successful in eroding the collective identity among vigil participants. If the moral power of the candlelight vigil is generated by the remembrance of Tiananmen as a collective, such power would have been undermined when this collectivity no longer holds together as tightly as before.

CONCLUSION

Collective memories play an important but understudied role in the mobilization of collective actions. People do not mobilize only when there are material resources or political opportunities; they are also influenced by collective memories, which give them a sense of who they are and shape their political preferences. By focusing on the relationship between collective memories and collective identity, this study seeks to contribute to a growing body of literature that examines the mnemonic process of social movements. Unlike previous studies exploring how collective memory acts as a resource or constraint for mobilization, we focus on the contentious impact of collective memory as a contested process. In particular, we examine how memory contestation under a changing context affects the formation of and change in collective identity. By proposing a dynamic model that comprises memory repository and repertoire as the basic building blocks of the memory process, we seek to understand why the memory process facilitates collective identity building at one point but not another and why memory contestation sometimes succeeds but sometimes fails.

Our case study on Hong Kong's three-decade Tiananmen candlelight vigil reveals the pivotal role of memory repertoires in the collective identity-building process of the vigil participants. On the one hand, the vigil's elaborate and mournful repertoires serve a performative role in evoking and enacting the memory repositories, which allow movement participants to recall, remember, and reexperience the Tiananmen event. On the other hand, they also serve a filtering role that enables memory entrepreneurs to strengthen and consolidate certain dimensions of the distant past, which can then be passed on in the future. Both help to generate meaning for participants, from which collective identity can be created or strengthened. Indeed, as we have demonstrated, both the Chinese funeral rituals and the sharing repertoires in the vigil play a crucial role in shaping the motivation of participants in attending the vigil and their memory about Tiananmen. In this sense, one may say that memory repertoire is a constitutive and inseparable part of collective memory. It provides a gateway to collectively revisiting a critical event—and only through that can collective identity be created and maintained, which partly explains why the anti-authoritarian consensus can be quickly built up in other protests including the anti-extradition bill movement in summer 2019.

Our findings also show that the enabling effect of memory repertoire at one point can become constraining at another point. Memory repertoire, once practiced for some time, can become inflexible. It can be constrained by its past trajectory, and it can also become interlocked with the memory repository that it serves to express. In our case, while this interlocking relationship enabled memory entrepreneurs to effectively address the memory contestations from pro-regime challengers and even appropriate them to strengthen collective identity, memory repertoire later became a burden when facing new memory challengers. The repertoire became a burden because it cannot deviate too much from what many existing participants had practiced. By rejecting the vigil's repertoire and creating alternative ones, nativists' memory challenges cannot be easily accommodated. As a result, they have effectively questioned the objectives laid out by the Alliance and hence the collective identity derived from it.

In short, the impact of collective memory on collective actions is not preordained. The memory process is, after all, constantly in movement. Not only does it simultaneously invoke and reshape the actual past, but it is also prone to contestation by mnemonic agents. How this process impacts collective actions and whether it fosters or destabilizes collective identities strongly depend on the ability of memory challengers to upend the relationship between memory repository and its repertoire and on the ability of memory entrepreneurs to defend it.

NOTES

1. Due to the lack of sampling frame, it was impossible to follow a probability sampling approach. The protocols and standardization outlined here should return the best available samples. The six surveys had 444 to 861 respondents, and the average response rate was 87 percent.

2. Interview 1, youth league member of the Alliance, May 5, 2018, Hong Kong; Interview 2, leader of Youngspiration, July 15, 2018, Hong Kong; Interview 3, leader of Demosisto, August 20, 2018, Hong Kong; Interview 4, volunteer of the Alliance, January 19, 2019; Interview 5, chairman of the Alliance, January 21, 2019, Hong Kong; Interview 6, vice-chairman of the Alliance, January 23, 2019, Hong Kong.

3. Independent surveys from academics suggested that the organizer overestimated the participation while the police underestimated the scale, especially in recent years.

4. The Alliance's five objectives are "Release the dissidents! Vindicate the 1989 pro-democracy movement! Demand accountability for the June 4 massacre! End one-party dictatorship! Build a democratic China!"

REFERENCES

Assmann, Jan, and John Czaplicka. 1995. "Collective Memory and Cultural Identity." *New German Critique* 65: 125–33.

Baumgarten, Britta, Priska Daphi, and Peter Ullrich, eds. 2014. *Conceptualizing Culture in Social Movement Research*. London: Palgrave Macmillan.

Benford, Robert D., and David A. Snow. 2000. "Framing Processes and Social Movements: An Overview and Assessment." *Annual Review of Sociology* 26(1): 611–39.

Brubaker, Rogers, and Margit Feischmidt. 2002. "1848 in 1998: The Politics of Commemoration in Hungary, Romania, and Slovakia." *Comparative Studies in Society and History* 44(4): 700–44.

Chan, Cecilia L. W., Amy Y. M. Chow, Samuel M. Y. Ho, Yenny K. Y. Tsui, Agnes F. Tin, Brenda W. K. Koo, and Elaine. W. K. Koo. 2005. "The Experience of Chinese Bereaved Persons: A Preliminary Study of Meaning Making and Continuing Bonds." *Death Studies* 29(10): 923–47.

Chan, Elaine, and Joseph Chan. 2014. "Liberal Patriotism in Hong Kong." *Journal of Contemporary China* 23(89): 952–70.

Cheng, Edmund W. 2016. "Street Politics in a Hybrid Regime: The Diffusion of Political Activism in Post-Colonial Hong Kong." *The China Quarterly* 226: 383–406.

Daphi, Priska. 2017. *Becoming a Movement: Identity, Narrative and Memory in the European Global Justice Movement*. London: Rowman & Littlefield.

Edy, Jill. 2006. *Troubled Pasts: News and the Collective Memory of Social Unrest*. Philadelphia, PA: Temple University Press.

Farthing, Linda, and Benjamin Kohl. 2013. "Mobilizing Memory: Bolivia's Enduring Social Movements." *Social Movement Studies* 12(4): 361–76.

Gabel, Ines. 2013. "Historical Memory and Collective Identity: West Bank Settlers Reconstruct the Past." *Media, Culture and Society* 35(2): 250–59.

Gillan, Kevin. 2018. "Temporality in Social Movement Theory: Vectors and Events in the Neoliberal Timescape." *Social Movement Studies*. DOI: 10.1080/14742837.2018.1548965.

Gongaware, Timothy B. 2003. "Collective Memories and Collective Identities: Maintaining Unity in Native American Educational Social Movements." *Journal of Contemporary Ethnography* 32(5): 483–520.

———. 2010. "Collective Memory Anchors: Collective Identity and Continuity in Social Movements." *Sociological Focus* 43(3): 214–39.

Goodwin, Jeff, and James M. Jasper. 1999. "Caught in a Winding, Snarling Vine: The Structural Bias of Political Process Theory." *Sociological Forum* 14(1): 27–54.

Goodwin, Jeff, James M. Jasper, and Francesca Polletta, eds. 2001. *Passionate Politics: Emotions and Social Movements*. Chicago: University of Chicago Press.

Halbwachs, Maurice. 1992. *On Collective Memory*. Chicago: University of Chicago Press.

Harris, Fredrick C. 2006. "It Takes a Tragedy to Arouse Them: Collective Memory and Collective Action during the Civil Rights Movement." *Social Movement Studies* 5(1): 19–43.

Hobsbawm, Eric, and Terence Ranger, eds. 1983. *The Invention of Tradition*. New York: Cambridge University Press.
Jansen, Robert S. 2007. "Resurrection and Appropriation: Reputational Trajectories, Memory Work, and the Political Use of Historical Figures." *American Journal of Sociology* 112(4): 953–1007.
Jasper, James. M. 1997. *The Art of Moral Protest: Culture, Biography, and Creativity in Social Movements*. Chicago: University of Chicago Press.
Jedlowski, Paolo. 2001. "Memory and Sociology: Themes and Issues." *Time & Society* 10(1): 29–44.
Johnston, Hank, and Bert Klandermans, eds. 2013. *Social Movements and Culture*. Minneapolis: University of Minnesota Press.
Juris, Jeffrey S. 2008. "Performing Politics: Image, Embodiment, and Affective Solidarity during Anti-Corporate Globalization Protests." *Ethnography* 9(1): 61–97.
Klandermans, Pieter G. 2014. "Identity Politics and Politicized Identities: Identity Processes and the Dynamics of Protest." *Political Psychology* 35(1): 1–22.
Kuan, Hsin-chi. 2015. "Memorial Participation in Hong Kong: The Case of the Tiananmen Crackdown in June 1989." In Joseph Y. S. Cheng, ed., *Whiter China and the Communist Party Regime?*, 35–62. Hong Kong: City University Press.
Lam, Wai-man. 2004. *Understanding the Political Culture of Hong Kong: The Paradox of Activism and Depoliticization*. New York: Routledge.
Lau, Siu-kai. 2015. *The Practice of One Country, Two Systems in Hong Kong*. Hong Kong: The Commercial Press.
Lau, Siu-kai, and Hsin-chi Kuan. 1988. *The Ethos of the Hong Kong Chinese*. Hong Kong: Chinese University Press.
Lee, Francis, and Joseph M. Chan. 2013. "Generational Transmission of Collective Memory about Tiananmen in Hong Kong: How Young Rally Participants Learn about and Understand 4 June." *Journal of Contemporary China* 22(84): 966–83.
———. 2016. "Collective Memory Mobilization and Tiananmen Commemoration in Hong Kong." *Media, Culture & Society* 38(7): 997–1014.
Leys, Simon, trans. 1997. *The Analects of Confucius*. New York: W. W. Norton & Company.
Li, Yee. 2015. "Candlelight Must Continue, but Only under the Priority of Nativism." *Apple Daily*, May 30, 2015.
Link, Perry. 2010. "June Fourth: Memory and Ethics." In Jean-Phillippe Beja, ed., *The Impact of China's 1989 Tiananmen Massacre*, 25–44. New York: Routledge.
Ma, Ngok. 2007. *Political Development in Hong Kong: State, Political Society, and Civil Society*. Hong Kong: Hong Kong University Press.
Melucci, Alberto. 1995. "The Process of Collective Identity." *Social Movements and Culture* 4: 41–63.
———. 1996. *Challenging Codes: Collective Action in the Information Age*. Cambridge: Cambridge University Press.
Meyer, David. 2006. "Claiming Credit: Stories of Movement Influence as Outcomes." *Mobilization: An International Quarterly* 11(3): 281–98.

Nepstad, Sharon. 2001. "Creating Transnational Solidarity: The Use of Narrative in the U.S.-Central America Peace Movement." *Mobilization: An International Quarterly* 6(1): 21–36.

Olick, Jeffrey K. 1999. "Genre Memories and Memory Genres: A Dialogical Analysis of May 8, 1945 Commemorations in the Federal Republic of Germany." *American Sociological Review* 64(3): 381–402.

Olick, Jeffrey K., and Daniel Levy. 1997. "Collective Memory and Cultural Constraint: Holocaust Myth and Rationality in German Politics." *American Sociological Review* 62(6): 921–36.

Polletta, Francesca. 1998. "'It was Like a Fever . . .' Narrative and Identity in Social Protest." *Social Problems* 45(2): 137–59.

———. 2006. *It Was Like a Fever: Storytelling in Protest and Politics.* Chicago: University of Chicago.

Polletta, Francesca, and James M. Jasper. 2001. "Collective Identity and Social Movements." *Annual Review of Sociology* 27(1): 283–305.

Pun, Lawrence. 2012. "The Scars of History—A Review of Hong Kong's June 4th Pop Songs." In Chung-hung Ng, Chi-wai Cheung, and Chung-kin Tsang, eds., *Pop Hong Kong: Reading Hong Kong's Popular Culture*, 249–53. Hong Kong: Educational Publishing.

Sawer, Marian. 2007. "Wearing Your Politics on Your Sleeve: The Role of Political Colours in Social Movements." *Social Movement Studies* 6(1): 39–56.

Schudson, Michael. 1989. "The Past in the Present versus the Present in the Past." *Communication* 11(2): 105–13.

———. 1993. *Watergate in American Memory: How We Remember, Forget, and Reconstruct the Past.* New York: Basic Books.

Shevel, Oxana. 2011. "Russian Nation-Building from Yeltsin to Medvedev: Ethnic, Civic or Purposefully Ambiguous?" *Europe-Asia Studies* 63(2): 179–202.

Staggenborg, Suzanne, and Amy Lang. 2007. "Culture and Ritual in the Montreal Women's Movement." *Social Movement Studies* 6(2): 177–94.

Szeto, Wah. 2011. *The River of No Return: A Memoir of Szeto Wah.* Hong Kong: Oxford University Press.

Taylor, Verta, and Nancy Whittier 1992. "Collective Identity in Social Movement Communities: Lesbian Feminist Mobilization." In Carol McClurg Mueller and Aldon D. Morris, eds., *Frontiers in Social Movement Theory*, 104–29. New Haven, CT: Yale University Press.

Veg, Sebastian. 2017. "The Rise of 'Localism' and Civic Identity in Post-Handover Hong Kong: Questioning the Chinese Nation-State." *The China Quarterly* 230: 323–47.

Wagner-Pacifici, Robin, and Barry Schwartz. 1991. "The Vietnam Veterans Memorial: Commemorating a Difficult Past." *American Journal of Sociology* 97(2): 376–420.

Wasserstrom, Jeffrey N. 2018. "History, Myth, and the Tales of Tiananmen." In Jeffrey N. Wasserstrom and Elizabeth J. Perry, eds., *Popular Protest and Political Culture in Modern China*, 2nd ed., 273–308. London: Westview.

Whittier, Nancy. 1995. *Feminist Generations: The Persistence of the Radical Women's Movement*. Philadelphia, PA: Temple University Press.

Yuen, Samson, and Sanho Chung. 2018. "Explaining Localism in Post-Handover Hong Kong: An Eventful Approach." *China Perspectives* 2018(3): 19–29.

Zamponi, Lorenzo. 2018. *Social Movements, Memory and Media. Narrative in Action in the Italian and Spanish Student Movements*. Gewerbestrasse, Switzerland: Palgrave Macmillan.

Zamponi, Lorenzo, and Priska Daphi. 2014. "Breaks and Continuities in and between Cycles of Protest: Memories and Legacies of the Global Justice Movement in the Context of Anti-Austerity Mobilisations." In Donatella della Porta and Alice Mattoni, eds., *Spreading Protest: Social Movements in Times of Crisis*, 193–226. Essex: ECPR-Press.

Zelizer, Barbie. 1995. "Reading the Past Against the Grain: The Shape of Memory Studies." *Review and Criticism* 12(2): 214–39.

Zerubavel, Eviatar. 1996. "Social Memories: Steps to a Sociology of the Past." *Qualitative Sociology* 19(3): 283–99.

Zerubavel, Yael. 1995. *Recovered Roots: Collective Memory and the Making of Israeli National Tradition*. Chicago: University of Chicago Press.

Part V

RELIGION

Chapter Eleven

The Public Transcript and the Rise and Fall of Urban Churches

Carsten T. Vala (Loyola University, Maryland)

For roughly a decade, from the early 2000s to the 2010s, unregistered Protestant religious groups, commonly called "house churches," achieved breakthroughs in several major cities in China. In previous decades, house churches in urban areas remained small and unobtrusive to avoid provoking state scrutiny and suppression and to nurture their members. In the early 2000s, new large and visible house churches developed, operating autonomously from the party-state hierarchy. These unregistered congregations, called "newly rising urban churches" (*xinxingshi chengshi jiaohui*, hereafter urban churches), gathered huge numbers of participants—as many as fifteen hundred people—for church services in one location as part of promoting an active, open presence in society. For years, they represented the largest nongovernmental organizations operating in mainland China.

The emergence of large, unregistered organizations with a public persona appeared to herald a decisive shift in church-state relations toward a more accommodating stance. Authorities seemed to accept a larger and more active religious presence apart from the official corporatist organizations established for Protestants, the Three-Self Patriotic Movement (TSPM) association, the China Christian Council (CCC), and official churches. But then, several years later, party-state authorities began cracking down. At first, they targeted only the most prominent urban churches. After staging outdoor worship services as religious protests, these congregations continued their activities in less obtrusive, scattered groups. Then, nearly a decade later, officials moved to suppress even these scattered groups and to shut down all other urban churches. What accounts for the urban churches' emergence? And why, after tolerating them for years, did authorities finally shut them down? Finally, what accounts for the delays in shuttering the last urban churches?

Social movement theory can help the analyst probe state-society dynamics, even in an authoritarian regime such as China. It offers ways to conceptualize the internal changes within Protestant organizations and the external shifts in the national political environment that made the breakthrough possible. In particular, McAdam and Tarrow's (2018) elaboration of the political process theory suggests three general factors to pay attention to: the political context of opportunities and constraints, the development of movement oppositional consciousness, and movement organizational capacities (2018: 21). They also emphasize the interaction between societal actors and state, conceptualizing it as a shifting dynamic that helps explain how activists judge when and how to expand their claims and advance their interests.[1] Drawing on these social movement concepts, this chapter brings together bottom-up factors of societal activism with state practices of control and social management to show that, in a period of more open political opportunities, churches negotiated with authorities, devising ways to preserve the appearance of regime domination while enabling them to grow rapidly—becoming the largest, most visible, and longest-lasting societal organizations to develop apart from the party's state corporatist hierarchy.

I argue that urban churches' initial growth and subsequent repression can be explained by the degree of public challenge they presented the image of Chinese Communist Party (CCP) rule. In the next section I explain how social movement theory helps to illustrate the church-state dynamic in authoritarian China. Then, I draw on religion-state literature on China to argue that a permissive political context—when top leaders signal to lower-level officials to use flexibility and discretion to manage religious activities and groups—opened opportunities for negotiation, rather than domination and resistance, in Protestant-state interactions. I borrow a term from James Scott to explain how a modus vivendi evolved between local officials and religious actors based on informal boundaries associated with the "public transcript," Scott's term for the "open interaction between subordinates and those who dominate [them]" (Scott 1990: 2). In short, when local officials and religious leaders accept explicit but informal limits on their behavior, they can each advance their interests despite the limitations set by scarce resources (not enough CCP manpower) or restrictive policies (against illegal religious activities). After discussing the public transcript concept, I highlight the novelty of urban churches as large, public, and unregistered religious organizations by juxtaposing them against traditional house churches and then turn to the empirical core of the chapter: the emergence of urban churches in the Hu Jintao era and their ultimate closure in the Xi Jinping era.

The data for the chapter come from months of fieldwork and eighty interviews that I conducted in Mandarin Chinese, most of them in the People's

Republic of China from 2003 to 2014. I conducted a few interviews in English; some took place in the U.S. All interviews are identified only by the regional location, year, and month in which they were conducted to protect the identity of the informants. Interviews were semistructured, typically lasted one to two hours, and were recorded with identifying information kept separately from the data itself. As soon as possible, I transcribed and translated the recorded interviews and then erased the original recordings. Other data come from Chinese-language scholarship, newspaper reports, faith-based organizations (Lausanne Congress 2010a, 2010b), and advocacy organizations (such as ChinaAid.org or BitterWinter.org). I also draw on social science scholarship on China in the fields of religion-state relations, contentious politics, and state-society relations. Whereas my previous work explained how resistance to shutdown varied among urban churches (Vala 2018), this chapter stresses how the political context, the rise of Xi Jinping, mattered for their development and shutdown.

SOCIAL MOVEMENT THEORY AND CHINA'S PROTESTANT CHURCHES

Applying social movement concepts to studying religious groups in China is helpful but also controversial. Scholars such as David Palmer (2009) have argued that religious groups in China do not constitute social movements because Chinese religious groups rarely engage in conflictual relations with the state, do not typically manifest a sharp break between state and society, and are remarkably capable of carving out space to protect and expand their religious interests, despite restrictive state control.[2] In Palmer's view, therefore, the frame of analysis should not be contestation and conflict between religion and state but instead it should stress the overlaps, negotiations, and mutual interests between state and religion.

Palmer is correct that religious groups are not social movements in the sense that they are not in sustained conflict with the state, but not all of his caveats apply to Protestants in China. In fact, Protestant groups and social movements share attributes that make applying social movement theory not only justified but insightful. The three general factors of the political process approach are key. First, while house churches, the larger set of autonomous, unregistered congregations of which urban churches are a subset, may sometimes share "zones of engagement" (Palmer 2009: 262) with the local state, these Protestant groups also sustain a form of "oppositional consciousness" toward aspects of state and society like social movements.[3] All unregistered Protestant groups to some extent mark off their activities and organizations as distinct from the tainted "world" of society, which includes party-state workings. This is an extension of how they contrast themselves and their theistic beliefs and practices from an avowedly atheistic communist regime. But urban churches do more to embrace engagement with authorities and prioritize their efforts to influence society and to preserve the theological boundary between themselves and non-Protestant affairs.

Second, the political process perspective stresses the organizational capacities that characterize both social movements and urban churches (McAdam and Tarrow 2018). As I will show, urban churches developed strategies for communication with officialdom as well as internal organizational procedures to operate under extreme duress. When communication broke down in moments of high tension with state actors, conflict spilled into open religious-service protests. Third, the importance of political context, broadly understood as the structures of political opportunities and threats, can help us make sense of the emergence of challenging groups, whether social movements or urban churches. Social movement scholarship offers then a conceptual and analytical framework with which to capture broad shifts in regime repression from the Hu Jintao era (2002–2012), when urban churches developed, to the Xi Jinping era (2012–now), when the last urban churches were shuttered.

URBAN CHURCHES IN PROTESTANT-PARTY-STATE RELATIONS

Before the Chinese Communist Revolution, many foreign mission-backed congregations worshipped in church buildings, but there were also indigenous Chinese congregations that worshipped in homes—the early antecedents of the house churches (Bays 1996). After assuming power in 1949, the CCP set about establishing national associations to ensure the political loyalty of all religious groups, but especially of Protestants and Catholics because of their close affiliation with the recently defeated Nationalist regime. Communists selected a few Protestant leaders to establish the TSPM, an association intended to bring millions of Protestant Christians in a range of denominations and spaces under party authority. Formed in the 1950s, the TSPM along with the CCC established branch offices that became the state-corporatist intermediaries between the party-state and the grassroots churches. Under the intense pressure of wartime public rallies, more than half of all 700,000 Protestants in the 1950s and their churches relinquished denominational identities and joined the TSPM association (Wu 1963: 34; Wickeri 1988: 131).

The remainder of the Protestants who rejected party-state oversight and the TSPM either were imprisoned for their open challenge or quietly stopped public worship. By the 1960s, the regime had forced the downsizing and merger of official churches, while TSPM leaders inside the remaining congregations politicized teaching so greatly that church attendance dwindled. With the onset of Chairman Mao Zedong's Cultural Revolution in 1966–1976, all public worship ended. From that period to the 1980s, however, the numbers of Protestants surprisingly appear to have grown because many Protestants reestablished religious activities at home or outdoors (Vala 2018: 32). With the death of Mao and the launch of economic reforms in the 1980s, the party reopened official churches and rehabilitated leaders of the TSPM, sparking an unprecedented growth rate in Protestant Christianity in world-historic terms (Yang 2012). Protestant Christianity came to be divided between two institutional expressions: official churches providing state-sanctioned venues for worship and unregistered house churches offering smaller, more numerous and intimate but less visible sites for Protestant activities. By the 2000s, most house churches in cities had remained small and hidden, so that the only large urban congregations operated as official churches under TSPM (and ultimately party-state) authority.

"GRAY ZONES" AND THE PUBLIC TRANSCRIPT

Sociological work has advanced our understanding of how these domains of house churches and official churches relate to each other. In particular, Fenggang Yang's (2006) influential framework categorized religious groups based on the dimension of the political context (legal status). He then theorized the interaction between different types of officially sanctioned and unsanctioned groups to explain the shifting sizes of their membership. Yang conceptualized different zones of state sanction, with the state-sanctioned official churches in a "red" zone at one end (red signifying CCP approval) and officially banned groups in a "black" zone at the other end. In between these two zones lies a large gray zone of questionable legality but de facto permissibility for many unregistered religious groups, including Protestant house churches (Yang 2012).[4] Yang extended religious market theory to cast the triple zones as a "triple market" model. This improved the classic domination-resistance model, in which the state controlled religious activities inside official churches and suppressed religious activities outside them, while unregistered house churches resisted the state as much as possible (e.g., Kindopp and Hamrin 2004).

Yang's triple market model accounted well for variations in the historical flow of participants between officially sanctioned churches and the gray zone of permissible but unsanctioned groups, widely acknowledged by scholars as the largest Protestant domain, where Protestant house churches existed. But Yang's formulation left unspecified how that gray market develops, what maintains the boundaries between official and "gray" organizations and activities, and how organizations with strictly illegal activities might be permitted to exist and even expand. Yang's analysis succeeded at connecting the macrolevel of state regulation to the mesolevel of zones of groups and activities, but he left unexplained the microlevel of how individuals and their organizations interact with local officials.

Unpacking the development of the gray zone up to the 2000s helps to elucidate what is novel about the urban churches from then onward, and it sheds light on the details of this political context. However, it requires beginning with bureaucratic details of religious officials' work and the trade-offs that Protestant house churches historically made with these authorities.

Local officials charged with managing religious affairs often sought to preserve the image of compliance with official policies rather than de facto enforcement. They resorted to merely maintaining appearances for several reasons. Most notably, religious affairs officials were chronically short-staffed and thus overwhelmed in numerical terms compared to the religious populations they were entrusted to monitor.[5] Relatedly, the officials were often unenthusiastic about implementing religion policies that were complex, requiring subtle theological distinctions between acceptable and unacceptable groups. Also, officials typically occupied their posts for a short time before being rotated elsewhere. Finally, the religious affairs bureaucracy was (and remains) a low prestige posting with few opportunities for distinction or advancement, worsening the weak morale. For all these reasons, local officials' interests resided in promoting an image of compliance with a minimum of effort.

Protestant house-church leaders, for their part, were (and still are) distinguished by a zeal for proselytization (or evangelism), a motivation that shapes their identity and activities. Their major interest is to increase the number of Protestant adherents in their own congregations as well as to establish new groups elsewhere through missionary work. House churches are also defined by their lack of registration with state offices. Congregational registration entails submitting extensive details to officials about who participates, who leads, where they gather, and other information as well as establishing streams of income and accounting (Homer 2010). For many house-church leaders, registration of Christian churches with an atheist party-state structure represented (and still represents) a dangerous compromise with "worldly" authorities. Even for less theologically conservative Protestants, however, registration presents serious downsides.

First, the multiple steps of registration paperwork compel Protestant leaders to create a formally recognized organization out of their worship services, an outcome that eases officials' ability to influence church activities, as a prominent religious affairs official explained (Zhou 2002). Second, while registration may provide congregations a degree[6] of state sanction and protection from harassment, it also incorporates house churches into spaces under state monitoring and exposes church staff to state control and dismissal. In fact, according to a religious affairs manual, authorities designed registration to contain rapid membership growth by restricting the number and type of worship services offered (Zhou 2002: 132). Additionally, congregational registration is laborious and time-consuming for church leaders.[7]

As a consequence, most leaders of small house churches in cities have consciously rejected registration and purposefully organized activities in ways to minimize the pressure from state officials to register (or at least submit detailed information to authorities). They do this by not institutionalizing congregations as organizations, such as by avoiding membership processes, leadership selection procedures, and any other hallmarks of formal organization. When faced with officials' inquiries about whether they have an "organization," they can plausibly respond that they are merely running informal gatherings (interview, northeast China, August 2010). Thus, on the one hand we have bureaucratic reluctance on the part of CCP officials, which combines with house churches' purposeful avoidance of organizational procedures (as well as large, open gatherings) on the other. Together, these work to preserve congregational autonomy and minimize state scrutiny and pressure. These are the mechanisms that work to create Yang's gray zone, as a way to achieve the interests of both state and society—of both religious affairs officials and Protestant house churches.

To conceptualize this process at the level of the behavior of individual religious leaders and local officials, I revitalize Scott's idea of a "public transcript" (Scott 1990: 2). The public transcript captures how a regime wishes its governance to appear, by "naturalizing" its power through an image of unanimity and political loyalty (Scott 1990: 4, 12, 18). Successfully symbolizing its domination through public demonstrations of power makes a regime's rule less costly because subordinates have learned to act deferentially, which releases dominants from costly monitoring and enforcement of subordinates (Scott 1990: 10).

Local officials expect that China's Protestants should at a minimum appear to obey the regime agenda, as reflected in formal party declarations and religion policies, ranging from state regulations, ideologies, and discourse. These expectations are informal understandings attached to the public transcript and can be summarized in three "red lines," or taboos: (1) organizing and promoting large-scale worship services, (2) involvement of foreign religious personnel, and (3) cross-jurisdiction organizing, especially of leaders from different church networks (Vala 2018: ch. 6). In exchange for observing these limits, regime officials tacitly agreed not to harass small groups of believers. These mutual understandings were linked to expectations of the performance of the public transcript, the public appearance of state domination. Observed by local officials and Protestant leaders alike, the public transcript in effect meant that Protestant Christianity from the 1980s to the 2000s grew in numbers of adherents at an enormous rate, spread across the country, and established groups of believers where none had previously existed. In this sense, observance of the public transcript encompassed mutual expectations of state and society and achieved interests of both sides.

EMERGENCE OF URBAN CHURCHES IN THE HU JINTAO ERA (2002–2012)

The emergence of urban churches in the 2000s theoretically broadened the gray zone because public congregations could now be found outside the red zone of official churches operating under the TSPM and Christian Council state-corporatist associations. The gray zone now included public, large-scale, but unregistered religious organizations. It also represented a shift in the boundaries implicit in the public transcript, which previously had forbidden these open or visible and large organizations. Underpinning these changes from traditional Protestant house churches to urban churches lay shifts in Tarrow and McAdam's three political process concepts: oppositional consciousness, organizational capacity, and political context.

First, urban-church leaders were characterized by a more complex oppositional consciousness than the previous generation of unregistered house-church leaders. To be sure, this oppositional consciousness has many dimensions which was shaped by the theological identities, specificities of experience, personalities, and many other traits of church leaders. Still, generally speaking, Protestant house-church leaders are theologically conservative and, as noted previously, many are wary of entanglements with the tainted "world" of striving, selfish desires, and corrupted society. Broadly speaking, house-church leaders also tend not to register their congregations. Sometimes this occurs because registration is unavailable in their area or they are unaware of registration requirements to legally operate as a congregation. Others, however, reject registration out of principle. At heart is their fear of submitting to what they view as a compromised "false" Christian organization, the Protestant TSPM associations (interview, coastal China, June 2003; also Vala 2018: 90). The official churches that operated under these associations' umbrella answer to an atheist authority and have been instruments for the persecution of Christians in the past. Avoidance of official associations and wariness toward the party-state more generally characterizes many house-church leaders' stance.

Urban-church leaders shared with traditional house churches a theological distinction between the church's sphere and the state and society (unlike some official churches), but they also promoted a more engaged and open stance toward society and authorities.[8] This manifested itself in a number of ways. First, they actively sought to be an influence in society, epitomized by the biblical image of a "city on a hill" (Matthew 5: 14–16) and by Jesus's call to teach followers to demonstrate their faith by doing good deeds (interview, north China, August 2010). This means that the congregations openly announced when and where services are held, unlike traditionally hidden house-church gatherings, and that they also welcomed authorities, whether police or officials, to attend their gatherings, so long as it was done respectfully. Also, and particularly for the urban churches with a Calvinist or reformed identity, they taught that all spheres of life, even politics, were part of God's kingdom, which meant that, unlike pietistic house churches, there was no stark division between church and culture or society or between where Christian values apply and where they do not (Fällman 2013). Most importantly in terms of official interactions, urban-church leaders deliberately engaged those authorities who were charged with monitoring them.

Second, in addition to oppositional consciousness, urban churches often exhibited higher levels of organizational capacity. Because many house-church leaders purposefully resist institutionalizing their congregations, they frequently employ a family-style authority structure, in which a single patriarchal leader makes key congregational decisions, controls the offerings, and installs family members to rule in succession. By contrast, a number of urban churches had clearly elaborated leadership selection procedures and decision-making processes, selected a church name, and established membership guidelines among other standardized processes to institutionalize their congregations with transparent, routine processes. They also developed modes of communication with local authorities to stabilize and attempt to safeguard their congregations from shutdown.

Last, the macrolevel of political context was critically important because Protestant urban churches worked to reshape the boundaries of the public transcript. The rise of the urban churches appeared to push the limits of the public transcript regarding the scale of religious activities and the public presence of Christianity. The larger congregations had a more visible institutional role in society. From the state's perspective, these accommodations seemed to confirm that a degree of independent social organizing was permissible and did not automatically spark instability or threaten the regime. At the same time, they did not mean that Protestant groups enjoyed a protected status that guaranteed their long-term existence. Indeed, the party-state's eventual closure of these congregations underscores how fragile and uncertain the new boundaries of the public transcript were, and how quickly churches' bargaining ability might evaporate in the face of concerted regime efforts to return Protestants to small, hidden gatherings.

Expanding the Public Transcript on Visibility and Congregational Size

Unlike smaller house churches, urban churches prioritized expanding congregations beyond a few dozen participants and operating as an open influence in society rather than as hidden groups. Instead of minimizing the risks of state intervention by avoiding authorities, Protestant urban leaders engaged local officials, and even cultivated ties among the police (Reny 2018) or the party-state religious affairs bureaucracy (Vala 2018). The goal was to persuade authorities that their large gatherings posed little threat to social stability or party-state power. The strategy was to nurture official ties and openly inform officials of church activities.

Greater visibility was also made possible by changes in the macrolevel political context. As Fu and Distelhorst (2018: 104) point out in a comparative study of repression under Hu and Xi governments, Hu Jintao's governance stressed social stability but allowed local variation in how to achieve it. Local authorities in the Hu Jintao era (2002–2012) had discretion to implement the CCP agenda as they saw fit, meaning that the political context presented greater opportunities and fewer threats to local Protestant groups. When authorities approached Protestant leaders of a dozen urban churches in multiple cities across China regarding their congregations, leaders responded by seeking to foster ties based on trust, transparency, and shared interests (see also Reny 2018). In the following examples, we see how this political context of local discretion facilitated a transformed consciousness to develop fresh communication strategies with authorities and novel organizational capacities.

One pastor in northern China who had previously worked in official churches alerted multiple leaders of the police and local government that he was establishing a congregation; he sent them meeting information along with all his personal, academic, and church credentials (interview, north China, 2009). Another pastor in central China had made connections to officials in his previous professional life and notified these officials about his foreign travels, specifying the identities of overseas pastors and congregations he planned to visit (interview, central China, 2009). Such connections came in handy in times of party-state pressure, as he learned to ward off lower-level authorities who made unannounced visits to his congregation's worship services. He threatened to call their superiors, with whom he had good relations, if inspectors did not show respect by giving him advance notice of their visits. An enterprising Protestant leader in the Northeast developed a relationship with a local official who had repeatedly detained him for organizing illegal religious activities (interview, northeast China, 2010). In planning a Christmas activity at a large public site, this Protestant leader called the official in advance to alert him of the activity; in doing so, he insisted that he was not seeking permission but rather conveying respect for the official. That official in turn advised the Protestant to keep the Christmas activity low key, presumably to avoid generating unwanted trouble for the official (interview, northeast China, 2010; Wright and Zimmerman-Liu 2013: 14).

This ambitious northeastern China Protestant leader, like other urban-church leaders, had clearly pushed the boundaries of the public transcript that prohibited public activities; furthermore, by notifying the official of his plans, he strategically signified that unregistered churches were not "out of control," as state propaganda often claimed but rather were "reliable and socially responsible" (interview, northeast China, 2010). Later, he launched an unregistered worship service in a three-star luxury hotel, inspired by the example of the large-scale urban church in Beijing, Shouwang Church (Vala 2018: 134).

Some leaders of urban churches did more than rely on transparency and communication to persuade authorities of their trustworthiness; they developed organizational strategies to demonstrate common interests by engaging in social welfare activities. While many house churches did such work as individual congregations, a few urban-church leaders also carried out "good works" in cooperation with local officials.[9] An urban-church leader in a central China capital mobilized his congregation to assemble aid packages for the poor, drawing from a list of poor people that local officials had given him (interview, central China, 2009). Together, the church leader and officials presented boxes with blankets, cooking oil, and books to needy families. In so doing, the church leader boosted the standing of officials in the public's eyes, presented an image of public cooperation between Christians and authorities, and fostered good will with officials.[10] In more common cases, such as that of an unregistered church in Beijing, congregations eagerly donated money to disaster relief drives led by lower-level state representatives (neighborhood residence committees) in buildings where Protestants gathered for worship services. By keeping religious gatherings unobtrusive and also joining in public-service activities sponsored by representatives of the regime, Protestants sought to prove themselves to be good neighbors. And by participating with authorities at all levels to solve societal problems, urban-church leaders hoped to allay officials' suspicions about their motives and demonstrated that they shared a sense of responsibility to serve society and a concrete commitment to act to benefit others. Using these channels of communication with officials, church leaders also sought to educate authorities about restrictive religion-management policies and, in rare opportunities, to influence policy making decisions. At times they also expressed personal concern for stressed cadres and their families, and even drew some party-state representatives into the Christian faith (Vala 2018: 140–141).

These pastor-cadre ties—vehicles of information, concern, and persuasion—originated in various ways. In the cases described, urban-church leaders either continued relationships with authorities from their previous work lives or they developed ties to authorities in the course of carrying out Christian work. These informal channels may also be initiated by party-state officials or other authorities (Reny 2018) wanting to avoid time-consuming, complex, and burdensome religion policies. Starting with an initial contact with a church leader and followed by congregational visits, party-state officials preferred to keep tabs on congregations by one-on-one lines of communication with pastors, through informal, adaptive mechanisms to bypass onerous church registration policies. The only other alternative—repression—is often seen as prohibitively costly and ineffective. For one, it requires marshaling already undermanned police and religion-management authorities to rein in numerous unregistered Protestant congregations. It also generates reams of unwelcome paperwork for the party-state bureaucrats. Experience has taught long-serving party-state authorities that compelling registration frequently heightens friction with unswerving religious devotees, invites their backlash and anger, and may further harden convictions that registration constitutes betrayal of Christian values in a compromise to "worldly" pressures. This was even more true for the urban-church congregations. They explicitly navigated a new third-way passage between traditional, small, unregistered house churches and official churches under TSPM authority, both of which were constrained by the limits linked to the preexisting public transcript (interview, northeastern China, 2010).

Transcending Restrictions on National Organizing and Foreigners

In addition to extending the limits on congregational size, pioneering urban-church leaders transcended a second public transcript restriction, in this case on cross-jurisdictional organizing, by setting up a national network to deliver disaster relief. Widespread flooding in 2007 sparked a discussion among urban-church leaders and other house-church Protestants on a Christian response to natural disasters. One well-connected urban-church pastor contacted 150 unregistered church leaders across China to gather for a meeting to establish a nongovernmental organization (NGO). By the time a massive earthquake struck Sichuan Province in May 2008, discussions had advanced far enough for the pastor to submit an application to the national government to establish a NGO called China ActionLove (*zhongguo aixing xingdong*) (Vala 2018: 144).

Eager to spring into action and unwilling to wait on slow bureaucratic approval, China ActionLove organizers dispatched several people from major urban churches within days of the earthquake. They established a headquarters in Sichuan's provincial capital city within a week, and within a year, China ActionLove had established four community centers to provide counseling, health services, community activities, and books for loan (Vala 2018: 145). Organizers claimed that their work drew an estimated fifteen hundred volunteers from 150 congregations in fifty cities and provinces by the three-year mark and that it eventually grew to involve participation and financial support from Christians in Hong Kong and even Taiwan.

The lead-up to the formation of the NGO suggests that these pioneering urban churches had also transcended a third political taboo circumscribing foreign Christian involvement in Chinese church affairs. In reality, although officials had long warned Chinese Protestants to avoid unsupervised[11] contacts with foreign Christians and their organizations, foreign Protestants have a far longer history of supporting Chinese Christianity, dating back at least to the 1920s.[12] Overseas missionary organizations had supplied religious materials and set up underground seminaries since the country became deeply entwined with the world economy in the 1980s (Vala 2018: 143). Foreign Christian involvement accelerated with China's 2001 accession to the World Trade Organization (Chan 2005).

What distinguished the involvement of foreign Protestants in the 2000s was their influence to encourage an urban-church agenda to openly influence society. One example of such influence was the Hong Kong-based Christian organization Asia Outreach. It brought pastors to Hong Kong for educational programs and referred them to seminaries in the U.S. for further training. In these trainings, it promoted the idea that churches in China should be like lights "shining on a hill," an image used throughout American political history, from colonial-era Puritans to U.S. President Ronald Reagan.[13] The founder of Asian Outreach explained that part of its emphasis on establishing churches with this public agenda was to spur church engagement in "holistic" ministry by embracing social engagement in welfare and relief work, thus becoming congregations "shining" in society (Vala 2018: 144; Wang 2011: 8). Concretely, Asian Outreach laid foundations for the NGO work by organizing a 2007 meeting of seventy leaders of unregistered house churches from across China to expand their work. The task lay in hitching congregations' wealth to conservative theological values in order to serve social needs. These large-scale gatherings inside China reportedly took place several times a year before the NGO work launched (interview, central China, July 2009).

In hindsight, after the closure of urban churches in 2018–2019, it appears that urban churches' challenge to certain limits of the public transcript may have hastened the party-state to shut them down. While all urban churches by definition pushed boundaries on congregational size and visibility, those changes plausibly can be understood as largely local in impact. By contrast, pioneering urban churches transcended limits on cross-jurisdictional organizing and foreigner involvement that may have been too challenging to party-state dominance. Also, superseding those limits undermined the regime's claim that the TSPM and CCC associations, the party-backed, state-corporatist associations, alone represented Chinese Protestant Christianity to the world.

SHUTTING DOWN THE URBAN CHURCHES IN THE HU JINTAO ERA

Hu's governance permitted local authorities to exercise discretion in implementing the broad goal of maintaining social stability (Fu and Distelhorst 2018: 104) in the sphere of religious affairs management as in other spheres. This discretion initially opened political opportunities for a kind of bargaining between state and society around the public transcript that allowed the emergence of large religious organizations outside state spaces. The bargaining had limits, however, which local authorities revealed in pressuring the most prominent urban churches that went beyond public activities and large-scale gatherings to challenge other elements of the public transcript.

As local authorities pursued similar strategies in cities across China to expel urban churches from rented spaces, urban churches shared counterstrategies to resist shutdowns and stage outdoor worship services in protest against the pressure.[14] Authorities typically first raided urban-church congregations to gather information on members and leaders and warn of illegal gatherings. Next, they officially banned the groups and blocked their use of rented office spaces. Finally, they detained leaders and harassed group members to leave the congregation altogether. Officials from western China to coastal China applied these strategies. In 2009, the churches' counterstrategies of outdoor worship services spilled into public conflict. The informal understandings and bargaining of the public transcript broke down first in Chengdu, capital of western China's Sichuan Province. Early Rain Covenant Church had been an important host congregation for the 2008 Sichuan earthquake relief effort, China ActionLove. Local officials banned Early Rain Church as an "unregistered social organization" in June 2009 and stopped them from using rented office space for meetings (ChinaAid 2009a). In response, Early Rain Church gathered outdoors for worship services and lodged legal challenges to the orders. Nine weeks of outdoor worship services followed until August 2009, when local authorities surprisingly acknowledged that they had wrongly enforced regulations and permitted the congregation to return to worship indoors (ChinaAid 2009a).

A few months later, in Beijing and in Shanghai, authorities separately pressured China's two largest urban churches to shut down. Officials worried about U.S. President Barack Obama's first state visit to China and the global publicity sure to follow. Unregistered Protestant congregations with public agendas would likely receive extensive overseas press coverage and substantial encouragement to remain outside the party-state hierarchy. Furthermore, in terms of the public transcript, Beijing Shouwang church ("Beijing Lookout") and Shanghai Wanbang Xuanjiao church ("All Nations Missionary") had each done much more than gather large numbers in publicized services in the months preceding the 2009 crackdowns.

In Shanghai, the pastor of Wanbang church had drawn official scrutiny for leading a nationwide pastoral network. Beginning a few years earlier, the pastor had cofounded a gathering of pastors and church staff from across China for mutual support, prayer, and consultation. Although it was established as a network to minimize chances that authorities would attack it as a "tightly organized" organization as they had other targeted religious groups, it still had a name, China Urban-church Pastors Fellowship, and hosted activities. And, by February 2009, when it met in Shanghai, it attracted more than seventy Protestants from multiple provinces. Shanghai authorities, accompanied by national officials of the Religious Affairs Bureau, raided the fourth biannual gathering that met in Wanbang church's building (Liu 2009). They pressured the pastor to cancel the gathering while he countered by trying to persuade them to relent. Neither side backed down, and the pastor moved the meeting to a new location to continue. Authorities in turn pressured Wanbang's landlord until he canceled their rental contract (Liu 2009). The challenge to the official Protestant associations' representational monopoly of national Protestant Christianity violated the informal understandings of the public transcript.

Similarly, in Beijing, local authorities began to closely monitor Shouwang church from the mid-2000s onward on the pretext of a new national religious-regulation policy. Officials heralded the 2005 Regulation on Religious Affairs as a "paradigm shift" that would permit unregistered house churches to gain legal status as registered religious organizations (Chou 2004). Shouwang decided to test that claim by reorganizing the congregation to satisfy all the registration requirements save one: acceptance of the authority of the Protestant associations over their church (interview, north China, August 2010; Vala 2018: 176). In 2007, while registration paperwork was passed from one Beijing office to another, Shouwang expanded its public influence by publishing a church magazine.[15] Months later, local authorities rejected the application. Approval would have overturned national regulations and the state-corporatist framework that banned autonomous organizations. It also would likely have led to other nonstate organizations, such as independent workers' unions, trying to register with the state (interview, coastal China, August 2010).

Following the strategies employed across China, in the months after the registration application, authorities tried a range of tactics to halt Shouwang's meetings. Their urgency was fed by the knowledge that foreign tourists, Christians and journalists who would arrive for the 2008 Beijing Summer Olympics, might well encourage the congregation's autonomy. The Beijing government issued a general notice prohibiting illegal religious meetings, and then officials and police raided a Shouwang worship service of several hundred worshippers (Wei and Li 2010, 53; Interview, north China, July 2010). After recording worshippers' personal information, they began harassing members at home and at work. In defense, Shouwang organized lawyers to explain how to use Chinese law to stop the harassment, a strategy that seemed to work for a time. Local officials then pressured Shouwang's landlord to evict them.

Finally, in November 2009 these two conflicts reached a head, as U.S. President Obama's visit neared. In Shanghai, authorities from multiple offices, including the State Security Bureau, broke the locks on the Wanbang church building, copied membership lists, and interrogated pastors (interview, coastal China, September 2010). The next day, they spread out across the city to find church members and their children at home, work, and school to warn them against returning to the church (ChinaAid 2009b). In Beijing, Shouwang, after a year of tense discussions with authorities and their landlord, responded to the official pressure by following through on months of warnings to authorities (interview, north China, July 2010) and escalated the challenge.

Nearly simultaneously, the two prominent urban churches in Beijing and Shanghai took the conflict public by staging outdoor worship services in protest. As the urban congregations gathered outdoors for worship services, authorities tried to detain church leaders, spread rumors about top church leaders' arrests, and block congregants from attendance. Congregants in both cities, however, were undeterred. They worshipped outdoors again and again until, days before President Obama's arrival in China, news of the outdoor services had apparently reached the highest level of government. President and Party Secretary Hu Jintao reportedly warned that he would take any measure necessary—including dispatching thousands of riot police—to prevent the church from causing embarrassment for him during Obama's visit (interview, north China, September 2010). Beijing Shouwang's organizational capacities were put to the test as the conflict worsened. Its leadership followed internal decision-making procedures and finally voted to return indoors for the third Sunday. In Shanghai, Wanbang church leaders learned that authorities had officially banned the congregation as an illegal religious group and that riot police had sealed off church buildings (interview, coastal China, September 2010, Wang 2010, 8), but the Wanbang congregation still worshipped outdoors, including the Sunday that President Obama arrived in China. When plainclothes police filmed the hundreds of believers who turned up and authorities detained the pastors for eight hours, Wanbang's leaders decided the pressure had grown too intense to withstand, and they relented by moving indoors to a space organized by authorities (Kahler 2009).

By the end of Hu Jintao's tenure, the fate of urban churches reflected mixed outcomes. While officials had shuttered two of the most prominent congregations, other urban churches continued to meet. The two urban churches in Beijing and Shanghai had effectively been shut down as single congregations. The senior pastor of Shouwang Church in Beijing had been put under home detention and large congregational services were blocked, although Shouwang's smaller congregational gatherings, Bible studies, and publication work still continued. The Shanghai congregation lacked the internal organization of Shouwang and suffered greater membership losses: two-thirds of its fifteen hundred members defected to an official church. Its remnant congregation however also continued meeting on a smaller scale. Beyond these two, however, other urban churches in Beijing, Chengdu, and elsewhere continued to function as single, large congregations. By the end of Hu's tenure in 2012, the national government's pressure had not eliminated all the discretion of local authorities (Fu and Distelhorst 2018).

XI JINPING (2012–PRESENT): SHUTTERING ALL URBAN CHURCHES

The ascendancy of Xi Jinping in 2012 dramatically decreased the relative openness of institutions and society and resulted in ever more centralized control (Madsen 2020, 26). Xi's increasingly authoritarian rule became apparent in multiple fields, from party governance to the media and activist lawyers and, of course, religious affairs. Soon after assuming power, Xi launched a wide-ranging anticorruption campaign that sacked hundreds of party officials and even targeted associates of a former top leader, upending decades of precedent that had protected high-level colleagues (and their families) from prosecution (Minzner 2018: 28–29). Xi reined in the official media by compelling them to treat the party as their most important constituency, rather than the public (See Vala 2019: 318 note 42). In civil society, he arrested human rights lawyers in the "709" crackdown on July 9, 2015 (Pils 2019: 69). Across the board, the new period under Xi heralded the "end of [a reform] era" (Minzner 2018).

In the area of religion-state relations, Xi has been no different. From promulgating stricter regulations to imposing ideological demands and compulsory practices on official churches to making consequential bureaucratic reorganizations, Xi has overhauled and tightened religious affairs management. First, under Xi's rule, the regime expanded the scope of the 2005 national religious regulation that had been challenged by the Beijing urban church. The new 2016 policy (in effect since 2018) encompassed bans on internet-based religious content and overseas training and fundraising (while also codifying curbs on officials' power) (ChinaLawTranslate 2017). The Party linked this regulatory expansion and hardening with an increasing emphasis on "sinicizing" religion, a catchall term for a variety of demands, that was formalized into a campaign in 2018. Among the demands, churches are now required to sing the national anthem as part of flag-raising rituals, teach "core socialist" values, promote the Chinese Constitution and other laws and regulations, and tout Chinese "traditional culture" (Zhang 2020).[16] Bureaucratic consolidation has further strengthened party control over religion. In 2018, the CCP office over religious affairs absorbed the government's State Administration of Religious Affairs, putting central and local officials of the Religious Affairs Bureaus under the CCP's United Front Work Department (Madsen 2020, 25). All these changes translated into more direct party control over religion.

These central government changes have unleashed powerful effects at the grassroots level. From 2013 to 2015, local authorities in Zhejiang Province along the southeast coast launched a campaign to remove or demolish prominent crosses and church buildings. Some campaign methods were familiar, such as the trial run of a controversial policy in a limited area to test popular reaction at home and abroad before spreading it nationwide (Yang 2020). And, local officials legitimated the campaign as a crackdown on illegally built structures, while obscuring its actual goal. Internal documents of the "Three Rectifications and One Demolition" campaign revealed that it not only targeted religion, but that it was also designed to use nonreligious means to take aim at Christianity's visibility.[17] In fact, as the demolition campaign proceeded in Zhejiang Province, the party intensified ideological pressures on Christian churches across the country, carrying out what one urban-church leader explained as "trying to 'party-fy' (*danghua*) religion" (Fifield 2018).

Some of the campaign's dimensions represented a new and heightened attack on Christianity, particularly in the targeting of official churches. While unregistered house churches had long been targeted in such campaigns, the primary target of cross demolition and removals were the state-sanctioned churches under official Protestant association authority. Officials claimed that as many as half of the almost four thousand Christian sites in Zhejiang Province failed to secure the necessary permits (Ying 2018: 50). Yet, if true, this claim also underscores the difficulty of securing construction approvals because dozens and dozens are needed from different departments and because local officials so frequently neglect to process them in a timely fashion.[18] In subsequent years, the southeastern China campaign has been nationalized such that local authorities across the country have demolished official churches in their home jurisdictions and even ones with valid approvals.[19]

Xi Jinping's efforts to rein in official churches resulted in the final shuttering of urban churches across the country. As we have already seen, the most pioneering urban churches had long been under intense pressure, yet they had still found some ways to continue as congregations. For example, despite the detention of its top leader and ban on single gatherings from 2009 onward, Beijing Shouwang had continued to operate in scattered groups. Under Xi's rule, however, all this changed, as even the remnant operations of the pioneering congregations and the remaining urban churches were now targeted. In September 2018, a prominent urban church in Beijing, founded by a former official church Protestant, was shuttered, after it refused authorities' demands to install security cameras to monitor its activities (Shellnutt 2018). Later that year, two more congregations in far-off locales were next: Early Rain Covenant Church in western China's Sichuan Province and Rongguili Church in the southeastern coastal capital Guangzhou of Guangdong Province (Lau 2018). Early Rain had not only formed a massive, public congregation outside state auspices, it had also created a denominational structure as part of the Presbyterian Church worldwide, developed a Christian school, and founded a seminary and college, among other pathbreaking initiatives.[20] Finally, in March 2019, authorities shut down the last gatherings of Beijing Shouwang church (Shellnutt 2018).

CONCLUDING THOUGHTS

The development of large-scale, public, unregistered Protestant churches in the mid-2000s, and their variable fates, points to the possibilities of organizational growth within the boundaries associated with the public transcript. The social movement framework points to the importance of oppositional consciousness, organizational capacities, and the overarching political context as important to explaining when the public transcript can be adjusted. Drawing on a fresh "oppositional consciousness" that empowered engagement with (rather than avoidance of) officialdom and savvy organizational capacities, urban-church leaders took advantage of bureaucratic permissibility to develop informal understandings with local officials to establish and increase the sizes, activities, and visibility of congregations in Beijing, Chengdu, Shanghai, Wuhan, and elsewhere. Protestant congregations met in rented office buildings where they gathered hundreds—even as many as fifteen hundred—worshippers at a time. Multiple congregations in Beijing, several in Chengdu, and a few in Shanghai and Wuhan had carved out a modus vivendi by trading information about their activities and attempting to build trust-filled ties with (or allay suspicions of) local authorities.

At the same time, the working boundaries of the public transcript were fragile and tenuous. Officials' acceptance of larger, more public urban-church congregations did not mean its terms were permanently settled. It is now clear that only under special conditions of an open political context, that is, when national-level directives were sufficiently permissive, as they had been under Hu's governance, could local authorities use their own discretion to accommodate and manage urban churches.

Pioneering urban churches such as the Beijing Shouwang and the Shanghai Wanbang congregations had pushed far beyond what other urban churches had sought to do. They challenged the regulations governing religious affairs and the public transcript's image that official Protestant associations were the main representatives of Chinese Christianity. Although some urban-church congregations had survived years into the Xi era, changes in the macrolevel of political context eventually restricted flexibility granted local authorities and imposed demands on them to bring to heel congregations outside the official Protestant associations. When such a regime-wide hardening took place, the negotiating space for bargaining over the public transcript was squeezed and ultimately disappeared. Theoretically, Xi's rule demonstrated the fragile and tenuous nature of negotiation and accommodation that had characterized the local official Protestant urban-church leader relationship.

The public transcript concept helps make sense of the boundary shifts between the official and unregistered congregations. Put another way, it offers one way to understand the broadening, maintenance, and squeezing of the gray zone or market (Yang 2006) as it incorporates negotiation dynamics into authoritarian church-state relations, not only for unregistered groups but also for official churches (Vala 2018). This conceptualization of authoritarian management of social and religious organizations is part of the broader scholarship that has refined understanding of the practice of authoritarianism and holds important implications for social organizations (Chen and Moss 2018: 668).

NOTES

1. For an example of this emphasis, albeit framed in terms of state-society relations, see Zhao 2001.
2. Instead, he proposes that such groups typically share overlapping spaces and interests with state actors (Palmer 2009: 259–62).
3. See Vala 2018, chapter 5, on distinctive Protestant values and activities.
4. The gray zone is also reminiscent of Tang Tsou's "zone of indifference" (1986) because of local officials' unwillingness to implement religion policies.
5. The ratio of religious affairs officials to believers of all religions is at least 2,500 to 1 and can be as high as 10,000 to 1 (Vala 2018: 42).
6. I insert "a degree" because registered churches during the mid 2010s anti-cross campaign in Zhejiang Province also faced state dismantling (Ying 2018).
7. It is laborious for local officials as well. After sifting through registration materials and processing applications, officials are then required to conduct annual inspections of all registered sites. Thus, officials have often preferred to avoid these bureaucratic procedures.
8. The changed attitudes of urban-church leaders also reflected local officials' greater understanding and acceptance of Christianity as a legitimate religion. In the mid-2000s, a Protestant leader declared that the party-state had "targeted" Christianity during the brutal anti-Falun Gong campaign (interview, northeast China, June 2006). But when interviewed again in 2010, he said that local officials no longer sought to harass unregistered churches, but rather officials "just want to talk to you, communicate [with] and understand you" (interview, northeast China, June 2010).
9. See Vala, Huang, and Sun (2015) on social welfare activities by house and official church congregations.
10. See McCarthy (2013) for how religious groups engage in social welfare work as a way to express their faith commitments.
11. Supervised contacts are another story because officials have eagerly courted foreign Christian investment in churches, seminaries, and other venues (Vala 2018: 98).
12. The Anti-Christian Movement of the 1920s led some foreign missionaries and their mission boards to turn over properties and leadership of churches to Chinese Christians, as part of an early expression of what would become institutionalized in political form under the People's Republic government as Three-Self (or Three Autonomies), meaning self-governance, self-support, and self-propagation (evangelism) (Lutz 1988).
13. The reference is to a biblical image used by Jesus to instruct followers, as the "light of the world," to be like a city on a hill, which cannot be hidden, and thus to "let your light shine before others, that they may see your good deeds and glorify your Father in heaven." (*New International Version* of the Bible; Reagan 1989).

14. It may well be that urban-church leaders, despite claiming different denominational or theological identities, also shared communications about how to handle regime pressure—like organizations that pursue disparate policy goals within a broad social movement.

15. *Almond Flowers*, as it was called, reached a small but influential circle of other house-church leaders and members. They discussed the thinking behind registration and other church-state and theological issues.

16. Other aspects include stocking church libraries with secular materials such as biographies of CCP leaders and accounts of wartime victory against Japanese invasion (Yang 2020).

17. Ying (2018: 51, 54) expertly analyzes how national security directives interpreted through local religious affairs officials' statements suggest that to some party officials "numerous Protestant and Catholic church buildings represent the chaos generated by overflowing Western religions and . . . a symbol of cultural colonization . . . in public spaces."

18. A *South China Morning Post* journalist (Chan 2014) reported a county church leader complaining that "at least 100 official seals" were required from different bureaucracies to build a church.

19. Official churches were demolished in two districts of the provincial capital Handan, Hebei Province, in June and July 2020 (Yang 2020).

20. Not one of the newly rising urban churches, Rongguili Church was founded decades earlier by a Protestant of an older generation and had operated independently of the party-state for years.

REFERENCES

Bays, Daniel H. 1996. "The Growth of Independent Christianity in China, 1900–1937." In Daniel H. Bays, ed., *Christianity in China: From the Eighteenth Century to the Present*, 307–16. Stanford, CA: Stanford University Press.

Chan, Kim-Kwong. 2005. "Religion in China in the Twenty-First Century: Some Scenarios." *Religion, State & Society* 33(2): 87–119.

Chan, Minnie. 2014. "Christians in Zhejiang Cross with Authorities over Church Demolitions." *South China Morning Post*. Retrieved January 7, 2021. https://www.scmp.com/news/china/article/1557359/christians-zhejiang-cross-authorities-over-church-demolitions.

Chen, Xi, and Dana M. Moss. 2018. "Authoritarian Regimes and Social Movements." In David A. Snow, Sarah A. Soule, Hanspeter Kriesi, and Holly J. McCammon, eds., *The Wiley Blackwell Companion to Social Movements*, 666–81. Hoboken, NJ: Wiley Blackwell

ChinaAid. 2009a. "Autumn Rain Church Members Worship Outdoors for the 9th Week." *ChinaAid*. Retrieved December 12, 2020. https://www.chinaaid.org/2009/08/autumn-rain-church-members-worship.html.

———. 2009b. "2,000 Wanbang Church Members Hunted, Interrogated, and Threatened After Stand-Off with Shanghai Psb." *ChinaAid*. Retrieved July 22, 2011. https://www.chinaaid.org/2009/11/2000-wanbang-church-members-hunted.html.

ChinaLawTranslate. 2017. "Religious Affairs Regulation 2017." *ChinaLawTranslate*. Retrieved January 8, 2021. https://www.chinalawtranslate.com/en/religious-affairs-regulations-2017/#_Toc492576019.

Chou Wiest, Nailene. 2004. "Religious Groups Get More Room to Move." *South China Morning Post*. Retrieved January 2, 2021. https://www.scmp.com/article/474793/religious-groups-get-more-room-move.

Fällman, Fredrik. 2013. "Calvin, Culture and Christ? Developments of Faith Among Chinese Intellectuals." In Francis K. G. Lim, ed., *Christianity in Contemporary China, Socio-Cultural Perspectives*, 153–68. New York: Routledge.

Fifield, Anna. 2018. "With Wider Crackdowns on Religion, Xi's China Seeks to Put State Stamp on Faith: The Biggest Christian House Church in Beijing has been Closed Down." *Washington Post*. Retrieved January 6, 2021. https://www.washingtonpost.com/world/asia_pacific/with-wider-crackdowns-on-religion-xis-china-seeks-to-put-state-stamp-on-faith/2018/09/15/b035e704-b7f0-11e8-b79f-f6e31e555258_story.html.

Fu, Diana, and Distelhorst, Greg. 2018. "Grassroots Participation and Repression Under Hu Jintao and Xi Jinping." *The China Journal* 79 (1): 100–22.

Homer, Lauren B. 2010. "Registration of Chinese Protestant House Churches Under China's 2005 Regulation on Religious Affairs: Resolving the Implementation Impasse." *Journal of Church and State* 52(1): 50–73.

Kahler, Annee. 2009. "500 Wanbang Church Members Meet Despite Leaders' Detentions." *ChinaAid*. Retrieved November 24, 2009. http://www.chinaaid.org/2009/11/500-wanbang-church-members-meet-despite.html.

Kindopp, Jason, and Carol Lee Hamrin. 2004. *God and Caesar in China: Policy Implications of Church-State Tensions*. Washington, DC: Brookings.

Lau, Mimi. 2018. "China Shuts Leading Underground Church, Third This Winter." December 16, 2018. Retrieved January 2, 2021. https://www.scmp.com/news/china/society/article/2178216/china-shuts-leading-underground-christian-church-third-winter?fbclid=IwAR2-P3Y9YB6MxZvWXk1lQNG4edCAhhm5EC9Pq0ruULlMiXzb36aCdeCmP44.

Lausanne Congress. 2010a. "Cape Town 2010: The Third Lausanne Congress on World Evangelization." *Lausanne Congress*. Retrieved October 9, 2020. https://www.lausanne.org/gatherings/congress/cape-town-2010-3.

———. 2010b. "Chinese Church Leaders' Exemplary Response Profoundly Impacts Cape Town 2010 Attendees." *Lausanne Congress*. Retrieved October 9, 2020. https://www.lausanne.org/news-releases/chinese-church-leaders-exemplary-response-profoundly-impacts-cape-town-2010-attendees.

Liu, Tongsu. 2009. "Buzhun Hefa Yu Buzhen Xinzhu–Guanyu 'wanbang' Shijian De Fenxi" [Not Allowed to Legalize Nor to Believe in God–an Analysis of the "wanbang" Incident]. *Gongfa Pinglun [Public Law Review]*. Retrieved April 5, 2014. http://www.gongfa.com/html/gongfazhuanti/gonggongshenxue/20091119/604.html.

Lutz, Jessie G. 1988. *Chinese Politics and Christian Missions: The Anti-Christian Movements of 1920–1928*. Notre Dame, IN: Cross Cultural Publications.

Madsen, Richard. 2020. "Religious Policy in China." In Stephan Feuchtwang, ed., *Handbook on Religion in China*, 17–33. Northampton, MA: Edward Elgar Publishing.

McAdam, Doug, and Sidney Tarrow. 2018. "The Political Context of Social Movements." In David A. Snow, Sarah A. Soule, Hanspeter Kriesi, and Holly J. McCammon, eds., *The Wiley Blackwell Companion to Social Movements*, 19–42. Hoboken, NJ: Wiley Blackwell.

McCarthy, Susan K. 2013. "Serving Society, Repurposing the State: Religious Charity and Resistance in China." *China Journal* 70(1): 48–72.

Minzner, Carl. 2018. *End of an Era: How China's Authoritarian Revival Is Undermining Its Rise*. London, UK: Oxford University Press.

Pils, Eva. 2019. "Legal Advocacy as Liberal Resistance: The Experience of China's Human Rights Lawyers." In Teresa Wright, ed., *Handbook of Protest and Resistance in China*, 62–74. Northampton, MA: Edward Elgar Publishing.

Palmer, David A. 2009. "Religiosity and Social Movements in China: Divisions and Multiplications." In Khun Eng Kuah-Pearce and Gilles Guiheux, eds., *Social Movements in China and Hong Kong, the Expansion of Protest Space*, 259–84. Amsterdam: Amsterdam University Press.

Reagan, Ronald. 1989. "Transcript of Ronald Reagan's Farewell Address to American People." *The New York Times*, January 12. Retrieved October 9, 2020. https://www.nytimes.com/1989/01/12/news/transcript-of-reagan-s-farewell-address-to-american-people.html.

Reny, Marie-Eve. 2018. *Authoritarian Containment: Public Security Bureaus and Protestant House Churches in Urban China*. New York: Oxford University Press.

Scott, James C. 1990. *Domination and the Arts of Resistance: Hidden Transcripts*. New Haven, CT: Yale University Press.

Shellnutt, Kate. 2018. "Beijing Shuts Down Another Big Beijing Church." *Christianity Today*. Retrieved January 2, 2021. https://www.christianitytoday.com/news/2018/september/china-bans-zion-beijing-house-church-surveillance-ezra-jin.html.

Tsou, Tang. 1986. *The Cultural Revolution and Post-Mao Reforms: A Historical Perspective*. Chicago: University of Chicago Press.

Vala, Carsten T. 2018. *The Politics of Protestant Churches and the Party-State in China, God Above Party?* New York: Routledge.

———. 2019. "Protestant Resistance and Activism in China's Official Churches." In Teresa Wright, ed., *Handbook of Protest and Resistance*, 316–31. Northampton, MA: Edward Elgar.

Vala, Carsten T., Jianbo Huang, and Jesse Sun. 2015. "Protestantism, Community Service and Evangelism in Contemporary China." *International Journal for the Study of the Christian Church* 15(4): 305–19.

Wang, David. 2011. "Getting Life-Long Returns in China." *Asian Report* AR304: 8.

Wei, Dedong, and Yi Li. 2010. "Preliminary Investigation into the Dynamic Mechanism of Mainland House Churches–Taking Beijing S Church as an Example" [*Dalu Jiating Jiaohui De Dongli Jizhi Chutan–Yi Beijing S Jiaohui Weili*]. 7th

Religious Social Scientific Symposium [*Diqijie Zongjiao Shehui Kexue Nianhui Huiyi Lunwen*]: 248–62.

Wickeri, Philip L. 1988. *Seeking the Common Ground: Protestant Christianity, the Three-Self Movement, and China's United Front*. Maryknoll, NY: Orbis Books.

Wright, Teresa, and Teresa Zimmerman-Liu. 2013. "Engaging and Evading the Party-State: Unofficial Chinese Protestant Groups in China's Reform Era." *China: An International Journal* 11(1): 1–20.

Wu, Yao-tsung. 1963. "The Present-Day Tragedy of Christianity." In Francis P. Jones, ed., *Documents of the Three-Self Movement, Source Materials for the Study of the Protestant Church in Communist China*, 1–5. New York: National Council of Churches of Christ in the USA.

Yang, Fenggang. 2006. "The Red, Black, and Gray Markets of Religion in China." *Sociological Quarterly* 47(1): 93–122.

———. 2012. *Religion in China, Survival & Revival Under Communist Rule*. New York: Oxford University Press.

Yang, Xiangwen. 2020. "Authorities in Hebei Province's Handan City Intensify Crackdowns on Protestant Churches with Valid, Government-Issued Religious Activity Certificates." *Bitter Winter*. Retrieved December 22, 2020. https://bitterwinter.org/state-run-churches-in-handan-city-destroyed/.

Ying, Fuk-tsang. 2018 "The Politics of Cross Demolition: A Religio-Political Analysis of the 'Three Rectifications and One Demolition' Campaign in Zhejiang Province." *Review of Religion and Chinese Society* 5(1): 43–75.

Zhang, Wenshu. 2020. "Crosses Removed from Numerous State-Run Churches." *Bitter Winter*. Retrieved December 22, 2020. https://bitterwinter.org/crosses-removed-from-numerous-state-run-protestant-churches/.

Zhao, Dingxin. 2001. *The Power of Tiananmen, State-Society Relations and the 1989 Beijing Student Movement*. Chicago: University of Chicago Press.

Zhou, Jiacai. 2002. *Zongjiao Gongzuo Tansuo* [Exploration of Religious Work]. Beijing: Zongjiao Wenhua Chubanshe.

Chapter Twelve

Religion and Protest Participation

Chengzhi Yi (Shanghai Jiaotong University),
Geping Qiu (East China University
of Political Science and Law), and
Tao Liang (Beijing Normal University)

Religion in China, its place in official political discourse, and its role in people's daily lives have recently received increased attention from researchers. Participation in religious activities has grown rapidly in China. According to China World Value Survey, the proportion of religious believers in 1990, 2001, 2007, 2012 was 3.2 percent, 6.1 percent, 11 percent, 14.77 percent respectively[1] (Inglehart et al. 2014a, 2014b, 2014c, 2014d, 2014e). However, recent efforts by the Chinese government to remove steeples and crosses or proceed with outright demolition of Christian churches for illegal construction or failure to secure proper permits in many regions reflect the regime's uneasy feelings toward the rapid growth of Western religions (Goldman 2018). Part of this uneasiness may be attributed to the relationship of religious practice to collective protests.

Although the role of religion on protest participation has long been debated in the social sciences (Jamal 2005), some important aspects remain underexplored in the Chinese context. First, religion can be measured by both religious affiliation and religious behaviors (Jones-Correa and Leal 2001), but its influence on protest participation seems to studied more from the perspective of reported affiliation than religious practice. Second, the direction of influence that religious beliefs may have on protest participation remains unclear and is much debated in literature. Third, research on the relationship between religion and protest participation is mostly based on data from Western countries and there is decidedly little research on this topic in China, the most populous country in the world.

FACTORS INFLUENCING PROTEST PARTICIPATION

Participation in protest movements and participation in institutionalized politics are often motivated by similar factors and often serve similar ends (McVeigh and Sikkink 2001), though the former is more contentious and disruptive than the latter. For example, Tarrow (2011) defined social movements as "collective challenges, based on common purposes and social solidarities, in sustained interaction with elites, opponents, and authorities" whereas protest movements include more disruptive collective actions (Klandermans 1997). Based on the contentious and disruptive nature of protests, protest movements may have destabilizing impacts on the social order.

Those who benefit less than others from existing social arrangements are often dissatisfied with social conditions and may address their grievances through participation in protest movements (Gurr 1970; Berkowitz 1972; Lind and Tyler 1988). However, little direct evidence is available to explain why protesters choose to address their grievances through protests rather than other means (McVeigh and Smith 1999). Literature from the West sheds some light on factors that facilitate protest participation. For example, Van Zomeren et al. (2004) point to the role of emotions stemming from relative deprivation and frustration. Others show that perceived efficacy, resources, and opportunities are factors that influence one's participation in protest activities (McCarthy and Zald 1977; Klandermans 1984; McAdam 2010; Galais and Lorenzini 2017). In addition, the manner that collective identity affects protest behavior has drawn researchers' attention (Reicher 1984; Simon et al. 1998; Klandermans and De Weerd 2000). Network ties (Tilly 1978; McAdam 1986) and organizational affiliations (McAdam 1986) can exert influence on protest participation.

As for China, various protest movements are also beginning to draw researchers' attention regarding the factors that influence participation. The existing literature has identified such factors as the work-unit system, expression of interests, political trust, self-efficacy, emotion, rationality, and hierarchy (Feng 2006; Wang and Huang 2008; Han 2012; Wei 2015; Xie and Chen 2014). Li (2004), for instance, found that Chinese villagers tend to have more trust in the central government than in the local government, which prompts them to participate in various types of collective action, such as collective petitions and tax resistance.

The Relationship of Religion to Protest Participation

The relationship between religion and protest participation is still much debated. For example, Collier and Hoeffler (2004) challenge the notion that religious divisions have an effect on civil conflicts. Many scholars believe that religion is a tranquilizing and dampening force that legitimizes the status quo (Marx 1967; Pope and Demerath 1942; Parsons 1991; Myrdal 2017). Religion provides a "cultural toolkit" (Swidler 1986) of collectively held meanings and symbols that may be used to mobilize believers to participate in protest movements. Religion can directly lead to social protest in two primary ways: through perceived threats to deeply held religious beliefs or values (Wallis 1977; Wood and Hughes 1984; Clarke 1987) and through specific religious beliefs that characterize life as a conflict between good and evil (McVeigh and Sikkink 2001), which can be used to mobilize believers in the struggle. Therefore, Huntington (1997) argues that the differences in religious beliefs can cause the clash of civilizations at the macro level and that religious beliefs are the key factor influencing individuals' participation in collective action at the micro level. Harris (1994) empirically challenges the claim that religion deters mobilization through data from the 1987 General Social Survey; he argues that religion among African Americans provided a psychological and organizational resource for collective action.

Specific religious beliefs are considered to have various degrees of impact on participation in protest movements, and among some religious sects, biblical literalism has a strong impact on participation in protest movements (Sherkat and Blocker 1994). Through data from the 1996 Evangelical Influence Survey, McVeigh and Smith (1999) conclude that conservative Protestants and liberal Protestants are substantially less likely than the nonreligious or moderate Protestants to engage in protests related to institutional politics. Although most research focuses on dominant religious groups and neglects religious minorities, Ayers and Hofstetter (2008) find in their study on American Muslim political participation that religious resources increase political participation but that religious beliefs show negative effects on political participation.[2]

While there is good evidence for a relationship between religion and protest participation, there is much debate on the directions and mechanisms of such influences (Marx 1967; Hunt and Hunt 1977; Wald, Silverman, and Fridy 2005). One view confirms that religion has a significant impact on participation (Harris 1994; Huntington 1997; Hasenclever and Rittberger 2000). Another view argues that religion has no influence on protest participation (Collier and Hoeffler 2004). Hasenclever and Rittberger (2000) distinguish three theoretical perspectives on the role religion plays in protest movements: (1) the primordialism emphasizing the importance of religious traditions in protest participation, (2) the instrumentalism admitting the aggravating role of religion but insisting that growing economic, social, and political inequalities result in social protests in most cases, and (3) constructivism, stressing the social definition of grievances that can draw on both primordial and instrumental perceptions. Many researchers have studied the impact of religion on Black militancy. Marx (1967) finds that religion generally plays a role of inhibiting the participation of Black civil rights protesters based on a nationwide sample. However, Hunt and Hunt (1977) find that religion actually inspires Black militancy through the reanalysis of Gary Marx's data. Alston et al. (1972) find that the relationship between religion and Black militancy varies among different segments of the Black population contingent on age, sex, and denomination.

Due to increased participation in religious activities and the rise of protest movements in recent China, Chinese scholars have begun to examine the relationship between religion and protest movements. There are several perspectives on the role of religion in protest participation. One view suggests that religious doctrines in general advocate patience and tolerance and, therefore, promote public tolerance, which in turn should reduce participation in protest movements. Therefore, religion plays a mediatory role in resolving collective conflicts and reducing collective protests (Liu et al. 2010). However, Ruan, Zheng, and Liu (2014) find the opposite; people with religious beliefs are more likely to participate in collective action than nonbelievers. In addition, researchers find that religion mobilizes villagers to participate in collective actions (Liu et al. 2010).

Theoretical Guidance for the Chinese Context

The relationship between religion and politics is an important part of studying Chinese politics (Goldman 1986; Potter 2003; Yang 2006; Tao 2015/2017, 2015/2018; Yi 2017), in which there are two dominant views. One view suggests that ideology is the main factor determining the relationship between religion and politics. The Chinese Communist Party (CCP) is a party guided by Marxism, of which atheism is an inherent part. After the CCP became the only ruling party in China with the success of the communist revolution, Marxism became the official ideology, which makes socialistic China innately reject religion. Some scholars (Goldstein 2017) use dichotomous frameworks of dominance and resistance to analyze the relationship between state and religion in China since 1949.

However, another view, based on the theory of rational choice, contends that it is the actual or anticipated benefits rather than ideology that is the decisive factor affecting the relationship between religion and politics. The role of religion is a complex one. Some scholars highlight the capacity of religion in providing public services (Tsai 2007), mediating local conflicts, and promoting social harmony (Tao 2015). However, with its organizational ability to mobilize its membership, religion also creates potentials for identity contentions due to intergroup conflicts (Seul 1999), which in turn threaten the state's power and political stability of the ruling communist party (Tao 2017). As a result, the state choses either to cooperate or struggle with religion based on different situations to serve its political needs (Tao 2015/2017).

Cao (2010) suggests that the traditional dominance and resistance model is unsuitable to explain the state-religion relationship in China because one finds both conflict and competition and adaptation and cooperation (Ashiwa and Wank 2009). This complexity has become more manifest in post-Mao China as the state displays more tolerance to religion. Official policies oscillate between management and curtailment, with strict restriction and control as the frequent response if a religious group is believed to threaten social stability (Kang and Han 2005; Guo and Zhang 2015). To suit its political needs, the CCP has different attitudes toward religion in different situations. When religion is believed to provide public services and promote societal harmony, the CCP adopts an attitude of tolerance, acceptance, and even support. However, when religion, as a potentially competitive political force, poses a challenge to the stability and ruling position of the regime, the CCP imposes strict control and regulation. These changing attitudes are not unique to the CCP; they were widely practiced in ancient dynasty politics (Tao 2017; Guo and Zhang 2015). Because the roles of religion are often difficult to separate, the relationship between politics and religion is often murky. And because some religions are better organized than others and have greater organizational capacity for mobilization, they are especially likely to become a potential competitor that challenges the state power. As a result, in modern times both the CCP and its earlier political rival the Nationalist Party were sensitive to organized religions such as Christianity. The best way to understand the relationship between religion and politics in China is perhaps through a utilitarian lens, with the state treating religion entirely based on its perceived usefulness to the political reality.

In analyzing the direction in which religion affects protest participation, existing research follows two approaches (Jones-Correa and Leal 2001). The first emphasizes the importance of religious beliefs and argues that religion matters in one's protest participation. The second emphasizes the instrumental and associational role of religion, that is, participation in religious activities plays a greater role than religious beliefs. Following this approach, religious activities are hypothesized to help develop protest participation skills (Jones-Correa and Leal 2001; Wald, Silverman and Fridy 2005), improve participation efficacy (Sobolewska et al. 2015), increase social capital (Brown and Brown 2003; King and Furrow 2004; Ruan, Zheng, and Liu 2014), and reduce organizational costs (Ran et al. 2014). In this study, we use a national sample from China to examine both hypotheses on the impact of religion on protest participation: (1) the role of religious beliefs, and (2) the role of actual participation in religious activities.

DATA AND METHODS

Data for this study are from the China World Values Survey (2010–2014) collected by the Research Center for Contemporary China at Peking University from November 2012 to January 2013.[3] The survey used a GPS-Assisted Area Sampling Method, covering thirty-one provinces in mainland China (excluding Hong Kong, Macao, and Taiwan) and 3,596 residential units. Based on the sampling frame, the research ultimately obtained 2,300 valid observations.

Dependent Variables

The dependent variable is participation in protest movements. Guided by previous research (Yi 2017), we separated participation in protest movements into: (1) propensity for participation and (2) actual participation. The questions for these measures in the questionnaire are: "I'm going to read out some forms of political action that people can take, and I'd like you to tell me, for each one, whether you have done any of these things, whether you might do it or would never under any circumstances do it: signing a petition, joining in boycotts, attending peaceful demonstrations, joining strikes or any other act of protest." Answers to these questions are: "have done," "might do," and "would never do." We create a dummy variable "propensity for participation in protest movements" to measure one's inclination to participate in protest movements, in which "might do" is regarded as "yes" and assigned the value of 1, while "would never do" is regarded as "no" and assigned the value of 0. We create a dummy variable "actual participation in protest movements" to measure one's actual participation in protest activities, in which "have done" is assigned the value of 1 and others the value of 0.

Primary Independent Variables

Our primary independent variable is religion. Religion is measured in two aspects: (1) subjective religious beliefs and (2) objective religious participation (Luckmann 1967). We create a dummy variable to measure the respondents' claim of religious faith, with having religious beliefs assigned the value of 1, none as 0. Other than Buddhism, most other religions have few observations. Our measure of religion includes three categories (0 = none, 1 = Buddhist,

2 = others). To measure the actual religious practice, we use the question, "Apart from weddings and funerals, about how often do you attend religious services these days?" The answers are, "more than once a week," "once a week," "once a month," "only on special holy days," "once a year," "less often," or "practically never." A continuous variable is constructed with values ranging from 1 to 7 (reverse coding).

Control Variables

Other control variables include gender, age, educational level, satisfaction with one's financial situation of the household, and marital status. Gender is set as a dummy variable, with male coded as 1 and female 0. Age is continuous. Educational level is measured as "No formal education," "Completing primary school," "Completing secondary school (technical/vocational type)," "Completing secondary school (university-preparatory type)," or "Completing university-level education (with degree)," and is assigned the value of 1–5, respectively. Satisfaction in one's household financial situation is assigned a value of 1–10, with 1 denoting the lowest level of satisfaction and 10 the highest. Marital status is a dummy variable with "not married" assigned the value of 0 and "married" assigned 1.

We define psychological factors as factors of subjective perception. They include confidence in the legal system, confidence in the central government, confidence in local governments, social trust, sense of deprivation, and social class. Confidence in the legal system, confidence in the central government and confidence in local governments are measured by questions directly asking about respondents' confidence in the courts, central government, and civil service. Social trust is measured by questions aimed to gauge the interviewee's degree of trust they have in others. This sense of deprivation is operationalized by asking if one feels they have been taken advantage by others. The following questionnaire item is how this is measured:

> Do you think most people would try to take advantage of you if they got a chance, or would they try to be fair? Please show your response on this card, where 1 means that "people would try to take advantage of you," and 10 means that "people would try to be fair."

We also construct an ordinal variable to reflect one's self-assessment of social class, ranging from lower class to upper class. The following question gathered this measure:

> People sometimes describe themselves as belonging to different social classes, the lower class, the lower-middle class, the middle class, upper-middle class, or the upper class. Which social class would you describe yourself as belonging to?

RESULTS

As shown in table 12.1, 47.78 percent of the respondents showed positive inclination to participate in protest movements, but only 7.68 percent actually took part in any protests. Only a small number of the respondents (14.77 percent) held religious beliefs,[4] with Buddhists accounting for the majority of them or 9.79 percent, and the remaining 4.99 percent accounting for all other religions.[5] Respondents showed high levels of confidence in major social institutions, with 80.11 percent reporting being confident in the legal system, 91.85 percent in the central government, and 77.44 percent in local governments. In comparison, fewer respondents (64.44 percent) reported trusting others in their social interactions. The sense of deprivation (as measured by a feeling being taken advantage of by others) has a mean of 4.095 (less than 5), suggesting that, overall, there is a tendency among respondents to feel that they have not been treated fairly by others and had been taken advantage of.

Table 12.1. Descriptive Statistics for Variables

Dependent Variable	Description and Coding	Value	N	%
Willingness to participate in protest movements	Does the interviewee tend to take an active part in protest movements? 1 = yes, 0 = no	0 1	1,140 1,043	52.26 47.78
Actual participation in protest movements	Does the interviewee take an active part in protest movements? 1 = yes, 0 = no	0 1	2,019 168	92.32 7.68
Primary Independent Variables				
Religious beliefs	Does the interviewee have religious beliefs? 1 = yes (14.77%), 0 = no (85.23%)	0 1	1,846 320	85.23 14.77
Religious denomination	Does the interviewee belong to a religious denomination? If yes, which one? 0 = no (85.%), 1 = Buddhist (9.8%), 2 = others (4.99%)	0 1 2	1,846 212 108	85.23 9.79 4.99
Religious participation	Frequency attending religious services? Assign the value of 1–7: 1 = the lowest, 7 = the highest		N = 2,239, Mean = 1.402, SD = 1.100[a]	
Control Variables				
Age	Continuous measure of age (in years) at the time of filling in questionnaires (from 18 to 75)		N = 2,300, Mean = 43.918, SD = 14.947[a]	

(continued)

Table 12.1. *Continued*

Dependent Variable	Description and Coding	Value	N	%
Gender	What is the interviewee's gender? 1 = male, 0 = female	0 1	1,174 1,126	51.04 48.96
Educational level	Interviewee's highest educational level? 1 = No formal education, 2 = Completes primary school, 3 = Completes secondary school (tech/vocational type), 4 = Completes secondary school (university-preparatory type), 5 = Completes university-level education (with degree)	1 2 3 4 5	175 534 708 494 389	7.61 23.22 30.78 21.48 16.91
Marital status	Marital status? 0 = not married (including living together as married, divorced, separated, widowed and single) 1 = married	0 1	423 1,877	18.39 81.61
Satisfaction in the financial situation of the household	Satisfied with household's financial situation? Assign value: 1 = the lowest, 10 = the highest		N = 2,245, Mean = 6.216, SD = 2.000[a]	
Confidence in the legal system	Does the interviewee have confidence in the courts? 1 = yes, 0 = no	0 1	403 1,623	19.89 80.11
Confidence in the central government	Does the interviewee have confidence in the central government, 1 = yes, 0 = no	0 1	171 1,926	8.15 91.85
Confidence in local governments	Does the interviewee have confidence in local governments? 1 = yes, 0 = no	0 1	436 1,497	22.56 77.44
Deprivation perception	Do you think most people try to be fair, or try to take advantage of you? Assign the value of 1–10: 1 = max unfairness, 10 = max fairness		N = 2121, Mean = 4.095, SD = 2.008[a]	
Social trust	Does the interviewee think that most people can be trusted? 1 = yes, 0 = no	0 1	781 1,415	35.56 64.44
Social class	Would you describe yourself as belonging to: 1 = lower class, 2 = lower-middle, 3 = middle class, 4 = upper-middle, 5 = upper class	1 2 3 4 5	440 952 704 91 5	20.07 43.43 32.12 4.15 0.23

SD, standard deviation.
[a] N means number of observations.

Table 12.2. The Difference in Protest Participation by Religious Beliefs

			Propensity to Participate in Protest Movements		
			No	Yes	Total
Religious Beliefs	No	Frequency	927	841	1,768
		Percent	85.2	84.61	84.92
	Yes	Frequency	161	153	314
		Percent	14.8	15.39	15.08
Total		Frequency	1,088	994	2,082
		Percent	100.00	100.00	100.00

Pearson $\chi^2(1) = 0.1434$ Pr = 0.705

			Actual Participation in Protest Movements		
			No	Yes	Total
Religious Beliefs	No	Frequency	1,639	130	1,769
		Percent	85.19	80.25	84.80
	Yes	Frequency	285	32	317
		Percent	14.81	19.21	15.20
Total		Frequency	1,924	162	2,086
		Percent	100.00	100.00	100.00

Pearson $\chi^2(1) = 2.8297$ Pr = 0.093 < 0.1

As shown in table 12.2, respondents claiming to hold religious beliefs were less likely to participate in protest movements than those without religious beliefs on both the propensity (inclination or willingness) to participate and actual participation. Among those without religious beliefs, the proportion of nonparticipation was higher than that of participation, while among those with religious beliefs, the proportion of participation in protest movements was higher than that of nonparticipation, regardless of inclined participation or actual participation. Our Pearson χ^2 test on the association between religious interviewees and interviewees without religious beliefs is marginally significant ($P = .093$) for *actual* participation in protest movements but is nonsignificant ($P = .705$) for propensity for participation in protest movements.

The Impact of Religion on Propensity for Protest Participation

In this section, we analyze the influence of religion on protest participation under the control of multiple factors. We first test the multicollinearity among the independent variables, and the results show there is no multicollinearity problem. We then choose propensity (inclination or willingness) for participation in protest movements as the dependent variable and use logistic regressions to estimate the relationship between religion and propensity for participation in protest movements.

Based on model 1, a series of factors affect propensity for participation in protest movements. Age, social trust, sense of deprivation, and self-assessment of social class all have an impact on propensity for participation in protest movements. As shown in table 12.3, a significant negative relationship exists between an interviewee's age and propensity for participation in protest movements, with the increase in age gradually reducing one's propensity for participation in protest movements.

Table 12.3. Binary Logistic Regression Model of Religion and Propensity to Protest[a]

Variables	Model 1	Model 2	Model 3	Model 4	Model 5[b]
Religious Beliefs		1.338*			1.174
		(0.195)			(0.218)
Religious denomination[c]					
Buddhism			1.168		
			(0.201)		
Other religions			1.813*		
			(0.446)		
Religious participation				1.129*	1.334**
				(0.054)	(0.139)
Religious beliefs					0.718*
*Religious participation					(0.102)
Gender	1.179	1.188	1.192	1.190	1.175
	(0.118)	(0.123)	(0.123)	(0.121)	(0.122)
Age	0.978***	0.979***	0.979***	0.978***	0.979***
	(0.004)	(0.004)	(0.004)	(0.004)	(0.004)
Educational Level[d]					
Complete primary school	1.463	1.610*	1.560	1.497	1.637*
	(0.332)	(0.373)	(0.364)	(0.344)	(0.382)
Complete secondary school (tech/vocational)	1.162	1.233	1.196	1.180	1.244
	(0.266)	(0.288)	(0.282)	(0.274)	(0.293)
Complete secondary school (university-prep)	0.949	1.053	1.026	0.957	1.046
	(0.229)	(0.258)	(0.253)	(0.233)	(0.258)
Complete university-level (with degree)	1.385	1.594	1.557	1.418	1.565
	(0.355)	(0.417)	(0.410)	(0.368)	(0.413)
Household's financial situation satisfaction	1.019	1.012	1.011	1.019	1.012
	(0.029)	(0.030)	(0.030)	(0.029)	(0.030)
Confidence in the legal system	0.954	0.937	0.943	0.949	0.940
	(0.150)	(0.151)	(0.152)	(0.151)	(0.153)
Confidence in local governments	0.696*	0.701*	0.707*	0.708*	0.707*
	(0.105)	(0.110)	(0.111)	(0.107)	(0.111)

Variables	Model 1	Model 2	Model 3	Model 4	Model 5[b]
Confidence in the central government	1.435 (0.313)	1.442 (0.322)	1.433 (0.319)	1.499 (0.328)	1.489 (0.330)
Social trust	1.350** (0.145)	1.340** (0.147)	1.334** (0.146)	1.348** (0.145)	1.369** (0.151)
Marital status	0.868 (0.118)	0.873 (0.121)	0.871 (0.121)	0.861 (0.119)	0.863 (0.121)
Deprivation perception	1.108*** (0.032)	1.118*** (0.033)	1.119*** (0.033)	1.112*** (0.032)	1.123*** (0.033)
Social class[e]					
Lower-middle class	1.397* (0.210)	1.429* (0.220)	1.442* (0.223)	1.389* (0.212)	1.427* (0.221)
Middle class	1.581 (0.422)	1.596 (0.436)	1.616 (0.441)	1.528 (0.414)	1.621 (0.445)
Upper-middle class	1.169 (0.174)	1.193 (0.183)	1.204 (0.185)	1.163 (0.175)	1.181 (0.182)
Upper Class	2.701 (3.140)	1.629 (2.114)	1.514 (1.923)	2.478 (2.810)	1.676 (2.183)
Constant	0.888 (0.376)	0.729 (0.317)	0.750 (0.326)	0.704 (0.306)	0.520 (0.235)
Pseudo R^2	0.039	0.041	0.042	0.041	0.045
Prob > χ^2	0.000	0.000	0.000	0.000	0.000
Observations	1,717	1,641	1,641	1,698	1,637

P value (two-tailed): ****P* < .001; ***P* < .01; **P* < .05.
[a]We use a heteroscedastic robust estimator to estimate. The standard error in heteroscedasticity robustness is shown in brackets.
[b]In model 5, to avoid the effect of multicollinearity, we center the variables of religious beliefs, religious participation and the interaction term of the two based on the method described in Jann (2004) and find the estimation results have no significant differences. Therefore, we do not report them.
[c]Reference group is no religion.
[d]Reference group is no formal education.
[e]Reference group is lower class.

We also find that social trust has a statistically significant positive effect on propensity for participation in protest movements. The data show that a one-unit increase in social trust will increase reported propensity for participation in protest movements by 35 percent. The model also shows one's sense of deprivation to be a significant factor; interviewees who feel they are treated more fairly and justly report a greater *willingness* to participate in protest movements. Confidence in local governments has a significantly negative influence on propensity for participation in protest movements: the more interviewees trust local governments, the lower their odds of propensity for participation. Specifically, a one-unit increase in confidence in local governments will decrease the odds of propensity for participation in protest movements by 30.4 percent. Being a member of the lower-middle class significantly increase the odds of propensity for participation in protest movements, with an odds ratio of 1.397 (*P* < .05).

In model 2, we examine the impact of religious beliefs on propensity for participation in protest movements. We find that religious beliefs have a significant effect on propensity for participation in protest movements when other variables are controlled for. Compared with people without religious beliefs, respondents with religious beliefs are 33.8 percent more likely to state that they would participate in protest movements. Other significant control variables (i.e., age, social trust, sense of deprivation, confidence in local governments and social status) remain significant in model 2.

Model 3 examines the impact of interviewees' stated religion on their propensity for participation in protest movements. With nonreligious interviewees as the reference group, respondents with other religious beliefs (i.e., other than Buddhists) are found to have greater propensity for participation in protest movements, with an odds ratio of 1.813 ($P < .05$). While there is some indication that Buddhist believers also report a higher willingness to participate in protest movements, the influence is not statistically significant.

Model 4 examines the impact of interviewees' frequency of religious participation on propensity for participation in protest movements. We find the frequency of religious participation to have a significant positive effect on propensity for participation in protest movements. The higher the frequency of religious participation, the higher the propensity for participation in protest movements, with an odds ratio of 1.129 ($P < .05$).

In model 5, we expand our analysis to include the variables of religious beliefs, religious participation and the interaction term between the two for estimation. The results again confirm that religious participation has a positive and significant impact on the propensity for participation in protest movements among both religious believers as well as the nonreligious respondents. Among religious believers, the higher the frequency of religious participation, the higher the propensity for participation in protest movements. Specifically, for religious believers, each unit increase in the frequency of religious participation will increase the odds of propensity for participation in protest movements by 5.2 percent.[6] This pattern is also found true among nonreligious respondents, although with a less pronounced coefficient.

The Impact of Religion on Actual Protest Participation

We examine actual participation in protest movements as an independent variable and use a logistic model to analyze the relationship between religion and participation. As shown in table 12.4, model 1 displays whether interviewees' participation is influenced by several control factors as discussed previously. Education, marital status, sense of deprivation, and social class all have a significant impact on protest participation. For education, with "no formal education" as a reference group, the odds of participation among interviewees with "complete university-level education (with degree)" is 6.416 times as likely as those with "no formal education" ($P < .001$). Relative to those with "no formal education," each higher level of educational attainment shows greater likelihood of participation in protests, although the impact are not statistically significant. These results suggest that increases in the level of education are likely to prompt increased odds of actual protest participation, but different education levels have different impacts. We also find that one's sense of deprivation has a significant impact on actual participation in protest movements. Those who feel they are treated more fairly or justly have increased odds of actual participation, with an odds ratio of 1.122 ($P < .05$).

Table 12.4. Binary Logistic Regression Model of Religion and Actual Protest Participation[a]

Variables	Model 1	Model 2	Model 3	Model 4	Model 5[b]
Religious Beliefs		1.550			1.546
		(0.367)			(0.442)
Religious denomination[c]					
Buddhism			1.325		
			(0.388)		
Other religions			2.084*		
			(0.719)		
Religious participation				1.190*	1.443**
				(0.082)	(0.172)
Religious beliefs *Religious participation					0.591**
					(0.110)
Gender	1.403	1.396	1.399	1.451*	1.351
	(0.255)	(0.259)	(0.260)	(0.267)	(0.254)
Age	1.000	0.998	0.998	1.000	0.999
	(0.007)	(0.007)	(0.007)	(0.007)	(0.007)
Educational Level[d]					
Complete primary school	3.469	3.383	3.240	3.659	3.512
	(2.579)	(2.525)	(2.425)	(2.706)	(2.560)
Complete secondary school (tech/vocational)	3.744	3.722	3.582	4.035	3.850
	(2.718)	(2.708)	(2.614)	(2.922)	(2.738)
Complete secondary school (university-prep)	4.081	4.140	4.005	4.333*	4.233*
	(2.974)	(3.030)	(2.934)	(3.153)	(3.035)
Complete university-level ed (with degree)	6.416*	6.251*	6.041*	6.853**	6.096*
	(4.698)	(4.621)	(4.470)	(5.021)	(4.423)
Household's financial situation satisfaction	1.081	1.093	1.091	1.082	1.087
	(0.060)	(0.061)	(0.061)	(0.059)	(0.061)
Confidence in the legal system	1.004	1.001	1.000	0.991	1.012
	(0.292)	(0.300)	(0.300)	(0.290)	(0.308)
Confidence in local governments	0.826	0.815	0.831	0.861	0.836
	(0.219)	(0.221)	(0.224)	(0.229)	(0.232)

(continued)

Table 12.4. *Continued*

Variables	Model 1	Model 2	Model 3	Model 4	Model 5[b]
Confidence in the central government	0.787 (0.288)	0.817 (0.306)	0.813 (0.305)	0.764 (0.276)	0.803 (0.293)
Social trust	0.789 (0.146)	0.794 (0.152)	0.790 (0.151)	0.785 (0.145)	0.836 (0.160)
Marital status	0.527** (0.111)	0.538** (0.115)	0.540** (0.117)	0.522** (0.111)	0.529** (0.115)
Deprivation perception	1.122* (0.058)	1.116* (0.059)	1.119* (0.059)	1.128* (0.059)	1.123* (0.061)
Social class[e]					
Lower middle class	1.829* (0.553)	1.852* (0.578)	1.878* (0.592)	1.772 (0.539)	1.807 (0.565)
Middle class	1.915 (0.935)	1.917 (0.957)	1.962 (0.984)	1.845 (0.903)	1.906 (0.942)
Upper middle class	1.570 (0.467)	1.604 (0.492)	1.630 (0.503)	1.521 (0.454)	1.521 (0.466)
Upper Class	5.480 (6.330)	5.662 (6.233)	5.194 (5.398)	4.658 (4.754)	6.141 (6.864)
Constant	0.012*** (0.011)	0.011*** (0.010)	0.011*** (0.010)	0.009*** (0.008)	0.007*** (0.007)
Pseudo R^2	0.052	0.054	0.055	0.057	0.066
Prob > χ^2	0.000	0.000	0.000	0.000	0.000
Observations	1,720	1,644	1,644	1,701	1,640

P value (two-tailed): ***P < .001; **P < .01; *P < .05. 2 3.
[a]We use a heteroscedastic robust estimator to estimate. The standard error in heteroscedasticity robustness is shown in brackets.
[b]In model 5, to avoid the effect of multicollinearity, we center the variables of religious beliefs, religious participation and the interaction term of the two based on the method described in Jann (2004) and find the estimation results have no significant differences. Therefore, we do not report them.
[c]Reference group is no religion.
[d]Reference group is no formal education.
[e]Reference group is lower class.

Marital status has a significant impact on protest participation. Respondents who are married show decreased odds of actual participation with an odds ratio of .527 ($P < .01$). Social class also has a significant impact on actual participation in protest movements. With lower class as a reference group, members of the lower-middle class have a much greater odds of actual protest participation (odds ratio = 1.829; $P < .05$) than other social classes.

Model 2 examines the impact of religious beliefs on actual protest participation. We find that compared with those interviewees without religious beliefs, religious interviewees' odds of *actual* participation in protest movements are 55 percent higher, although the effect is not statistically significant.

Model 3 in table 12.4 examines the impact of interviewees' religion. With nonreligious interviewees as the reference group, we find that Buddhist interviewees are 1.325 times that of nonreligious interviewees to actually participate in protests, but the impact of religion in this case is not statistically significant. However, believers of other religions are 2.084 times as likely as those nonreligious interviewees to have actually participated in protest movements ($P < .05$). This finding suggests religious believers of "other" religions rather than Buddhism are more inclined to participate in protests. Buddhists' participation is lower than that of interviewees following other religions but is not significant.

Model 4 examines the impact of interviewees' frequency of participation in religious activities on protest participation. We find the frequency of participation in religious activities has a significant positive effect. The higher the frequency of religious participation, the higher the odds of actual participation in protest movements, with each unit increase in the frequency of religious practice bringing about 19 percent increase in the odds of protest participation.

In model 5, we expand our analysis to include the variables of religious beliefs, participation in religious activities, and the interaction term between the two for estimation. Again we find that religious participation has a positive and significant impact on actual participation in protest movements among both religious believers and their nonreligious peers, all other things being equal. Among respondents with religious beliefs, the higher the frequency of their religious practice, the higher the odds of actual participation in protest movements.

DISCUSSION

Findings from this study clearly suggest that beliefs have a significantly positive effect on one's inclination to participate in protest movements, which helps explain why the state remains wary of the expansion of religious activities in China, particularly religions from the West. Those who participate in religious activities are even more likely to have actually participated in protest movements. Furthermore, all other things being equal, believers in "other" religions (in most cases denominations in Christianity) are even more likely to participate in protest movements than those who practice Buddhism.

The relationship between the state and religion remains contentious in China. Culturally speaking, Christianity has always been associated with Western colonialism, thus inviting suspicion as well as hostility from the state. Christian missionaries have long been regarded as agents of the Western powers that brought nothing but disaster to modern China, and this history of humiliation results in the communist regime's distrust of Christianity (Goldman 1986; Tsai 2007). Although Buddhism is also an exogenous religion, it was introduced into China from another Eastern culture, and compared to Christianity, Buddhism is viewed as more indigenous and is more tolerated by the state. As Tsai (2007) has observed in rural China, although both are solidary social settings, in general Buddhist temples rather than Christian churches enjoy a much closer relationship with village officials visiting and patronizing the religious ceremonies. Another important difference between the Buddhist temple and Christian churches is in their organizational structures. Buddhist temples are loosely organized, while Christian churches are more closely organized. Goldman (1986) explains that Buddhism is not centrally organized and monks and nuns often return to secular life. Kurtz (2015) argues Buddhism over time can become intertwined with indigenous religions of China (e.g., Confucianism and Taoism). Because organized religion is stronger in terms of mobilization and organizational capacity, it is more likely to arouse suspicions from the state.

It should be noted that mere claims of religious belief does not necessarily influence one to actually participate in protest movements. It is the actual participation in religious activities that seems to matter the most when it comes to actual protest participation. Our analysis shows that, after controlling religious beliefs, religious participation has a significantly positive effect on participation in protest movements. In other words, the greater the religious practice, particularly in non-Buddhist religions, the more likely believers will challenge state policies via protest. In terms of limiting protests and maintaining social harmony and popular quiescence, it is utilitarian that the CCP carefully watches and, where and when it deems necessary, impede and disrupt the growth of certain religious organizations.

Our findings bear several important implications. First, we use Chinese data to analyze the relationship between religion and protest participation. The results support the general view that religious participation is more important than religious beliefs. Second, existing studies have identified the influence of religion on general protest participation, but elements of the relationship still remain underexplored. Our analysis examines two dimensions of taking part in protests: propensity to participate—that is, expressed willingness or intention to take part in a movement and actual participation. Our results find that religious beliefs and religious participation have different impacts on both.

We acknowledge that the present study has several limitations, which can be addressed by further research. First, the study uses cross-sectional data that limit the analysis of the cause-and-effect relationship between religion and participation in protest movements. For example, religious beliefs are measured at the time of participants' interviews, while participation in protest movements might have happened before interviewees started believing in a religion. Therefore, a temporal sequence mismatch may exist. Second, the operationalization of some variables may be rough—constrained by our data set—for example, one's sense of deprivation and social trust—resulting in imprecision about the connotation of these variables. Finally, additional factors that influence protest participation may interact with religion in ways we have not explored. Further inquiry can explore these important and complex processes.

There is much to be explored on the topic of protest movements in China. Understanding the causes and correlates will be the first step toward effective mediation and conflict resolution. Although we have learned from this study that participation in religious activity appears to increase one's involvement in protest movements, much more empirical work is needed to unpack this relationship and explain why that may be the case. Furthermore, people protest for different reasons, and not all grievances share the same causes. Future research can explore what elements of religious participation contribute to what types of protest activity. Although considerations of social order may lead the state to curtail unauthorized religion in China, particularly those of Western origin, our understanding of the relationship between religion and protest movements can be much more nuanced.

NOTES

1. China WVS is part of the worldwide research project World Value Survey that conduct representative surveys to explore human beliefs and values. It is to be noted that the first round WVS was not implemented in China and the data of religious denomination was missed in the third round survey in 1995, for detailed information of World Value Survey, please visit http://www.worldvaluessurvey.org/wvs.jsp. Based on the data from China General Social Survey (CGSS), the proportion of religious believers in China in 2008, 2010, and 2012 was 9.45 percent, 12.91 percent, and 14.67 percent, respectively. See http://cgss.ruc.edu.cn/. The two different data are consistent and could confirm each other.

2. Political participation includes but is not limited to "signing a petition, participating in a boycott of a product or a business, attending a rally in support of a politician or a cause."

3. For further details on sampling methodology, questionnaire, and data sets used in this chapter's analysis are available at the website: http://www.worldvaluessurvey.org/wvs.jsp.

4. China's General Social Survey (CGSS 2010) conducted by Renmin university of China together with academic institutions across the country is another influential database. According to the database, 12.03 percent of interviewees have religious beliefs, which is close to our statistical conclusion. For information on the CGSS 2010 database, refer to: http://cnsda.ruc.edu.cn/index.php?r=projects/viewand id=15553986.

5. Due to the few observations, all other religious denominations are combined.

6. $(1.334 - 1) + (0.718 - 1) = 0.052$.

REFERENCES

Alston, Jon P., Charles W. Peek, and C. Ray Wingrove. 1972. "Religiosity and Black Militancy: A Re-appraisal." *Journal for the Scientific Study of Religion* 11(3): 252–61.

Ashiwa, Yoshiko, and David L. Wank. 2009. "Making Religion, Making the State in Modern China: An Introductory Essay." In Yoshiko Ashiwa and David L. Wank, eds., *Making Religion, Making the State: The Politics of Religion in Modern China*, 1–21. Stanford, CA: University of Stanford Press.

Ayers, John W., and C. Richard Hofstetter. 2008. "American Muslim Political Participation Following 9/11: Religious Belief, Political Resources, Social Structures, and Political Awareness." *Politics and Religion* 1(1): 3–26.

Berkowitz, Leonard. 1972. "Frustrations, Comparisons, and Other Sources of Emotion Arousal as Contributors to Social Unrest." *Journal of Social issues* 28(1): 77–91.

Brown, R. Khari, and Ronald E. Brown. 2003. "Faith and Works: Church-Based Social Capital Resources and African American Political Activism." *Social Forces* 82(2): 617–41.

Cao, Nanlai. 2010. *Constructing China's Jerusalem: Christians, Power, and Place in Contemporary Wenzhou*. Stanford, CA: Stanford University Press.

Clarke, Alan. 1987. "Moral Protest, Status Defence and the Anti-Abortion Campaign." *The British Journal of Sociology* 38(2): 235–53.

Collier, Paul, and Anke Hoeffler. 2004. "Greed and Grievance in Civil War." *Oxford Economic Papers* 56(4): 563–95.

Feng, Shizheng. 2006. "Protest Mobilization under Unit System in China" [in Chinese]. *Sociological Studies* (3): 98–134.

Galais, Carol, and Jasmine Lorenzini. 2017. "Half a Loaf Is (Not) Better than None: How Austerity-Related Grievances and Emotions Triggered Protests in Spain." *Mobilization* 22(1): 77–95.

Goldman, Merle. 1986. "Religion in Post-Mao China." *The Annals of the American Academy of Political and Social Science* 483(1): 146–56.

Goldman, Russel. 2018. "Chinese Police Dynamite Christian Megachurch." *New York Times*, January 12. Retrieved April 2, 2020. https://www.nytimes.com/2018/01/12/world/asia/china-church-dynamite.html.

Goldstein, Warren S. 2017. "The Mandate of Heaven on Earth: Religious and Secular Conflict in China." *Journal of Religious and Political Practice* 3(1–2): 25–45.

Guo, Changgang, and Fengmei Zhang. 2015. "Religion and Social Stability: China's Religious Policies in the Age of Reform." *Third World Quarterly* 36(11): 2183–95.

Gurr, Ted R. *1970. Why Men Rebel*. Princeton, NJ: Princeton University Press.

Han, Zhiming. 2012. "Interest Expression, Resource Mobilization and Agenda Setting: A Descriptive Analysis on the NAO-DA Phenomenon" [in Chinese]. *Journal of Public Management* 2(1): 52–66.

Harris, Fredrick C. 1994. "Something Within: Religion as a Mobilizer of African-American Political Activism." *The Journal of Politics* 56(1): 42–68.

Hasenclever, Andreas, and Volker Rittberger. 2000. "Does Religion Make a Difference? Theoretical Approaches to the Impact of Faith on Political Conflict." *Millennium* 29(3): 641–74.

Hunt, Larry L., and Janet G. Hunt. 1977. "Black Religion as Both Opiate and Inspiration of Civil Rights Militance: Putting Marx's Data to the Test." *Social Forces* 56(1): 1–14.

Huntington, Samuel P. 1997. *The Clash of Civilizations and the Remaking of World Order*. London: Penguin.

Inglehart, Ronald, et al. 2014a. World Values Survey: Round Two—Country-Pooled Datafile Version.1990–1994. Madrid: JD Systems Institute. http://www.worldvaluessurvey.org/WVSDocumentationW.

———. 2014b.World Values Survey: Round Three—Country-Pooled Datafile Version.1995–1998. Madrid: JD Systems Institute. http://www.worldvaluessurvey.org/WVSDocumentationW.

———. 2014c.World Values Survey: Round Four—Country-Pooled Datafile Version. 2000–2004. Madrid: JD Systems Institute. http://www.worldvaluessurvey.org/WVSDocumentationW.

———. 2014d.World Values Survey: Round Five—Country-Pooled Datafile Version. 2005–2008. Madrid: JD Systems Institute. http://www.worldvaluessurvey.org/WVSDocumentationW.

———. 2014e. World Values Survey: Round Six—Country-Pooled Datafile Version. Madrid: JD Systems Institute. www.worldvaluessurvey.org/WVSDocumentationWV6.jsp.

Jamal, Amaney. 2005. "The Political Participation and Engagement of Muslim Americans: Mosque Involvement and Group Consciousness." *American Politics Research* 33(4): 521–44.

Jann, Ben. 2004. "CENTER: Stata Module to Center (or Standardize) Variables." Statistical Software Components S4444102, Boston College Department of Economics, revised April 13, 2017.

Jones-Correa, Michael A., and David L. Leal. 2001. "Political Participation: Does Religion Matter?" *Political Research Quarterly* 54(4): 751–70.

Kang, Xiaoguang, and Heng Han. 2005. "The Classification of Control: Current Research on the Relationship between State and Society in Mainland China." *Sociological Studies* 20(6): 73–89.

King, Pamela Ebstyne, and James L. Furrow. 2004. "Religion as a Resource for Positive Youth Development: Religion, Social Capital, and Moral Outcomes." *Developmental Psychology* 40(5):703–13.

Klandermans, Bert. 1984. "Mobilization and Participation: Social-Psychological Expansions of Resource Mobilization Theory." *American Sociological Review* 49(5): 583–600.

———. 1997. *The Social Psychology of Protest*. Oxford: Blackwell.

Klandermans, Bert, and Marga de Weerd. 2000. "Group Identification and Political Protest." In Sheldon Stryker, Timothy Owens, and Robert White, eds., *Self, Identity and Social Movements*, 68–90. Minneapolis: University of Minnesota Press.

Kurtz, Lester R. 2015. *Gods in the Global Village: The World's Religions in Sociological Perspective.* Thousand Oaks, CA: Sage.

Li, Lianjiang. 2004. "Political Trust in Rural China. *Modern China.*" 30(2): 228–58.

Lind, E. Allan, and Tom R. Tyler. 1988. *The Social Psychology of Procedural Justice.* Heidelberg: Springer Science and Business Media.

Liu, Mingxing, Liu Yongdong, Tao Yu, and Tao Ran. 2010. "Farmers' Associations, Contention Mediation and Collective Petitions in Rural China" [in Chinese]. *Sociological Studies* 6: 178–200.

Luckmann, Thomas. 1967. *The Invisible Religion: The Problem of Religion in Modern Society.* New York: Macmillan.

Marx, Gary T. 1967. "Religion: Opiate or Inspiration of Civil Rights Militancy among Negroes?" *American Sociological Review* 32(1): 64–72.

McAdam, Doug. 1986. "Recruitment to High-Risk Activism: The Case of Freedom Summer." *American Journal of Sociology* 92(1): 64–90.

———. 2010. *Political Process and the Development of Black Insurgency 1930–1970.* Chicago: University of Chicago Press,

McCarthy, John D., and Mayer N. Zald. 1977. "Resource Mobilization and Social Movements: A Partial Theory." *American Journal of Sociology* 82(6): 1212–41.

McVeigh, Rory, and David Sikkink. 2001. "God, Politics, and Protest: Religious Beliefs and the Legitimation of Contentious Tactics." *Social Forces* 79(4): 1425–58.

McVeigh, Rory, and Christian Smith. 1999. "Who Protests in America: An Analysis of Three Political Alternatives—Inaction, Institutionalized Politics, or Protest." *Sociological Forum* 14(4): 685–702.

Myrdal, Gunnar. 2017. *An American Dilemma: The Negro Problem and Modern Democracy, Volume 1.* London: Routledge.

Parsons, Talcott. 1991. *The Social System.* New York: The Free Press.

Pope, Liston, and Nicholas Jay Demerath. 1942. *Millhands and Preachers: A Study of Gastonia* (Vol. 15). New Haven, CT: Yale University Press,

Potter, Pitman B. 2003. "Belief in Control: Regulation of Religion in China." *The China Quarterly* 174: 317–37.

Reicher, Stephen D. 1984. "The St. Pauls' Riot: An Explanation of the Limits of Crowd Action in Terms of a Social Identity Model." *European Journal of Social Psychology* 14(1): 1–21

Ruan, Rongping, Fengtian Zheng, and Li Liu. 2014. "Religious Believing and Social Conflict: Origin or Instrument?" [in Chinese]. *China Economic Quarterly* 13(2): 793–816.

Seul, Jeffrey R. 1999. "'Ours Is the Way of God': Religion, Identity, and Intergroup Conflict." *Journal of Peace Research* 36(5): 553–69.

Sherkat, Darren E., and Jean Blocker. 1994. "The Political Development of Sixties' Activists: Identifying the Influence of Class, Gender, and Socialization on Protest Participation." *Social Forces* 72(3): 821–42.

Simon, Bernd, Michael Loewy, Stefan Stürmer, Ulrike Weber, Peter Freytag, Corinna Habig, Claudia Kampmeier, and Peter Spahlinger. 1998. "Collective Identification and Social Movement Participation." *Journal of Personality and Social Psychology* 74(3): 646–58.

Sobolewska, Maria, Stephen D. Fisher, Anthony F. Heath, and David Sanders. 2015. "Understanding the Effects of Religious Attendance on Political Participation among Ethnic Minorities of Different Religions." *European Journal of Political Research* 54(2): 271–87.

Swidler, Ann. 1986. "Culture in Action: Symbols and Strategies." *American Sociological Review* 51(2): 273–86.

Tao, Yu. 2015. "Unlikely Friends of the Authoritarian and Atheist Ruler." *Politics and Religion* 8(1): 86–110.

———. 2015/2017. "The Historical Foundations of Religious Restrictions in Contemporary China." *Religions* 8(12): 263–82.

———. 2015/2018. "Agitators, Tranquilizers, or Something Else: Do Religious Groups Increase or Decrease Contentious Collective Action?" *Religions* 9(7): 213.

Tarrow, Sidney G. 2011. *Power in Movement: Social Movements and Contentious Politics*. New York: Cambridge University Press.

Tilly, Charles. 1978. *From Mobilization to Revolution*. Reading, MA: Addison-Wesley Publishing.

Tsai, Lily L. 2007. "Solidary Groups, Informal Accountability, and Local Public Goods Provision in Rural China." *American Political Science Review* 101(2): 355–72.

Van Zomeren, Martijn, Russell Spears, Agneta H. Fischer, and Colin Wayne Leach. 2004. "Put Your Money Where Your Mouth Is! Explaining Collective Action Tendencies through Group-Based Anger and Group Efficacy." *Journal of Personality and Social Psychology* 87(5): 649–64.

Wald, Kenneth D., Adam L. Silverman, and Kevin S. Fridy. 2005. "Making Sense of Religion in Political Life." *Annual Review of Political Science* 8: 121–43.

Wallis, Roy. 1977. "A Critique of the Theory of Moral Crusades as Status Defense." *Scottish Journal of Sociology* 1(2): 195–203.

Wang, Jinhong, and Zhenghui Huang. 2008. "The Deviation between Institution Supply and Behavior Selection: The Empirical Analysis of Rural Migrant Workers' Interest Expression in the Pearl River Delta Region" [in Chinese]. *Open Times* 3(1): 60–76.

Wei, W. Q. 2015. "Emotion, Rational Choice, Class Identity: Multiple Mechanisms of the Participation of Collective Action Based on the Data of CGSS 2006. "*Sociological Review of China* 3: 82–96.

Wood, Michael, and Michael Hughes. 1984. "The Moral Basis of Moral Reform: Status Discontent vs. Culture and Socialization as Explanations of Antipornography Social Movement Adherence." *American Sociological Review* 49(1): 86–99.

Xie, Qiushan, and Shixiang Chen. 2014. "Political Efficacy and Contentious Interest Express: An Quantitative Analysis Based on CGSS2010" [in Chinese]. *Journal of Gansu Administration Institute* (3): 88–95.

Yang, Fenggang. 2006. "The Red, Black, and Gray Markets of Religion in China." *Sociological Quarterly* 47(1): 93–122.

Yi, Chengzhi. 2017. "Religious Belief and Collective Action Participation: An Empirical Study Based on CGSS2010 Data" [in Chinese]. *Fudan Journal (Social Sciences edition)* 1: 171–84.

Index

action stage, in Beijing TGD petitioning campaign: CCDI approach, 67, 70, 77–78, 83n18; LVOCG approach, 67, 70, 77–78; LVOTG approach, 67, 71, 77–78

activists: feminist structure of abeyance, 230; grassroots environmental, 194, 201, 216n7; institutional, 120, 196–99; mobilization tactics, 61

ACWF. *See* All-China Women's Federation

ADV. *See* anti-domestic violence

AI. *See* artificial intelligence

All-China Federation of Trade Unions, 12, 25n16

All-China Women's Federation (ACWF), 108, 109

Alliance. *See* Hong Kong Alliance in Support of Patriotic Democratic Movements of China

antagonistic contradictions between people, Mao era and, 104–5

Anti-Christian Movement, of 1920s, 301n12

anti-domestic violence (ADV) organizations, 109

anti-extradition movement, 225, 228–31, 243–44, 246; black-bloc tactic, 235–36; COVID-19 and, 227; government emergency powers in, 227; growth of, 226; occupation zones and, 232–37, *233*, *241–42*, 245; police brutality in, 227; Telegram and LIHKG internet platforms, 236, 240; violence in, 226, 238, 244. *See also* umbrella movement

anti-PX chemical plant protests in Xiamen and Kumming, 195, *200*, 200–202, *201*, *202*, 214–15; Kunming pervasive participation, 206–8, *214*; Xiamen minimal presence, 203–4, *214*

anti-waste incinerator protests in Beijing and Guangzhou, 195, *200*, 200–202, *201*, *202*, 214–15; Beijing invisible involvement, 204–5, *214*; Guangzhou creative coordination, 205–6, *214*

appeals, collective actions logic of, 8–10

Arab Spring (2011), 113, 225

arrests: feminist five, 113–14; by police, 6, 50–51, 55; rights lawyers and dissidents, 6, 152–53; violence and, 50–51

artificial intelligence (AI) surveillance, 16–17

328 *Index*

atheism, of CCP, 309
attributional explanations, for ENGOs participation, 209–10
authoritarian states: activist mobilization tactics in, 61; civic activism as threat in, 93; constrained environments in, 61, 115; political participation and social instability in, 55–56; POS in, 171; repression in, 145; soft repression in, 142; state elites in, 171, 175
autocracy: civic and noncivic activism under, 91–116; of Xi regime, 91

Beijing, 199; anti-waste incinerator protests in, 195, *200*, 200–202, *201*, *202*, *214*, 214–15; ENGOs invisible involvement, 204–5, *214*; national ENGOs lack of anti-waste incinerator support in, 195, 202; WeChat on floods in, 20
Beijing TGD petitioning campaign, 65–66; action stage, 67, 70–71, 77–78, 83n18; evaluation and repercussion stage, 67–68, 72–73, 75–76; retreat stage in, 67, 69, 71–72
biblical literalism, religion protest participation influenced by, 308
Big V bloggers, Great Firewall interception of, 19
black-bloc tactic, 235–36
Black militancy, religion relationship with, 309
brokerage, 215; defined, 216n3; durable coordinated action in, 197; in ENGOs popular protests participation, 197–99, 208–13, *214*; gatekeeping, 198; Kumming protest example of, 210–11; in relational model, 197; resource sharing and, 197
Bruun, Ole, 82n6
Buddhism, 311, 321
buffering, 215; in ENGOs popular protests participation, 197–99, 208–13, *214*

bureaucrat-assisted contention, 136; collective action facilitation, 122; description of, 121–23; framing of, 128–32; historical precedents for, 123–24, 136n1; institutional tensions in, 123–26; local socioeconomic elites in, 124–25; opportunities for, 127–28; ordinary leadership cadres and, 124–25; party secretaries influence on, 124, 127–28, 134; petition repression undermined through, 122; repression sabotage in, 121–22; social movements and, 134; as state power struggle weapon, 120–22; structures mobilization, 132–33; study methods and variation, 126–27; theory consequences and implications, 133–35
buying stability strategy, for limiting protests, 38

CCC. *See* China Christian Council
CCDI. *See* Central Commission for Discipline Inspection
CCP. *See* Chinese Communist Party
CEN. *See* China Environmental News
censorship: of COVID-19 Wuhan outbreak, 15, 24n9; Cybersecurity Law on internet communication, 19, 39; Cybersecurity Law on self-, 19; by security state, 15
Central Commission for Discipline Inspection (CCDI), TGD petitioning campaign and, 67, 70, 77–78, 83n18
central government: laws and regulations for labor issues protest type, 35; local government tension with, 34–35, 121; local protests tolerance by, 35; nonpolitical actions tolerance, 35; POS and, 34; regime stability concern of, 35
CGSS. *See* China General Social Survey
Charter 08 movement, 94, 96, 150
China: fast-growing economy, 31; FWCW hosted by, 108, 114;

powerful government and upper
class, 31; Western countries research
on religion protest participation, 306
China Christian Council (CCC), 281,
284–85
China Environmental Journal, 179
China Environmental News (CEN),
SEPA newspaper of, 180, 182; on
Wen comment, 186
China General Social Survey (CGSS),
323n4
China Labor Bulletin NGO, labor
activism monitoring by, 114
China Youth Daily, of CYL, 179, 182
Chinese Communist Party (CCP), 7;
atheism of, 309; Central Committee
economism protesters repression,
105–6; citizenship obligations
definition by, 155; Deng leadership
position in, 171; digital corporations
social control by, 16; on FWCW
hosting, 108; law popularization
policies by, 156; lawyers informal
political dependence, 148; legal
discourses in speeches of, *153*; on
mediation, 154; moral and social
management by, 19; nationalist
movement caution, 94; Nu River
Hydropower Dam support by, 176;
petition system support, 66; pre-Xi
reform mass line politics, 107; rule
of law reform dedication by, 146;
state scrutiny of behaviors by, 17
Chinese Lawyers Society (CLS), 148,
150
Chinese People's Political Consultative
Conference (CPPCC), 182, 188n11
Chinese Women's Daily, 108
citizenship (*gongmin*): CCP obligations
definition of, 155; human rights
connection with, 155
citizenship bargaining: collective
rights transformation into individual
interests, 158–60; in lawyering
repression, 147; lawyers citizen
education for, *156*, 156–58; on
national interest and collectivism,
158–59; petitioners divisions in,
159–60; petitioners pacifying in,
158; pragmatism in, 159; rights
consciousness and, 155, 156; rules
consciousness and, 155, 156
civic activism: authoritarian states
on threat of, 93; in democracy,
7, 93; examples of, 94; Mao era
polarization, 100; mass mobilization
in, 93; pre-Xi reform era lenience,
100; for public interests, 91; Xi
strong repression of, 92, 100, 101,
113
civic and noncivic activism under
autocracy, 91–93, 116; Cultural
Revolution and economism
protests, 104–6; historical change
and variation, 99–102; Mao social
activism, 102–4; POS, 94–98; pre-Xi
reform era, 106–12; social activism
under Xi, 112–15
civic organizations, state restriction of,
37
civil disobedience, in umbrella
movement, 236
civil rights, Xi oppression of, 39
civil society, Xi attacks on, 91
civil society groups, 12
claims: government accommodation and
facilitation of SOE, 110–11; lawyers
grievances mediation and, 146,
161n2; social protest targets and, *46*,
46–47, *47*
CLS. *See* Chinese Lawyers Society
coercive activities, private agents
engagement in, 144–45
cognitive praxis, of social movements,
225
collective action: bureaucrat-assisted
contention facilitation of, 122;
collective or individual litigation in,
145; contained contention as start
of, 7; in contemporary China, 5–6;

downturn since 2014, 21; emotional charge to, 37; framing processes and, 33; government response to, 32; of HCAs, 21; mobilization spontaneity, 37; modernized economy and increase in, 5; of peasants, 307; petitioning upward in, 146; petitions and appeals logic in, 8–10; from POS, 33–36; protest events increase, 5; resource mobilization and, 33; social media and internet communication impact on, 7, 37; state facilitation of, 99; street protests in, 146
collective memory, dynamic model of, 255–57, *257*
collective petitioning, social mobilization and, 81n2
collective protests: mobile networks and social media blocked during, 39; as national security issue, 39; of SOE employees from restructuring, 110; worker NGOs and, 36
collective resistance, shared values violation for, 37
collective rights into individual interests, in citizenship bargaining, 158–60
collectivism: communist ideology on, 154; lawyering in, 154–55; national interest and, 158–59
commemoration vigils, for Tiananmen Square, 259; collective identity through memory repertoire, 262–67, *263*, *265*, *266*, *267*; Mnemonic Agent participatory experience, 260–62; vigil participation and donation patterns, 260–61, *261*; vigil participation history, 2010-2018, *261*
communist ideology, on collectivism, 154
Communist Party Central Military Commission protests, 13
Communist Youth League (CYL), 179, 182
community disarticulation, for TGD migrants, 64–65

comprehensive surveillance policies, 6
confiscated properties, rural transformation protests on, 11
Confucianism, petitioning upward in, 146
Constitution 1980 rewriting, 152
constitutional discourses, in legal consensus construction, 152–53
constrained environments, in authoritarian states, 61, 115
construction industry, labor issue protests in, 12
consultative authoritarianism, in pre-Xi reform era, 107
contained contention, as collection action start, 7
contentious actions: from petitioning upward escalation, 146; from POS, 33–36
contentious politics, 91, 214; lawyering repression in, 160; POS and, 92
corruption, rural transformation protests against, 11
COVID-19, 39; anti-extradition movement and, 227; social media response to, 19; Wuhan outbreak censorship, 15, 24n9; youth on coverups of, 23
CPPCC. *See* Chinese People's Political Consultative Conference
criminal organizations, in Hong Kong, 246n1
Crossley, Nick, 61, 78–80
cultural approach, in social movements, 251–55
cultural framing, 160
Cultural Revolution: economism protests and, 104–6; Mao violence during, 103
Cybersecurity Law (2017), 19–20, 39
Cyberspace Administration of China, 19
CYL. *See* Communist Youth League

decentralization, POS and Chinese, 34
demobilization: lawyering repression relationship with, 160; rule of law

authoritarianism and, 144–46; in soft repression, 143, 144
democracy: civic activism in, 7, 93; collective resistance and, 33, 51; demonstrations, marches, and rallies in, 61; POS in, 93, 171; social protests in, 31
Democracy Wall movement, Deng support of, 171
demonstration effect, in protests, 225
Deng Xiaoping, 171
detentions, in security state, 15
digital dimensions, of social control, 15
digital surveillance, by Xi, 39, 112
disaster response, 24n4
dislocated persons, rural transformation protests for, 11
displacement, from TGD building, 62
disruption and repression of social protests: police presence and actions in, 48–49, *49*; violence in, 47–48, *48*; in Xi administration, 49
dissent and protest actions restriction, by Xi: comprehensive surveillance, 6; increased propaganda, 6; minority national regions repression, 6; NGOs closures and prohibitions, 5; rights lawyers and dissidents arrests, 6
dissent groups, Mao brutal repression of, 103
DOC. *See* dynamics of contention
durable coordinated action, in brokerage, 197
dynamic model, of collective memory, 255–57, *257*
dynamics of contention (DOC) approach, in lawyering repression, 143–44, 160–61

economic marginalization, of TGD migrants, 64
economic protests: for economic rights, 47, *47*; localized as popular contention, 94; for rights, 47, *47*; state tolerance of, 94–95; in umbrella movement, 237
economism (1966-1967): CCP Central Committee protesters repression, 105–6; Cultural Revolution and protests of, 104–6; former city residents protests, 104; Mao tolerance for, 104–5; workers with inferior status protests, 104
economy: China fast-growing, 31; China market-based, 6, 106–7; collective actions increase for modernized, 5
education: *laojiao* system of reeducation, 24n11; lawyers citizen, *156*, 156–58; parent social media connections for, 13
EIA. *See* Environmental Impact Assessment
elites, 83n22; Nu River Hydropower Dam and SEPA, 172–73, 181–83. *See also* state elites
emotional charge, to collective action and social protests, 37
emotion work mobilization tactic, 183
ENGOs. *See* environmental nongovernmental organizations
environmental activism: of grassroots activists, 194, 201, 216n7; NGOs and popular protests in, 200–202; for Nu River Hydropower Dam project, 172; state-movement interaction in, 173–74; topics for, 174
Environmental Impact Assessment (EIA) Law (2003): Pan promotion of, 180; SEPA enforcement of, 172, 177–78, 180; Wang Yongchen on enforcement of, 184–85
environmental movements, 62; SEPA support of, 34
environmental nongovernmental organizations (ENGOs): attributional explanations, 209–10; environmental movements driven by, 173; media engagement with, 173, 179, 186; Nu River Hydropower Dam

influenced by, 172–73, 184–85, 201; participation variations, 208–14, *214*; popular protests participation, 195, 197–99, *200*, 200–215, *201*, *202*, *214*; relational explanation, 210–13; SEPA alliance with, 179–80, 200; study methods and data, 199–200. *See also specific ENGOs*
environmental protests, 14; institutional alliance relational approach, 196–99; NGOs relational mechanisms in, 194–216
environmental public interest litigation, 217n9, 217n11
environmental social organizations, 201
ethno-nationalist movements, 24n7
evaluation and repercussion stage, in Beijing TGD petitioning campaign, 67–68, 72–73, 75–76
Evangelical Influence Survey (1996), 308
"Experts Call for Preserving the Nu River," of SEPA, 183

facial recognition, in techno authoritarianism, 17, 18
factory: automation and unemployment, 12; protests against pollution by, 14
Falun Gong protests, 33
FDI. *See* foreign direct investment
feminist activism, 14, 94; ACWF as representative for women, 108, 109; ADV organizations, 109; *Chinese Women's Daily* and, 108; feminist five arrest, 113–14; against gender discrimination, 96; government narrow understanding of, 108–9; as national security issue, 111; performance art advocacy, 109; pre-Xi reform era rise of, 108–9; SOE worker mobilization compared to, 111–12; structure of abeyance in, 230; Tiananmen Square incident and, 108; in Xi era, 113–14
feminist five arrest, 113–14

financial investment, for lawyers informal political dependence, 148–49, *149*
fishball revolution, 246n2
foreign direct investment (FDI) firms, protests by, 45, 53
fourth World Conference on Women (FWCW), in 1995, 108, 114
framing: of bureaucrat-assisted contention, 128–32; cultural, 160; of grievances as injustice, 128–29; localist flavor for, 129, 130; protect our hometown discourse in, 131
frauds, misrepresented products, and consumer safety protest type: consumer market regulatory oversight, 12; in housing market, 13; P2P lending firms collapse, 12; Ponzi schemes, 12–13; school building poor construction, 12
free spaces allowances, for security monitoring, 22
Friends of Nature ENGO, 200, 204–6
FWCW. *See* fourth World Conference on Women

Gansu Province, bureaucrat-assisted contention in, 122
gatekeeping, in brokerage, 198
GCBL. *See* governing the country by law
gender issues: feminist activism against discrimination, 96; global activism for, 109
Golden Shield. *See* Great Firewall
Golden Snubnosed Monkey Protection Movement (1995-1996), 173, 201
gongmin. *See* citizenship
Google, Great Firewall closing of, 18
governing the country by law (GCBL), 151–52
government: China powerful, 31; department inconsistencies, 34; emergency powers in anti-extradition movement, 227; feminist activism narrow understanding, 108–9; labor

laws and regulations from, 35; local governance tensions with, 34–35, 121; nonpolitical actions tolerance from, 35; persistent grievances pressure on, 55; repression for protest containment, 55; rights defense lawyers as threat to, 97; social governance measures, 32; social protests tolerance by, 34; SOE claims accommodation and facilitation by, 110–11; stability maintenance measures, 32. *See also* central government; local government; state

grassroots environmental activists: NIMBYism of, 194, 201, 206; social organizations and, 216n7

grassroots petitioning campaign on TGD building: Beijing petitioning, 65–66; making trouble motive in, 62; migrants grievances, 63–65; mobilization process, 62; *nao* habitus and outcomes, 61, 78–80; *nao* resistance logic, 75–78; petitioner tactics for, 62, 68–74; repertoire selection motives in, 62; state counterpetition moves in, 62, 68–69; study data structure, 67–68; violent tactics support in, 73

grassroots resistance: *nao* habitus and, 80; parties in, 80; repression-concession-escalation dynamics of, 80; state authority challenge and compliance, 81n2

Great Firewall, 21–23, 24n13; Big V bloggers interception, 19; Cybersecurity Law (2017), 19–20, 39; Google, YouTube, Twitter closing down, 18; internet sovereignty intent, 19, 39; strategic objective of, 18–19; VPN service and, 24n15

Green Beagle ENGO, 204–6

Green Earth Volunteers, 179; Wang Yongchen of, 186

Green Forum, 184–85

Green Kumming ENGO, 207–8

Green Watershed, 207–8

grid system, in Xi era, 112

Guangzhou, 199; anti-waste incinerator protests in, 195, *200*, 200–202, *201*, *202*, *214*, 214–15; creative coordination in anti-waste incinerator protests in, 205–6, *214*; national NGOs anti-waste incinerator involvement, 195, 202

hard repression, social and political risks of, 142

HCA. *See* high-capacity authoritarian

health, education and welfare issues protest type: profit seeking motives in, 13; for SOE worker pensions, 13; veterans PLA protests, 13

He Damin, 176, 178

Henan Province, bureaucrat-assisted contention framing in, 131

hierarchy, religion protest participation influenced by, 307

high-capacity authoritarian (HCA): collective actions of, 21; protest movements, 4; repression tactics, 15; states, 3; variability in, 14–15

Ho, Denise, 225

Hong Kong: anti-extradition movement of 2019, 225–46; criminal organizations, 246n1; fugitives transfer to PRC, 226; pro-democracy camp in, 231, 262, 269; prostitution tolerance, 246n3; rule of law in, 226; Tiananmen movement vigils, 250–74; youth participation in 2019 mobilizations, 23

Hong Kong Alliance in Support of Patriotic Democratic Movements of China (Alliance), 250, 274n2; activities of, 271–72; challenges of, 269; committee of, 265; Hong Kong Federation of Students member of, 271; objectives of, 271, 274, 274n4;

study on, 258–59; vigil memory repertoire, 271–72
Hong Kong Federation of Students, as Alliance member, 271
Hospital Authorities Employee Alliance, 240
housing market fraud, 13
Hubei Province: bureaucrat-assisted contention framing in, 131; bureaucrat-assisted contention in, 122–23
Hu era (2002-2012), urban churches emergence in, 288–94
Hu Jintao: institutionalized participation under, 91; limited repression by, 52, 55; national organizing and foreigners restrictions, 292–94; on rule of law, 152; scientific development emphasis, 181; urban churches shutting down in, 294–97
human agency, reflexivity of, 225
human rights: citizenship connection with, 155; global activism, 109; legal reforms protection of, 152
Hunan Province, bureaucrat-assisted contention in, 127, 133

ideological pluralism, Mao absence of, 108
impoverishment risks, from TGD building, 63
industrial restructuring, during pre-Xi reform era, 109–12
informal markets, local government regulation of, 12
informal political dependence, of lawyers: personal incentives for, 148–50; political dynamics of, 150–51
informal repression, 145
information: protests as government source of, 32, 34, 35, 37; repression facilitation from, 39
institutional activists, 120; in social movements, 196–99

institutional allies, in POS, 194, 216n1
institutional changes, protest groups impacted by, 33, 54
institutionalization: Hu and participation of, 91; of lawyers, 145; of social conflicts, 40, 49–50
institutional tensions, in bureaucrat-assisted contention, 123–26
internet communication: collective action impacted by, 7, 37; Cybersecurity Law censorship of, 19, 39; Telegram and LIHKG internet platform, 236, 240. *See also* WeChat

Jiangsu Province, bureaucrat-assisted contention framing in, 130–31
Jiang Zemin, 55
Jiangzi Province, bureaucrat-assisted contention framing in, 129–30

Kumming, 199; anti-PX chemical plant protests in, 195, *200*, 200–202, *201*, *202*, *214*, 214–15; brokerage protest example, 210–11; ENGOs pervasive participation in, 206–8, *214*; local and national ENGOs relationship for anti-PX protest, 195, 202

labor activism, 94; China Labor Bulletin NGO monitoring of, 114–15; in Xi era, 114–15
labor issues protest type, 33; from central government laws and regulations, 35; in construction industry, 12; factory automation and unemployment, 12; private domestic owned business concentration, 11–12; socialism and, 11
labor nongovernmental organizations (NGOs), 112, 113; Xi administration assaults on, 92
labor strikes, by unorganized workers, 36
land expropriations, rural transformation protests on unjust, 11, 47

Index

landlessness problems, for TGD migrants, 64
Lao Tzu, 131–32
late popularization policies, of CCP, 156
lawyering repression mechanism: citizenship bargaining in, 147, 155–60; in contentious politics, 160; demobilization relationship with, 160; DOC approach in, 143–44; interview participants for, 147–48; lawyers organized by regime in, 145; legal consensus construction, 147, 151–55; politics informal lawyer dependence in, 147, 148–51; process-mechanism approach, 144; strategy for, 143
lawyers: citizen education, *156*, 156–58; claims and grievances mediation by, 146, 161n2; domestication of, 150, 151; informal political dependence of, 148–51; institutionalization of, 145; in lawyering repression regime organization of, 145; mediation public service by, 155; petitioning upward participation by, 152; radical rights, 150, 151; soft repression use of, 142, 160
lawyers informal political dependence: case defense cost reductions, 149; CCP and, 148; CLS and, 148, 150; financial investment for, 148–49, *149*; lawyer domestication, 150, 151; MOJ and, 150–51; personal incentives for dependence, 148–50; personal safety incentive for, 149–50; political dynamics of, 150–51; POS and, 150; symbiotic exchange process, 148
Lawyers Law (1996), 148, 161n3
legal consensus construction: Chinese characteristics for rule of law, 153–54; collectivism lawyering, 154–55; constitutional discourses invention, 152–53; GCBL for, 151–52
legal discourses in speeches of CCP, *153*

legal reform: Constitution 1980 rewriting, 152; human rights protection in, 152; in post-Mao era, 152
Lennon Walls, in umbrella movement, 226, 234
Letters and Visits Office of the Central Government (LVOCG), TGD petitioning campaign and, 67, 70, 77–78
Letters and Visits Office of the Three Gorges Project Construction Committee (LVOTG), TGD petitioning campaign and, 67, 71, 77–78
Leung, Edward, 236, 242, 246n2
liberalized authoritarian contexts, 194–95
LIHKG internet platform, 236, 240
litigation: individual or collective, 146; mediation advantages over, 153
local government, 7; central government tension with, 34–35, 121; framing, 129, 130; informal market regulations from, 12; popular contention and, 94, 113; pre-Xi reform era civic activism and, 107; relational connections for protests reduction, 38; repression threat by, 37–38; social mobilization and state tensions with, 121; social protests information collection by, 37; socioeconomic elites in bureaucrat-assisted contention, 124–25; soft repression of, 145; TGD counterpetition tactics by, 68–69; worker harassment by, 12; Xi repression and, 38
localized economic protests, as popular contention, 94
local protests, central government tolerance of, 35
LVOCG. *See* Letters and Visits Office of the Central Government
LVOTG. *See* Letters and Visits Office of the Three Gorges Project Construction Committee

making trouble (*nao*) motive, in TGD petitioning campaign, 62; characteristics of, 77; grassroots resistance and, 80; habitus and outcomes, 61, 78–80; resistance logic, 75–78

making trouble (*nao*) tactics: illegal, 76–77; in labor activism, 115; for mobilization, 79–80; for SOE complaints, 111

Mao era (1949-1978): on antagonistic contradictions between people, 104–5; civic activism polarization, 100; Cultural Revolution violence during, 103; mass mobilization in, 101–3; mediation during, 154; mobilization tactics during, 104–5; national liberation goal, 102; on nonantagonistic contradictions among people, 104; noncivic activism moderate repression, 100, 103; political campaigns and dissent groups brutal repression, 103; popular contention in, 101, 104–6; social activism in, 102–4; social transformation goal, 102; totalitarian regime of, 101, 102; work-unit system organized dependency, 103. *See also* post-Mao era

Maoist-Marxist chat rooms, 25n16

Mao Zedong, 102; economism protests tolerance, 104–5; ideological pluralism absence, 108; on rebellion against revisionist authorities, 104; social movements support by, 171

marginalization, of TGD migrants, 63–64

market-based economy, 6; in pre-Xi reform era, 106–7

market reforms, protest groups impacted by, 33, 54

Marxist-Leninist regimes, 15; protest movements in, 3, 21; resistance repertoire of, 6, 23n3

mass line politics: CCP in pre-Xi reform era on, 107; state online involvement with digitalized, 20

mass mobilization: in civic activism, 93; Mao era, 101–3; in pre-Xi reform era, 106; social mobilization and, 81n2

materialist contention, 91, 96–98, *97*, *98*

May Fourth Movement, 94

media: ENGOs engagement with, 173, 179, 186; soft repression and stigmatization of, 144; Wang Yongchen and Zhang Kejia campaign, 182

mediation (*tiaojie*), 158–59; advantages over litigation, 153; CCP on, 154; lawyers public service in, 155, 161n5; during Mao era, 154; post-Mao era de-emphasis on, 154; rule of law and, 153; SEPA Nu River Hydropower Dam project, 176, 183–87

memory repertoire, Tiananmen Square collective identity through, 262–67, *263*, *265*, *266*, *267*

MEP. *See* Ministry of Environmental Protection

migrants from TGD building, 81n3; collective petitions of, 65; community disarticulation for, 64–65; grievances of, 63–65; impoverishment risks for, 63; landlessness problems, 64; marginalization of, 63–64; Partnership Support Scheme failure for, 64; unemployment of, 64

Ministry of Environmental Protection (MEP), 208, 215; environmental activism and, 200

Ministry of Justice (MOJ): CLS affiliation with, 150; on lawyers and collectivism, 154; lawyers informal political dependence and, 150–51

Ministry of Propaganda, social media postings analysis by, 20

Ministry of Public Security, 19;
  on popular uprisings focus, 32;
  repressive crackdown in 2015, 152;
  rights lawyers arrests in 2015 by,
  152–53
Mnemonic Agent participatory
  experience, for Tiananmen Square
  commemoration, 260–62
mobile networks, collective protests
  blocking of, 39
mobilization tactics: of activists, 61; in
  authoritarian states, 61; bureaucrat-
  assisted contention structures,
  132–33; emotion work, 183; during
  Mao era, 104–5; *nao* use of, 79–80;
  in TGD petitioning campaign, 62;
  violence and anti-regime, 144
MOJ. *See* Ministry of Justice
movement actors: state actors alliances
  with, 174; state-led alliances and,
  175

nao. *See* making trouble motive
National Development and Reform
  Commission (NDRC), on Nu River
  Hydropower Dam project, 176–78,
  182, 186, 188n3
national infrastructure projects, rural
  transformation protests on, 11
national interest, collectivism and,
  158–59
nationalist movements: CCP caution in,
  94; May Fourth Movement, 94; as
  popular contention, 94
national liberation goal, of Mao era, 102
national security issue: of collective
  protests, 39; of feminism, 111
National Security Law, 39
NDRC. *See* National Development and
  Reform Commission
networked authoritarianism, of state,
  69–70
NGOs. *See* nongovernmental
  organizations
NIABY. *See* not in anyone's backyard

NIMBY. *See* not in my backyard
nonantagonistic contradictions among
  people, Mao era on, 104
noncivic activism: Mao era moderate
  repression, 100, 103; pre-Xi reform
  era facilitation of, 107; for private
  interests, 91; of SOE employees,
  109; Xi moderate repression
  increase, 101, 112–13, 114
nonconfrontational events, 41
nongovernmental organizations
  (NGOs): challenges by, 55;
  closing and prohibitions of, 5, 93;
  collective protests and worker, 36;
  corporatist relationship with regime,
  6; environmental protests relational
  mechanisms, 194–216; human
  rights groups threatened, 6; labor,
  112, 113; pre-Xi reform era three-
  no policy, 106, 203; restrictions
  against, 6, 81n2, 195; state symbiotic
  relationship with, 195; for women,
  108, 111, 114; Xi assaults on labor,
  92
nonmaterialist contention, 91, 96–98,
  97, 98
nonmaterialist social movement,
  feminist movement as, 14
nonpolitical actions, central government
  tolerance of, 35
nonstate actors: rule of law
  authoritarianism and, 144–46; in
  soft repression, 143; state actor
  interactive dynamics with, 174
nonviolent protest: forceful police and,
  50, 51–52; tolerant police and, *50,* 51
not in anyone's backyard (NIABY)
  protests, 206
not in my backyard (NIMBY) protests,
  14; environmentalism and, 206;
  grassroots environmental activists
  and, 194, 201; for housing market,
  13
Nu River Hydropower Dam:
  CCP support of, 176; EIA law

mobilization, 180–81; ENGOs protest participation, 172–73, 184–85, 201; environmental NGOs influence, 172–73, 184–85; He opposition to, 176, 178; NDRC on, 176–78, 182, 186, 188n3; post-EIA law, 177–79; pre-EIA law, 176–77; project for, 175–80; SEPA and, 176–87; SEPA elites-movement alliance, 172–73, 181–83; SEPA mediation, 176, 183–84, 187; SEPA mediation after Wen comment, 185–87; state elites and movement alliances against, 171–88; state-movement interaction in environmental activism, 173–74; temporary suspension in 2004 of, 172, 173, 186; Thirteenth Five-Year Plan and, 187; Wang Yongchen and, 182, 189n13; Wen suspension of, 173, 186; Zhang Keijia and, 182

occupation zones, in umbrella and anti-extradition movements, 232–37, *233*, 241–42, 245
opposition lawmakers, in umbrella movement, 243
ordinary leadership cadres, bureaucrat-assisted contention and, 124–25
organized dependency, of Mao work-unit system, 103
overt protests, repression decrease of, 4

P2P. *See* peer-to-peer
Pan Yue: EIA law promotion by, 180; of SEPA, 179–80, 182, 187, 188n9, 204
Partnership Support Scheme, TGD migrant failure from, 64
party secretaries, bureaucrat-assisted contention influenced by, 124, 127–28, 134
party-state. *See* state
peasants: collective actions of, 307; protest repression for, 38; rights awareness foundation of, 79

peer-to-peer (P2P) lending firms collapse, 12
People's Daily, 182–83
People's Republic of China (PRC) history: Hong Kong fugitives transfer to, 226; Mao era (1949-1978), 100–106, 154; pre-Xi reform era (1978-2012), 100, 106–15, 203; Xi era (after 2012), 39, 92, 100–101, 112–15
performance art advocacy, 109
petitioners: citizenship bargaining division of, 159–60; citizenship bargaining pacifying, 158; TGD tactics against state, 62, 68–74
petitioning upward (*Xinfang*): in Confucianism and populism, 146; contentious action escalation from, 146; lawyers participation in, 152; political agents monitoring through, 146
petitions, 4, 41; Bruun on, 82n6; bureaucrat-assisted contention repression undermining of, 122–23; CCP support of, 66; collective actions logic of, 8–10; migrants from TGD building collective, 65; state on illegality of collective, 66
phone tracking, in techno authoritarianism, 17, 18
police: arrests by, 6, 50–51, 55; brutality, 7, 13, 32, 50, 227; nonviolent protests and forceful, *50*, 51–52; nonviolent protests and tolerant, *50*, 51; rural protests repressive actions, 48; at social protests, 48–49, *49*, 81n2; urban protests response by, 48; violent protests and forceful, *50*, 52; violent protests and tolerant, *50*, 51
political agents, petitioning upward monitoring of, 146
political campaign groups, Mao brutal repression of, 103
political dynamics, of lawyer dependence, 148–51

political elites. *See* state elites
political mediation model, 172, 174–75, 188n8
political opportunity structure (POS), 92, 230; in authoritarian states, 171; central and local government disparities, 34–35; central government social protests tolerance, 34; in Chinese decentralization, 34; collective and contentious action from, 33–36; in democracies, 93, 171; from government department inconsistencies, 34; institutional allies in, 194, 216n1; in lawyering dependence, 150; for social protests, 35–36; social stability maintenance and, 34; state tensions within, 127; structures of, 94–98
political participation, in authoritarian states, 55–56
political protest movements: as popular contention, 94; repression toward, 95
political space, historical periods and shift of, *99*, 99–100
politics: informal lawyer dependence of, 147; of recognition, 95–96; of redistribution, 95; social media and mass line, 20
Ponzi schemes, 12–13
popular contention: local government control of, 113; localized protests on economic entitlements as, 94; Mao era and, 101, 104–6; nationalist movements as, 94; protest movements with political or religious agenda as, 94; umbrella movement incident, 228
popular protests, 2000-2019, 55–56; characteristics of, 31; collective protest dynamics, 38–40; data and methods on, 40–42; diminishment reasons, 37–38; escalation reasons, 33–37; news events data for, 42; nonconfrontational events exclusion, 41; social protests dynamics, 31, 42–54; structures mobilization for, 36–37
popular protests, ENGOs participation in, 202–8; for anti-PX chemical plant protests in Xiamen and Kumming, 195, *200*, 200–204, *201*, *202*, 206–8, *214*, 214–15; anti-waste incinerator protests in Beijing and Guangzhou, 195, *200*, 200–202, *201*, *202*, 204–6, *214*, 214–15; brokerage and buffering in, 197–99, 208–13, *214*; decline in, 217n15; MEP and, 200; SEPA and, 179–80, 200
populism, petitioning upward in, 146
POS. *See* political opportunity structure
post-Mao era: legal reform, 152, 154; mediation de-emphasis in, 154; religion tolerance in, 310
post-umbrella organizations, 237–38, 241, 245; Hospital Authorities Employee Alliance, 240; Spark Alliance, 240; union leaders and, 239–40
pragmatism, in citizenship bargaining, 159
PRC. *See* People's Republic of China
pre-Xi reform era (1978-2012): civic activism extreme repression, 100; civic activism leniency response, 100; civic and noncivic activism under, 106–12; consultative authoritarianism in, 107; feminist activism rise, 108–9; local governments and civic activism, 107; market economy transition, 106–7; mass mobilization in, 106; NGO three-no policy in, 106, 203; noncivic activism state facilitation, 107; political environment tolerance, 106; post-totalitarianism in, 106; social activism in, 112–15; SOE worker protest during industrial restructuring, 109–12; work-unit system decline in, 106–7
prison terms, in security state, 15

private agents, coercive activities engagement by, 144
private domestic owned business, labor issue protests for, 11–12
process-mechanism approach, in lawyering repression, 144
pro-democracy camp, in Hong Kong, 231, 241
propaganda: increased, 6; state online involvement use of, 20; Xi practices of, 24n14
prostitution, Hong Kong tolerance for, 246n3
protect our town discourse, in bureaucrat-assisted contention framing, 131
Protestant churches, social movement theory and, 283–84
Protestant-party-state relations, urban churches and, 284–85
protest repertoire, governance structure and, 6–8
protests: buying stability strategy for limiting, 38; demonstration effect, 225; disaster response and, 24n4; against factory pollution, 14; by FDI firms, 45, 53; as government information source, 32, 34, 35, 37; growth during 1990s, 3; over SOEs, 96; peasant repression in, 38; by public-sector employees, 53–54; relational model for institutional alliances in, 196–99; response to, 40; social organizations participation in, 217n8; state repression decrease of, 3; umbrella legacy evolution of, 225–46; WeChat coordination of, 20; West comparison for, 6. *See also* economic protests; *specific protest types*
public policy, social movements influence on, 171
public-sector employees, protests by, 53–54
Putin, Vladimir, 93

radical habitus, Crossley application of, 61, 78–80
radical rights lawyers, 150, 151; Ministry of Public Security 2015 arrests of, 152–53
rallies, 4, 49–50
rational choice, religion protest participation and, 309–10
reeducation system of *laojiao*, 24n11
reflexivity, of human agency, 225
reform era, central leadership and local authorities conflict in, 7
regime stability concern, of central government, 35
relational explanation, for ENGOs participation, 210–13
relational model: brokerage in, 197; ENGOs, 210–13; environmental protests institutional alliance, 196–99; NGOs relational mechanisms, 194–216; for protests institutional alliance, 196–99; for social movements, 196
relational repression, 145
religion protest participation: by affiliation, 306; from beliefs and, 308, 322; biblical literalism impact on, 308; Black militancy relationship, 309; CGSS on, 323n4; China WVS on, 306, 311, 323n1; Chinese context in theoretical guidance, 309–11; factors influencing, 307–11; hierarchy influence on, 307; politics and, 309; post-Mao era religion tolerance, 310; rational choice and, 309–10; study on, 311–23; Western countries research on China, 306; Western religion rapid growth, 306; work-unit system influence on, 307
religion protest participation study: data and methods, 311–12; discussion, 321–23; results, *313–17*, 313–21, *319–20*

religious protest movements: as popular contention, 94; state response to, 94–95

repertoires of contention: peasant rights awareness, 79; repressive state fight by, 61; Tilly on, 61

repression: in authoritarian states, 145; bureaucrat-assisted contention sabotage of, 121–22; government containment of, 55; through Great Firewall, 18–19; hard types of, 142; information facilitation of, 39; local government threat of, 37–38; location impact on, 54; overt protests decrease from, 4; relational, 145; selective components of, 32; toward political protest movements, 95; typology in social protests, 49–54, *50*, *53*; Xi era increased, 112; Xi strong, 52, 55. *See also* soft repression

repression-concession-escalation dynamics, of grassroots resistance, 80

repression-tolerance facilitation continuum, 99

repressive state, repertoires of contentions to fight, 61

resistance repertoire, 4, 61; of Marxist-Leninist regimes, 6; societal-specific, 62

resources: brokerage sharing of, 197; collective action mobilization of, 33; social movements organization, networking of, 7

retreat stage, in Beijing TGD petitioning campaign, 67, 69, 71–72

rightful resistance, 8, 24n5, 174; in rural protests, 34

rights awareness foundation, of peasant repertoires of contention, 79

rights consciousness, 146, 156

rights defense lawyers: challenges by, 55; dissident arrests of, 6; government threat from, 97; Xi administration assaults on, 92, 101

rule consciousness, 146, 156

rule of law: CCP reform dedication to, 146; with Chinese characteristics, 153–54; in Hong Kong, 226; Hu and Xi on, 152; mediation tradition in, 153

rule of law authoritarianism, 161; CCP reform dedication, 146; citizenship bargaining, 155–60; demobilization and, 144–46; in lawyering repression, 147; lawyering repression mechanism, 146–48; lawyers informal political dependence, 148–51; legal consensus construction, 151–55; nonstate actors and, 144–46; reforms in, 142–43; soft repression and, 144–46. *See also* governing the country by law

rural protests, 6–7; about environment, 14; land-related, 5, 47; protest forms, 47–48, *48*; repressive police actions, 48; rightful resistance and, 34; violence in, 47–48, *48*

rural transformation protest type: on confiscated properties, 11; against corruption, 11; for dislocated persons, 11; on national infrastructure projects, 11; on unjust land expropriations, 11, 47

scientific development, Wen emphasis on, 181

security state: censorship by, 15; detentions and prison in, 15–16; fear and social control in, 15; Great Firewall, 18–23, 24n13; techno authoritarianism, 17–18; in twenty-first century, 14–18

self-censorship, 19

SEPA. *See* State Environmental Protection Administration

sequential interviewing method, 199–200

Sichuan Province, bureaucrat-assisted contention in, 134
social activism: international intervention and, 96; in Mao era (1949-1978), 102–4; totalitarian regimes suppression of, 101; in Xi era (after 2012), 112–14
social conflict: government stability maintenance measures, 32; institutionalization of, 40, 49–50; stability preservation offices screening for, 39
social control: digital corporations CCP, 16; digital dimensions of, 15; security state on fear and, 15
social governance measures, 32
social harmony, in lawyering repression, 147
social identity, social media sources on, 17
socialism, labor issue protests and, 11
social media: collective action impacted by, 7, 37; collective protests blocking of, 39; COVID-19 response on, 19; mass line politics review, 20; Ministry of Propaganda analysis of postings on, 20; sources on social identity, 17; structure mobilization through, 36
social mobilization: central and local government tensions, 121; collective petitioning, mass protest and, 81n2; WeChat closed networks and, 81n1
social movements: bureaucrat-assisted contention and, 134; cognitive praxis, 225; cultural approach in, 251–55; Deng support of, 171; feminist movement as nonmaterialist, 14; institutional activism in, 196–99; Mao support of, 171; as organized, networked and resource dependent, 7; public policy influenced by, 171; relational model for, 196; research, 3; society, 40; state elites in, 171

social movement theory, 132, 282; China Protestant churches and, 283–84
social organizations, 216nn6–7; protests participation by, 217n8; Xi era increase of, 113
social protests: central government POS for, 35–36; emotional charge to, 37; government toleration for, 32; local government information collection on, 37
social protests dynamics, 2000-2019, 31, 54; for disruption and repression, 47–49; frequency distribution for, 42, *43*; large-scale protests, 42, *43*; participants distribution, 44, 44–45; protest targets and claims, *46*, 46–47, *47*; repression and violence typology, 49–54, *50*, *53*
social stability: authoritarian states instability, 55–56; POS and maintenance of, 34
social transformation goal, of Mao era, 102
societal-specific resistance repertoire, 62
SOE. *See* state-owned enterprises
soft repression: in authoritarian states, 142; informal repression and, 145; lawyers use of, 142, 160; of local government, 145; media stigmatization and, 144; movements demobilization, 143, 144; nonstate actors and demobilization in, 143; relational repression and, 145; rule of law authoritarianism and, 144–46
Songjiang District, bureaucrat-assisted contention framing in, 130
Spark Alliance, 240
stability preservation offices, social conflict screening by, 39
Stalin, Joseph, 93
state: behaviors scrutiny by CCP, 17; citizen interest organizations prohibition, 36; civic organization restrictions by, 37; collective

Index

action facilitation, 99; on collective petitions illegality, 66; economic protests tolerance, 95; on grassroots environmental protests, 195; grassroots resistance challenge and compliance with, 81n2; of Hu, 52, 55; intensified surveillance, 38–39; of Jiang Zemin, 55; multifarious strategies by, 81n2; networked authoritarianism by, 69–70; NGOs symbiotic relationship with, 195; petitioning ambivalence from, 66; POS and tensions within, 127; social mobilization and local tensions with, 121; student activism allowance by, 94; surveillance strategies, 82n7; TGD counterpetition moves by, 62, 68–69; TGD petitioner tactics against, 62, 68–74; trade union affiliations with, 12, 25n16, 36. *See also* security state

state actors: movement actors alliances with, 174; nonstate actors interactive dynamics with, 174. *See also* nonstate actors

state elites: in authoritarian regimes, 171, 175; as decision makers, 174; against Nu River Dam, 171–88; in social movements, 171

State Environmental Protection Administration (SEPA): CEN of, 180, 182, 186; EIA enforcement by, 172, 177–78, 180; environmental activism and, 200; environmental movement support by, 34; "Experts Call for Preserving the Nu River" of, 183; on Nu River preservation, 172–73, 177–87; Pan of, 179–80, 182, 187, 188n9, 204

State Information Office, for intelligence gathering, 39

state-led alliances, movement actors and, 175

state-movement interaction, in environmental activism, 173–74

state online involvement: digitalized mass line politics, 20; negative news events monitoring, 20; propaganda through social media tools, 20

state-owned enterprises (SOE): employees collective protests from restructuring of, 110; government accommodation and facilitation of claims of, 110–11; noncivic activism of employees of, 109; pre-Xi reform era industrial restructuring, 109–12; protests over, 96; reform and laid-off workers protests, 33; worker mobilization compared to feminist activism, 111–12; worker pensions in closed, 13; Zhu sympathy for complaints of, 110–11

state repression, under Xi: from post facto to preemptive, 92; from social stability to national security framing, 92; from sporadic harassment to criminalization, 92

street: politics, 4; protest, 146

structure of abeyance: in feminist activists, 230; in umbrella movement, 231

structures mobilization, for protests, 37; organization for citizen interest protection prohibition, 36; through social media, 36

student activism, state allowance of, 94

surveillance: AI, 16–17; comprehensive policies on, 6; state intensified, 38–39; state strategies of, 82n7; Xi era modern technology use for, 39, 112

symbiotic exchange process, in lawyers informal political dependence, 148

taxation, rural transformation protest on high, 11, 33

techno authoritarianism: AI surveillance, 16–17; optimistic view of, 22; phone tracking and facial recognition, 17, 18; points and penalties in, 17; for policing, 18; social media sources on social identity, 17; state scrutiny of behaviors, 17; VPN access restrictions, 20, 22

Telegram internet platform, 236, 240

TGD. *See* Three Gorges Dam

Thirteenth Five-Year Plan (2016–2020), 187

Three Gorges Dam (TGD) building: dimensions of, 63; displacement at, 62; forced migrants from, 63–65; local government counterpetition tactics, 68–69; WeChat on petitioning against, 62, 66–68, *68*, 71–77, *74*, 82n5, 82nn8–16

three-no policy, for NGOs, 106, 203

Three-Self Patriotic Movement (TSPM) association, 281, 284–85

Tiananmen Square (1989): commemoration vigils for, 250–74, *261*, *263*, *265*, *266*, *267*; Hong Kong commemoration of, 257–58; international criticism on, 108; massacre at, 107; nativist challenges, 269–73, *272*; regime loyalist challenges, 268–69; repression at, 18; youth and, 23

Tilley, Charles, 61

totalitarian regimes, 93; in Mao era, 101, 102

trade unions, state affiliation with, 12, 25n16, 36

triple market model, of Yang, 284–85

TSPM. *See* Three-Self Patriotic Movement

Twitter, Great Firewall closing of, 18

umbrella movement (2014), 225, 246; anti-extradition movement impacted by, 227–28; black-bloc tactic during, 235–36; civil disobedience in, 235–36; criminal organizations in, 246n1; economic protests in, 237; failure lessons, 241–44; Lennon Walls, 226, 234; occupation zones in, 232–37, *233*, 241–42, 245; opposition lawmakers and, 243; organization development in, 230–31; popular contention incident of, 228; post-umbrella organizations, 237–41, 245; structure of abeyance in, 231

unemployment: factor automation and, 12; of TGD migrants, 64

union leaders, post-umbrella organizations and, 239–40

urban churches, rise and fall of, 300–301; CCC and, 281, 284–85; gray zones and public transcript in, 285–88; Hu emergence of, 288–94; national organizing and foreigners restrictions, 292–94; in Protestant-party-state relations, 284–85; TSPM association and, 281, 284–85; visibility and congregational sizes of, 290–92; Xi shuttering of, 297–99

urban protests: environmental, 14; forms of, 47–48, *48*; police response to, 48

urban space, Xi era monitoring and controlling of, 112

vigils. *See* commemoration vigils, for Tiananmen Square

violence: in anti-extradition movement, 226, 238, 244; anti-regime mobilization from, 144; arrests and, 50–51; during Cultural Revolution, 103; forceful police and, *50*, 52; police brutality, 7, 13, 32, 50, 227; police responses to, *50*, 50–51; in rural protests, 47–48, *48*; in social protests, 47–48, *48*; TGD petitioning campaign support for, 73; tolerant police and, *50*, 51; typology in social protests, 49–54, *50*, *53*

virtual private network (VPN) services: Great Firewall and, 24n15; restriction in Western countries of, 20, 22

Wang Qishan, 78

Wang Yongchen, 186; on EIA law enforcement, 184–85; Nu River

Hydropower Dam media campaign, 182, 189n13
WeChat: on Beijing floods, 20; power bloggers detention, 16; protests coordination through, 13; social mobilization and closed networks of, 81n1; on TGD petitioning, 62, 66–68, *68*, 71–77, *74*, 82n5, 82nn8–16
Wen Jiabao: on Nu River Hydropower Dam, 185–87; Nu River Hydropower Dam suspension by, 173, 186; scientific development emphasis, 181
Western countries: China religion protest participation research, 306; China religion rapid growth from, 306; human rights and gender issues global activism, 109; protests comparison for, 6; riots and public disturbances rarity in, 40; VPN services restriction for, 20, 22
women: ACWF as representative for, 108, 109; FWCW and, 108, 114; NGOs for, 108, 111, 114. *See also* feminist activism
Wong, Joshua, 243
workers: economism protests by former city residents, 104; economism protests by inferior, 104; labor strikes by unorganized, 36; local government harassment of, 12; NGOs role, 36
work-unit system: Mao era organized dependency in, 103; pre-Xi reform era decline of, 106–7; religion protest participation influenced by, 307
World Value Survey (WVS), on religion protest participation, 306, 311, 323n1

Xiamen, 199; anti-PX chemical plant protests in, 195, *200*, 201, *201*, *202*, *214*, 214–15; ENGOs minimal presence in, 203–4, *214*; local ENGO on PX information, 195, 202

Xi era (after 2012): civic activism brutal crackdown, 92, 100, 101, 113; feminist activism, 113–14; grid system development, 112; increased repression during, 112; labor activism in, 114–15; modern technology surveillance in, 39, 112; social activism in, 112–14; social organizations increase in, 113. *See also* pre-Xi reform era
Xi Jinping: autocracy of, 91; civic activism strong repression, 92, 100, 101, 113; civil rights oppression, 39; civil society attacks by, 91; dissent and protest actions restriction by, 5, 32, 44–45; local government repression and, 38; propaganda practices of, 24n14; protests decrease in mid-2010s, 31, 32; on rule of law, 152; social protests disruption and repression by, 49; strong repression by, 52, 55; urban churches shuttering, 297–99
Xinfang. *See* petitioning upward

Yang, Fenggang, 284–85
YEPB. *See* Yunnan Environmental Protection Bureau
youth: on COVID-19 coverups, 23; Tiananmen Square repression and, 23
YouTube, Great Firewall closing of, 18
Yunnan Environmental Protection Bureau (YEPB), Nu River Hydropower Dam campaign, 176
Yunnan Province, bureaucrat-assisted contention in, 123, 128, 133

Zero Waste Alliance, 205
Zhang Gaoli, 78
Zhang Kejia, 182
Zhejiang Province, bureaucrat-assisted contention in, 132–33
Zhongze Women's Legal Counseling Service Center, 114
Zhu Rongji, 110–11